Chronicles of the Crusades: Contemporary Narratives of the Crusade of

Richard Coeur de Lion, and of the Crusade of Saint Louis

By Richard of Devizes , Geoffrey of Vinsauf , and Jean de Joinville

PROLOGUE

Sect. 1. After you had happily proceeded to the Charter House from our church of Winchester, much and often did I desire to follow you who had thus departed, peradventure to remain with you, but certainly to behold what you were about, how you lived, and whether the Carthusian cell is more exalted and nearer heaven than the cloister of Winchester. It pleased God at length to satisfy my wish. I came, and oh that I had come alone! I went thither making the third, and those who went with me were the cause of my return. My desire displeased them, and they caused my fervor, I will not say error, to grow cold. I saw with you that which elsewhere I had not seen, which I could not have believed, and which I could not sufficiently admire. In each of your cells there is one door according to custom, which you are permitted to open at pleasure, but to go out by it is not permitted, except so much as that one foot should always remain in the cell, within the threshold. The brethren may step out with one foot, whichever they please, but the other must remain in the cell. A great and solemn oath is to be taken that the door by which it is not permitted to enter or depart should be kept open. I am astonished also at another thing; abounding in all the good things of this world, as having nothing, yet possessing all things, more compassionate and humane than all men, having the most perfect love one to another, you divide the affection of charity to strangers, you bless without giving supplies to your guests. Nor do I less admire, in the third place, that living to yourselves apart out of society, and singly, you understand all the great things achieved in the world as they happen, and even sometimes you know them prior to their being accomplished. Do not, however, consider it want of respect in me to your more than Pythagorean taciturnity, if I shall dare presume to address men of so great gravity, and so arduous profession, rather with the trifles of the world than mere idle gossip.

Sect. 2. Nevertheless, although, as it is thought, the Omniscient God is with you and in you, and through Him you know all things, and not from man, nor yet by man, you were pleased, as you said, that my essay would be a solace to you, inasmuch as in the first place I should write to you a history of the fresh changes, which the world has produced, turning squares into circles (more especially since your transmigration to the celled heaven, by means of which the world may appear more worthless to you, having its fickleness before your eyes), and, secondly, that a well-known hand might recall to you the memory of one beloved.

Oh! What delight! If that holy spirit, if the angel of the Lord, if the deified man who is become already of the number of the gods, should deign to remember me before the great God, me, who am scarcely worthy to be accounted a man. I have done that which you desired, do that which you have promised. And that the little book may have a commencement of some importance, I have begun a little higher than was stipulated, making our Royal house troubled like that of Aedipus, the bounds of my work, commencing at the latter part, not daring to hope to unravel the whole. Why, and how, and when, the father may have crowned his son; how great things and of what importance thence ensued; who and how often and what regions they embroiled; with what success they all ended I have left to those who produce greater works: my narrative serves only for the living.

RICHARD OF DEVIZES IN THE YEAR OF THE LORD MCLXXXIX

Richard, the son of King Henry II by Eleanor, brother of Henry III, was consecrated king of the English by Baldwin, archbishop of Canterbury, at Westminster, on the third of the ones of September (3 Sept.). On the very day of the coronation, about that solemn hour, in which the Son was immolated to the Father, a sacrifice of the Jews to their father the devil was commenced in the city of London, and so long was the duration of this famous mystery, that the holocaust could scarcely be accomplished the ensuing day. The other cities and towns of the kingdom emulated the faith of the Londoners, and with a like devotion dispatched their bloodsuckers with blood to hell. In this commotion there was prepared, although unequally, some evil against the wicked, everywhere throughout the realm, only Winchester alone, the people being prudent and circumspect, and the city always acting mildly spared its vermin. It never did any thing overspeedily; fearing nothing more than to repent, it considers the result of every thing before the commencement. It was unwilling, unprepared, to cast up violently through the parts the indigestion by which it was oppressed to its bodily peril, and it was careful for its bowels, in the mean time temperately concealing its uneasiness, until it should be possible for it, at a convenient time for cure, to cast out the whole cause of the disease at once and once for all.

Sect. 4. Not without the anxious solicitude and amazement of many, a bat was seen, in the middle and bright part of the day, to flutter through the monastery, inconveniently recircling in the same tracks, and especially around the king's throne.

Sect. 5. William de Longchamp, who had been the chancellor of the earl of Poitiers before his accession, when the earl was crowned king, considered his office to we profited as much for the better, as a kingdom is superior to an earldom.

Sect. 6. A circumstance happened on the selfsame day of the coronation in Westminster Abbey, a presage of such portentous omen, as then was hardly allowable to be related even in a whisper. At Complin, the last hour of the day, the first peal that day happened to be rung, neither by any agreement, nor even the ministers of the church themselves being aware of it, till after it was done; for Prime, Tierce, Sext, Nones, and the solemn service of vespers and two masses were celebrated without any ringing of peals.

Sect. 7. Stephen de Marzia, seneschal of Anjou, under the king lately deceased, he great and mighty, singularly fierce, and the master of his lord, being taken and cast into chains, was dragged to Winchester, where being made a gazing-stock to angels and to men, emaciated with woeful hunger, and broken with the weight of his irons, he was constrained to the payment of thirty thousand pounds of money of Anjou, and the promise of fifteen thousand pounds, for his ransom. Ralph de Glanville, justiciary of the realm of England and the king's eye, a man not inferior to Stephen, except in manners and riches, being deprived of authority and given into custody, redeemed merely his liberty to go and come for fifteen thousand pounds of silver. And whereas this name, Glanville, had been so great the day before, a name as it were above every name, so that whosoever, to whom it should be given by the Lord, would converse among princes, and would be adored by the people, yet the next morning there remained not one in the land who could be called by this name. That was the ruin of those two, to wit, of Stephen and Ralph, which also it is certain has been the ruin of thousands before them, and which hereafter may ruin others, namely, a suspicion arising from the confidence of their former lord.

Sect. 8. John, the king's brother, who alone of the sons of his mother, queen Eleanor, survived his brother, besides the earldom of Mortain, which, by his father s gift, he had long enjoyed, was so greatly enriched and increased in England by his brother, that both privately and publicly it was affirmed by many that the king had no thoughts of returning to the kingdom, and that his brother, already no less powerful than himself, if he should not restrain his innate temper, would, impelled by the desire of sovereignty, endeavor to drive him vanquished from the realm.

Sect. 9. The time of commencing his journey pressed hard upon King Richard, as he, who had been first of all the princes on this side the Alps in the taking up of the cross, was unwilling to be last in setting out. A king worthy of the name of king, who, in the first year of his reign, left the kingdom of England for Christ, scarcely otherwise than if he had departed never to return. So great was the devotion of the man, so hastily, so quickly and so speedily did he run, yea fly, to avenge the wrongs of Christ. However, whilst he kept the greater matter in his mind, giving himself in some little measure to deliberation for the kingdom, having received power from the pope that he might withdraw the cross from such of his own subjects, as he should desire, for the government of his kingdom, he first appointed Hugh Pudsey, bishop of Durham, to be chief justice of the whole realm, and with design, as is thought by many, further creating him a young earl of Northumberland out of an old bishop, the custody of as many castles as he liked being yielded to him, he diligently cleared from his coffers ten thousand pounds of silver. Geoffrey Fitz Peter, William Briwere, and Hugh Bardulf being permitted to remain at home, the cross being withdrawn from them, the king's treasurer transferred the whole collections of the three as three nuts into the Exchequer. All the sheriffs of the kingdom, on any trivial accusation falling under the king's displeasure, were deprived of their unlucky power, and scarcely permitted to see his face, even by the mediation of inestimable treasure. Ralph de Glanville, than whom none of his time was more subtle whilst he was in power, now being reduced to a private person by his prince, was so stupefied through grief, that his son-in-law, Ralph de Ardenne, utterly lost, by reason of his careless talk, whatever he had previously acquired by the judgment of his mouth. He too, himself, because he was an old man, and not able to bear fatigue, if he had been willing to give the king that little which remained after the payment of the fine, as a gratuity would easily have obtained a remission of the peril of the journey. The king received security from the tributary kings of the Welsh and of the Scots, that they would not pass their borders for the annoyance of England during his absence.

Sect. 10. Godfrey, son of that renowned Richard de Luci, Richard (Fitz Neale) the treasurer, Hubert Walter, and William de Longchamp, four men of no small virtue, and of no mean praise, were elected at Pippewelle to the four vacant sees, viz. Winchester, London, Salisbury, and Ely. They all obtained sufficient canonical nomination, and especially the elect of

Winchester, who obtained his nomination to the dignity on the seventeenth of the kalends of October (Sept. 15), while the election of the other three was delayed till the morrow, the king consenting and the archbishop confirming what was done, although at the first he would rather have had it somewhat otherwise: concerning which it wonderfully happened that he, who had been nominated to one of the sees by the archbishop's means, died that very day. William, bishop elect of Ely, retained the king's seal on the payment of three thousand pounds of silver, although Reginald the Italian had bid one thousand more. The bishops elect of Winchester and Salisbury were consecrated at Westminster, by Baldwin, archbishop of Canterbury, on the eleventh of the kalends of November (Oct. 22). On that day, Hugh de Nonante, bishop of Coventry, laid his complaint before the archbishop and bishops assembled at the consecration of the bishops elect, against his monks of Coventry, for having laid violent hands on him and drawn his blood before the altar. He also expelled the greater part of the congregation before his complaint, nor did he cease from his importunity until he had obtained the sanction of all the bishops in attestation to the pope against the monks.

Sect .11. Godfrey, bishop of Winchester, mindful of his profession, suing for the restoration of the possessions of his church, which had been taken away, as no one had any right of replaying against the church of Winchester with respect to its two manors, namely Meones and Weregrave, recovered them by judicial decree, three thousand pounds of silver being privately given to the king. Nor did the considerate man omit at the same time to pay a fine to the king for the indemnity of the church's treasure, for his patrimony, for the county of Hampshire and for the custody of the castles of Winchester and Porchester. And because the time for the payment of so much money was nigh at hand, as he could not pass over the day fixed for the payment without detriment to the whole business, and he could find no nearer resource under heaven, although against his will, he laid his hand on the treasure of his church, to restore which, however, he obliged himself and his successors, providing security to the convent by the testimony of a sealed bond. A man of such courtesy and moderation, who not even when angry ever did any thing to those who were under him, but what savored of mildness: truly of his family, and one of his familiars, of whom it is said, under whom to live is to reign.

Sect. 12. The king readily disburdened all, whose money was a burthen to them, such powers and possessions as they chose being given to anybody at pleasure; wherewith also on a time an old acquaintance in the company joking him, he broke off with this evasion, "I would sell London if I could find a chapman." Many a one might have been forewarned by that expression, had it been uttered sooner, not to learn to be a wise merchant, after the English proverb, by buying for a dozen, and selling for one and a half."

IN THE YEAR OF THE LORD MXCX

Sect. 13. In the year from the incarnation of the Lord 1190, the king crossed the Channel to Neustria (Normandy), the care of the whole kingdom being committed to the chancellor.

Richard, bishop elect of London, and William of Ely, were consecrated by Archbishop Baldwin at Westminster, the second of the kalends of January (Dec. 31, 1189). William de Mandeville, earl of Albemarle, being seized with delirium in an acute semi tertian fever, died at Gisorz whose relict, a woman almost a man, who was deficient in nothing masculine but manhood, William de Fortibus, a knight a thousand times approved in arms, received to wife by King Richard's gift, together with all the honors of her former husband.

Sect. 14. William, bishop of Ely, and the king's chancellor, by nature a second Jacob, although he did not wrestle with the angel, a goodly person, making up in mind for his shortness in stature, secure for his master's love, and presuming on his favor, because all power was, is, and will be impatient of a partner, expelled Hugh de Pusac from the Exchequer, and barely leaving him even his sword with which he had been invested as an earl of the king's hand, after a short time, deprived him of the honor of his earldom also. And lest the bishop of Durham alone should bewail his misfortunes, the villain, who was now crueler than a wild beast, and spared nobody, fell upon the bishop of Winchester also. The custody of the castles and county taken away from him, nor is he even permitted to enjoy his own patrimony. The kingdom is disturbed, and the discontented are charged with disaffection to the king. Everybody crosses the sea to importune the king against the tyrant, but he having crossed first of all, briefly related before the king a partial account of his entire proceeding and expulsion; by whom also he was fully instructed in all things to be done; he thus foiled the adverse wishes of his rivals, and was on his return before those who assailed him could obtain admission to the king's presence. So he returns to the English not less powerful and prosperous, than one who has accomplished all things whatsoever he desired. The king having returned from Gascony, where he had forcibly put down the thieves, and captured the holds they had occupied, all those whom the chancellor had injured assembled before him, who satisfying every one as then to each seemed good, sent them all back to the chancellor with such letters as they then desired. John, bishop of Norwich, being also one of those who threatened Saladin, amply furnished for his journey and the cause, whilst proceeding on his way in the borders of Burgundy, fell among robbers, who took from him all his substance and, as he had no means left wherewith he might proceed, he turned his course towards the pope, and when with his insinuation he had bemoaned his mischance and poverty to him, the clemency of the Holy See dismissed him home, absolved from his vow.

Sect. 15. The bishop of Winchester, being affected with a serious disease, remained some time beyond the sea. The bishop of Durham in haste proceeded direct to London, but not being received by the barons of the Exchequer, he hastily, as if sure to triumph, pursues his way after the chancellor, who at that time had gone on an expedition towards Lincoln; whom having overtaken, he saluted in the king's name, not freely nor without a frown, and then questioned him seriously concerning the affairs of state, and, indeed, as if he would not suffer any thing to be done without his consent. He neglected fine language and long words, and while he boasted too much of power not yet received, not considering with whom he was speaking, he loosely uttered whatever he ought to have kept secret. At the conclusion of his address, the staff is put forth to silence talk, the king's solemn act much to be reverenced is exhibited for recital. The mountains travail, the silly mouse is produced. The observance of strict silence is enjoined during the king's mandate; all were hushed and attentive held their tongues. The epistle is read in public, which would have been much more to be feared if it had not been so soon read; he (Longchamp), well able to conceal his device, shrewdly deferred to answer what he had heard till the seventh day, appointing their place of conference at Tickhill. On the day appointed the bishop of Durham comes to the castle, and his attendants being commanded to wait for him before the gates, he goes into the chancellor quite alone; he who before had held his peace, speaks first, and compels the deceived to recite with his own mouth letters he had obtained after the former against whatever he had hoped. As he was preparing to answer, he added, "The other day while you were speaking it was time for me to be silent; now that you may discern why I have taken a time for speaking, you being silent; as my lord the king lives, you shall not depart hence until you have given me hostages for all the castles which you hold being delivered up to me, for I do not take you as a bishop a bishop, but as a chancellor a chancellor!" The ensnared had neither the firmness nor the opportunity to resist; the hostages are given, and at the term assigned he castles are given up for the restoring of the hostages. William, bishop of Worcester, who succeeded next to Baldwin, went the way of all flesh.

Sect. 16. The lord bishop of Winchester, at length recovering in Neustria, and also desiring to receive back the things taken from him, recrossed with all the speed he could, and found the chancellor besieging the castle of Gloucester. Whose arrival being known, the chancellor goes forth to meet him as he comes and having heartily embraced and kissed him, says, "You have come at a most desirable time, dear friend! Are we to prosecute the siege or desist. To whom the bishop replies, "If you desire peace, lay down arms/' He, quick of apprehension, perceived the force of the words, and commanded the heralds to sound the retreat; he also restored to the bishop his patrimony without dispute, but that only. All the others, who had crossed the sea against the chancellor, profited less than nothing. William, legate of the Apostolic See, held a council at Westminster, in which, lest there should be nothing done to be reported of him hereafter, he sentenced all religion to be expelled from Coventry cathedral, and prebendary clerks to be substituted in place of the monks.

Sect. 17. William, the wonderful bishop of Ely, chancellor of the king, justiciary of the kingdom, of threefold charge and threefold title, that he might use both hands as the right, and that the sword of Peter might succour the sword of the ruler, took upon himself the office of legate of all England, Scotland, Wales, and Ireland, which he obtained from the pope at the instance of the king, who would not otherwise set out, by Reginald, bishop of Bath. Therefore successful in every office which he craved, he passed to and fro through the kingdom with the rapidity of a flash of lightning.

The King of Darkness, that old incendiary, having added fresh fuel, fanned the ancient spark between the church of Salisbury and the monastery of Malmesbury into renewed flames. The abbot is roused not now to make the profession of pontiff, but to disavow the very title of the bishop as well as his crosier. Royal letters to the chancellor were obtained, by which the abbot should be compelled to respond at law to the motions of the bishop. Nor did the man whose affairs were at stake forget himself; no peril could ever overtake him unprovided, who never knew the loss of any thing through sloth. He repelled one nail by another, being presented by the king with letters invalidating the former letters. The chancellor having perceived the shameful contrariety of the mandates of his prince, lest the king's fame should be injured by the fact, if he proceeded in the cause, deferred all process of both the one party and the other till the king's return.

Sect. 18. King Richard exacted an oath from his two brothers, John, his own brother, and

Geoffrey, a bastard, that they would not enter England within three years from his departure, the three years to be reckoned from the day of his starting from Tours; through the entreaties of his mother, however, dispensing so far concerning John, that passing into England with the chancellor's approbation, he should abide his judgment, and at his pleasure he should either remain in the kingdom, or live in exile.

Queen Eleanor's dowry was recognized throughout the king's territories by a solemn act, and delivered up to her, so that she who had before lived on the Exchequer might thenceforward live on her own.

The king's fleet, having left its own shores, sailed round Spain, and from the ocean having entered the Mediterranean, which further on is called the Grecian Sea, by the Straits of Africa, steered on to Marseilles, there to await the king.

The king of France and the king of England, having held a council at Tours and again at Yezelay, and confirmed the treaty between themselves and their kingdoms, and having settled and disposed of all things on both sides according to their pleasure, depart from each other with their respective armies. The Frenchman, being subject to sickness at sea, marches by land to Sicily; the Englishman, on the contrary, about to proceed by sea, comes to Marseilles to his ships. Baldwin, archbishop of Canterbury, and Hubert Walter, bishop of Salisbury, being the only bishops of all England who accomplished their vows, follow the king to Sicily, and arrive first in the land of Juda.

Sect. 19. The monks of the order of Cluni were not wont to supplant one another in their priories and government either by entreaty or bribes, and although some of them have sometimes attempted something of that sort that however we have seen visited with condign punishment. There was a certain venerable man elected prior of Montacute solely on account of his worth, Josceline by name, in whom you could discern nothing but what was praiseworthy. To supplant this so good a man there came a certain one, whose name it is not necessary to mention, one of his false brethren, with letters, obtained by great cunning from the abbot of Cluni, by which it was commanded that the prior should resign to the bearer of the present letters, and the congregation receive him for their prelate. The prior by some means foreknew what commodity the dealer had come to seek, wherefore, without awaiting the mandate, he vacated his seat in the chapter, and the congregation being present, addressed him, "Friend, for what art thou come?" He, having tarried long that he might appear unwillingly to receive that, which he had come to take by violence, at length betook himself to his seat, and anon imprecated himself, saying, " O thou, who with unalterable purpose governest the world, whose power takes its pastime in human affairs, who puttest down the mighty and exaltest the humble! O thou just judge Jesu Christ, if wrongfully I here preside, without delay and manifestly do thou vouchsafe to show! "Behold the miracle! On that same day he lost his speech; on the next, his life; on the third, being consigned to the earth, he learnt by experience, and taught by example, that sordid plunder is never followed by prosperous results.

A certain monk of Glastonbury, in hopes of promotion, courted Earl John with many presents but just as he should have come to receive it, a certain beam having suddenly given way, fell in his face, so that, bruised and wholly disfigured, he lost both his eggs (expectations) and his money together.

Sect. 20. The ships which the king found already prepared on the shore were one hundred in number, and fourteen busses, vessels of great magnitude and admirable swiftness, strong vessels and very sound, whereof this was the equipage and appointment. The first of the ships had three spare rudders, thirteen anchors, thirty oars, two sails, three sets of ropes of all kinds, and besides these double whatever a ship can want, except the mast and the ship's boat. There is appointed to the ship's command a most experienced steersman, and fourteen subordinate attendants picked for the service are assigned him. The ship is freighted with forty horses of value, trained to arms, and with arms of all kinds for as many horsemen, and forty foot, and fifteen sailors, and with an entire year provisions for as many men and horses. There was one appointment for all the ships, but each of the busses received a double appointment and freight. The king's treasure, which was very great and inestimable, was divided amongst the ships and busses, that if one part should experience danger, the rest might be saved. All things being thus arranged, the king himself, with a small household, and the chief men of his army, with his attendants, having quitted the shore, advanced before the fleet in galleys, and being daily entertained by the maritime towns, taking along with them the larger ships and busses of that sea, arrived prosperously at Messina. So great was the splendor of the approaching armament, such the clashing and brilliancy of their arms, so noble the sound of the trumpets and clarions, that the city quaked and was greatly astounded, and there came to meet the king a multitude of all ages, people without number, wondering and proclaiming with what exceeding glory and magnificence that king had arrived, surpassing the king of France, who with his forces had arrived seven days before. And forasmuch as the king of France had been already received into the palace of Tancred, king of Sicily, within the walls, the king of England pitched his camp without the city. The same day the king of France, knowing of the arrival of his comrade and brother flies to his reception, nor could their gestures sufficiently express in embraces and kisses how much each of them rejoiced in the other. The armies cheered one another with mutual applause and intercourse, as if so many thousand men had been all of one heart and one mind. In such pastimes is the holiday spent until the evening, and the weary kings departing, although not satiated, return every one to his own quarters. On the next day the king of England presently caused gibbets to be erected without the camp to hang thereon thieves and robbers. The judges delegated spared neither sex nor age; the cause of the stranger and the native found the like law and the like punishment. The king of France, whatever transgression his people committed, or whatever offence was committed against them, took no notice and held his peace; the king of England esteeming the country of those implicated in guilt as a matter of no consequence, considered every man his own, and left no transgression unpunished, wherefore the one was called a Lamb by the Griffones, the other obtained the name of a Lion.

Sect. 21. The king of England sent his messengers to the king of Sicily, demanding Johanna his sister, formerly queen of Sicily, and her dowry, with a golden seat and the whole legacy which King William had bequeathed to his father, King Henry, namely, a golden table of twelve feet in length, a silk tent, a hundred of the best galleys with all their necessaries for two years, sixty thousand silinas of wheat, sixty thousand of barley, sixty thousand of wine, four and twenty golden cups, and four and twenty golden dishes. The king of Sicily, setting little by the demands of the king of the English, and still less considering his own exigencies, sent him back his sister with the ordinary furniture of her bed, having given her, however, with royal consideration, a thousand terrini for her expenses. On the third day following, the king of England, having passed over the great river Del Far, which separates Calabria from Sicily, entered Calabria in arms, and took therein the well-fortified town which is called La Banniere, and having expelled the Griffones, established his sister there, and secured the place with an armed garrison. Again the king took a very strong castle, which is called the Griffones' Monastery, on same river Del Far, situated between La Banniere and Messina, and fortified it when taken and having without mercy dispatched by various tortures the Griffones who had resisted, caused them to be exhibited as a gazing-stock to their friends. Wido, king of Jerusalem, sent word to Philip, king of the French, and Richard, king of the English, whilst wintering in Sicily, that the residue of the Christians who lay before Acre would, on account of their weakness and the violence of the pagans, either be obliged to depart or perish, unless very shortly sustained. To aid whom, the kings sent forward Henry, count of Champagne, and Baldwin, archbishop of Canterbury, and Hubert, bishop of Salisbury, and Ralph de Glanville, with a strong army; of whom Archbishop Baldwin and Ralph de Glanville died at the siege of the city, which the Latins call Acre and the Jews Accaron, while the kings still remained in Sicily.

Sect. 22. The Griffones, before King Richard's arrival in Sicily, were more powerful than all the mighty of that region and having moreover always hated the people beyond the Alps, and now irritated by recent occurrences more inveterate than ever, kept the peace with all who claimed the king of France for their master, but sought to wreak the entire vengeance of their wrongs on the king of the English and his tailed followers, for the Greeks and Sicilians followed that king about and called them tailed English. Thereupon all intercourse with the country is denied the English by proclamation; they are murdered both day and night by forties and fifties, wherever they are found unarmed. The slaughter was daily multiplied, and it was madly purposed to go on until they should either destroy or put them all to flight. The king of England, excited by these disorders, raged like the fiercest lion, and vented his anger in a manner worthy that noble beast. His fury astounded his nearest friends and his whole court, the famous princes of his army sat around his throne, each according to his rank, and if any one might dare to raise his eyes to look him in the face, it would be very easy to read in the rulers countenance what he silently considered in his mind. After a long and deep silence, the king disburdened his indignant lips as follows.

Sect. 23. "O, my soldiers! My kingdom's strength and crown! Who have endured with me a thousand perils, you, who by might have subdued before me so many tyrants and cities, do you now see how a cowardly rabble insults us? Shall we vanquish Turks and Arabs? Shall we be a terror to nations the most invincible? Shall our right hand make us a way even to the ends of the world for the cross of Christ? Shall we restore the kingdom to Israel, when we have turned our backs before vile and effeminate Griffones? Shall we, subdued here in the confines of our own country, proceed further, that the sloth of the English may become a by word to the ends of the earth? Am I not right, then, O my friends, in regarding this as a new cause of sorrow? Truly, methinks I see you deliberately spare your pains that perchance you may the better contend with

Saladin hereafter. I, your lord and king, love you; I am solicitous for your honor; I tell you, I warn you again and again, if now you depart thus unrevenged, the mention of this base flight will both precede and accompany you. Old women and children will be raised up against you, and assurance will yield a double energy to every enemy against the runaways. I know that he who saves any one by constraint, does the same as kill him; the king will retain no man against his will. I am unwilling to compel any one of you to stay with me, lest the fear of one should shake another's confidence in the battle. Let every one follow what he may have chosen, but I will either die here or will revenge these wrongs common to me and you. If hence I depart alive, Saladin will see me only a conqueror; will you depart, and leave me, your king, alone to meet the conflict?"

Sect. 24. The king had scarcely well concluded his harangue, when all his brave and valiant men burst out, troubled only that their lord appeared to mistrust his men. They promise that they will comply from their souls with whatever he shall enjoin; they are ready to penetrate mountains and walls of brass, should he but give a nod: all Sicily, at his command alone, shall be subjected to him by their labor; if he should but desire it, as far as the Pillars of Hercules shall be steeped in blood. As the clamor, hushed by the ruler's gravity, subsided, "I am pleased," said he, "with what I hear; you refresh my spirits by your readiness to cast off your disgrace. And, as delay has always been hurtful to those who are prepared, we must make haste, so that whatever we design may be sudden. Messina shall be taken by me in the first place; the Griffones shall either ransom themselves, or be sold. If King Taucred, do not more speedily satisfy me for my sister's dowry and the legacy of King William, which falls to me in right of my father after the depopulation of his kingdom, he shall be compelled to restore them fourfold. Whatever belongs to the inhabitants shall be a prey for everybody to whom it shall fall; only with my lord the king of the French, who lodges in the city, and with all his followers, shall perfect peace be preserved. Let two thousand bold knights, the choice of the entire army and a thousand foot, archers, be made ready within two days. Let the law be enforced without remission; let the footman, who flies full speed, lose his foot, the knight be deprived of his girdle. Let every man, according to military discipline, be disposed in line in exact array, and on the third day, at the sound of the horn, let them follow me. I will head them and show them the way to the city." The assembly separated with the greatest applause; the king, having relaxed the sternness of his countenance, was seen returning thanks for their good-will with his wonted affability of expression.

Sect. 25. It wonderfully fell out that not even the king's enemy could pretend that his cause was unjust. On the third day on which the army was to have been led forth to battle, very early in the morning, Richard, archbishop of Messina, the archbishop of Montreal, the archbishop of Pisa, Margaritus Admiralis, Jordan de Pin, and many other of King Tancred's familiar friends, having taken with them Philip, king of the French, the bishop of Carnot, the duke of Burgundy, the counts of Nevers and Perch, and many followers of the king of France, also, the archbishops of Rouen and Auch, the bishops of Evreux and Bayonne, and all who were supposed to have any influence with the English, came reverently to the king of England, that they might cause satisfaction for all his complaints to be given to his content. The king, after long and earnest solicitation, is prevailed on by the entreaty of such honorable men, and commits the matter to be settled by their arbitration. They would consider well the enormity of what he had had to brook, and would provide that the satisfaction should be answerable to the offence. Whatever their general deliberation should have determined to be sufficient would be satisfactory to him, if only, from that very moment, none of the Gridlines would lay hands on his men. Those who had come were even more astonished than rejoiced at this unhoped-for clemency, and giving him at once what he had last propounded they retired from the king's presence and were assembled at some distance to treat of the rest.

Sect. 26. The king's army having on the previous day been numbered according to the aforementioned order, was with solemn silence in arms before the camp, awaiting the herald, from the rising of the sun, and the framers of the peace, not so easily coming to a determination, had protracted the day till full the third hour, when behold, suddenly and unexpectedly, there was proclaimed by a voice, too distinctly heard, before the gates, "To arms, to arms, men! Hugo Brunus is taken and being murdered by the Griffones, all he has is being plundered, and his men are being slaughtered. The cry of the breach of peace confounded those who were treating for the peace, and the king of France broke forth in the following speech: "I take it that God has hated these men, and hardened their hearts that they may fall into the hands of the destroyer: and having quickly returned, with all who were with him, to the king's pavilion, he found him already girding on his sword, whom he thus briefly addressed: "I will be a witness before all men, whatever be the consequence, that thou art blameless, if at length thou takest arms against the cursed Griffones." When he had said this, he departed; those who had accompanied him followed, and were received into the city. The king of England proceeds in arms; the terrible standard of the dragon is borne in front unfurled, while behind the king the sound of the trumpet excites the army. The sun shone brightly on the golden shields, and the mountains were resplendent in their glare; they marched cautiously and orderly, and the affair was managed without show. The Griffones, on the contrary, the city gates being closed, stood armed at the battlements of the walls and towers, as yet fearing nothing, and incessantly discharged their darts upon the enemy. The king, acquainted with nothing better than to take cities by storm and batter forts, let their quivers be emptied first, and then at length made his first assault by his archers who preceded the army. The sky is hidden by the shower of arrows, a thousand darts pierce through the shields spread abroad on the ramparts, nothing could save the rebels against the force of the darts. The walls are left without guard, because no one could look out of doors, but he would have an arrow in his eye before he could shut it.

Sect. 27. In the mean time, the king with his troops, without repulse, freely and as though with permission, approached the gates of the city, which, with the application of the battering-ram, he forced in an instant, and having led in his army, took every hold in the city, even to Tancred's palace and the lodgings of the French around their king's quarters, which he spared in respect of the king his lord. The standards of the victors are planted on the towers through the whole circuit of the city, and each of the surrendered fortifications he entrusted to particular captains of his army, and caused his nobles to take up their quarters in the city. He took the sons of all the nobility both of the city and surrounding country as hostages that they should either be redeemed at the king's price, or the remainder of the city should be delivered up to him without conflict, and he should take to himself satisfaction for his demands from their king Tancred. He began to attack the city about the fifth hour of the day, and took it the tenth hour and having withdrawn his army, returned victorious to his camp. King Tancred, terrified at the words of those who announced to him the issue of the transaction, hastened to make an agreement with him, sending him twenty thousand ounces of gold for his sister's dowry, and other twenty thousand ounces of gold for the legacy of King William and the observance of perpetual peace towards him and his. This small sum is accepted with much ado and scornfully enough, the hostages are given back, and peace is sworn and confirmed by the nobles of both nations.

Sect. 28. The king of England, now having little confidence in the natives, built a new wooden fort of great strength and height by the walls of Messina, which, to the reproach of the Griffones, he called "Mategriffun." The king's valor was greatly extolled, and the land kept silence in his presence. Walter, who from a monk and prior of St. Swithin's church at Winchester, had been advanced to be abbot of Westminster, died on the fifth of the calends of October.

Sect. 29. Queen Eleanor, a matchless woman, beautiful and chaste, powerful and modest, meek and eloquent, which is rarely wont to be met with in a woman, who was advanced in years enough to have had two husbands and two sons crowned kings, still indefatigable for every undertaking, whose power was the admiration of her age, having taken with her the daughter of the king of the Navarrese, a maid more accomplished than beautiful, followed the king her son, and having overtaken him still abiding in Sicily, she came to Pisa, a city full of every good, and convenient for her reception, there to await the king's pleasure, together with the king of Navarre's ambassadors and the damsel. Many knew what I wish that none of us had known. The same queen, in the time of her former husband, went to Jerusalem. Let none speak more thereof; I also know well. Be silent.

IN THE YEAR OF THE LORD MCXCI

Sect. 30. The first conference between the earl of Mortain, the king's brother, and the chancellor, respecting the custody of certain castles and the money out of the Exchequer conceded to the earl by his brother, was held at Winchester on Lester Jerusalem.

Robert, prior of St. Swithin's, at Winchester, having left his priory and forsaken his profession, cast himself into the sect of the Carthusians, at Witham, for grief (or shall I say for devotion?)

Walter, prior of Bath, with a like fervor or distraction, had before presumed the selfsame thing but once withdrawn, he seemed as yet to think of nothing less than a return.

Sect. 31. The king, although he had long ago sworn to the king of France that he would accept his sister as a consort, whom his father King Henry had provided for him, and for a long time had taken care of, because he was suspicious of the custody had of her, contemplated marrying the princess his mother had engaged. And that he might accomplish the desire without difficulty, with which he vehemently burned, he consulted the count of Flanders, a most eloquent man, and one who possessed an invaluable power of speech, by whose mediation the king of France released the king of England from his oath to marry his sister, and quit-claimed to him for ever the whole territory of Vaegesin and Gisorz, having received from him ten thousand pounds of silver.

Sect. 32. The king of France, with his army, departing for Jerusalem before the king of England, put to sea the third of the calends of April. The king of England, about to leave Sicily, caused the fort which he had built to be taken down, and stowed the whole of the materials in his ships to take along with him. Every sort of engine for the attack of fortifications, and every kind of arms which the heart of man could invent, he had all ready in his ships. Robert, son of William Fitz Ralph, was consecrated for the bishopric of Worcester by William de Longchamp, as yet legate, at Canterbury, on the third of the nones of May. The convent of Canterbury deposed their prior, whom Archbishop Baldwin had set over them, and substituted another in the place of the deposed.

Sect. 33. Walter, archbishop of Rouen, because, as is usual with the clergy, he was pusillanimous and timorous, having bidden adieu to Jerusalem from afar, resigned, unasked, all indignation against Saladin, and gave to the king all the provision he had brought for attacking him, and the cross; whilst, forgetting shame, he pretended, with that devotion which diffidence, the most wretched of mothers, brought forth, that pastors of the church should rather preach than fight, and that it is not meet for a bishop to wield other arms than those of virtue. But the king, to whom his money appeared more necessary than his personal presence, as if convinced by the overpowering argument, approved the allegations, and having arranged concerning the three years' contribution that he should furnish of a certain number of men and horses, sent him back again into England with his letters to William the chancellor; this being added at the end of the letters for honor and for all, that the chancellor should use his counsel in affairs of state. The king, having gained experience from the proceedings of this archbishop, purified his army, not permitting any one to come with him but such as could bear arms, and with a ready mind would use them nor did he suffer those who returned to take back with them their money, which they had brought thus far, or their arms. The queen, also, his mother, who had been received with all honor, as it was meet and after affectionate embraces had been led forth with great splendor, he caused to return with the archbishop having retained for himself the princess whom he had sought, and entrusted her to the safe custody of his sister, who had now returned to the camp to meet her mother.

Sect. 34. John, bishop of Exeter, closed his last day. Savaricus, archdeacon of Northampton, being also one of the many who had followed the king of England out of England to Sicily, was supplied by the king with letters patent, in the presence of the king's mother, to the justiciaries of England, containing the king's assent, and something more than an assent, that he should be promoted to whatever vacant diocese he could be elected to. These honorable acquisitions Savaricus sent to his kinsman, the bishop of Bath, into England, but he himself retired to Rome as one who had been best known among the Romans.

Sect. 35. Richard, king of England, in letters destined for England, taking leave of his whole kingdom, and giving strict injunction for the chancellor to be honored by all, his fleet, more to be prized for its quality than its numbers, being in readiness, with a chosen and brave army, with his sister Johanna and the princess he was to marry, with all things which could be necessary for those going to war, or going to set out on a long journey, set sail on the fourth of the ides of April. In the fleet, moreover, there were one hundred and fifty-six ships, four-and-twenty busses, and thirty and nine galleys; the sum of the vessels two hundred and nineteen.

Sect. 36. The archbishop of Rouen came to England to the chancellor, by whom he was received and treated honorably, and much better than the king had commanded. Others also followed with many mandates, in all of which the conclusion was, that the chancellor should be obeyed by all. To his brother John especially, he sent word by every messenger, that he should adhere to the chancellor that he should be a support to him against all men, and that he should not violate the oath he had given him. The king of England sent orders to the chancellor, and to the convent of Canterbury, and to the bishops of the province, that they should canonically and jointly provide for the metropolitan see, because, Baldwin being dead, it had been bereft of its prelate for the abbacy, however, of Westminster, now vacant, it is permitted to the chancellor alone to ordain as he pleases. There happened an eclipse of the sun about the third hour of the day: those who were ignorant of the causes of things were astonished, that in the middle of the day, no clouds obstructing the sun, the sun's rays should give a much feebler light than usual but those whom the motion of the universe occupies, say that the making deficiencies of the sun and moon does not signify any thing.

Sect. 37. John, the king's brother, who had long kept his ears open for it, when he knew for certain that his brother had turned his back on England, presently perambulated the kingdom in a more popular manner, nor did he forbid his followers calling him the king's heir. And as the earth is dreary in the sun's absence, so was the face of the kingdom altered at the king's departure. The nobles are all stirred up in arms, the castles are closed, the cities are fortified, entrenchments are thrown up. The archbishop of Rouen, not foreseeing more of the future than the fuel of error which was praised, knew well how so to give contentment to the chancellor, that at the same time he might not displease his rivals. Writs are privately dispatched to the heads of the clergy and of the people and the minds of everybody are excited against the chancellor. The knights of parliament willingly, though secretly, consented but the clergy, more fearful by nature, dared not swear obedience to either master. The chancellor, perceiving these things, dissembled, disdaining to know that any one would presume any how to attempt any thing against him.

Sect. 38. At length the pot is uncovered; it is announced to him, that Gerard de Camville, a factious man and reckless of allegiance, had done homage to Earl John, the king's brother, for the castle of Lincoln, the custody whereof is known to belong to the inheritance of Nicholas, the wife of the same Gerard, but under the king. The deed is considered to infringe upon the crown, and he resolves to go and revenge its commission. So having quickly collected numerous army, he came into those parts, and having first made an attack against Wigmore, he compelled Roger de Mortimer, impeached for a conspiracy made against the king, with the Welsh, to surrender the castles, and abjure England for three years. As he departed, he was blamed by his associates for want of courage, because, while supported by the numerous soldiery of the castles, and abounding in advantages, he had given way, without a blow, at the bare threats of the priest. Reproof was too late after the error; Roger leaves the kingdom, and the chancellor gives orders to besiege Lincoln. Gerard was with the earl and his wife Nicholaa, proposing to herself nothing effeminate, defended the castle like a man. The chancellor was wholly busied about Lincoln, whilst Earl John occupied the castle of Nottingham and that of Tickhill, both very strong, the warden being compelled to the surrender by fear alone. He proceeded, moreover, to send word to the chancellor that he must raise the siege, or otherwise he would avenge the cause of his vassal that it was not proper to take from the loyal men of the kingdom, well known and free, their charges, and commit them to strangers and men unknown; that it was a mark of his folly that he had entrusted the king's castles to such, because they would expose them to adventurers; that if it should go with every barbarian with that facility, that even the castles should be ready at all times for their reception, that he would no longer bear in silence the destruction of his brothers kingdom and affairs.

Sect. 39. The chancellor, incredibly troubled at these threats, having summoned before him the peers and chiefs of the army, begins: "Never trust me if this man seeks not to subjugate the kingdom to himself; what he presumes is exorbitant, even if he had a right to wear the crown by annual turns with his brother, for Eteocles has not yet completed a full year in his government. He uttered many words of anguish after this manner and then again having taken heart, as he was greater in moral courage than in physical, conceiving great things in his mind, he sent the archbishop of Rouen to the earl, demanding in an imperative manner that he should deliver up the castles, and that he should answer before the court of King's Bench for the breach of his oath to his brother. The archbishop, skilful in working with either hand, praised the constancy of the chancellor; and having proceeded to the earl, after the delivery of the mandates, he whispered in his ear, that whatever others might say, he should dare something great, worthy of Gyara and the dungeon, if he desired to be any thing. In public, however, he advised that the earl and the chancellor should agree to an interview, and that a reference to arbitration should end their disagreement.

Sect. 40. The earl, greatly exasperated at the impropriety of the mandates, was so altered in his whole body that a man would hardly have known him. Rancour made deep furrows in his forehead, his flaming eyes glistened, paleness discolored the rosy complexion of his face, and I know what would have become of the chancellor, if in that hour of fury he had fallen as an apple into his hands while frantically raging. His indignation increased so much in his stifled breast that it could not be kept from bursting out at least in part. "This son," said he, "of perdition, the worst of the evil ones, who first borrowed from the pleasantry of the French, and introduced among the English, the preposterous practice of kneeling, would not harass me, as you perceive, if I had not refused to learn the new craft offered to me!" He would fain have said more, whether true or false, but recalling his presence of mind, and repressing his rage, "If I have spoken amiss," said he, "O archbishop, I ask pardon." After these frivolous expressions, they applied themselves to the weighty matters. They consulted about the demands of the chancellor; and the counsel of the archbishop, that there should be a meeting of them both, was agreed to, about the middle of the day. The day was fixed for the fifth of the calends of August; the place without Winchester. The chancellor allowed what they had settled to stand, and, having broken up the siege, returned to London.

Sect. 41. The earl, however, fearing his craftiness, brought thither four thousand Welsh, that, if the chancellor should endeavor to take him during the truce, they, being placed in ambush close beside the conference, might thwart his endeavors by a sally. Moreover, he commanded that it should be summoned, and required that every one of his men, and others, his adherents, should be prepared to go to battle, should attend him at the place and on the day of the engagement, so that as the interview between himself and the lord of the whole land had been undertaken, at least he might escape alive, if he, who was more than a king, though less in his eyes, should transgress against the law, or should not consent to an arrangement. The chancellor, however, on the other hand, commanded that one-third of the soldiery, with all the arms of all England, should proceed to Winchester by the day appointed; moreover, at the expense of the king's revenue he also hired some Welsh, that if it should come to a contest with the earl, he might have an equal array, and javelins threatening javelins.

Sect. 42. They came to the interview as was' before agreed on, and it happened to terminate better than was feared. The agreement, moreover, made between the earl and the chancellor was thus, and in this way provided. First of all were named the three bishops of Winchester, London, and Bath, in whose fidelity each party considered himself secure. The bishops chose for the chancellors part the three earls of Warren, of Arundel, of Clare, and certain other eight by name. For the easy part, Stephen Ridel, the earl's chancellor, William de Yenneval, Reginald de Wasseville, and certain other eight by name. These all, some beholding some touching the holy gospels, swore that they would provide satisfaction between the earl and the chancellor concerning their quarrels and questions to the honor of both parties and the peace of the kingdom. And if hereafter any disagreement should happen between them, they would faithfully end it. The earl also, and the chancellor, swore that they would consent to whatever the aforesaid jury should settle; and this was the provision. Gerard de Camville, being received into the chancellor's favor, the custody of the castle of Lincoln was reserved to him in peace and safety; the earl gave up the castles which he had taken, and the chancellor having received them, gave them over to the king's faithful and liege men, namely, to William de Wenn the castle of Nottingham, and to Reginald de Wasseville the castle of Tickhill and each of them gave an hostage to the chancellor, that they would keep those castles in the safe peace and fidelity of their lord the king, if he should return alive. If, however, the king should die before his return, the aforesaid castles should be delivered up to the earl, and the chancellor should restore the hostages. The constables of the castles of the earl's honors should be changed by the chancellor, if the earl should show reason for their being changed. The chancellor, if the king should die, should not seek the disherison of the earl; but should promote him to the kingdom with all his power. Concluded solemnly at Winchester, on the seventh of the calends of May.

Sect. 43. The chancellor, by wonderful importunity and earnestness, persuaded first a part of the monks and after wards the whole congregation of Westminster, to permit his brother, a monk of Cadomo, to profess a cohabitation in Westminster, and to be elected by all for their abbot for his profession and cohabitation on a day appointed; and that this election should not be broken, security was taken by a bond, with the church's seal affixed as a testimony.

Sect. 44. Geoffrey, a brother of King Richard and Earl John, but not by their mother, who had been consecrated archbishop of York at Tours, by the archbishop of Tours, by the pope's command, continually solicited by message John the king's brother and his own, that at the least it might be permitted him to return to England and having obtained his consent, he prepared to return. The intercourse of the brothers did not escape the chancellor's knowledge, who providing, lest their natural genuine perverseness should increase, commanded the keepers of the coasts, that wherever that archbishop, who had abjured England for the three years of the king's travels, should disembark within the bounds of the kingdom, he should not be permitted to proceed, but by the will of the jury, to whose award the earl and the chancellor had taken oath to stand concerning every thing that should happen.

Sect. 45. A certain Robert, prior of Hereford, a monk who did not think very meanly of himself, and gladly forced himself into other people's business that he might intermix his own, had gone into Sicily to the king on the chancellor's messages, where after the rest he did not forget his own interests and having by some means or other worried everybody, succeeded in obtaining the abbacy of Muchelney to be granted to him and confirmed by the king. Into possession of which, by the chancellors means, he entered, against the will of the convent, neither canonically, nor with a benediction and presently on the first day, at the first dinner, by greedily partaking of fresh eels without wine, and more than was proper, he fell into a languor, which the food, undigested and lying heavily on an inflamed stomach, brought on. And lest the languor should be ascribed to his gluttony, he caused the monks of that place to be slandered of having given him poison.

Sect. 46. Geoffrey, archbishop of York, presuming upon the consent of his brother Earl John, his shipping being ready, came to Dover, and presently having landed, first sought a church for prayer. There is there a priory of monks of the profession of Canterbury, whose oratory he entered with his clerks to hear mass, and his household was intent about unlading the ships. No sooner had the whole of his goods been landed, than suddenly the constable of the castle caused whatever he thought was the archbishop's to be brought into the town, understanding more in the command of his lord the chancellor than he had commanded. Certain also of the soldiers, armed under their tunics, and girt with swords, came into the monastery, that they might apprehend the pontiff; whom when he saw, their intention being foreknown, he took a cross in his hands, and first addressing them and extending his hands towards his followers, he says, "I am the archbishop; if ye seek me, let these go their way. And the soldiers reply, " Whether you be an archbishop or not, it is nothing to us; one thing we know, that you are Geoffrey, the son of King Henry, whom he begot on some strange bed, who before the king, whose brother you make yourself, have forsworn England for three years; if you are not come into the kingdom as a traitor to the kingdom; if you have brought letters of absolution, either say, or take the reproach. Then said the archbishop, "I am not a traitor, neither will I show you any letters. They then laid their hands on him there before the very altar, and violently dragged him out of the church against his will, and resisting, but not with force; who immediately being set without the threshold, excommunicated by name those who had laid hands on him, both present and whilst they were still holding him nor did he receive the horse that they offered him that he might ride with them to the castle, because it was the property of the excommunicated. And so, outraging humanity, they dragged him on foot by the hands, and carrying the cross, all through the mud of the streets to the castle. After this they desired of their own good will to deal humanely with their captive, bringing him some of the best provisions which they had prepared for themselves; but he, being firmly resolved, by what he had now suffered, rejected their victuals as if it were an offering to idols, and refused to live on any thing but his own. The report spread over the kingdom more rapidly than the wind, those who had followed their lord at a distance came after, relating and complaining to all that the archbishop, the king's brother, thus landed, had been so treated and detained in prison.

Sect. 47. The archbishop was already three days in custody, and the chancellor, as soon as the case was made known to him, restored to him all his goods, and set him at liberty to depart whithersoever he should desire. He wrote, moreover, to Earl John, and to all the bishops, asserting, with an oath, that the aforesaid man had suffered the above-written injuries without his knowledge. The excuse profited little, because the occasion, which had been long sought and which spontaneously offered itself against him, was most eagerly and tenaciously laid hold of.

The authors of this daring act, who laid hands on the archbishop, as well as those who consented thereto, were all specially excommunicated in every church of the whole kingdom, that at least the chancellor, who was hateful to everybody, might be involved in the general malediction.

Sect. 48. Earl John, gnashing his teeth with anger against the chancellor, whom he hated, brought a weighty complaint before all the bishops and lords of the kingdom, of the infringement of the convention by the adverse party, by the arrest of his brother, to his own dishonor. The jurors are summoned and are sworn to stand by their plighted promise, and to bring it to pass as quickly as possible, that the perjurer and breaker of his faith should repair what he had done amiss by giving ample satisfaction. The affair, hitherto confined to trifles, now bears a serious aspect; the chancellor is summoned by the powerful authority of all his and the earl's mediators, to meet him and answer to the earl's accusations, and to submit to the law, the place at Lodbridge, the day the third of the nones of October.

Sect. 49. The earl, with the greatest part of the nobility of the kingdom all favoring him, had awaited the chancellor two days at the place of meeting, and on the third, in the morning, he sent on certain of his followers to London, still waiting at the place of meeting in case he who was expected should either dare or deign to come. The chancellor, dreading in himself the earl, and being suspicious of the judges, delayed to come to the place for two days on the third (because as every one feels conscious in his mind, so does he conceive in his breast both hope and fear for his deeds), half way between hope and fear, he attempted to go to the meeting. And behold! Henry Biset, a faithful man of his, who had seen the above-mentioned party of the earl's friends passing on, putting frequently the spur to his horse, comes to meet the chancellor, and tells him that the earl, before daylight, had gone in arms to take Loudon and who was there, on that day, that did not take every thing as gospel, which that honorable man told them? but yet he was not guilty of falsehood, because he thought that what he had said was true. The chancellor, deceived, as all men are liable to be, immediately caused all the force that was with him to arm and thinking that he was following close upon the earl, came before him to the city. The citizens being asked by him, for the earl was not yet come, that they would close the gates against him when he should come, refused, calling him a disturber of the land, and a traitor. For the archbishop of York, conscious of what would happen, whilst he was tarrying there some days that he might see the end of the matter, by continual complaints and entreaties had excited them all against him and then, for the first time, perceiving himself betrayed, he betook himself to the

Tower, and the Londoners set a watch, both by land and water, that he might not escape. The earl, having knowledge of his flight, following him up with his forces, was received by the joyful citizens with lanterns and torches, for he came to town by night and there was nothing wanting in the salutations of the flattering people, save that barbarous Chaire Basileus which is, "Hail, dear lord!"

Sect. 50. On the next day, the earl and all the nobles of the land assembled in St. Paul's church, and first of all was heard the archbishop of York's complaint after that, whosoever had aught against him was admitted. The accusers of the absent had an attentive and diligent hearing, and especially Hugh, bishop of Coventry, so prolix in words, who the day before had been his most familiar friend, who, as the worst pest, is a familiar enemy, having harangued more bitterly and perversely than all the rest, against his friend, did not desist until it was said by all, " We will not have this man to reign over us." So the whole assembly, without any delay, elected Earl John, the king's brother, chief justiciary of the whole kingdom, and ordaining that all the castles should be delivered to the custody of such as he should choose, they left only three of the weakest, and lying at a great distance from each other, to the now merely nominal chancellor. The chief justice after the earl, the justices itinerant, the barons of the Exchequer, the constables of castles, all new, are appointed afresh. Amongst others then gainers, both the bishop of Winchester received the custodies which the chancellor had taken from him, without diminution, and the lord bishop of Durham received the county of Northumberland.

Sect. 51. That unlucky day was declining towards evening, when four bishops, and as many earls, sent on the part of the assembly to the chancellor, explained to him, to the letter, the acts of the whole day. He was horror-struck at such unexpected presumption and arrogance, and, his vigor of mind failing, he fell to the earth so exhausted, that he foamed at the mouth. Cold water being sprinkled on his face, he revived, and having risen on his feet, he addressed the messengers with a stern countenance, saying, "There is one help for the vanquished, to hope for no help." You have conquered and you have bound incautiously. If the Lord God shall grant me to see my lord the king with my two eyes, be sure this day has shone inauspiciously for you. As much as in you lay, you have now delivered to the earl, whatever was the king's in the kingdom. Say to him, Priam still lives. You, who forgetful of your still surviving king, have elected to yourselves another to be lord, tell to that your lord, that all will turn out otherwise than he supposes. I will not give up the castles, I will not resign the seal." The messengers, having returned from him, related to the earl what they had received, who ordered the Tower to be more closely besieged.

Sect. 52. The chancellor was sleepless the greater part of the night (because he who does not set his mind on honest studies and pursuits will toss about wakeful through hate or love) and at the same time his people disturbed him more than his conscience, falling prostrate at his feet, and entreating with tears that he would yield to necessity, and not stretch forth his arms against the torrent. He, though harder than iron, is softened by the piteous counsel of those who were weeping round him again and again having fainted with grief, at last, lie with much ado assented that that should be done, which, being entirely destitute of aid, he was compelled to do. One of his brothers, and three, not ignoble, of his adherents, being permitted, not commissioned, announced to the earl at that time of night, that the chancellor, with what readiness it does not matter, was prepared to do and suffer whatever had been determined. He should avoid delay, because it has always been injurious for those who are prepared to defer. It should be done the next day, lest the wind should so veer, that it might be deferred for a year. These return to the Tower, and before day, the earl made known to his adherents that these things had passed.

Sect. 53. Meanwhile, the rising dawn left the ocean, and the sun having now appeared, the earl, with his whole troop, withdrew to the open field, which is without London towards the east; the chancellor went thither also, but less early than his adversaries. The nobles took the centre, around whom was next a circle of citizens, and beyond an attentive populace, estimated at ten thousand men. The bishop of Coventry first attacked the chancellor, rehearsing the several accusations of the preceding day, and ever adding something of his own. "It is not" said he, "either fit or bearable that such gross incapacity of one should so often cause so many noble and honorable men, and from such remote parts, to assemble for nothing. And since it is better to be troubled once for all, than always, I will conclude all in few words. It does not please, because it is not convenient, that you should any longer bear rule in the kingdom. You will be content with your bishopric, and the three castles with which we have indulged you, and the shelter of a great name. You will in the next place give hostages for giving up all the other castles, and for not seeking increased power or making tumults, and afterwards you will be able to depart freely whithersoever you may desire. Many spoke much in favor of this, none against the lord of Winchester, although he was more eloquent than most of them, alone observed continued silence. At length the chancellor, scarcely permitted to speak, exclaimed, "Am I always to be a hearer only and shall I never answer? Before all things, know ye each and every one, that I feel myself guilty of not ing that I should fear the mouth of any of you. I solemnly declare that the archbishop of York was taken, without either my knowledge or my will that I will prove in the civil courts- if you wish, or in the ecclesiastical. Respecting the deficiencies of the king, if I have done any thing amiss in that matter, Geoffrey Fitz-Peter, William Briwere, and Hugh Bardolf, whom I received from the king as councilors, would, if it were permitted them to speak, give satisfaction for me. Why and in what I have spent the king's treasure, I am ready to give account to the utmost farthing. I do not refuse to give hostages for delivering up the castles, though in this I ought rather to fear the king yet as I must, I must. The name which you are not able to take away, and I am still to bear, I do not set light by. In short, I give you all to know, that I depose myself from no administration given me by the king. You, being many, have besieged me alone; you are stronger than I, and I, the king's chancellor and justiciary of the kingdom, am condemned against all form of law; it is through necessity I yield to the stronger." The sun declining to the west, put an end to the allegations of the parties; the two brothers of the chancellor that was, and a certain third person, his chamberlain, who had also been his secretary, were received in hostage. The assembly is dissolved, the keys of the Tower of London being given up on the sixth of the ides of October. The chancellor started for Dover, one, to wit, of the three castles of which mention was made and the earl delivered, to those he chose and whom he trusted most, all the fortresses of the land which had been given up to him.

Sect. 54. Messengers are immediately dispatched to the Land of Promise, to the king himself, both by the condemned and the condemners, each by his own party, sufficiently instructed to accuse or excuse. The chancellor, being uncomfortable here under the appellation of his lost authority, and the recollection of his present state, whilst he endeavored by all means to elude the prohibition of his going abroad, got scoffed, not uniformly, nor once only. I will not recount how he was taken and detained, both in the habit of a monk and in that of a woman, because it is enough and more than enough, to recollect what inestimable property and immense treasures the Flemish stripped him of, when at length he arrived in Flanders. His passage over being known, whatever revenue he had possessed in England was confiscated. A most dreadful contention is carried on between the mighty. The chancellor suspends his diocese which had been taken from him, and he denounces his anathema upon all those who trespassed against him. Nor was the archbishop of Rouen more remiss in the same way, for in revenge for his presumptuous excommunication of the Exchequer barons, he commanded it to be announced throughout Normandy that William de Longchamp should be held as excommunicated. He was, however, unwilling to seem to fear the malediction uttered against the invaders of the aforesaid bishopric, nor did he believe that the sentence of a fugitive prelate could find its way before his majesty's throne. So the face of the church of Ely was disfigured, they ceased throughout the diocese from every work of the Lord, the bodies of the dead lay unburied by all the ways. In Normandy, the like being returned, none under the archbishop's authority communicated with the chancellor on his entry every church was suspended, and on his departure all the bells were rung, and the altars where he officiated cast down.

Sect. 55. Two legates dispatched into France by the pope, at the instigation, though secret, as is reported, of the king of the French, came to Gisorz to visit Normandy, which they understood was a chief part of the kingdom of the French but both the constable of the castle and the seneschal of Normandy would not admit them, excusing themselves with this shadow of a reason, that the visitation of any province should not be made unless with the approbation or in the presence of the lord of the land all the kings of the English, and particularly Richard, being especially indulged with this privilege by the Holy See. No allegation, whether real or probable, availed with the legates their almost divine power rose and swelled with rage, though against those who heeded them not the contemned authority of Roman majesty is exercised they lay aside high-flown sentences and long words. They threaten their adversaries with much bitterness; but, however, as they had not to plead with boys, the castle gates being shut against them, they stood without the doors. But their solace was not wanting, though they were repulsed. They reached with their power, where they could not approach in person. They excommunicated by name the constable of Gisorz and the seneschal of Normandy, there present, and suspended the whole of Normandy from every administration of the rites of the church. It was necessary to yield to their power; the church was silent immediately, and so remained the space of three weeks, until, the pope being supplicated, both the sentence against those named was remitted, and the suspension given out against Normandy. The book of liberty was restored to Normandy, and the voice of gladness, and the legates were prohibited to set foot therein.

Sect. 56. The Westminster monks, who before those days had so greatly excelled in magnanimity, that they would not stain their deeds for death itself, as soon as they saw a new era, changed also with the time, putting behind their backs whatever they had covenanted with the chancellor for his brother with the connivance of the earl, they elected the prior of their house to be abbat, who also received immediately the benediction and staff from the bishop of London. The chancellor's brother, who by agreement should have been elected abbat, seeing the convent break their engagement, troubled thereat, departed with his half-modesty, carrying off with him, however, the bond of security, having made an appeal prior to the second election before legitimate witnesses, that nothing should be done against his stipulated promotion.

The monks of Muchelney, after the example of those of Westminster, though not altogether in a similar way, expelled their principal, I do not know whether abbat or abbat elect, whom they had been forced to accept, casting forth the straw of his bed after him, and thrust him with much insult out of their island to the four winds of heaven.

Sect. 57. The archbishop of Rouen being constituted by the earl justiciary of the kingdom, and supreme over affairs, having convoked, at Canterbury, the clergy and people, as the king himself had enjoined him, directed them to proceed to the election of an archbishop. The bishops of London and Winchester, however, were not present, being detained at London by the king's business, and the question being broached among the bishops who had assembled, which of them should be esteemed the greater, whose the election ought to be, as the two aforesaid of chief dignity were absent, the prior of Canterbury solving the point of difficulty, made all equal in choosing a pontiff, and proceeding forth in public with his monks, in the face of the whole church, elected, as archbishop, Reginald, bishop of Bath, from the midst of the clergy.

Sect. 58. Reginald, elect of Canterbury, who would have proceeded to Rome for his pall, had the fates permitted, having completed the solemnities which are usually celebrated for the elect at Canterbury, came to set things in order in the diocese of Bath, which he greatly loved, and by which he was more beloved. It is reported also, that he had obtained, as he desired, the assent of the prior and convent for electing and substituting in his place, Savaricus, archdeacon of Northampton, and had received the security. Returning from thence, he fell sick by the way, and was laid up very ill at his manor of Dokemeresfeld and seeing nothing more likely to happen to him than death, he took the habit of a monk at the hands of his prior Walter, then tarrying with him and receiving it, spoke these words, "God willed not that I should be archbishop, and I will not God willed that I should be a monk, and I will!" Moreover, being in the last extremities, he took the king's letters to the justices, for conceding to Savaricus whatever diocese he should be elected to, and gave them to the prior of Bath, that by the authority of this instrument he might the sooner be promoted. Then having accomplished all things which relate to faith and penitence devoutly and with a sane mind, he fell asleep in the Lord on the seventh of the calends of January.

Walter, prior of Bath, and his convent, without the clergy, elected to themselves for their future bishop Savaricus, archdeacon of Northampton, who was absent, and as yet ignorant of the decease of his fellow-pontiff; and although the clergy resisted, they carried it out.

Sect. 59. The fleet of Richard, king of the English, put out to sea, and proceeded in this order. In the forefront went three ships only, in one of which was the queen of Sicily and the young damsel of Navarre, probably still a virgin; in the other two, a certain part of the king's treasure and arms in each of the three, marines and provisions. In the second line there were, what with ships and busses and men-of-war, thirteen; in the third, fourteen; in the fourth, twenty; in the fifth, thirty; in the sixth, forty; in the seventh, sixty; in the last, the king himself, followed with his galleys. There was between the ships, and between their lines, a certain space left by the sailors at such interval, that from one line to another the sound of the trumpet, from one ship to another, the human voice, could be heard. This also was admirable, that the king was no less cheerful and healthy, strong and mighty, light and gay, at sea, than he was wont to be by land. I conclude, therefore, that there was not one man more powerful than he in the world, either by land or sea.

Sect. 60. Now, as the ships were proceeding in the aforesaid manner and order, some being before others, two of the three first, driven by the violence of the winds, were broken on the rocks near the port of Cyprus; the third, which was English, more speedy than they, having turned back into the deep, escaped the peril. Almost all the men of both ships got away alive to land, many of whom the hostile Cypriotes slew, some they took captive, some, taking refuge in a certain church, were besieged. Whatever also in the ships was cast up by the sea, fell a prey to the Cypriotes. The prince also of that island coming up, received for his share the gold and the arms and he caused the shore to be guarded by all the armed force he could summon together, that he might not permit the fleet which followed to approach, lest the king should take again what had been thus stolen from him. Above the port, was a strong city, and upon a natural rock, a high and fortified castle. The whole of that nation was warlike, and accustomed to live by theft. They placed beams and planks at the entrance of the port, across the passage, the gates and entrances; and the whole land, with one mind, prepared themselves for a conflict against the

English. God so willed, that the cursed people should receive the reward of their evil deeds by the hands of one who would not spare. The third English ship, in which were the women, having cast out its anchors, rode out at sea, and watched all things from opposite, to report the misfortune to the king, lest haply, being ignorant of the loss and disgrace, he should pass the place unrevenged. The next line of the king's ships came up after the other, and they all stopped at the first. A full report reached the king, who, sending heralds to the lord of the island, and obtaining no satisfaction, commanded his entire army to arm, from the first even to the last, and to get out of the great ships into the galleys and boats, and follow him to the shore. What he commanded, was immediately performed; they came in arms to the port. The king being armed, leaped first from his galley, and gave the first blow in the war but before he was able to strike a second, he had three thousand of his followers with him striking away by his side. All the timber that had been placed as a barricade in the port was cast down instantly, and the brave fellows went up into the city, as ferocious as lionesses are wont to be when robbed of their young. The fight was carried on manfully against them, numbers fell down wounded on both sides, and the swords of both parties were made drunk with blood. The Cypriotes are vanquished, the city is taken, with the castle besides; whatever the victors choose is ransacked, and the lord of the island is himself taken and brought to the king. He, being taken, supplicates and obtains pardon; he offers homage to the king, and it is received and he swears, though unasked, that henceforth he will hold the island of him as his liege lord, and will open all the castles of the land to him, make satisfaction for the damage already done and further, bring presents of his own. On being dismissed after the oath, he is commanded to fulfill the conditions in the morning.

Sect. 61. That night the king remained peaceably in the castle and his newly-sworn vassal flying, retired to another castle, and caused the whole of the men of that land, who were able to bear arms, to be summoned to repair to him, and so they did. The king of Jerusalem, however, that same night, landed in Cyprus, that he might assist the king and salute him, whose arrival he had desired above that of any other in the whole world. On the morrow, the lord of Cyprus was sought for and found to have fled. The king, seeing that he was abused, and having been informed where he was, directed the king of Jerusalem to follow the traitor by land with the half of the army, while he conducted the other part by water, intending to be in the way, that he might not escape by sea. The divisions reassembled around the city in which he had taken refuge, and he, having sallied out against the king, fought with the English, and the battle was carried on sharply by both sides. The English would that day have been beaten, had they not fought under the command of King Richard. They at length obtained a dear-bought victory, the Cypriote flies, and the castle is taken. The kings pursue him as before, the one by land, the other by water, and he is besieged in the third castle. Its walls are cast down by engines hurling huge stones; he, being overcome, promises to surrender, if only he might not be put in iron fetters. The king consents to the prayers of the supplicant, and caused silver shackles to be made for him. The prince of the pirates being thus taken, the king traversed the whole island, and took all its castles, and placed his constables in each, and constituted justiciaries and sheriffs and the whole land was subjected to him in every thing just like England. The gold, and the silk, and the jewels from the treasures that were broken open, he retained for himself; the silver and victuals he gave to the army. To the king of Jerusalem also he made a handsome present out of his booty.

And because Lent had already passed, and the lawful time of contract was come, he caused Berengaria, daughter of the king of Navarre, whom his mother had brought to him in Lent, to be affianced to him in the island.

Sect. 62. After these things, having taken again to the ships, whilst sailing prosperously towards Acre, he falls in with a merchant ship of immense dimensions, destined by Saladin to the besieged, laden with provisions and full of armed soldiers. A wonderful ship, a ship than which, with the exception of Noah's ark, we do not read of any being greater. The intrepid king here rejoices, because everywhere he meets with a fit object for valor; he, first of his warriors, having summoned to his, the galleys of his followers, commences the naval action with the Turks. The ship was fortified with towers and bulwarks, and the desperate fought furiously, because "the only hope for the conquered is to have nothing to hope for." The assault was dreadful and the defense stout; but what is there so hard, that the sturdy man who stoutly perseveres shall not subdue? The followers of Mahomet are vanquished that ship, the queen of ships, is shattered and sunk, as lead in the mighty waters, and the whole property perished with its possessors.

The king, proceeding thence, came to the siege of Acre, and was welcomed by the besiegers with as great joy as if it had been Christ that had come again on earth to restore the kingdom of Israel. The king of the French had arrived at Acre first, and was very highly esteemed by the natives but on Richard's arrival he became obscured and without consideration, just as the moon is wont to relinquish her luster at the rising of the sun.

Sect. 63. Henry, count of Champagne, whose whole store that he had brought both of provision and money was now wasted, comes to his king. He asks relief, to whom his king and lord caused to be offered a hundred thousand of Paris money, if, in that case, he would be ready to pledge to him Champagne. To that the count replied, "I have done what I could and what I ought; now I shall do what I am compelled by necessity. I desired to fight for my king, but he would not accept of me, unless for my own; I will go to him who will accept me: who is more ready to give than to receive." The king of the English, Richard, gave to Henry, count of Champagne, when he came to him, four thousand bushels of wheat, four thousand bacons, and four thousand pounds of silver. So the whole army of strangers out of every nation under heaven bearing the Christian name, who had already assembled to the siege long before the coming of the kings, at the report of so great a largess, took King Richard to be their general and lord the Franks only who had followed their lord remained with their poor king of the French.

Sect. 64. The king of the English, unused to delay, on the third day of his arrival at the siege, caused his wooden fortress, which he had called "Mate Griffon," when it was made in Sicily, to be built and set up, and before the dawn of the fourth day the machine stood erect by the walls of Acre, and from its height looked down upon the city lying beneath it and there were thereon by sunrise archers casting missiles without intermission on the Turks and Thracians. Engines also for casting stones, placed in convenient positions, battered the walls with frequent volleys. More important than these, sappers making themselves a way beneath the ground undermined the foundations of the walls; while soldiers bearing shields, having planted ladders, sought an entrance over the ramparts. The king himself was running up and down through the ranks, directing some, reproving some, and urging others, and thus was he everywhere present with every one of them, so that whatever they all did, ought properly to be ascribed to him. The king of the French also himself did not lightly assail them, making as bold an assault as he could on the tower of the city which is called Cursed.

Sect. 65. The renowned Carracois and Mestocus, after Saladin the most powerful princes of the heathen, had at that time the charge of the besieged city, who, after a contest of many days, promised by their interpreters the surrender of the city, and a ransom for their heads but the king of the English desired to subdue their obstinacy by force and wished that the vanquished should pay their heads for the ransom of their bodies, but, by the mediation of the king of the French, their life and indemnity of limbs only was accorded them, if, after surrender of the city and yielding of every thing they possessed, the Holy Cross should be given up.

Sect. 66. All the heathen warriors in Acre were chosen men, and were in number nine thousand. Many of whom, swallowing many gold coins, made a purse of their stomachs, because they foresaw that whatever they had of any value would be turned against them, even against themselves, if they should again oppose the cross, and would only fall a prey to the victors. So all of them come out before the kings entirely disarmed, and outside the city, without money, are given into custody and the kings, with triumphal banners, having entered the city, divided the whole with all its stores into two parts between themselves and their soldiers; the pontiff's seat alone its bishop received by their united gift. The captives, moreover, being divided, Mestocus fell by lot to the portion of the king of the English, and Carracois, as a drop of cold water, fell into the burning mouth of the thirsty Philip, king of the French.

Sect. 67. The duke of Austria, who was also one of the ancient besiegers of Acre, followed the king of the English as a participator in the possession of his portion, and because, as his standard was borne before him, he was thought to take to himself a part of the triumph; if not by command, at least with the consent, of the offended king, the duke's standard was cast down in the dirt, and to his reproach and ridicule trampled under foot by them. The duke, although grievously enraged against the king, dissembled his offence, which he could not vindicate and having returned to the place where he had carried on the siege, betook himself that night to his tent, which was set up again, and afterwards, as soon as he could, returned to his own country full of rancor.

Sect. 68. Messengers on the part of the captives having been sent to Saladin for their ransom, when the heathen could by no entreaty be moved to restore the Holy Cross, the king of the English beheaded all his, with the exception of Mestocus only, who on account of his nobility was spared and declared openly without any ceremony that he would act in the same way towards Saladin himself.

Sect. 69. A certain marques of Montferrat, a smooth-faced man, had held Tyre, which he had seized on many years ago, to whom the king of the French sold all his captives alive, and promised the crown of the region which was not yet conquered but the king of the English withstood him to the face. "It is not proper," said he, "for a man of our reputation to bestow or promise what is not yet obtained but further, if the cause of your journey be Christ, when at length you have taken Jerusalem, the chief of the cities of this region, from the hand of the enemy, you will without delay or condition restore the kingdom to Guy, the legitimate king of

Jerusalem. For the rest, if you recollect, you did not obtain Acre without a participator, so that neither should that which is the property of two be dealt out by one hand." Oh! oh! How fine for a godly throat ! The marques, bereft of his blissful hope, returns to Tyre, and the king of the French, who had greatly desired to strengthen himself against his envied ally by means of the marques, now fell off daily; and this added to the continual irritation of his mind,—that even the scullion of the king of the English fared more sumptuously than the cupbearer of the French. After some time, letters were forged in the tent of the king of the French, by which, as if they had been sent by his nobles out of France, the king was recalled to France. A cause is invented which would necessarily be respected more than it deserved his only son, after a long illness, was now despaired of by the physicians; France exposed to be desolated, if, after the son's death, the father (as it might fall out) should perish in a foreign land. So, frequent council being held between the kings hereupon, as they were both great and could not dwell together, Abraham remaining, Lot departed from him. Moreover, the king of the French, by his chief nobles, gave security by oath for himself and his vassals, to the king of the English, that he would observe every pledge until he should return to his kingdom in peace.

Sect. 70. On that day the commonalty of the Londoners was granted and instituted, to which all the nobles of the kingdom, and even the very bishops of that province, are compelled to swear. Now for the first time London, by the agreement conceded to it, found by experience that there was no king in the kingdom, as neither King Richard himself, nor his predecessor and father Henry, would have suffered it to be concluded for one thousand marks of silver. How great evils forsooth may come forth of this agreement, may be estimated by the very definition, which is this. The commonalty is the pride of the common people, the dread of the kingdom, the ferment of the priesthood.

Sect. 71. The king of the French, with but few followers, returning home from Acre, left at that place the strength of his army to do nothing, to the command of which he appointed the bishop of Beauvais and the duke of Burgundy. The English king, having sent for the commanders of the French, proposed that in the first place they should conjointly attempt Jerusalem itself but the dissuasion of the French discouraged the hearts of both parties, and dispirited the troops, and restrained the king, thus destitute of men, from his intended march upon that metropolis. The king, troubled at this, though not despairing, from that day forth separated his army from the French, and directing his arms to the storming of castles along the sea-shore, he took every fortress that came in his way from Tyre to Ascalon, though after hard fighting and deep wounds. But to Tyre he deigned not to go, because it was not in the compass of his part of the campaign.

IN THE YEAR OF THE LORD MCXCII

Sect. 72. Philip, king of the French, having left his companion, Richard, king of the English, in the territory of Jerusalem amongst the enemies of the cross of Christ, returned to France, without obtaining either the liberation of the Holy Cross or of the Holy Sepulchre. Godfrey, bishop of Winchester, restored to his church a great part of the treasure, which, as related above, he had appointed, on the third of the calends of February. The feast of the Purification of the Blessed Mary was celebrated on the very Sunday of Septuagesima at Winchester. But the Sunday had nothing belonging to Sunday but its memory at vespers and matins, and the morning mass. One full hide of land at the manse which is called Morslede, of the village of Ciltecumba, was let to a certain citizen of Winchester of the name of Pentecuste, to hold for twenty years for the annual and free service of twenty shillings, without the privily of the convent.

Sect. 73. Queen Eleanor sailed from Normandy and landed at Portsmouth on the third of the ides of February. The chancellor repaired to the king of the French, and deposed before him his complaint relative to the loss of his treasures in Flanders, but he got nothing more there than what makes men ridiculous.

The king of the French caused all manner of arms to be fabricated both day and night throughout his whole realm, and fortified his cities and castles, as was thought, by way of preparation for a struggle against the king of the English, if he should return from his journey. Which being known in the territories of the king of the English, his constables throughout Normandy, Le Mans, Anjou, Tours, Bourges, Poitou, and Gascony, of themselves fortified every place that could be fortified in the fullest manner. Moreover, the son of the king of Navarre, to spite the French, ravaged the country about Toulouse. A certain provost of the king of the French, desiring to become greater than his forefathers, set up a castle on the confines of Normandy and France, where there had never yet been any fortification which, ere it was built, the Normans, by the impulse of their natural anger, totally overthrew, and tore the provost himself to pieces.

Sect. 74. Queen Eleanor, a lady worthy of repeated mention, visited certain houses appertaining to her dower within the diocese of Ely. To meet her there came out of all the hamlets and manors, wherever she passed, men with women and little children, not all of the lowest class, a piteous and pitiable company, with their feet bare, their clothes unwashed, and their hair unshorn. They speak in tears, for which, in very grief, they had failed to utter words, nor was there need of an interpreter, as more than they desired to say might be read in the open page. Human bodies lay unburied everywhere throughout the country, because their bishop had deprived them of sepulture. The queen, on understanding the cause of so great severity, as she was very compassionate, taking pity on the people's misery for the dead, immediately neglecting her own, and following other men's matters, repaired to London; she entreated, nay, she demanded, of the archbishop of Rouen, that the confiscated estates of the bishop should be restored to the bishop, and that the same bishop should in the name of the chancery be proclaimed absolved from the excommunication denounced against him, throughout the province of Rouen. And who could be so harsh or obdurate that that lady could not bend him to her wishes? She, too, forgetful of nothing, sent word into Normandy to the lord of Ely, of the public and private restitution which she had obtained for him, and compelled him to revoke the sentence of excommunication he had pronounced against the Exchequer barons. So by the queen's mediation there was peace between the implacable, though their vexation was apparent, as the disaffection of their minds, contracted in their former hatred, could not be changed, without each giving some utterance to his feelings.

Sect. 75. Earl John, sending messengers to Southampton, commanded shipping to be made ready for him to depart, as was thought, to the king of the French but the queen his mother, fearing lest the light-minded youth, by the counsels of the French, might go to attempt something against his lord and brother, with anxious mind takes in hand with her utmost ability to divert the intention of her son. The fate of her former sons, and the untimely decease of both under their oppressing sins, recurring to her mind, moved, or rather pierced, the maternal bowels of compassion. She desired that their violence might be enough, and that, at least, good faith being kept amongst her younger children, she, as their mother, might end her days more happily than had fallen to the lot of their deceased father. So having assembled all the peers of the realm, first at Windsor, secondly at Oxford, thirdly at London, and fourthly at Winchester, she with her own tears and the entreaties of the nobles with difficulty obtained that he would not cross the sea for this time. The earl, therefore, being in effect frustrated of his proposed passage, did what he could that way, and received the castles from the king's constables of Windsor and Wallingford, whom he had secretly called to him and having received them, he delivered them over to his lieges to keep for him.

Sect. 76. By command of the archbishop of Rouen, there assembled at London, the pillars of the church, the oracles of the laws, to discuss either something or nothing, as it often falls out, in matters of state. There was but one mind among all, to convene Earl John for the pre-occupation of the castles but, because no one of them durst commit himself to another, every one desired in himself that the question should be proposed rather by a deputy than by his own mouth. So whilst they all clamor to this end, and with this purpose, Aeacus alone is wanting, to whom they all simultaneously agreed to resort; but even whilst among other matters they only casually discoursed of the late chancellor, behold again is Crispinus at hand. The messengers of the chancellor, now again legate, enter the assembly, saluting the queen, who was present, and all the rest, whom by chance they found together, on the part of their lord, who had safely arrived the day before at Dover. The last clause of the mandates prohibited him from following up the ministration of his legation. Long were they all silent, and greatly astonished, intently kept their peace. At length it came to be the vote of all that they should humbly entreat him to be their dictator and lord, whom they had assembled to judge as a perjurer and transgressor against their lord. So many of the nobles, of whom one was Echion, are sent, and that repeatedly, to Earl John, then staying at Wallingford, and laughing at their conventions. Humbly, and without austerity, they beg that he would hasten to meet the goat. "Lord!" say they, "he wears horns, beware!"

Sect. 77. The earl, not greatly moved, long suffered himself to be reverently entreated but at length, satiated with the honor offered him, he came to London with the last intercessors, whom he most loved, sufficiently taught to answer to every question that might chance to be asked. The court rises up and compliments him on his entry, no order either of age or rank being observed; everybody that first can, first runs to meet him, and desires himself to be first seen, eager to please the prince, because to have been acceptable to the great is not the last of praises. The leaders were at a stand. Of the castles, no mention is made; the whole discussion and consultation was about the chancellor. Should the earl advise, all are ready to proscribe him. They strive by all means to soften the earl to consent, but they had a wild beast on their right hand. The earl, on being asked to answer, briefly declares, "The chancellor fears the threats of none of you, nor of you altogether, nor will he beg your love, if only he may succeed to have me alone his friend. He is to give me seven hundred pounds of silver by the seventh day, if I shall not have meddled between you and him. You see I am in want of money. To the wise, a word is sufficient." He said, and withdrew, leaving the conclusion of his proposition in the midst. The court, placed in a great strait, strained its counsel: it appeared expedient to every one to propitiate the man with more than was promised; the gift or loan of the money is approved, but not of their own, and so in the end it all falls upon the treasury of the absent king. Five hundred pounds of silver sterling out of the Exchequer are lent to the earl by the barons, and letters to their liking against the chancellor are received. Nor is there delay; the queen writes, the clergy write, the people write, all unanimously advertise the chancellor to bolt, to cross the sea without delay, unless his ears are ticklish to hear rumors, unless he wishes to take his meals under the charge of armed soldiers.

Sect. 78. The chancellor stood aghast at the severity of the mandates, and was as pale as one who treads a snake with his bare feet. But, on retiring, is reported to have made only this manly reply:—"Let all who persecute me, know they shall see how great is he whom they have offended. I am not destitute of all counsel, as they reckon. I have one who serves me as a fine ear by true dispatches. As long as I am an exile, said he, patiently endure the things which you suffer. Every land is a home to the brave, believe one who has found it so by experience; persevere and preserve your life for a better day. A grateful hour, which is not hoped for, will overtake both you and me. Unlooked for, I shall return and triumph over my enemies, and again shall my victory make thee a citizen in my kingdom, forbidden thee, and now not obeying me; haply it may hereafter be gratifying to us to reflect on this event.

Sect. 79. Because Winchester ought not to be deprived of its due reward for keeping peace with the Jews, as in the beginning of this book is related, the Winchester Jews (after the manner of the Jews), studious of the honor of their city, procured themselves notoriety by murdering a boy in Winchester, with many signs of the deed, although, perhaps, the deed was never done. The case was thus:—A certain Jew engaged a Christian boy, a pretender to the art of shoemaking, into the household service of his family. He did not reside there continually to work, nor was he permitted to complete any thing great all at once, lest his abiding with them should apprise him of the fate intended for him and, as he was remunerated better for a little labor there, than for much elsewhere, allured by his gifts and wiles, he frequented the more freely the wretch's house. Now, he was French by birth, under age, and an orphan, of abject condition and extreme poverty. A certain French Jew, having unfortunately compassioned his great miseries in France, by frequent advice persuaded him that he should go to England, a land flowing with milk and honey; he praised the English as liberal and bountiful, and that there no one would continue poor who could be recommended for honesty. The boy, ready to like whatever you may wish, as is natural with the French, having taken a certain companion of the same age as himself, and of the same country, got ready to set forward on his foreign expedition, having nothing in his hands but a staff, nothing in his wallet but a cobbler s awl.

Sect. 80. He bade farewell to his Jewish friend; to whom the Jew replied, "Go forth as a man. The God of my fathers lead thee as I desire." And having laid his hands upon his head, as if he had been the scapegoat, after certain muttering of the throat and silent imprecations, being now secure of his prey, he continued,—" Be of good courage; forget your own people and native land, for every land is the home of the brave, as the sea is for the fish, and as the whole of the wide world is for the bird. When you have entered England, if you should come to London, you will quickly pass through it, as that city greatly displeases me. Every race of men, out of every nation which is under heaven, resort thither in great numbers; every nation has introduced into that city its vices and bad manners. No one lives in it without offence; there is not a single street in it that does not abound in miserable, obscene wretches; there, in proportion as any man has exceeded in wickedness, so much is he the better. I am not ignorant of the disposition I am exhorting; you have, in addition to your youth, an ardent disposition, a slowness of memory, and a soberness of reason between extremes. I feel in myself no uneasiness about you, unless you should abide with men of corrupt lives; for from our associations our manners are formed. But let that be as it may. You will come to London. Behold! I warn you, whatever of evil or of perversity there is in any, whatever in all parts of the world, you will find in that city alone. Go not to the dances of panders, nor mix yourself up with the herds of the stews; avoid the talus and the dice, the theatre and the tavern. You will find more braggadocios there than in all France, while the number of flatterers is infinite. Stage-players, buffoons, those that have no hair on their bodies, Garamantes, pick thanks, catamites, effeminate sodomites, lewd musical girls, druggists, lustful persons, fortunetellers, extortioners, nightly strollers, magicians, mimics, common beggars, tatterdemalions, —this whole crew has filled every house. So if you do not wish to live with the shameful, you will not dwell in London. I am not speaking against the learned, whether monks or Jews; although, still, from their very dwelling together with such evil persons, I should esteem them less perfect there than elsewhere.

Sect. 81. "Nor does my advice go so far, as that you should betake yourself to no city; with my counsel you will take up your residence nowhere but in a town, though it remains to say in what. Therefore, if you should land near Canterbury, you will have to lose your way, if even you should but pass through it. It is an assemblage of the vilest, entirely devoted to their know not whom, but who has been lately canonized, and had been the archbishop of Canterbury, as everywhere they die in open day in the streets for want of bread and employment. Rochester and Chichester are mere villages, and they possess nothing for which they should be called cities, but the sees of their bishops. Oxford, scarcely, I will not say satisfies, but sustains, its clerks. Exeter supports men and beasts with the same grain. Bath is placed, or rather buried, in the lowest parts of the valleys, in a very dense atmosphere and sulfury vapor, as it were at the gates of hell. Nor yet will you select your habitation in the northern cities, Worcester, Chester, Hereford, on account of the desperate Welshmen. York abounds in Scots, vile and faithless men, or rather rascals. The town of Ely is always putrefied by the surrounding marshes. In Durham, Norwich, or Lincoln, there are very few of your disposition among the powerful; you will never hear any one speak French. At Bristol, there is nobody who is not, or has not been, a soap maker, and every Frenchman esteems soap makers as he does night men. After the cities, every market, village, or town, has but rude and rustic inhabitants Moreover, at all times, account the Cornish people for such as you know our Flemish are accounted in France. For the rest, the kingdom itself is generally most favored with the dew of heaven and the fatness of the earth and in every place there are some good, but much fewer in them all than in Winchester alone.

Sect. 82. "This is in those parts the Jerusalem of the Jews, in it alone they enjoy perpetual peace; it is the school of those who desire to live well and prosper. Here they become men here there is bread and wine enough for nothing. There are therein monks of such compassion and gentleness, clergy of such understanding and frankness, citizens of such civility and good faith, ladies of such beauty and modesty, that little hinders but I should go there and become a Christian with such Christians. To that city I direct you, the city of cities, the mother of all, the best above all. There is but one fault, and that alone in which they customarily indulge too much. With the exception I should say of the learned and of the Jews, the Winchester people tell lies like watchmen, but it is in making up reports. For in no place under heaven so many false rumors are fabricated so easily as there; otherwise they are true in every thing. I should have many things too still to tell you about business but for fear you should not understand or should forget, you will place this familiar note in the hands of the Jew my friend, and I think, too, you may some time be rewarded by him." The short note was in Hebrew. The Jew made an end of his speech, and the boy having understood all things for good, came to Winchester.

Sect. 83. His awl supplied him, and his companion as well, with food, and the cruel courtesy and deceitful beneficence of the Jew was by the letter unfortunately obtained to their relief. Wherever the poor fellows worked or eat apart by day, they reposed every night in one little bed in the same old cottage of a certain old woman. Days follow days, and months months, and in the same way as we have hitherto so carefully described, our boys hasten the time of their separation that they may meet again. The day of the Holy Cross had arrived, and the boy that same day, whilst working at his Jew's, being by some means put out of the way, was not forthcoming. Now the Passover, a feast of the Jews, was at hand. His companion, during the evening, greatly surprised at his absence, not returning home to bed, was terrified that night with many visions and dreams. When he had sought him several days in all corners of the city without success, he came to the Jew and simply asked if he had sent his benefactor anywhere whom when he found violently enraged beyond his general disposition, from having been so courteous the day before, and noticed the incoherence of his words and change of countenance, he presently fired up, and as he was of a shrill voice and admirable readiness of speech, he broke out into abuse, and with great clamor challenged him with taking his companion away. "Thou son of a sordid harlot," said he; "thou robber, thou traitor, thou devil, thou hast crucified my friend. Alas, me! Wherefore have I not now the strength of a man! I would tear you to pieces with my hands." The noise of his quarrelling in the house is heard in the street, Jews and Christians come running together from all quarters. The boy persists, and now, deriving courage from the crowd, addressing those present, he alleged his concern for his companion as an excuse. "O you good people," said he, "who are assembled, behold if there is any sorrow like my sorrow. That Jew is a devil; he has stolen away my heart from my breast—he has butchered my only companion, and I presume too that he has eaten him. A certain son of the devil, a Jew of French birth, I neither know nor am acquainted with that Jew gave my comrade letters of his death-warrant to that man. To this city he came, induced, or rather seduced. He often gave attendance upon this Jew, and in his house he was last seen." He was not without a witness to some points, inasmuch as a Christian woman, who, contrary to the canons, had nursed up the young Jews in the same house, constantly swore that she had seen the boy go down into the Jew's store, without coming up again. The Jew denies it—the case is referred to the judges. The accusers are defective; the boy because he was under age, the woman because the service of Jews had rendered her ignominious. The Jew offered to clear his conscience of the evil report. Gold contented the judges. Phineas gave and pleased, and the controversy ceased.

Sect. 84. The bishop of Chester, who, from his detestation of religion, had expelled the monks from Coventry, entirely broke down all the workshops there were in the monastery, that by the altered appearance of the place, all remembrance of its past state might be taken away from posterity. And further, lest the ruin of the walls should some day bespeak their author, the church of the place, which had not been finished, was found a ready plea, and having bestowed the materials upon it, without charge, he began to build. More over, lie appointed the masons and 'plasterers their hire out of the chattels of the monastery. He selected two principal manors of the monks for his own proper use; this arrangement being made for their abuse—that wherever he should eat, some special delicacy provided out of the issues of the aforesaid manors should be presented to him to eat, that he might glory in the victory, and might batten, as it were, on the viscera of the monks, whom he had by his wickedness overcome. But all the rest of their revenues he allotted to the prebends, some of which he conferred and settled for ever on the Romish church, appropriated to certain cardinals of the Apostolic See, appointing them and their canonical successors in the same titles to be canons of the church of Coventry, that if by any chance there should be any delay to the transactions before the pope, he should make the whole court the more ready in the defense of his part; he conferred the other prebends on others, but not one on any whom he did not know for certain to be an advocate of no religion. They built eagerly, even the absent canons, around the church spacious and lofty villas, perhaps for their own use, if even once in their lives any chance should offer a cause for visiting the place. None of the prebendaries regularly resided there any more than they do elsewhere; but doing great things for the gates of palaces, they have left to poor vicars, induced by a trifling remuneration, to insult God to them have they entrusted the holy chant and vanquished household gods and bare church walls.

Sect. 85. This forsooth is true religion; this should the church imitate and emulate. It will be permitted the secular canon to be absent from his church as long as he may please, and to consume the patrimony of Christ where, and when, in whatsoever luxuries he may list. Let them only provide this, that a frequent vociferation be heard in the house of the Lord. If the stranger should knock at the doors of such, if the poor should cry, he who lives before the doors will answer (he himself being a sufficiently needy vicar), "Pass on, and seek elsewhere for alms, for the master of the house is not at home." This is that glorious religion of the clerks, for the sake of which the bishop of Chester, the first of men that durst commit so great iniquity, expelled his monks from Coventry. For the sake of clerks irregularly regular—that is to say, of canons, he capriciously turned out the monks; monks who, not with another's, but with their own mouth praised the Lord, who dwelt and walked in the house of the Lord with unanimity all the days of their life, who beyond their food and raiment knew nothing earthly, whose bread was always for the poor, whose door was at all times open to every traveler nor did they thus please the bishop, who never loved either monks or their order. A man of bitter jocularity who even, though he might sometimes spare, never ceased to worry the monks. O what a fat morsel, and not to be absorbed, is a monk many a thousand has that bit choked, while the wicked at their death have had it for their viaticum. If as often as a monk was calumniated and reproached he was consumed, all religion would be absorbed before many ages. At all times and in every place, whether the bishop spoke in earnest or in jest, a monk was some part of his discourse. Nor did the expulsion of his own monks satisfy him, but ever after, true to himself, he continued censuring the monks as before. But as he could not desist from speaking of them, lest he should incur the opprobrium of a detractor, if in their absence he should carp at their order, he resolved to keep some monk abiding with him in his court; that his conversation about them might be made less offensive, by the presence and audience of one of them. So he took as his quasi chaplain a certain monk, scarcely of age, but yet who had professed at Burton, whom to the scandal of religion he generally took about with him. O excess of sorrow! Even among the angels of God is found iniquity. The monk, wise and prudent, seduced to the delusion, hardened his forehead as a harlot that he a monk should not blush when monks were reviled. Alas! How great a thirst for roving and riding! Hear me and attend a little; you shall see how the riding of his rider concluded. On a certain day, as the bishop was standing over his workmen at Coventry, his monk attending close by his side, on whom the bishop familiarly resting, said, "Is it not proper and expedient, my monk, even in your judgment, that the great beauty of so fair a church, that such a comely edifice, should rather be appropriated to gods than devils?" And while the monk was hesitating at the obscurity of the words, he added, "I," said he, "call my clerks gods, and monks devils!" And presently putting forth the forefinger of his right hand towards his clerks, who were standing round him, he continued, "I say ye are gods, and ye are all the children of the Highest!" And having turned again to the left, concluded to the monk, " But ye monks shall die like devils and as one and the greatest of your princes ye shall fall away into hell, because ye are devils upon earth. Truly if it should befall me to officiate for a dead monk, which I should be very unwilling to do I would commend his body and soul not to God, but to the devil." The monk, who was standing in the very place that the monks had been plundered of, did not refute the insult on the monks, and because on such an occasion he was silent, met, as he deserved, with the reward of eternal silence being imposed upon him. For suddenly a stone falling from the steeple of the church, dashed out the brains of the monk who was attending on the bishop, the bishop being preserved in safety for some greater judgment.

Sect. 86. The king of the English, Richard, had already completed two years in conquering the region around Jerusalem, and during all that time there had no aid been sent to him from any of his kingdoms. Nor yet were his only and uterine brother, John, earl of Mortain, nor his justiciaries, nor his other nobles, observed to take any care to send him any part of his revenues but they did not even think of his return. However, prayer was made without ceasing by the church to God for him. The king's army was decreased daily in the Land of Promise, and besides those who were slain with the sword, many thousands of the people perished every month by the too sudden extremities of the nightly cold and the daily heat. When it appeared that they would all have to die there, every one had to choose whether he would die as a coward or in battle. On the other side, the strength of the Gentiles greatly increased, and their confidence was strengthened by the misfortunes of the Christians their army was relieved at certain times by fresh troops; the weather was natural to them ; the place was their native country; their labor, health; their frugality, medicine. Amongst the Normans, on the contrary, that became a disadvantage which to the adversaries brought gain. For if our people lived sparingly even once in a week, they were rendered less effective for seven weeks after. The mingled nation of French and English fared sumptuously every day, and (saving the reverence of the French) even to loathing, at whatever cost, while their treasure lasted; and the well-known custom of the English being continually kept up even under the very clarions and the clangor of the trumpet or horn, they gaped with due devotion while the chalices were emptied to the dregs. The merchants of the country, who brought the victuals to the camp, were astonished at their wonderful and extraordinary habits, and could scarcely believe even what they saw to be true, that one people, and that small in number, consumed threefold the bread and a hundred-fold the wine more than that whereon many nations of the Gentiles had been sustained, and some of those nations innumerable. And the hand of the Lord was deservedly laid upon them according to their merits. So great want of food followed their great gluttony that their teeth scarcely spared their fingers as their hands presented to their mouths less than their usual allowance. To these and other calamities, which were severe and many, a much greater was added by the sickness of the king.

Sect. 87. The king was extremely sick, and confined to his bed; his fever continued without intermission; the physicians whispered that it was an acute semi tertian. And as they despaired of his recovery even from the first, terrible dismay was spread from the king's abode through the camp. There were few among the many thousands who did not meditate on flight, and the utmost confusion of dispersion or surrender would have followed, had not Hubert Walter, bishop of Salisbury, immediately assembled the council. He obtained by forcible allegations that the army should not break up until a truce was demanded of Saladin. All well armed stand in array more steadily than usual, and with a threatening look concealing the reluctance of their mind, they feign a desire for battle. No one speaks of the indisposition of the king, lest the secret of their intense sorrow should be disclosed to the enemy; for it was thoroughly understood that Saladin feared the charge of the whole army less than that of the king alone; and if he should know that he was dead, he would instantly pelt the French with cow dung, and intoxicate the best of the English drunkards with a dose which should make them tremble.

Sect. 88. In the meantime, a certain Gentile, called Saffatin, came down to see the king, as he generally did he was a brother of Saladin, an ancient man of war of remarkable politeness and intelligence, and one whom the king's magnanimity and munificence had charmed even to the love of his person and favor of his party. The king's servants greeting him less joyfully than they were accustomed, and not admitting him to an interview with the king, "I perceive," said he by his interpreter, "that you are greatly afflicted ; nor am I ignorant of the cause. My friend, your king, is sick, and therefore you close his doors to me." And falling into tears, with his whole heart, he exclaimed, "O God of the Christians, if thou be a God, do not suffer such a man, so necessary to thy people to fall so suddenly." He was entrusted with their avowal, and thus spoke on: "In truth I forewarn you, that if the king should die while things stand as they are at present, all you Christians will perish, and all this region will in time to come be ours without contest. Shall we at all dread that stout king of France, who before he came into battle was defeated,— whose whole strength, which three years had contributed, the short space of three months consumed? Hither will he on no account return any more; for we always esteem this as a sure token (I am not speaking craftily, but simply), that those whom at first we think cowardly, we ever after find worse. But that king, of all the princes of the Christian name whom the round circle of the whole world encompasses, is alone worthy of the honor of a captain and the name of a king, because he commenced well, and went on better, and will be crowned by the most prosperous result, if only he shall remain with you a short time.

Sect. 89. "It is not a new thing for us to dread the English, for fame reported to us his father to be such, that had he come even unarmed to our parts, we should all have fled, though armed, nor would it have appeared inglorious to us to be put to flight by him. He our terror, a wonderful man in his day, is dead but, like the phoenix, renewed himself, a thousand times better, in his son. It was not unknown to us how great that Richard was, even while his father lived; for all the days of his father, we had our agents in those parts, who informed us both of the king's deeds, and of the birth and death of his sons. He was justly beloved for his probity by his father above all his brothers, and preferred before them to the government of his states. It was not unknown to us that when he was made duke of Aquitaine he speedily and valiantly crushed the tyrants of the province, who had been invincible before his grandfather and great grandfather;—how terrible he was even to the king of France himself, as well as to all the governors of the regions on his borders. None took of his to himself, though he always pushed his bounds into his neighbors. It was not unknown to us, that his two brothers, the one already crowned king, the other duke of Bretagne, had set themselves up against their dear father, and that he ceased not to persecute them with the rigor of war, till he had given them both eternal repose, vanquished as they were by the length of the prosecution. Besides, as you will the more wonder at, we know all the cities of your parts by name nor are we ignorant that the king of your country was beaten at Le Mans through the treachery of his own people; that he died at Chinon, and was buried at Fontevraud.

Sect. 90. "It is not through ignorance that I do not relate who made himself the author of such unusual and mighty slaughter against us if that Richard, whom although I love yet I fear, if he were dispatched out of the way, how little should we then fear, how very little should we make account of that youngest of the sons, who sleeps at home in clover! It was not unknown to us, that Richard, who nobly succeeded his great father in the kingdom, immediately set forward against us even in the very year of his coronation. The number of his ships and troops was not unknown to us before his setting forth. We knew, even at the very time, with what speed he took Messina, the well-fortified city of Sicily, which he besieged and although none of our people believed it, yet our fears increased, and fame added false terrors to the true.

Sect. 91. "His valor, unable to rest in one place, proceeded through a boundless region, and everywhere left trophies of his courage. We questioned among ourselves whether he made ready to subdue, for his God, the Land of Promise only, or, at the same time, to take the whole world for himself. Who shall worthily relate the capture of Cyprus? Verily had the island of Cyprus been close to Egypt, and had my brother Saladin subdued it in ten years, his name would have been reckoned by the people among the names of the gods. When, however, we at last perceived that he overthrew whatever resisted his purpose, our hearts were melted as the hoar frost melts at the appearance of the approaching sun, forasmuch as it was said of him that he ate his enemies alive. And if he were not presently, on the very day of his arrival before Acre, received freely into the city with open gates, fear alone was the cause. It was not from their desire to preserve the city, but through dread of the torments promised them and their despair of life that they fought so bravely, or rather desperately, fearing this more than death, endeavoring this by all means, namely, that they should not die unrevenged. And this was not from sheer obstinacy, but to follow up the doctrine of our faith. For we believe that the spirits of the unavenged wander for ever, and that they are deprived of all rest. But what did the rashness and timidity of the devoted profit them? Being vanquished by force, and constrained by fear to surrender, they were punished with a more lenient death than they had expected. And yet, oh! shame on the Gentiles their spirits wandered unavenged! I swear to you by the Great God, that if, after he had gained Acre, he had immediately led his army to Jerusalem, he would not have found even one of our people in the whole circuit of the Christians' land on the contrary, we should have offered to him inestimable treasure, that he might not proceed, that he might not prosecute us further.

Sect. 92. "But, thanks be to God! he was burdened with the king of the French, and hindered by him, like a cat with a hammer tied to its tail. To conclude, we, though his rivals, see nothing in Richard that we can find fault with but his valor; nothing to hate but his experience in war. But what glory is there in fighting with a sick man? And although this very morning I could have wished that both you and he had all received your final doom, now I compassionate you on account of your king's illness. I will either obtain for you a settled peace with my brother, or at the least a good and durable truce. But until I return to you, do not by any means speak of it to the king, lest, if he should be excited, he may get worse, for he is of so lofty and impatient a disposition, that, even though he should needs presently die, he would not consent to an arrangement, without seeing the advantage on his side!" He would have spoken further, but his tongue, languishing and failing for sorrow, would not continue his harangue, so with his head resting in his clasped hands he wept sore.

Sect. 93. The bishop of Salisbury, and such of the most trusty of the king's household as were present, who had secretly deliberated with him upon this subject, reluctantly consented to the truce which before they had determined to purchase at any price, as if it had been detested, and not desired by them. So their right hands being given and received, Saffatin, when he had washed his face, and disguised his sorrow, returned to Jerusalem, to Saladin. The council was assembled before his brother, and after seventeen days of weighty argument, he with difficulty succeeded in prevailing on the stubbornness of the Gentiles to grant a truce to the Christians. The time was appointed and the form approved. If it please King Richard, for the space of three years, three months, three weeks, three days, and three hours, such a truce shall be observed between the Christians and the Gentiles, that whatever either one party or the other in anywise possesses, he shall possess without molestation to the end; it will be permitted during the interval, that the Christians at their pleasure may fortify Acre only, and the Gentiles Jerusalem. All contracts, commerce, every act and every thing shall be mutually carried on by all in peace. Saffatin himself is dispatched to the English as the bearer of this decree.

Sect. 94. Whilst King Richard was sick at Jaffa, word was brought him that the duke of Burgundy was taken dangerously ill at Acre. The day was the day for the king's fever to take its turn, and through his delight at this report, it left him. The king immediately with uplifted hands imprecated a curse upon him, saying, "May God destroy him, for he would not destroy the enemies of our faith with me, although he had long served in my pay/' On the third day the duke died as soon as his decease was known, the bishop of Beauvais, having left the king with all his men, came in haste to Acre; the French out of all the towns assembled before him, all but Henry, count of Champagne, King Richard's nephew by his sister. And the bishop, being made their leader and bully, set forth a proclamation and commanded them all to return home.

Sect. 95. The fleet was made ready, and the glorious prince retreating with his cowardly troop, sails over the Etruscan Sea. Having landed on the German coast, he spreads abroad among the people, during the whole of his journey, that that traitor the king of England, from the first moment of his arrival in Judea, had endeavored to betray his lord the king of the French to Saladin that, as soon as he had obtained Tyre, he caused the marques to be murdered that he had dispatched the duke of Burgundy by poison that at the last he had sold generally the whole army of the Christians who did not obey him; that he was a man of singular ferocity, of harsh and repulsive manners, subtle in treachery, and most cunning in dissimulation that on that account the king of the French had returned home so soon that on that account the French who remained had left Jerusalem unredeemed. This report gained strength by circulation, and provoked against one man the hatred of all.

Sect. 96. The bishop of Beauvais, having returned to France, secretly whispered in the king's ear, that the king of England had sent assassins to France who would murder him. The king, alarmed at that, appointed, though against the custom of his country, a chosen bodyguard; he further sent ambassadors to the emperor of Germany with presents, and carefully persuaded his imperial majesty to a hatred of the king of England. So it was enjoined by an imperial edict, that all cities and princes of the empire should take the king of the English by force, if by chance in his return from Judea he should happen to pass through their countries, and present him to him alive or dead. If any one spared him he should be punished as the public enemy of the empire. All obeyed the emperor's charge and especially that duke of Austria whom the king of England had dismissed at Acre.

Sect. 97. Henry, count of Champagne, now the only one of the French nobles left in Judea, returned to the king of the English, to Jaffa and when he announced to him both the death of the duke of Burgundy and the departure of the French, the hope of the king so revived, that he presently experienced a perfect convalescence with a healthy perspiration and having resumed his strength of body more by the high temper of his mind than by repose or nourishment, he issued a command through the whole coast from Tyre to Ascalon, that all who were able to serve in the wars should come to the service at the king's charges. There assembled before him a countless multitude, the greater part of whom were foot which being rejected, as they were useless, he mustered the lords had perished. And not mistrustful on account of their small number, he being a most excellent orator, strengthened the minds of the fearful in a seasonable harangue. He commanded that it should be proclaimed through the companies that on the third day they must follow the king to battle, either to die as martyrs or to take Jerusalem by storm. This was the sum of his project, because as yet he knew nothing of the truce. For there was no one who durst even hint to him, who had so unexpectedly recovered, that which, without his knowledge, they had undertaken through fear of his death. However, Hubert Walter, bishop of Salisbury, took counsel with Count Henry concerning the truce, and obtained his ready concurrence in his wishes. So having deliberated together by what stratagem they might be able without danger to hinder such a hazardous engagement, they conceived one of a thousand, namely, to dissuade the people if possible from the enterprise. And the matter turned out most favorably the spirit of those who were going to fight had so greatly failed, even without dissuasion, that on the appointed day, when the king, according to his custom leading the van, marshaled his army, there were not found of all the knights and shield-bearers above nine hundred. On account of which defection, the king, greatly enraged, or rather raving, and champing with his teeth the pine rod which he held in his hand, at length unbridled his indignant lips as follows:—"O God!" said he, "O God, my God, why hast thou forsaken me? For whom have we foolish Christians, for whom have we English come hither from the furthest parts of the earth to bear our arms? Is it not for the God of the Christians? O fie! How good art thou to us thy people, who now are for thy name given up to the sword; we shall become a portion for foxes. O how unwilling should I be to forsake thee in so forlorn and dreadful a position, were I thy lord and advocate as thou art mine! In sooth, my standards will in future be despised, not through my fault but through thine; in sooth, not through any cowardice of my warfare, art thou thyself, my King and my God, conquered this day, and not Richard thy vassal."

Sect. 98. He said, and returned to the camp extremely dejected and as a fit occasion now offered, Bishop Hubert and Henry, count of Champagne, approaching him with unwonted familiarity, and as if nothing had yet been arranged, importuned under divers pretexts the king's consent for making such overtures to the Gentiles as were necessary. And thus the king answered them: "Since it generally happens that a troubled mind rather thwarts than affords sound judgment—I, who am greatly perplexed in mind, authorize you, who have as I see a collected mind, to arrange what you shall think most proper for the good of peace." They having gained their desires chose messengers to send to Saffatin upon these matters; Saffatin, who had returned from Jerusalem, is suddenly announced to be at hand the count and the bishop go to meet him, and being assured by him of the truce, they instruct him how he must speak with the lord their king. Saffatin being admitted to an interview with the king as one who before had been his friend, could scarcely prevail with the king not to make himself a sacrifice, and to consent to the truce. For so great were the man's strength of body, mental courage, and entire trust in Christ, that he could hardly be prevailed upon not to undertake in his own person a single combat with a thousand of the choicest Gentiles, as he was destitute of soldiers. And as he was not permitted to break off in this way, he chose another evasion, that, after a truce of seven weeks, the stipulations of the compact being preserved, it should remain for him to choose whether it were better to fight or to forbear. The right hands are given by both parties for faithfully observing this last agreement and Saffatin, more honored than burdened with the king's present, goes back again to his brother, to return at the expiration of the term for the final conclusion or breaking off of the above truce.

Sect. 99. Richard, king of England, held a council at Acre, and there prudently regulating the government of that state, he appointed his nephew, Henry, count of Champagne, on whom he had formerly conferred Tyre, to be captain and lord of the whole Land of Promise. Only he thought proper to defer his consecration as king till haply he might be crowned at Jerusalem. King Richard now thinking to return home, when with the assistance of Count Henry he had appointed chosen men for all the strongholds that had been taken in his territories, found Ascalon alone without ward or inhabitant for want of people. Wherefore, taking precaution that it might not become a receptacle of the Gentiles, he caused the ramparts and fortifications of the castle to be cast down. The seventh day of the seventh week appeared, and behold Saffatin, with many mighty ones who desired to see the face of the king, drew near the truce was confirmed on both sides by oath, this being added to that which had been previously settled, that during the continuance of the truce no one, whether Christian or Gentile, should inhabit Ascalon, and that the whole of the tillage pertaining to the town should remain to the Christians. Hubert, bishop of Salisbury, and Henry, captain of Judea, together with a numerous band, went up to Jerusalem to worship in the place where the feet of Christ had stood. And there was woeful misery to be seen—captive confessors of the Christian name, wearing out a hard and constant martyrdom; chained together in gangs, their feet blistered, their shoulders raw, their backsides goaded, their backs weald, they carried materials to the hands of the masons and stone layers to make

Jerusalem impregnable against the Christians. When the captain and bishop had returned from the sacred places, they endeavored to persuade the king to go up but the worthy indignation of his noble mind could not consent to receive that from the courtesy of the Gentiles which he could not obtain by the gift of God.

GEOFFREY DE VINSAUF'S ITINERARY OF RICHARD I AND OTHERS TO THE HOLY LAND

PROLOGUE

It sometimes happens, that exploits, however well known and splendidly achieved, come, by length of time, to be less known to fame, or even forgotten among posterity. In this manner the renown of many kings has faded, and their deeds have sunk with them into the grave where their bodies lie buried—deeds that had been performed with great splendor, and were much celebrated in their own times, when their novelty brought them into favor, and unanimous applause set them up as models before the people. The ancient Greeks, aware of this, were wise enough to use the pen as a remedy against oblivion, and zealously stimulated their writers, whom they termed historiographers, to compile histories of noble deeds. Thus the silence of the living voice was supplied by the voice of writing, so that the virtues of men might not die with them. The Romans, emulating the Greeks, with the view of perpetuating merit, not only employed the service of the pen, but also added sculpture and thus by exhibiting the ancients they excited their descendants, and impressed the love of virtue the more strongly on the minds of its imitators, conveying it in various ways, both through their eyes and through their ears. Who would now know anything about the voyage of Jason, the labors of Hercules, the glory of Alexander, or the victories of Caesar, if it had not been for the service which writers have rendered? And, to adduce the examples of the Holy Fathers, I may say, that neither the patience of Job, the liberality of Abraham nor the gentleness of David, would have remained as an example among the faithful of after-ages, if antiquity, with a due appreciation of truth, had not bequeathed history for our perusal. Indeed, kings formerly, when they became the objects of praise, were most anxious, that, whilst they stood high in the estimation of their contemporaries, they might also descend to the knowledge of posterity. However numerous have been the historians, most of them have recorded what they heard; few what they have seen. If Dares Phrygius is more readily believed about the destruction of Troy, because he was an eyewitness of what others related only on hearsay, we also, who treat of the history of Jerusalem, are justly entitled to credit; for we testify what we have seen, and celebrate these deeds with the pen, whilst our memory of them retains its freshness. If the fastidious readers require a more elegant style, let him consider that we wrote while in the camp and that the noise of war did not admit of calm and silent meditation. Truth has charms enough in herself, and even though not decked out in pompous array, still possesses sufficient attractions for all who are desirous of learning her secrets.

BOOK I

CHAPTER I - In the year of the Incarnate Word 1187, when Urban III held the government of the Apostolic See, and Frederic was emperor of Germany; when Isaac was reigning at Constantinople, Philip in France, Henry in England, and William in Sicily, the Lord's hand fell heavy upon his people, if indeed it is right to call those Ms people, whom un cleanness of life and habits, and the foulness of their vices, had alienated from his favor. Their licentiousness had indeed become so flagrant that they all of them, casting aside the veil of shame, rushed headlong, in the face of day, into crime. It would be a long task and incompatible with our present purpose to disclose the scenes of blood, robbery, and adultery, which disgraced them, for this work of mine is a history of deeds and not a moral treatise but when the ancient enemy had diffused, far and near, the spirit of corruption, he more especially took possession of the land of Syria, so that other nations now drew an example of uncleanness from the same source which formerly had supplied them with the elements of religion. For this cause, therefore, the Lord seeing that the land of his birth and place of his passion had sunk into an abyss of turpitude, treated with neglect his inheritance, and suffered Saladin, the rod of his wrath, to put forth his fury to the destruction of that stiff-necked people; for he would rather that the Holy Land should, for a short time, be subject to the profane rites of the heathen, than that it should any longer be possessed by those men, whom no regard for what is right could deter from things unlawful. The approach of future destruction was foretold by divers events: famine, earthquakes, and frequent eclipses, both of the sun and of the moon. And that strong wind also, which astronomers prophesied would spring out of the conjunction of the planets, became changed to the signification of this event. It was a mighty wind indeed; it shook the four cardinal points of the earth, and foreshowed that the whole of the globe was about to be stirred up to troubles and wars.

CHAPTER II – *How Saladin invaded Palestine*

Saladin, therefore, having assembled his bands of warriors, violently assailed Palestine, and sent forward Manafaradin, admiral of Edessa, with 7,000 Turks, to ravage the Holy Land. This man, when he had marched as far as the parts about Tiberias, was there encountered by Gerard de Riddeford, master of the Templars, and Roger de Moulins, master of the Hospital; one of whom they routed and put to flight and slew the other in a sudden attack. In this battle a few of our soldiers were cut off and surrounded by an immense multitude, which led to an achievement of distinction which deserves to be recorded. A certain knight of the Temple, by birth a German, named Jakeline de Maille, by his extraordinary valor provoked the enemy to turn all their attacks on him. His fellow-soldiers, who were estimated about 500 in number, were all either taken or slain, and he alone sustained the weight of the whole battle,—a glorious champion for God's law! At length, hemmed in by the enemy's troops, and destitute of all human aid, seeing so many thousands rushing upon him on every side, he gathered up his whole courage for an effort, and bravely faced the foe alone. His valor attracted the admiration of his enemies;

they were filled with compassion for him, and called earnestly to him to surrender. He, however, turning a dear ear to their exhortations, was not afraid to die for Christ, but overwhelmed with the load of javelins, stones, and lances, rather than vanquished, he at length was with difficulty slain, and his soul fled triumphant, bearing the palm of martyrdom, to the heavenly kingdom. His death indeed was rendered glorious, since by his single sword so large a circle of dead bodies had been heaped around him. It was sweet for a man to die thus, himself in the centre, surrounded by the unbelievers whom his brave arm had slaughtered. And inasmuch as he rode on a white horse and fought that day in white armor, the idolaters who knew St. Gregory to have fought in such costume, boasted that they had slain the knight of the white armor, who was the bulwark of the Christians. There was, in the place of this conflict, some stubble which the reaper had left after the ears had been cut off a short time before, but the Turks had rushed over it in such multitudes and this single champion had held out so long against them, that the field in which they stood was wholly trampled to dust, and showed no signs of a crop of corn ever having grown there. It is said, there were some who sprinkled the limbs of the dead man with dust, which they afterwards placed on their own heads, believing that they derived force from the contact and one man, as is said, more ardent than the rest, cut off certain members of the man, and kept them for his own use, that even though dead they might perchance produce a successor to such distinguished valor.

CHAPTER III – *Of the Origin of Saladin*

At this victory Saladin rejoiced greatly; and fired with the ambition of gaining the kingdom turned his thoughts to still greater deeds. But that future ages may know more of this persecutor of the Christian name, I will premise a few particulars of his origin, as far as the brevity at which I aim will allow. He was of the race of the Mirmurseni, the son of parents who were not noble, though not a plebeian of obscure birth. His father was called Job, and his own name was Joseph. For according to the tradition of Mahomet, it is customary among many of the heathens, when they circumcise their children, to give them Hebrew names also but their princes, that they may be admonished by their names to be zealous defenders of the Mahometan law, take their own names from the very name of that law. Now, law in their language, is Hadin. Hence Saladin is so called as the upholder of the law; and, as our princes are called either emperors or kings, so theirs are called sultans (soldani), as it were sold-dominants. Now Saladin, under Noradin, sultan of Damascus, as a first omen of his power, began by raising an infamous tribute for himself out of the venal courtesans of that city; for he would not allow them to exercise their profession until they had first purchased of him a license. Whatever money he obtained by this base patronage, he lavishly expended on players, and so under the plea of largess, he concealed the design of obtaining the venal favor of the multitude. He was led to aspire at sovereignty by the prediction of a certain Syrian, that he should obtain the government of Damascus and Babylon. Thus he arranged in his own mind the different steps to power, and soon began to aim at more than a kingdom of small or limited dimensions. In process of time, when his years were matured and he was fit for military service, he came to Enfrid of Tours, the illustrious prince of Palestine, to be mantled, and after the manner of the Franks received from him the belt of knighthood.

CHAPTER IV – *How Saladin seized on the kingdoms of Egypt and Damascus, with India and other countries*

At that time a certain Mahometan, named Sewar, governed all Egypt, under Molanus, whom they called Lord in the language of their country, and he had been compelled to pay tribute to Amalric, the victorious king of Jerusalem. Now Molanus showed himself only three times a year to the Egyptians, who made adoration to him on those occasions, and all his subjects thought him so powerful, that it was said the Nile overflowed at his command. Moreover, in obedience to the statutes of the heathen law, he had as many concubines as there are days in the year, and so passing his life in his harem, he gave up all the business of his kingdom to Sewar. At this time Saladin, with his uncle, Saracun, was serving in Egypt, and by an act of treachery, he put to death Molanus and Sewar, and thus gained for himself the sovereignty of Egypt. Not long after, Noradin died, and Saladin, marrying the widow, expelled the lawful heirs, and secured for himself through her the possession of their kingdom. Thus the caprice of fortune brought about the establishment of his great power; she is able to make a rich man out of a poor one: a great man out of a little one and a lord out of a peasant. If things were measured by judgment, and not by opinion, all earthly power, which can be gained by the wicked and the unworthy, would be estimated as dross. That patron of prostitutes, whose power was among stews, his campaigns in a tavern, his studies among dice and garlic, is suddenly lifted up; he sits among princes, and is even greater than princes; he rules on the throne of Egypt; subdues Damascus; occupies the lands of Roasia and Gesyra, and carries his sovereignty to the centre of India Citerior. Wherefore he assails also and subdues the neighboring kingdoms, at one time by arms, at another time by deceit, and making one monarchy out of several scepters, arrogates to himself alone the power of so many kings. Neither is the tyrant's cupidity ever gratified; the more he gets the more he covets, and strives with all his power to occupy the land which is the inheritance of our Lord. At length an opportunity arose favorable to his wishes, and he hoped to obtain what he never before presumed to hope for. For Raimund, count of Tripoli, and Guy, the eighth king of the Latins, quarreled for the sovereignty, and a fatal sedition arose among the people.

CHAPTER V - *Of the immense army with which Saladin attached the army of the Christians, and captured our Lord's cross with the king Guy, and Acre, and reduced to submission the Land of Promise.*

The opportunity above mentioned at once roused his ambitious mind, and promised him a brilliant and sure success. Moreover it was not altogether without cause that the sultan declared war; Reginald, prince of Antioch, having broken the terms of truce, which had been agreed upon between our people and the unbelievers. For once upon a time, when a large and wealthy caravan of Mahometans were passing from Damascus to Egypt, and, trusting to the truce, did not hesitate to pass over the frontiers of the Christian territories, the aforesaid prince suddenly attacked them, and dishonorably carried them off prisoners, together with all their baggage. The sultan, excited on one side by his ambition and on the other moved with indignation at the outrage, raised all the strength of his kingdom, and assailed with power and impetuosity the territories of Jerusalem. If the number of men, the variety of nations, and the diversity of religions were fully described, as the law of history demands, my plan of brevity would be interrupted by the ample details of such a narrative; Parthians, Bedouins, Arabs, Medes, Cordians, and Egyptians, though differing in country, religion, and name, were all aroused with one accord to the destruction of the Holy Land. As our troops were marching to meet them, and the fatal day approached, a fearful vision was seen by the king's chamberlain, who dreamt that an eagle flew past the Christian army, bearing seven missiles and a balista in its talons, and crying with a loud voice, "Woe to thee, Jerusalem!" To explain the mystery of this vision, we need, I think, only take the words of Scripture; "The Lord hath bent his bow, and in it prepared the vessels of death." What are the seven missiles, but a figure for the seven sins by which that unhappy army was soon to perish? By this number, seven, may also be understood the number of punishments that impended over the Christians, which was some time after fulfilled by the event, that too faithful and terrible interpreter of omens. The battle had not begun, when, the armies having been drawn out at a short distance from Tiberias, at a place called the Marescallia, the Lord hemmed in his people with the sword, and as a punishment for the sins of men, gave over his inheritance to slaughter and devastation. What need I say more? Neither the plan of my work, nor the immensity of the calamity, allows me to find lamentations for all its details. However, to sum all up in few words, so many were slain there, so many wounded, and so many cast into prison, that the destruction of our people drew pity even from the enemies. That vivifying wood of the cross of our salvation, on which our Lord and Redeemer hung, and down whose shaft the holy blood of Christ flowed, the sign of which is adored by angels, venerated by men, and feared by devils, under whose protection our men have always been victors in war, alas is now captured by the enemy and the two bearers of the cross, the bishop of Acre, and the presenter of our Lord's tomb (the bishop of St. George), fell with it, the one slain, the other a prisoner. This was the second indignity, since Chosroes, king of the Persians, which that holy cross endured for our sins; it had redeemed us from the old yoke of captivity, and now it was captured from us, and soiled by the profane hands of the unbelievers.

Let him that hath intelligence consider how fierce must have been God's wrath, how great the iniquity of his servants, when unbelievers were deemed less unworthy than Christians to become its guardians. Nothing ever happened so lamentable in all ancient times for neither the captivity of God's ark, nor that of the kings of Judah, can compare with the calamity of our own times, by which the king and the glorious cross are taken captive together. Of the other prisoners, whose number was both extraordinary and lamentable, part were reserved unhurt to be placed at the victor's disposal, part were dispatched with the sword, and so found a happy and short byroad to heaven! Among others was Reginald prince of Antioch: he was led into the presence of the sultan, and that tyrant, either following the impulse of his passion, or envious of the great excellence of the man, cut off with his own hand that veteran and aged head. All the Templars also who were taken, except their master, he ordered to be decapitated, wishing utterly to exterminate those whom he knew to be valiant above all others in battle. O what faith, what fervor of mind was theirs! How many assumed the tonsure of the Templars, and flocked eagerly round their executioners, joyfully presenting their necks to the sword, in the pious fraud of this new costume! Among these soldiers of Christ was a Templar, named Nicholas, who had so induced others to aspire to martyrdom, that, by reason of their emulation to be beforehand with him, he could hardly succeed in first obtaining the mortal stroke which he coveted. Nor did the Divine mercy withhold its miraculous manifestation, for during the three following nights, when the bodies of the holy martyrs were lying still unburied, a ray of celestial light shone over them from above.

When the noise of battle had ceased, Saladin seeing prisoners carried off in all directions, and the ground on all sides covered with the slain, lifting up his eyes to heaven, gave thanks to God for the victory which he had gained. This was his practice in all cases; but at present among other things, he is reported to have said, that it was not his own power but our crimes which had given him the victory; and it was proved to be so by the character of the event. In other engagements, our army, however moderate in size, with the Divine aid always conquered; but now, because we were not with God, nor God with us, our people were altogether defeated, even before the conflict, though they were reckoned at more than 1,000 knights and more than 20,000 footmen: so entirely had the whole force of the kingdom flocked together at the king's command to that fatal campaign, that those only remained to guard the cities and castles, whom weakness of sex or age rendered unfit to bear arms. This disastrous battle was fought on the day of the translation of St. Martin, and in one moment all the glory of the kingdom passed from it and was extinguished. The sultan, therefore, trusting that the fortresses of the kingdom would be easily taken, now that their defenders were slain, carried the captive king in triumph through the castles of Syria, reserving him as a mark for his ridicule, to be shown to the cities which he wished to take and to enforce their surrender. With this view he marched first to Acre, and took it without a blow, granting the citizens leave to remove themselves and their effects to whatever place they pleased.

CHAPTER VI - *Of the capture of the Christians, who unwarily put in at the port of Acre.*

Meanwhile our sailors were proceeding on their customary voyage to Acre, coming from Christian countries and laden some with merchandise, others with pilgrims. Alas! They had not heard what had happened, and they entered the hostile port to be made prisoners. It was indeed a sad destiny: they hailed the sight of land, where chains were prepared for them on landing they rejoiced to have passed the dangers of the sea, and the sword awaited them they hoped for repose after their fatigues, and they found persecution some of them were kept as prisoners, many of them were made objects of derision, a few were allowed to escape, but designedly naked and helpless, that others might be deterred by their example.

CHAPTER VII - *How the Marquis Conrad escaped being taken in the same snare, and proceeded to Tyre.*

Among others, the marquis, on his way from Constantinople, dropped his sails outside the port of Acre, and, as it was near sunset, lay to till the morning. For the silence which prevailed in the city created suspicion, since at other times there was a general shout of congratulation when any vessel appeared; the ensigns of the sultan, seen in different parts of the city, gave still more cause for apprehension. Some of the Saracen galleys were now seen approaching, but the rest of the crew becoming alarmed, the marquis commanded them to be silent, and stood forth as their spokesman. When, therefore, those who were sent asked who they were, he said it was a merchantship, and he was the master; that he had heard what had happened and being a devoted servant of the sultan, would wait on him at break of day and exhibit his wares. That same night, the wind being favorable, he sailed to Tyre, and undertook the task of defending it: his arrival was alike a protection to all other Christians who should come, and would have contributed to his own glory, if he had only persevered to the end in the same line of conduct. This was the marquis Conrad, an Italian by birth, a man of singular activity, and brave in all he undertook. But however noble the beginning, when it is tarnished by a disgraceful end, it merits shame rather than glory.

The sultan, after the capture of Acre, followed by the surrender of Berytus and Sidon, expected to take Tyre with the same ease, but was shamefully repulsed from its walls, and raised the siege.

CHAPTER VIII - *How Saladin, after the capture of Berytus and Sidon, was repulsed from the walls of Tyre, and took Ascalon by a false treaty.*

Saladin, taking the king with him, proceeded thence to Ascalon, and planting his machines for throwing stones, began to assail it. The town is easy to be taken if defended by a weak garrison, though its great strength renders it invincible if sufficiently garrisoned. The insatiable invader, eager above all things to obtain this city, nevertheless distrusted his ability to take it by force, for he did not know how things were within its walls, nor how deficient it was both in arms, men, and victuals. He therefore agreed to a capitulation, by which the citizens were to depart freely with their effects, and the king, with fifteen other distinguished captives, were to be set at liberty as soon as possible. On the same day that this capitulation gave him possession of the city, the sun, as if in sympathy, was eclipsed, and withdrew its light from the city and from the world. The perjured and perfidious tyrant, too, was faithless in the performance of part of his agreement; for the king was carried to Damascus, and was there held in chains until the ensuing month of May nor was he released from his captivity until he had first consented to abjure his crown.

CHAPTER IX - *Jerusalem is taken and treated with indignity: the people who ransom themselves are expelled, the rest are made slaves.*

The fall of Jerusalem was now impending the victor advancing with speed equal to his hatred, laid siege to the city and erecting his machines, with sacrilegious irreverence profaned all the holy places. There was a certain cross of stone, which our soldiers formerly, when, after the capture of Antioch, they had gloriously taken this city, had erected on the wall in commemoration of the deed. The ferocious invaders destroyed this cross with a blow from one of their machines, and at the same time struck down a great part of the wall. The citizens interposed such defenses as they were able, but all the exertions of our men were ineffectual bows, balistas, and slings were used to no purpose; both arms and machines visibly declared that the Lord was wroth and foretold the fall of the city. A large number of people had flocked together to the city from the neighboring fortresses, trusting rather in the sanctity of the place than in the strength of its defenses; but in so great a multitude hardly fourteen knights could be found. The priests and clerks, although it was contrary to their profession, discharged the duties of soldiers, according to the emergency, and sought bravely for the Lord's house, bearing in mind the maxim, that to repel force by force is allowed by all laws both human and divine. But the populace, alike ignorant and timorous, flocked in numbers round the patriarch and the queen, who were left in charge of the city, bitterly complaining and earnestly entreating that they might treat with the sultan for peace, as soon as possible. Their capitulation, however, was one to be deplored, rather than praised: for each of them had to pay the ransom of his own life; a man was valued at ten bezants, a woman at five, a child at one; and whoever was unable to pay, was made a slave. It thus happened that when many of them, either out of their own property or by aids gathered from other sources, had paid the price of their safety, there remained 14,000, who could not redeem themselves, and were made slaves for life. To those who purchased their liberty, the choice was given, either to proceed to Antioch, or to be carried under safe conduct to Alexandria, and thence to cross the sea. That day was indeed a bitter day, on which the exiles separated, each on his different road, and left that sacred city, that city which had been the queen of cities, but which was now reduced to slavery that city which was the inheritance of its children, but was now in the hands of strangers, on account of the wickedness of those who dwelt therein.

Glorious was Jerusalem, the city of God, where the Lord suffered, and was buried, and where he displayed the glory of his resurrection but she is now subject to contamination at the hands of her baseborn foe nor is there any grief like that grief, that they should possess the sepulchre, who persecuted Him that lies buried in it and those, who had despised the Crucified, have made themselves masters of his Cross! This most holy city had been, for about ninety six years, in the hands of our people, ever since the victorious arms of the Christians had taken it, at the same time as Antioch; when it had been forty years before in the possession of the unbelievers. When the city was taken, the crier of the Mahometan law proceeded to the summit of the rock of Calvary, and there published their false law, in the place where Christ had consummated the law of death upon the cross. Another diabolical act was perpetrated by the enemy. They fastened ropes round a certain cross, which stood upon the pinnacle of the church of the Hospitallers, and dragged it to the ground, where they spat upon it, and hacked it, and drew it, in derision of our faith, through all the filth of the city.

CHAPTER X - *How Saladin besieged Tyre by sea and land.*

Now the queen, who was the daughter of King Amalric, and was named Sibula, together with Heraclius the patriarch, the Templars, the Hospitallers, and an immense multitude of fellow exiles, directed their course towards Antioch. How she had a sad interview at Neapolis with the captive king her husband and how the marquis violently carried off to Tyre the ship in which she intended to embark, brevity compels us to pass over. But we must not omit to mention how Saladin, burning with desire to take the city of Tyre, went against it a second time with all his army and not content with besieging it by land, he blockaded it from the sea with his galleys, and prepared to attack it on every side. That nothing might be left untried, he brought forward the marquis's father, whom he had taken prisoner in the battle before mentioned, trusting that the son, moved by filial affection, would give up the city in exchange for his parent. At one moment he offers him in exchange, at another he threatens him with death, and tries various means of working upon his feelings. All, however, is in vain, for the marquis, inflexible, derides his offers and despises his threats. Whenever, to move his compassion, they show him his father in chains, he immediately seizes a balista, and aims a shaft obliquely towards him, intending indeed that his hand shall err, but feigning to take good aim. And when the sultan's messengers came to threaten that his father should be slain, he replied that he wished it by all means; that the wicked man, after so many crimes, might at length find a good end, and he might himself have a martyr for his father. Thus the tyrant, failing in his expectation of gaining the city by these means, tried his fortune in another way and where art failed, determined to see what could be done by arms.

Tyre is situated in the heart of the sea, and is surrounded on all sides by walls. A small part of it, where it is not washed by the waves, is fortified by several lines of walls. It was once famous for its kings, and gave birth to the founders of Thebes and Carthage. When Solomon was king of Judea, Tyre had her own sovereign, and though she was then the head of her own dominions, in process of time she became a part of the kingdom of Jerusalem. This city its eager foe now assailed by land and sea and, whilst it suffered within from hunger, it was exposed to manifold assaults from without. On the morning after Innocent's day, namely on the feast of the blessed martyr Thomas, the citizens gained an important victory, for at dawn of day they sailed out with a few small vessels, and in a naval engagement obliged the enemy to raise the siege on the side of the sea. They seemed indeed more fitted for flight than fighting and on the first onset, all the enemy's fleet, by the power of the Almighty, were so panic-struck, that some of them were carried into the city with their crews the rest in their flight ran aground and there perished. The unbelievers, seeing this engagement by sea, supposed that all the defenders of the city had left it, and thus, confident of victory, they attacked the town with impetuosity. Already their troops had reached the fortifications, and numbers were hasting to mount them, when the marquis ordered the gates to be thrown open, and followed by Hugh of Tiberias, with his brothers and a noble company of men besides, struck down multitudes with his small band. Saladin seeing the fortunes of the day against him gave orders that his remaining engines and galleys should be burnt, and retreated ingloriously. Afterwards, about the beginning of May, he released the king from captivity, and, having broken his former agreement, imposed, as we have already mentioned, a new and hard condition.

CHAPTER XI - *Of the meeting of the Icing and queen.*

There is an island called Arados, having a city named Antharados, but commonly, called Tortosa. Hither the queen came to meet the king: they kiss and embrace one another, shedding tears of joy, and rejoice at having escaped the calamities which had caused them so much grief. The king remained the following year, partly at Antioch, partly at Tripoli, waiting for the

Christians who were preparing to come from beyond the sea to the succour of the Holy Land.

CHAPTER XII - *Of the money which king Henry formerly deposited with the Templars.*

Among other things we think it ought not to be passed over in silence, that Henry, king of England, had formerly deposited a large sum of money with the Templars and Hospitallers, to defend Tyre, and provide for other matters concerning the kingdom. This money that magnificent king, by a provision as pious as necessary, had transmitted to Jerusalem, during a period of many years, to be used in the service of the Holy Land: its total, as is said, amounted to 30,000 marks.

CHAPTER XIII - *How Saladin, retreating from Tyre, took several towns, both in Palestine, and near Antioch.*

Now Saladin leaving Tyre, occupied several castles in Palestine, and thence marched with rapidity into the country round Antioch and took, by assault rather than by siege, Gebeli, Laodicea, and several other fortresses of that province. The city itself was thrown into no small alarm but the patriarch and prince, with the common consent of the citizens, promised the tyrant to surrender, if they should not within a given period receive the assistance which they expected. Inconsolable would have been the grief of all Christ's followers, if a city so renowned, and honored by the first origin of the Christian name, had again become subject to the impure heathen, whom, after a long and dreadful chance of war, our victorious troops had formerly expelled. But whence are the expected reinforcements to come and when or how shall they come? There is no road open for them by land, and the sea is blockaded by their enemies. The ships of the Christians abstain from approaching, for fear of falling among the galleys of the unbelievers, which they see lying in wait for them. But what the Lord has resolved to save will not be allowed to perish. Behold, the hoped-for troops arrive the expected ones are coming. Lo! William, the illustrious king of Sicily, sends the first auxiliaries to the Holy Land, consisting of two earls, five hundred knights, and fifty galleys!

CHAPTER XIV - *How William, king of Sicily, sends Margaritus with fifty galleys and five hundred knights to the assistance of the Holy Land.*

To whom else, then, can we give the glory of having saved Antioch, Tripoli, and Tyre, but to Him who preserved from famine and the sword the inhabitants of these cities secure in his strength? At the head of the royal fleet was Margaritus, a very brave man, who, proceeding in advance with the galleys, repressed piratical attempts and having ascertained that the coast was clear, encouraged the others to follow him. Keeping in check the distant islands, and happily escaping all the dangers of the sea, he had gained such credit by his numerous victories, that he was called the king of the sea, and by some a second Neptune. Already Tripoli appeared in sight to his sailors: the citizens, on the other hand, beheld in the distance his spreading sails. Though they come the heralds of safety, yet fear, that worst prognosticator at critical moments, raises apprehensions. Without delay they man their walls and mount the bulwarks, uncertain, however, whether to offer a surrender or to try the chance of battle. But when the ships arrive near, and the ensigns of the Cross and other emblems of the Christian religion are beheld on their lofty sterns, a loud shout is raised the waves echo the sound of their mutual congratulations; the shore is covered with the crowds who flock to meet them, and joy unspeakable fills the breasts of all. Among others, Henry of Dantzic, especially distinguished by the celebrity of his deeds, contributes his veteran wisdom to the defense of that land and so in a short time, many a valiant band flocked thither, and the coast was preserved from the power of the enemy.

CHAPTER XV - *Saladin takes the town Erathrum, and Mount Royal is surrendered to him after a siege of two years, in exchange for Remfrid de Tours, and Girard, the master of the Temple.*

There is a castle called Erathrum, where once stood the city of Petras. It is still a metropolitan see, and the prelate of it, retaining his ancient title, is still called the archbishop of Petras. This castle, lying in the innermost parts of the kingdom, was long held in siege by the admirals of the sultan. If it were not for famine, which conquers all places however secure, this fortress would be impregnable. There is also a castle called Mount Royal, distant about twenty leagues from the aforesaid city, lying further towards Egypt. Against this also the sultan had sent his admirals at the beginning of the war; trusting to reduce it by famine, though he could not by arms. They did not, therefore, erect machines or try to assault it for it would be ridiculous to try to scale heaven and to carry by storm a place which could not be approached. The siege was protracted two years, when our people began to feel want, and they endured all the horrors which the Spaniards are said in ancient times to have suffered at Saguntum or the Romans at Perusium but they still kept up their courage, nor did they decline to eat food at which man's usual habits and nature revolt. Fatherly affection renounces its rights love, too, heeds no longer what it had once delighted in the father rejects his son, the son his decrepit parents, and the husband his newly-married bride. They are driven out weeping from the walls and exposed without protection to the enemy, that the remaining stock of food may the longer maintain the fighting men. At last, worn out and half dead with hunger, they enter into terms of capitulation, but yet such as honor would sanction; for they obtained a free passage for themselves and liberty for their lord Remfrid of Tours who had been taken prisoner. By a similar fortune, Gerard de Riddeford, master of the Temple, was also released on the surrender of certain fortresses and the father of the marquis obtained his liberty in exchange for some of the Mahomedan captives.

CHAPTER XVI - *How Saladin, extolling the live of Mahomet, is reproved by a jester.*

Saladin by these means had got possession of nearly all the kingdom, and every thing succeeded to his wishes. Elevated with his proud triumphs, he talked in magnificent terms of the law of Mahomet, and pointed to the result of his enterprise as a proof that it was superior to the law of Christ.

These insolent vaunts he often threw out in the presence of the Christians, one of whom, well known to him for his loquacity, on a certain occasion, inspired by the Almighty, turned him into ridicule by the following reply: "God, who is the father of the faithful, judging the Christians worthy of reproof and correction for their crimes, has chosen thee, O prince, as his agent in this matter thus sometimes a worldly father in anger seizes a dirty stick out of the mire, wherewith when he has chastised his erring sons, he throws it back among the filth where he found it."

CHAPTER XVII - *First of Richard, earl of Poitou, then of Henry, king of the English, and of Philip, king of the French.*

Whilst these things were done in Palestine, the archbishop of Tyre had embarked on ship-board, and already reported to Christendom the news of this great calamity, and the affliction of so small a kingdom was felt as a calamity over many countries. Fame had carried to the ears of all the kings, and of all the faithful, that the inheritance of Christ was occupied by the heathen some were affected to tears by the news, and some were stimulated to vengeance. First of all, Richard the brave earl of Poitou, assumed the cross to revenge its wrongs, and took the lead of all, inviting others by his example. His father Henry, king of England, was now declining in years; yet the young man was not deterred by either his father's advanced age, or his own right to the throne, or the difficulties of so long a voyage no arguments could deter him from his purpose. The Almighty, to reward the valor of this brave man, whom he had chosen to be the first inciter of the others, reserved him, after the other princes were dead or returned to their own country, to achieve his great work. Some time after, Philip, king of France, and Henry, king of England, take the cross at Gisors, followed by the nobles of both kingdoms, with numbers of the clergy and laity,—all, with equal aspirations, bent upon the same design. So great was the ardour of this new pilgrimage, that it was no longer a question who would take the cross, but who had not yet taken it. Several persons sent a present of a distaff and wool to one another, as a significant hint that whosoever declined the campaign would degrade himself as much as if he did the duties of a woman wives urged their husbands, mothers their sons, to devote themselves to this noble contest and they only regretted that the weakness of their sex prevented themselves from going also. The renown of this expedition spread so extraordinarily, that many migrated from the cloister to the camp, and exchanging the cowl for the cuirass, showed themselves truly Christ's soldiers, and quitting their libraries for the study of arms. The prelates of the churches publicly preached to one another the virtue of abstinence, admonishing all men that, laying aside all extravagance in eating and dress, they should refrain from their accustomed luxuries. It was agreed also both among nobles and bishops, by common consent, that to maintain the pilgrims who were poor, those who remained at home should pay tithes of their property but the flagitious cupidity of many took advantage of this to lay heavy and undue exactions upon their subjects. In those days William, king of Sicily, yielded to the lot of mortality; and his death was the cause of so much the greater sorrow to all the faithful, because he had always been prompt and ready to lend assistance to the Holy Land.

CHAPTER XVIII - *The emperor of the Romans {Frederic Barbarossa) takes the cross.*

In process of time, Frederic, the Roman emperor, assumed the insignia of the holy pilgrimage, and displayed both outwardly in his dress, and inwardly in his heart, the form of a true pilgrim. So great a king, whose empire was bounded on the south by the Mediterranean Sea, on the north by the Northern Ocean, whose glory was augmented by continual victories, whose fortune had experienced no check, resigns every pleasure and blandishment of the world, and humbly girds on his sword to fight for Christ. His bravery, especially in his declining years, is no less to be wondered at than praised; for though he was an old man and had sons, whose age and valor seemed better adapted to military service, yet esteeming them insufficient, he took upon himself the charge of defending Christianity but when his sous urged him to let them discharge the task which he had undertaken, either in his stead or in his company, he left his eldest son to govern his empire, and the younger, whom he had created duke of Suabia, he took with him on the expedition and because the imperial majesty never assails any one without sending a defiance, but always gives notice of war to his enemies, a herald is dispatched from the emperor to Saladin, calling upon him to give full satisfaction to Christendom, which he has injured, or, failing to do so, to prepare himself for war.

THE EPISTLE OF FREDERIC TO SALADIN

Frederic, by the grace of God emperor of the Romans, ever august, the magnificent triumpher over the enemies of the empire and the fortunate governor of the achole monarchy, to the illustrious Saladin, formerly governor of the Saracens. May he take warning from Pharaoh and touch not Jerusalem!

The letters which your devotion sent to us a long time ago, on weighty and important matters, and which would have benefited you if reliance could have been placed on your words, we received, as became the magnificence of our majesty, and deemed it meet to communicate by letter with your greatness. But now that you have profaned the Holy Land, over which we, by the authority of the Eternal King, bear rule, as guardian of Judea, Samaria, and Palestine, solicitude for our imperial office admonishes us to proceed with due rigor against such presumptuous and criminal audacity. Wherefore, unless, before all things, you restore the land which you have seized, and give due satisfaction, to be adjudged according to the holy constitutions, for such nefarious excesses, that we may not appear to wage unlawful war against you, we give you, from the first of November, a period of twelve months, after which you shall experience the fortune of war, in the field of Zoan, by the virtue of the vivifying cross, and in the name of the true Joseph. For we can scarcely believe that you are ignorant of that which all antiquity and the writings of the ancients testify. Do you pretend not to know that both the Aethiopias, Mauritania, Persia, Scythia, Parthia, where our general Marcus Crassus met with a premature death, Judea, Samaria, Maritima, Arabia, and Chaldaea, also Egypt, where, shame to say a Roman citizen, Antony, a man endowed with signal virtues, passing the bounds of temperance, and acting otherwise than as became a soldier sent from so great a state, submitted to the unchaste love of Cleopatra;—do you pretend not to know that Armenia, and other innumerable countries, have been subject to our sway? This is well known to those kings in whose blood the Roman sword has been so often steeped; and you, God willing, shall learn by experience the might of our victorious eagles, and be made acquainted with our troops of many nations—the anger of Germany the untamed head of the Rhine—the youth from the banks of the Danube, who know not how to flee—the towering

Bavarian—the cunning Suabian—the cautious Franconian—Saxony, that sports with the sword—Thuringia—Westphalia —the active Brabantine—the Lorrainer unused to peace— the fiery Burgundian—the nimble mountaineer of the Alps—the Frison with his javelin and thong— the Bohemian ever ready to brave death—Bolonia fiercer than her own fierce beasts—Austria— Syria—Ruwennia—Istria—Rocumphia—Illyria—Lombardy Tuscany— the march of Ancona— the resolute Venetian and the Pisan sailor—and lastly, also, you shall assuredly be taught how our own right hand, which you suppose to be enfeebled by old age, can still wield the sword upon that day of reverence and gladness which has been appointed for the triumph of Christ's cause.

We think it right to insert in our history the letter which Saladin sent in reply to the foregoing. The proud boasting of the tyrant, which he had conceived in his opposition, is sufficiently manifest in it. However, we give it in the simple form of words in which it was written, without changing a syllable of it.

To the great king, his sincere friend, the illustrious Frederic, king of Germany:—In the name of God the merciful by the grace of the one God, the powerful, the surpassing, the victorious, the everlasting, of whose kingdom there is no end.

We give continual thanks to Him, whose grace is over all the world we pray that he may pour out his inspiration over all his prophets, and especially on our teacher, his messenger the prophet, Mahomet, whom he sent to teach the true law, which he will make to appear above all laws. But we make it known to the sincere and powerful king, our great, amicable friend, the king of Germany, that a certain man, named Henry, came to us, professing to be your envoy, and he gave us a letter, which he said was from your hand. We caused the letter to be read, and we heard him speak by word of mouth, and to the words which he spake by word of mouth we answered also in words. But this is the answer to your letter:—You enumerate those who are leagued with you to come against us, and you name them and say—the king of this land and the king of that land—this count and that count, and such archbishops, marquises, and knights. But if we wished to enumerate those who are in our service, and who listen to our commands, and obey our words, and would fight for us, this is a list which could not be reduced to writing. If you reckon up the names of the Christians, the Saracens are more numerous and many times more numerous than the Christians. If the sea lies between us and those whom you name Christians, there is no sea to separate the Saracens, who cannot be numbered between us and those who will come to aid us, there is no impediment. With us are the Bedouins, who would be quite sufficient singly to oppose our enemies and the Turkomans, who, unaided, could destroy them even our peasants, if we were to bid them, would fight bravely against the nations which should come to invade our country, and would despoil them of their riches and exterminate them. "What! Have we not on our side the warlike Soldaru, by whom we have opened and gained the land, and driven out our enemies? These and all the kings of Paganism will not be slow when we shall summon them, nor delay when we shall call them. And whenever your armies shall be assembled, according to the import of your letter, and you shall lead them, as your messenger tells us, we will then meet you in the power of God. Nor will we be satisfied with the land which is on the sea-coast, but we will cross over with God's good pleasure, and will take from you all your lands, in the strength of the Lord. For if you come, you will come with all your forces, and will be present with all your people, and we know that there will remain none at home to defend themselves or fight for their country. And when the Lord, by his power, shall have given us victory over you, nothing will remain for us to do but freely to take your lands, by His power, and with His good pleasure. For the union of the Christian faith has twice come against us in Babylon; once at Damietta, and again at Alexandria: it was also in the coast of the land of Jerusalem while in the hand of the Christians, in the land of Damascus, and in the land of the Saracens in each fortress there was a lord who studied his own interests. You know how the Christians each time returned, and to what an issue they came. But these our people are assembled together with their countries, and the Lord has associated with us countries in abundance, and united them far and wide under our power: Babylon, with its dependencies, and the land of Damascus, and Jerusalem on the sea-coast, and the land of Gesireh with its castles, and the land of Roasia with, its dependencies, and the land of India with its dependencies —by the grace of God, all this is in our hands, and the residue of the Saracenic kings is in our empire. For if we were to command the illustrious kings of the Saracens they would not withdraw themselves from us. And if we were to admonish the caliph of Bagdad (whom God preserve) to come to our aid, he would rise from the throne of his great empire and would come to help our excellence. We have obtained, also, by the virtue and power of God, Jerusalem and its territory and of the three cities which still remain in the hands of the Christians, Tyre, Tripoli, and Antioch, nothing remains but that we should occupy them also. But, if you wish for war, and if God so will of his good pleasure that we occupy the whole land of the Christians, we will meet you in the power of the Lord, as is written in this our letter. But, if you ask us for the boon of peace, you will command the warders of the three places above mentioned to deliver them up to us without resistance and we will restore to you the holy cross, and will liberate all the Christian captives who are in all our territories and we will be at peace with you and will allow you to have one priest at the sepulchre, and we will restore the abbeys which used to be in the time of Paganism, and will do good to them, and will permit the pilgrims to come during all our life, and we will be at peace with you. But if the letter which came to us by the hand of Henry be the letter of the king, we have written this letter for answer, and may God give us counsel according to his will. This letter is written in the year of the coming of our prophet Mahomet, by the grace of the only God. And may God save our prophet Mahomet and his race, and may he save the salvation of our Savior, illustrious Lord, and victorious King; the giver of unity; the true word; the adorner of the standard of truth; the corrector of the world and of the law sultan of the Saracens and Pagans; the servitor of the two holy houses, and of the holy house of Jerusalem; the father of victors; Joseph the son of Job; the reviver of the progeny of Murmurasnus!

CHAPTER XIX - *How the emperor Frederic Barbarossa assembled his army throughout Hungary.*

This letter of the proud and faithless tyrant, with its absurdities, the magnificent emperor treated with contempt; and, filled with indignation worthy of a prince, prepared all his forces for the war. The princes of all the empire followed him, and when they were met at Mayence, according to the imperial edict, all of them joined with one acclaim in taking the vow of so noble a pilgrimage. This was the Lord's doing, of Him whose inspiration blow where it list, who inclines the hearts of men at his will. For these great princes were neither allured by a desire of vain glory, nor induced by bribes or entreaties, but solely by desire of the heavenly reward by the Lord, and the Lord alone, were they led to buckle on their armor for this warfare. For the loftiness of the heavenly wisdom had provided that, as they were enlisted of their own free will, they rendered a service agreeable to God, and the imperial magnificence was accompanied by a train of worthy followers. Thus, then, led by the Holy Spirit, they flocked together on every side; and whoever could have seen so many nations and princes under one commander, must have believed that the ancient glory of Rome was not yet departed. In this army of Christ were pontiffs, dukes, earls, marquises, and other nobles, without number for if we were to recapitulate their names and territories, the writer would become tedious, his reader be disgusted, and his plan of brevity be overthrown. It was determined by a prudent counsel that no one should go on this expedition whose means could not provide him with supplies for one year. A large number of carriages were constructed for the use of the pilgrims who should be sick, that they might neither give trouble to the sound, nor be left behind and perish. It had long been a question whether the mass of the army should proceed by sea or land. But it seemed that any number of ships, however large, would be insufficient to transport so great a multitude. The emperor, therefore, urging on the task which he had undertaken, determined to march through Hungary, and so, though he was the last sovereign who took the vow of pilgrimage, he was the first to carry it into effect.

CHAPTER XX - *Bela, king of the Hungarians, receives the king hospitably.*

The king of the Hungarians, Bela by name, came out with joy to meet the emperor. He was a man endowed by nature with many good qualities tall in stature, of a noble countenance, possessing a combination of virtues, and worthy of the highest panegyric who, if he had no other merit, would be thought worthy of sovereignty by his dignified appearance. He received Christ's army with hospitality, met them in a triumphant procession, and followed them with good will, testifying by his deeds the fervor of his friendship. The people in large numbers, burning with their sovereign's example, contemplate the sacred army and are eager to enlist; they look forwards to the prizes of the combat, and fear no dangers at once they form the wish, they take the vow, and follow with the army, so that it is evident the workings of Holy Inspiration knew no impediment or delay. Crossing the Danube they reached the furthest passes of Bulgaria, where Huns, Alans, Bulgarians, and Pincenates rushed suddenly from their ambush upon the Lord's host, encouraged to the attack by the rugged and inaccessible nature of the ground.

CHAPTER XXI - *How Frederic, having crossed the Danube, found the Huns and Alans hostile to him.*

The outlet from Bulgaria into Macedonia is fortified on both sides by high rocks, covered with thorns and bushes, through which wind narrow and rugged paths. To these the inhabitants have added lofty artificial defenses. These passes were seized by the nations before mentioned, who had been sent for this purpose by the wicked emperor Conrad that they might destroy the army, or at least stop its further approach. Our soldiers, however, courageously overcame both the enemy and the road, and passing through Macedonia, arrived at Philippopolis, a city which had before been called Pulpudeba, but took the name of Philippopolis in honor of the Roman emperor Philip, who first of all the emperors became a Christian, and by the profession of the Christian faith conferred additional luster upon the imperial dignity. The Greeks, hearing of the approach of the Latin army, deserted the city, fearing where there was no need of fear; for which their only reason was that they feared all whom they did not love for the pilgrims had not come to plunder others, as they had sufficient of their own nor had they taken arms against the faithful, but only to crush the errors of an infidel race. But the ancient and inexorable hatred which the Greeks entertained of old against the Latins had been handed down by the tenacity of ages to their posterity. If a motive or reason of this enmity be sought — It were no wrong, if it a plea had found. Yet this may, perhaps, be urged as an excuse, that whereas the Latins were flourishing in arts and arms, they themselves were altogether ignorant and unwarlike: this gives a motive to their enmity, and they pine with jealousy at the prosperity of others. They are a perfidious race, a wicked generation, and utterly degenerate the more illustrious they once were, the more signal is their degradation; their gold is converted into dross, their wheat into chaff, their purity to filth, their glory to corruption. The old Greeks attempted and achieved much, both in arts and arms but all their zeal for virtue has chilled in their posterity and has passed over to the Latins, so that where once fountains were there now are rivulets, or rather, dry and exhausted channels. Their virtues have found no heirs, but their crimes many they still retain the deceit of Sinon, the falseness of Ulysses, and the atrocity of Atreus. If I be asked concerning their military science, this turns on stratagems rather than on battles if concerning their good faith, the man should beware who has them for his friends, though their hostility can do him no harm. That nation, unable to impede the march of our army at the aforesaid passes, did what lay in their power to do it all the natives fled to the mountaintops and carried with them every comfort which we could have bought of them for money, leaving their empty houses without an article of furniture in them to our army that was approaching, The emperor indeed, on the plea of peace, had already sent forwards the bishop of Munster, with some other princes, to Constantinople; but the wicked and cruel tyrant cast them into prison, daring to violate the sanctity of an ambassador, which, even among barbarians, has been respected from all antiquity by the sanction of usage and the laws of honor. Afterwards, however, influenced more by fear than a regard for right, he released the ambassadors from prison for he feared the destruction of his capital if he should not speedily pacify our wrath. It would have been right, indeed, that the city should have been razed, even to the ground for, if we believe report, it was polluted by new mosques, which its perfidious emperor allowed to be built, that he might strengthen the league which he had entered into with the Turks. The season of the year was now ripening towards autumn, and the constellation Libra was balancing the day and night in nearly equal lengths. The magnificent emperor of the Romans marched to take up his winter-quarters at Adrianople, which he found empty and deserted by its inhabitants. Here he took up his position, and waited for the season when he should lead his army forwards.

CHAPTER XXII - *Of the emperor Frederic's entering in Greece, and of the peace between him and the emperor Isaac of the deceitful embassy sent to him by the sultan of Iconium, and of his passage through St. George's Arm*

The duke of Suabia, son of the emperor, fearing lest ease should produce luxury, and luxury generate indolence, determined to find employment for the army during the inactivity of winter and for this purpose, he formed a plan to storm a fortress which was situated at no great distance from the aforesaid city. The Greeks had assembled together in it, trusting in its fortifications, that they might from thence direct their schemes against the Latins but in this expectation they were confounded, for they were speedily defeated and vanquished, thrown into chains and kept prisoners. When the Byzantine emperor heard of these things, he feared that something still worse would happen and apprehending the destruction of all his empire, he hastily sent ambassadors to our emperor, promising hostages for peace, a market for the sale of provisions, and ships to transport all who wished to cross. The emperor, although many of them thought it dangerous to make peace at all with a tyrant, yet preferred to accept the offered treaty rather than longer delay his expedition. And now that Easter was approaching, he crossed over the narrow sea, generally called by the name of "St. George's Arm." Although but a narrow strait, this sea enjoys no little reputation, because it washes so great a city, and flows between the two divisions of the world, Asia and Europe. The sultan of Iconium, a deceitful man, and thirsting after Christian blood, under a fraudulent pretext professed friendship towards us, and concealing the malignant venom of his heart, sought thereby to destroy us when off our guard. He had sent frequent messengers to the emperor, whilst still in Greece, entreating him to cross over; and whilst he accused the Greeks and their prince of treachery, he promised that he would be a devout and faithful servant to the Christians, and that he would place himself and all that he had at their disposal, and furnish to all of them a market to buy provisions, and a safe passage through his dominions. The emperor, too credulous, and estimating others by his own knowledge of himself, made a proclamation, in which he threatened all with punishment who, when they entered the territories of the Turks, should commit depredations, or fail to observe the peace which had been concluded. Thus then it happened, that our men passed on without touching the great booty which the sultan had, intentionally, left at the very entrance of his dominions. Alas, how blind are men and ignorant of the future! If they could have foreseen the famine which they were about to suffer, the difficulties of the road, and the deceitfulness of the tyrant! Chance had thrown in their way the means of providing for themselves against these great and imminent dangers. However, our people did not so far listen to the words of that faithless prince, as, neglecting their own security, to march in disorder, or without their arms. When, therefore, they were about to enter Parthia, all of them seized their arms, in number 3,000 knights; of the rest there were about 80,000. There were seven bishops, one archbishop, two dukes, nineteen counts, and three marquises and this splendid army seemed neither to have had its like before or after. But to prevent disaffection or confusion in so large a mass, the whole army was divided into three bodies: the first was led by the duke of Suabia, the last by the emperor that in the centre was charged with the care of the Sumpter horses and baggage. The army advanced judiciously arranged, to the delight of the beholder, neither crowded together, nor yet dispersedly, but in bodies and though there were many officers over each body, yet there was but one commander-in-chief. This is the best for a camp, an important circumstance in war: for as an army perishes without a leader, where no one is preeminent above the rest, so it is generally inefficient, where there are many leaders who contend for pre-eminence. Happy empire! happy Germany! the parent of so many nations, so many brave warriors of Christ, a source of pride to herself, and destruction to her enemies!

CHAPTER XXIII - *Of the discomforts which the Christians endured through the sultan, and how they reached Iconium*

Our army, having entered the territories of the Turks, experienced no hostility during several days the sultan wished by his forbearance to allure them into the heart of his dominions, until want of food and the asperities of the road should give him more ready means of annoying them. That nefarious traitor had seized the rugged mountain tops, the thickets of the woods, and the impassable rivers and whilst he professed to observe the treaty which he had made, he opposed arrows and stones to our passage. This was the market and the safe-conduct which he had promised us such is the faith that must be placed in the unbelievers; they always esteem valor and treachery as equally praiseworthy towards an enemy. Moreover, they avoid, above all things, coming to close quarters and fighting hand to hand but they shower their arrows from a distance; and with them it is no less glory to flee, than to put their enemy to flight. They attack both extremities of the army, at one time the rear, at another time the van that, if by any chance they can separate them, they may attack either the one or tho other by itself. Night brought with it neither sleep nor rest for a terrific clamor disturbed the army on every side. A shower of javelins pierced through their tents, numbers of them were slain asleep, and the enemy hung on them so incessantly, that for six weeks, they ate their meals under arms, and slept under arms, without taking off their coats of mail. At the same time they were assailed by such violent hunger and thirst, that when they lost their horses by the chances of war, it was to them a consolation and source of delight, to feed on horse-flesh and drink the blood in this manner, by the ingenuity which necessity teaches, they found out an additional use for the animals on which they rode.

There was a place between high rocks which was rendered so difficult to pass by reason of the steep ascent and the narrowness of the paths, that when the first division of the army, led by the emperor's son, had passed through, the Turks suddenly rushed from their ambush on the last division, and in their confidence of victory, attacked them with lance and sword. The alarming news was carried to the duke, who returned with headlong haste upon his march, eagerly retracing all the difficulties which he had a little before rejoiced at having surmounted. His rage heeded not danger; his cavalry were made to gallop where they could not even walk. In this manner, whilst he was anxiously and incautiously seeking for his father on every side, and incessantly shouting his father's name, his helmet was struck off by a stone, and his teeth knocked out, yet he still remained immoveable and unshaken. Happy the son, who, to save his father, was so prodigal of his own life, and exposed himself to so many dangers! As a consolation for the wound which he then received, he retains a lasting mark of it ; for whenever he opens his mouth, the bare gum testifies the glory of his victory. At last, after many severe attacks, the army arrives at Iconium, where that wicked traitor had shut himself within the walls of the city: our soldiers pitched their tents at no great distance, uncertain what new disaster the morrow might bring with it. It was now about the end of Whitsuntide, and that same night so violent and sudden a storm burst upon them, that its fury was felt even within the camp. In the morning, when the clouds were dispersed, the sky became clear, and behold the Turkish army appear around on every side with trumpets, drums, and horrid clang, ready to attack. They had never before been seen in such multitudes, nor could they have been conceived to have been so numerous. If any one should read that there were three hundred thousand or more of them, it was only an estimate of the amount, for it was impossible to number them. All this multitude had been roused to arms by the sultan's son Melkin, who wished to anticipate his father-in-law Saladin's victory, and, trusting in the number and valor of his men, was confident of success. Meanwhile the sultan had ascended a lofty tower, where he sat in expectation, eyeing the country beneath him and the armies that were ready to engage, and hoping in a short time to see accomplished what his sanguine mind had promised. The emperor, seeing some of his men alarmed at the unusual multitude of the enemy, displayed the confidence of a noble chieftain, and raising his hands to heaven, gave thanks to God in the sight of all, that the inevitable necessity was at length arrived for that combat which had so long been deferred by the flight of the enemy. At these words, ail were inspired with fresh ardour, as they looked on the emperors placid countenance and one old man, weak though he was, supplied an incentive of valor to many who were young and strong. What God is so great as our God? All that multitude who were so sure of victory that they brought chains with them rather than swords, were overthrown in a moment and at once the city was taken and occupied, and the enemy without vanquished everywhere were blood and death, and heaps of slain their number impedes their flight, and they fall by those very means on which they had counted for triumph. The battle is now fought hand to hand the bows are snapped asunder the arrows no longer fly, and they have scarcely room to wield their swords. Thus everything is thrown into confusion by the multitude, and what our enemies intended for our ruin turns out to our greater glory; the flying war, which had been waged among brambles and the gorges of rocks, is now carried on in a fair and open field the Christians satiate their fury, which had so often been put forth in vain. The Turks experience, against their will, how well their enemies can fight hand to hand whom they had so often provoked at a distance.

This splendid victory was not granted unworthily by the Divine excellence to His faithful servants for they observed chastity in the camp, and discipline when under arms in all, and above all, was the fear of the Lord; with all was the love of their neighbor; all were united in brotherly affection, as they were also companions in danger. The sultan, when the city was taken, seeing that there remained to him truly the tower in which he was, sent hastily to the emperor, throwing all the blame upon his son, and professing his own innocence; promising, moreover, as much gold as he should demand, and whatsoever persons he should name as hostages for his observance of the treaty. The emperor, alas! Too easy, accepted what was offered and gave what was asked in this less worthy of praise, because he let go that man of blood and treachery whom he had almost in his possession, when it would have been more honorable to slay him than to keep alive so great an enemy to the Christian name. The hostages were given and the treaty confirmed but the wickedness of that malignant traitor did not rest there for, whilst the Christians were continuing their march far beyond Iconium, he attacked them, sometimes by ambuscade, sometimes openly in the field. The hostages were asked what this meant, and they told a falsehood which suited their own purpose they said that the Turks were a wild race whom no one could govern that they wandered about with no fixed habitation, having no property of their own, and always trying to obtain that of others either by robbery or theft. They attacked us however less boldly, knowing that many of their men had fallen for, by a moderate computation, 22,000 of the Turks had been slain in former conflicts.

CHAPTER XXIV - *How the Emperor Frederic, arriving in Armenia, is drowned in the river Selesius, and his son, the duke of Suabia, takes the command of the army*

The victorious army now enters the Armenian territories all rejoice at having quitted a hostile kingdom, and at their arrival in the country of the faithful. But, alas! A more fatal land awaits them, which is to extinguish the light and joy of all. Let man take thought and investigate, if he may, the counsels of the Lord, whose judgments are unfathomable. Things will occur sometimes to cause him astonishment, sometimes confusion, yet so that in every circumstance man may recognize the author of all things. On the borders of Armenia there was a place, surrounded on one side by steep mountains, on the other side by the river Selesius. Whilst the Sumpter horses and baggage were passing this river, the victorious emperor halted. He was indeed an illustrious man, of stature moderately tall, with red hair and beard his head was partly turning grey, his eyelids were prominent and his eyes sparkling his cheeks short and wide his breast and shoulders broad in all other respects his form was manly. There was in him, as is read of Socrates, something distinguished and awful for his look denoted the firmness of his mind, being always immovably the same, neither clouded by grief, nor contracted by anger, nor relaxed by joy. He so much reverenced the native language of Germany, that although he was not ignorant of other languages, yet he always conversed with ambassadors from foreign countries by means of an interpreter. This great man, having halted some time, in consequence of the Sumpter horses crossing the river, became at last impatient of the delay and wishing to accelerate the march, he prepares to cross the nearest part of the stream, so as to get in front of the Sumpter horses and be at liberty to proceed. O sea! O earth! O heaven! The ruler of the Roman empire, ever august, in whom the glory of ancient Rome again flourished, its honor again lived, and its power was augmented, was overwhelmed in the waters and perished and though those who were near him hastened to his assistance, yet his aged spark of life was extinguished by a sudden though not premature death. If love of swimming, as several have asserted, be said to have caused his death, yet the gravity of the man argues the contrary; nor does it merit belief that, a bad swimmer, he would have committed to the deceitful waters the safety of so many. The conscience is witness that death is less painful than the cause of death, but this is our consolation as it is written the just, by whatever death he shall be surprised, will be refreshed. If the mountains of Gilboa, where the brave ones of Israel were slain, deserved to be deprived of the dew and rain, what imprecations may we not deservedly utter upon this fatal river, which overthrew a main pillar of all Christendom? There were some who said that the place had been marked by a fatality from ancient times, and that the nearest rock had long borne upon it these words inscribed, "Here the greatest of men shall perish." The lamentable report of his death was spread around and filled all with dismay. If we search all the annals of antiquity, the traditions of history, and the fictions of romance, concerning the sorrows of mothers, the sighs of brides, or the distresses of men in general, the present grief will be found to be without example, never before known in any age, and surpassing all tears and lamentations. There were many of the emperor's domestics present, with some of his kinsmen and his son but it was impossible to distinguish them amid the general lamentation, with which all and each lamented the loss of their father and their lord. This, however, was a consolation to all, and they all returned thanks for it to Divine Providence that he had not died within the territories of the infidels. When his funeral-rites were performed, they left the fatal spot as soon as possible, bearing with them the body of the emperor adorned with royal magnificence, that it might be carried to Antioch. There the flesh, being boiled from the bones, reposes in the church of the Apostolic see, and the bones were conveyed by sea to Tyre, thence to be transported to Jerusalem. It was fit indeed and wonderfully contrived by God's providence, that one who had contended gloriously for Christ, should repose in the two principal churches of the Christian religion, for both of which he had been a champion,—part of him in the one, and part in the other,—the one that which our Lord's burial rendered the most distinguished, the other that which was honored by being the see of the chief of the apostles. The Christians arriving at Antioch, after many and long fastings, gave way too plentifully to their appetites, and died of sudden repletion and so, after they had resisted both famine and the swords of their enemies, repose was fatal to them, and a pernicious abundance cut them off. In this shameful manner, then, the greater part of that great army perished, and most of the survivors returned to their own countries: a small body of them, ashamed to return, served under the emperor's son, to whom the prince of Antioch surrendered his city with all its defenses. For on the plea of greater protection, he offered of his own accord to commit his city to the duke, that this brave man might defend his territories against the frequent assaults of the enemies.

CHAPTER XXV - *Acre is besieged. King Guy is freed from his oath.*

In the mean time Christ's soldiers, who had been conveyed by sea to the succour of the Holy Land, were laying siege to Acre. That the order of the siege may be better understood, we will relate it from the beginning. Guy, king of Jerusalem, after he had been a year in captivity at Damascus, was released by Saladin on the strict promise that he should abjure his kingdom, and, as soon as possible, go into exile beyond the sea. The clergy of the kingdom determine to release the king from the bond of his oath both because what is done under compulsion deserves to be annulled, and because the bands of the faithful who were on their way would find in him a head and leader. It was right indeed that art should overreach art, and that the treachery of the tyrant should be deceived by its own example for one who is faithless in his promises, gives encouragement to similar faithlessness in him whose promise he exacts. The faithless unbeliever, having broken his previous agreement, had extorted from the captive king, after many injuries, an oath that on being restored to liberty he would go into exile. A sad condition this, of liberty accompanied with exile and the renunciation of a kingdom. But God so ordered it that the counsel of Belial was brought to naught; for the tyrant was baffled in his hopes of retaining the kingdom, and the king was released by the sentence of the clergy from the enormity of his promise. Men also had arrived, who would nobly vindicate the wrongs which had been done to Christ's cross, distinguished champions, whose devout zeal had stirred them up to bring consolation to thee, O Jerusalem! Behold, the whole world is in arms for thy service, and the word is fulfilled which was spoken by the prophet Isaiah: "I will bring thy seed from the north, and from the west I will gather thee together: I will say to the north, Give and to the south, Do not forbid." Thus, then, when numbers had flocked together to meet the king at Tripoli, the minds of all were inspired with bravery, so that they strove not only to keep what they had retained, but also to recover what they had lost. Moreover, whilst they were remaining at Tripoli, they did not pass the time in idleness for they assailed the enemies in that neighborhood, and defeated at one time three hundred, at another time a larger number, with their victorious band. Among the rest was the king's brother who had lately landed his name was Geoffrey, and he distinguished himself especially amongst the combatants by his valor, for, in addition to the common cause, which influenced all alike, he was roused to action by his own private wrongs and the injury which had been done to his brother.

CHAPTER XXVI - *How the king, arriving at Tyre, is not received by the marquis, but dissembling the insult, proceeds with the men of Pisa and a small army to Acre, which the Christians besiege by sea and land*

After a while the king assembled his army and proceeded to Tyre but demanding admittance, was refused by the marquis, though the city had been committed to his custody on the condition that it should be restored to the king and the heirs of the kingdom. Not content with this injury, he adds insult to breach of faith, for whenever the king's messenger, or any pilgrims, endeavored to enter the town, they were treated harshly, and were in his sight no better than Gentiles and Publicans. But the Pisans, who possessed no small part of the city, would not be induced to consent to his perfidy, but with commendable rebellion stood up for the king's rights. The marquis directed not only insults, but civil war against them, and they, prudently withdrawing for a time, retired with others from the city to the army. The troops had pitched their camp in an open plain; but none of them were allowed to enter the city, even to buy provisions and they all found an enemy where they had hoped to find an ally. Whilst these events were going on, the marquis was afflicted by a complaint to which he had long been subject but, as it chanced to assail him this time with greater violence than usual, he conjectured that he had taken poison. Upon this, he issued a harsh edict against physicians who make potions; innocent men were put to death on false suspicions, and those whose province it was to heal others, now found the practice of their art lead to their own destruction. The king was urged by many to attack the city, but he prudently dissembled his own wrong, and hastily marched, with all the army he could collect, to besiege the town of Acre. There were seven hundred knights and others more numerous stilly collected out of all Christendom; but if we were to estimate the whole army, its strength did not amount altogether to nine thousand men. At the end of August, on St. Augustin's day, two years after the city had been taken they bravely commenced that long and difficult siege which was protracted during two years longer before the city surrendered. The Turks from the battlements of the walls, beheld the army approach, but without knowing who they were, or for what they came. When they learnt the truth, they feared not their approach, and treated their intentions with derision. The men of Pisa, who chose to proceed by sea, as shorter and easier, approached Acre in due order in their ships, and bravely occupied the shore; where they had no sooner secured a station, than they formed the siege on the side towards the sea with equal courage and perseverance. The king, with the rest of his army, fixed his tents on a neighboring hill commonly called Mount Turon, from which, by the eminence of the ground, he overlooked the approach both by sea and land. This hill was higher on the eastern side of the city and, as it allowed the eye to rove freely round, it gave a prospect over the plain on all sides, far and wide.

CHAPTER XXVII - *The Christians assault the city, hut are attacked by Saladin in the rear, and whilst they are thus between two enemies, they are encouraged by receiving a reinforcement of 12,000 northern warriors*

On the third day after their arrival the Christians made an assault upon the town; and deeming it tedious to await the effect of engines for throwing stones, together with other machines, they trusted to the defense of their shields alone, and carried scaling ladders to mount the walls. That day would have put a happy termination to the toil of so many days, if the malice of the ancient enemy, and the arrival of false information, had not frustrated their achievement when it was almost completed for it was reported that Saladin was at hand, and our men returned with speed to the camp; but when they perceived that it was only a small body that had come in advance, they expressed indignation rather than complaint that the victory had been snatched from them.

They were indeed few that had come, but fear had reported that an innumerable multitude was at hand for it is not unusual, that things should be magnified through terror. The sultan, at this time, was besieging the castle of Belfort and when he heard what was going on, he marched in haste with a large army to Acre. Our men, unequal to cope with him, kept themselves within the limits before described. The Turks assailed them perseveringly, both morning and evening, trying every means to penetrate to the hilltop and thus, those who came to besiege others, were now besieged themselves. In this position, then, were our men, when the Morning Star visited them from on high for behold fifty ships, such as are commonly called coggs, having twelve thousand armed men, on board, are seen approaching,—a grateful sight to our men, on account of the strait which they were in. Grateful is that which comes when prayed for more grateful still is that which comes contrary to our hope but grateful beyond all is that which comes to aid us in the last necessity yet off times we suspend our belief concerning a thing we so much long for, and cannot credit what we too much desire. Our army from the top of the hill sees the reinforcements coming, and dare not hope for an event so joyful and the new comers, also, look upon the camp as an object of suspicion. When, however, they came nearer and saw the ensigns of the Christian faith, a shout is raised on both sides—their joyful feelings find vent in tears they eagerly flock together and leap into the waves to go and meet them. O happy fleet, which, sailing from the Northern Ocean, and encountering a voyage never before tried, passed over so many seas, so many coasts, so many dangers, and came from Europe, along the shores of Africa, to succour Asia in her distress. The crews of these ships were Danes and Frisons, men inured to labor by the rigors of the north, and having three qualities good in war—large limbs, invincible minds, and devout fervor for the faith. They had sailed from their country, and the kindly breeze had wafted them on the waves, as well as winds were benignant, such as give delight to sailors, and so the merciful Lord brought his champions safe and uninjured through so many dangers. But the inhabitants of the lands by which these vessels sailed, were excited when they saw the fleet, and, embarking on ship-board, both Englishmen and Flemings followed them in haste. Nor must I pass in silence a gallant action which was performed by them as they passed they courageously attacked a city called Silvia, on the sea-coast of Spain, and having quickly made themselves masters of it, and slain the Gentile inhabitants, they delivered the city up to the Christians, appointed there a bishop, and proceeded victorious on their voyage. To Acre, then, they came and having pitched their camp between the city and Mount Turon, they turned their invincible prowess to the destruction of the enemy, whom they assailed, not by frequent skirmishes, but by one continued conflict—for their prodigal valor and reckless fury exposed them to so many dangers that afterwards, when the city was taken, hardly a hundred men remained alive out of the twelve thousand.

CHAPTER XXVIII - *Of the arrival of James d'Avennes the siege of the city is pressed with greater vigor the fiction of Saladin*

The night after the landing of the Prisons and Danes, James d'Avennes reached the desired shore, a man endowed with threefold qualifications,—in counsel a Hector, in arms an

Achilles, and in honor surpassing Regulus. He pitched his camp opposite the tower they call the Cursed (Maledicta), and a little further on lay the Templars; still the greater part of the city was not besieged, but there was a free communication open to the enemy. Our men, anxious as to their movements, liked not this freedom of entrance and exit; but the extended circuit of the walls and the paucity of soldiers allowed not of a continued blockade. They therefore divided their forces into troops, and by turns watched the approaches of the city in arms; and thus, for some days, obstructed the passage of those who would go out. The Turks, however, issuing from city and camp, and having collected their strength from all quarters, attacked our men and prevailed for a divided line of battle is easily broken through, and scattered strength quickly yield. On that day the Hospitallers were on guard, and on giving way, were relieved by the Templars, who checked the enemy, and hindered them, though pressed severely, from bursting into the camp. Moreover, day by day the army of the faithful increased and a multitude of ships coming together, struck no small terror into the Mahometan army. But Saladin, by means of a fiction, lessened the fears thus excited, asserting that the Christians took away their ships by night, and brought them back again at dawn of day as if they were newly arrived, for the purpose of making a display of strength. He himself was not, however, ignorant of the real state of the case, and grieved bitterly at our daily increase of strength; but, dissembling the cloud on his mind under a haughty aspect, he exhibited a calm and fearless countenance.

CHAPTER XXIX - *Of the arrival of the French, English, and Germans*

Very many indeed had already come from the kingdom of France and amongst others the bishop of Beauvais, a man more devoted to the camp than the closet, and one who gloried in warfare and strove to be like Turpin if he could but find a Charles. There is a part of France called Champagne and though the whole country is famous for the pursuit of arms, this one, by a sort of privilege of chivalry, excels and surpasses the rest. Hence its warlike youth marching out in power displayed the strength which it had exercised in the gymnasium with greater boldness against the foe and having laid aside the playful game of battle, they turned their bellicose spirits to the realities of war. So, indeed, English as well as French are led on by the warmth of their devotion, so that not waiting for their own kings they march forward to perform their duty to the King of kings. From Germany, also, there came an illustrious and powerful man, whom in their language they call Landgrave; which, according to the sense of the word, appears to mean count of the land, as if so entitled par excellence. He persuaded the marquis, who had a difference with

King Guy, to repair to Acre, though at first he had declined to do so on account of the disagreement. "We know that the rules of history sometimes require us to commit to writing, seriatim, the names of the chiefs who assist in the management of affairs, to which, indeed, they themselves, in a sort of itch for glory, sometimes lay claim; whilst, on the other hand, the fastidious reader may think the work too long in this particular, and so reject a narrative which, runs to wearisomeness. We therefore will be as brief as possible in enumerating the chiefs. But when the course of affairs shall offer an opportunity, we will mention the illustrious actions of each. After the numbers of the faithful were considerably increased, and when the army was fitter for setting about its arduous undertaking, it was unanimously determined to attack the neighboring camp of the unbelievers. A certain mount stood opposite to Mount Turon, which we have before described; here the enemy had pitched their pavilions, and a large intervening space of plain presented far and wide an area well adapted for battle. Hither the army descended from the camp to the plain and there being put in array, were divided into troops, so that the light-armed soldiers with the bowmen and arbalesters went first next to them followed the body of the army, glittering with horses, arms, and the various insignia of war. Their countenance and bearing indicated the disposition of their minds; the faithful had recourse to prayer, whilst the enemy trembled. There were those who, abandoning themselves to excessive exultation at the sight of the battle-array, presumed to say,—"What power shall prevail, what multitude shall withstand us? Let the Lord assist neither us nor our adversaries; the victory rests in our own valor." Certainly a most impious and utterly detestable sentiment, for it placed the issue of the battle in man and not in the Deity, when man can do nothing without God which, indeed, the issue of affairs proved by sad experience.

The Turks stood resolute for the defense of their camp but when our men approached nearer, they opened the body of their infantry who stood first, and boldly charged the enemy with their horse. The unbelievers were put to flight and abandoned their camp the Christians desisted from the pursuit, and were eager after the spoil; the cords of the pavilions were cut, and the tent of the sultan himself was seized upon by the fiery Count de Bar. Meanwhile, an immense multitude of the enemy burst out from the city, and marching from that part which was not besieged, proceeded towards the mountain by a circuitous path. Indeed, they purposely marched by a tortuous circuit, that while our men were in doubt whether they meant to attack the camp or the army, they might fall suddenly upon the latter, and close them in from the rear. The

Templars, inferior to none in renown, devoted to slaughter, had by this time burst through the enemies' squares, and, if the remainder of the army had pressed on in pursuit, they would that day have been the fortunate conquerors as well of the city as of the battle but when the Templars in their ardour had advanced too far in following up their fortune, they were suddenly attacked by the townsmen and although multitudes overcame them, it was not without great slaughter of their own men that the enemy triumphed. There Gerard de Riddeford the master of the Templars, of whom we have made mention before, was slain; happy he on whom the Lord conferred so great glory, that he should gain the laurel which he had earned in so many wars, and be admitted into the fellowship of martyrs. In another part, while the Germans were too eagerly bent upon plunder, the old deceiver offered to their view a horse escaping and seeing them pursue him in a crowd, the rest supposed that they were running away. By this slight but fatal accident the whole army was thrown into a panic, and all turned their thoughts to flight. At the same time, a new rumor increased their fear for there was a cry that the townsmen had gone forth to plunder the baggage. The army was at once thrown into confusion the battalions dispersed, and abandoned their standards even the commanders fly headlong, and scarce any have courage to resist.

CHAPTER XXX - *The flight and slaughter of the Christians*

The Turks, on seeing the confusion of the Christians, wondered at the circumstance, but were ignorant of the cause and having regained the victory unexpectedly, they turned their horses and resumed the courage which they had more from use than nature, yielding to those who pressed, and pressing on those who yielded; for they will fly from those who attack, and pursue those who fly. In this lamentable and disastrous tumult, Andrew de Brienne, while calling upon his comrades to resume the battle, was slain by the Turks who were pursuing this man was so superior to all the other Frenchmen that they awarded him the crown of chivalry, while others were content to strive for the honor of being second to him. His brother, the Count de Brienne, though he had seen him fall, passed him as he lay on the ground, and though called upon, feared to stop, and, like a coward, left him to his fate. Different from this was the conduct of a soldier, who, seeing James d'Avennes thrown from his horse, gave him the one on which he was escaping, and nobly by his own death saved the life of his lord. King Guy, also, was on the point of being slain by the foe, had not the marquis come to his assistance who forgot the wrongs he had received from him, to discharge the duties of humanity, though to one undeserving of it, and rescued him from destruction. Geoffrey, the king's brother, seeing the army in confusion, and all hastening to fly, at last abandoned the care of the camp which he had undertaken to defend and, anxious for his brother's safety, rushed forward to arrest the fugitives. O miserable change of affairs the Christians had gone forth with confidence—they return in confusion they had marched in order—they return in disorder ; victorious, they had routed the foe—yet they run back vanquished. Man's presumption at length acknowledged what man and what man's strength can effect if it rely not on the Lord's right hand for he powerfully works victory amongst his own people, who gives confidence to the warrior, and a crown to the victor. Our men had presumed on their own strength, they believed no enemy could be found who could put them in fear, and yet they found that enemy too near them, for they lost one thousand five hundred men. There was a knight named Ferrand, who having been left behind naked and nearly lifeless, after lying hid amongst the slain, returned by night to the camp, but was so disfigured by his wounds, that he could not be recognized by his friends, and with difficulty gained admission. The license of the poet or a lengthy dissertation might depict the various incidents of the battle and the divers modes of death but we are obliged to be brief, and must say, not how, but what occurred. Saladin ordered the bodies of the Christians to be collected and cast into the river which flowed near that, being carried down by the current, the sight of them might occasion terror, or becoming decomposed they might infect the water.

CHAPTER XXXI - *How our men, increasing in number daily, suffer severely from the Turks while occupied in carrying a trench round the city*

After this, our chiefs, thinking it best to abstain for the present from open war, occupy themselves in strengthening their camp, and carry round an embankment of turf, with deep ditches from sea to sea, for the protection of the tents while the marquis and the Hospitallers boldly seized upon the space free from siege, and thus the city was blockaded by sea and by land. While our men were thus sedulously employed in making the trenches, the Turks harassed them incessantly, and one party relieving another continued to annoy them from morn till night. It was necessary, thus, that one part of our men should defend the other while at work from their attacks. Such as we thought worth while to bear with, we did, without returning them, although the air was darkened with their missiles and darts, which exceeded all computation. Our men, however, worked away with their utmost endeavor and the Turks lamented their progress. You might see in their frequent encounters, now these now those (according to the chances of war) overthrown and borne down. While our men were thus for a considerable time struggling, the

Lord above grieved over them, and by strengthening and increasing our numbers from day to day, deserted not altogether those who trusted in him. There came together, therefore, from different parts of the world, princes, dukes, counts, besides many of inferior degree whose names were the Count of Ferrara, Nargenot du Bourg, Anselm de Montreal, Geoffrey de Grenville, Otho de la Fosse, William Goez, the Viscount de Chatellerault, the Viscount de Turome, the Chastellan of Bruges, the Archbishop of Pisa, also the Count Bertulf, the Count Nicholas of Hungary, the Count Bernard, the Count Jocelyn, the Count Richard of Apulia, the Count Alebrand, Engelran de Vienne, Hervey de Gien, Theobald de Bar, the Count John of Loegria, another Count John of Seis, with a nephew of the king of Denmark. There came also some chiefs of the Danes, with 400 of their countrymen. At the same time came Guy de Dampierre, the bishop of Verona, and a few Roman citizens. All these, and a great many future martyrs and confessors, were added to the number of the faithful. Martyrs truly they were, a great part of whom died in a short time by the stench of the dead bodies which corrupted the air, and by the fatigue of constant watchings while others were overcome by the injuries they received, as neither rest nor breathing time was allowed them, for the Turks harassed without intermission those who were working at the ditch, and reduced their spirits by unexpected attacks, until it was at length completed. They then made an attempt to relieve the city from the threatened blockade.

CHAPTER XXXII - *The description of the city of Acre and the places round about it*

We do not think it foreign to our purpose to give at times, as the order of our matter requires, the description of places, in order that a city, so famous for its magnificence, as well as the various incidents of war, may gain additional celebrity by our labors. For if a ten years' war made Troy celebrated if the triumph of the Christians made Antioch more illustrious, Acre will certainly obtain eternal fame, as a city for which the whole world contended. In the form of a triangle, it is narrow on the western side, while it extends in a wider range towards the east, and full a third part of it is washed by the ocean on the south and west. The port, which is not so convenient as it should be, often deceives and proves fatal to the vessels which winter there for the rock which lies over against the shore, to which it runs parallel, is too short to protect them from the fury of the storm. And because this rock appeared a suitable place for washing away the entrails, the ancients used it as a place for offering up sacrifices, and on account of the flies which followed the sacrificial flesh, the tower which stands above it was called the Tower of Flies. There is also a tower called the Cursed, situated on the wall which surrounds the city and if we are to credit common report, it received its name because it is said that the pieces of silver for which Judas betrayed his Lord, were made there. The city, then named Ptolemais, was formerly situate upon Mount Turon, which is close to the city, whence, by an error of antiquity, some call Acre Ptolemais. There is a hill called the Mosque, near Mount Turon, where the ancients say is the sepulchre of Memnon but by whose kind offices he was brought thither, we have learnt neither by writing nor by hearsay. The river which flows by the city is named Belus, and although its bed is narrow and not deep, Solinus has rendered it celebrated by numbering it amongst the wonders of the world, as being enriched with glassy sand. For there was a certain sandy foss, the sand of which supplied materials for making glass these, if taken out, were altogether useless; but, if let in, from the secret virtue of the place assumed a glassy nature. Not far from the river is pointed out a low rock near the city, at which it is said that the three divisions of the world, Asia, Europe, and Africa meet and though it contains separately the other parts of the world, the place itself, dependent on none, is distinct from and independent of all three. Mount Carmel rises aloft on the southern side of the city, where Elijah the Tishbite is known to have had an habitation of modest cost, as his cave still testifies but although we are often wont in a description to wander away to the pleasant parts of the circuit, we must at present overlook the attractions of the surrounding places, while we turn our attention to the course of the war.

CHAPTER XXXIII - *How the people of the city were reduced to such starvation that they offered to surrender the Sultan comes to their assistance with fifty galleys they capture and put to flight our galleys*

When therefore our men had encompassed Acre on all sides with a blockade, the townspeople, having consumed their provisions, began to be severely pressed by famine, so that they offered to surrender the city on condition that they should be allowed to depart, with their property, unmolested. These conditions did not satisfy the chiefs, who had determined, either to compel them by extreme necessity to submit to their will, or to gain, by every means in their power, the glory of storming the city. But whilst they were slowly negotiating for the surrender of the city, the sultan had fully equipped at Alexandria fifty galleys, with men, provisions, and arms, which he sent to succour Acre. These arrived on All Saints' Eve, and when they were seen at a distance, vague rumors distracted the people with various forebodings. Some report that the enemy is at hand others that subsidies are come for the Christians. While they were still doubting, the enemy threw themselves into the city, and even carried with them, by force, one of our ships laden with provisions, which they found in the port and being long sustained with those provisions, pressed upon us with the greater courage. Not content with plundering our ship of burden, they put to death without mercy the crew and every one else they had found therein, and hung them round the walls on the day of All Saints. Moreover, the galleys of the enemy kept watch over both the exit and entrance of the port of the city that no one dared to come to our assistance for fear of falling into their hands. And on the morrow of the Nativity of our Lord, one of our galleys deeming the fleet an arrival of Christians, went for the purpose of making inquiries after our succors, incautiously to meet this Babylonian fleet as it approached, and with it a smaller vessel, called a galleon; this taking the lead, owing to its lightness, fell suddenly into the midst of the enemy, instead of meeting with friends as was supposed. The voice of some who answered and the suspicious silence of others, undeceived them upon which the terrified sailors cast themselves into the sea, and escaped, by means of swimming, according as each was able. Thus then occupying that part of the sea, and our galleys which were by far the least numerous, having gone away secretly to Tyre, the enemy had free and open communication with the city by sea. At that time the Germans, making a large mill for the grinding of corn, turned by horses, while the millstones grated as they were drawn round, the Turks, gazing with great earnestness at the mill at work, thought that it was some instrument for their destruction, or for storming their city for never before had a mill of that description been seen in that land.

CHAPTER XXXIV - *Of the sea-fight between the fleet of the marquis and our men and that of the enemy, and how we gained the victory*

At a season of calm, when Easter was close at hand, the marquis at our request returned from Tyre with a large equipment and supplies of men, arms, and provisions. For by the provident care of the chiefs, the king and marquis were pacified on the pretext that the marquis should have possession of Tyre, Berytus, and Sidon, and on condition that he should be faithful and strenuous for the interests of the king and his kingdom. But rash ambition always turns to evil the avaricious and iniquitous heart for inflamed with the desire of obtaining the kingdom, he broke the faith he had pledged and while to the outward eye he appeared a friend, within his breast he concealed the foe. At length the townspeople liked not their privation of liberty, and determined to try the issue of a sea-fight. They therefore led forth their galleys by twos, and keeping good order, they rowed into the offing to meet and attack those that were coming our men prepared to meet them as they came on, and since there was no means of getting away, prepared to face them with greater resolution. On the other hand our men got on board our war ships, and straining to the left by an oblique course, retreated to a distance, and gave the enemy free means of egress. And now that mention is made of a sea-fight, we judge it right to describe briefly the fleet, and what difference there is between those of the moderns and ancients. With the ancients, a larger number of oars was required in ships of this kind, which were arranged in stories, so that some plied the oars at a longer, others at a shorter distance from the sea. These vessels had frequently three or four banks of oars each, some even five and a few of the ships used at the battle of Actium between Antony and Augustus, are said to have had six. Furthermore, ships of war were called liburnce for the ships used in the battle of Actium were chiefly built at Liburnia in Dalmatia; whence it became usual among the ancients to call them liburnce. But all that ancient magnificence has passed away for ships of war, which once had six banks of oars, have now seldom more than two. But what the ancients used to call a liburna, we call a galea, with the middle syllable lengthened it is long and graceful, not high out of water, and has a piece of wood at the prow, which is commonly called the spur with which the enemy's ships are struck and pierced. Galleons are vessels with one bank of oars manageable from their shortness, easily turned, and light for running to and fro they are better suited for throwing fire. When, therefore, they went forth on both sides to light, our men drew not up their ships in a straight line, but in the form of a crescent that if the enemy should charge the inner ships, he might be shut in and crushed. They placed their most powerful ships at the points of the crescent, as against them would be directed the enemy's most vigorous attack on the upper row of benches were arranged shields close together; and in one the rowers sat, in order that those who were on deck might have free space for fighting. The sea was perfectly calm and tranquil, as if it favored the battle, and the rippling wave impeded neither the shock of the attacking ship, nor the stroke of the oars. As they closed, the trumpets sounded on both sides. A terrific clang is roused, and the battle is commenced by the throwing of missiles. Our men implore the Divine assistance, and ply their oars strenuously, and dash at the enemy's ships with their beaks. Soon the battle began the oars become entangled and they fight hand to hand, having grappled each other s ships together and they fire the decks with burning oil, which is vulgarly called Greek fire. That kind of fire with a detestable stench and livid flames consumes both flint and steel it cannot be extinguished by water, but is subdued by the sprinkling of sand, and put out by pouring vinegar on it. But what can be more dreadful than a fight at sea? What more savage, where such various fates await the combatants? Some are tortured by the burning of the flames; some falling overboard are swallowed in the waves; others wounded perish by the enemy's weapons. One galley, unskillfully managed by our men, exposed its flank to the foe and being set on fire, received the Turks as they boarded her on all sides. The rowers in their fright fall into the sea but a few soldiers, impeded by their heavy armor, and restrained by ignorance of swimming, took courage from desperation, and commenced an unequal fight and trusting in the Lord's valor, a few of them overcame numbers and having slain the foe, they brought back the half-burnt vessel in triumph. Another ship was boarded by the enemy, who had driven the combatants from the upper deck while those who were below strove to escape by the help of their oars. Wondrous and terrible was the conflict for the oars being pulled different ways, the galley was drawn first one way, then the other, as the Turks drove it; yet our men prevailed, and the enemy, who rowed on the upper deck, being overcome and thrust down by the Christians, yielded. In this naval contest, the enemy lost both the galley and a galleon, together with their crews and our men, unhurt and joyful, gain a glorious triumph. Having drawn the captured galley on shore, they gave it up to be plundered by both sexes who came to meet them. On this our women, dragging the Turks by the hair, after treating them shamefully and cutting their throats in a disgraceful manner, beheaded them. And the weaker the hand to strike, so much the more lengthened was the punishment inflicted for they used knives, and not swords, for cutting off their heads. A like sea-fight was never seen, so destructive in its issue, accomplished with so much danger, and completed with so much cost.

CHAPTER XXXV - *Meanwhile the Turks from without, eager to fill our breach with earth fiercely attack our men who were within*

In the mean time the Turkish army from without, though deeply bewailing our victory, persisted in making attacks upon our men who were within the trench, endeavoring either to fill up the completed portion by casting back the earth, or to slay those who resisted. Our men, sustaining their attack, though with difficulty, fight under great disadvantages, for they seemed unequal to contend against so countless a multitude,—for the numbers of the assailants continually increased, and we had to take precautions on the side of the city lest they also should rush in and assault us. There was amongst the assailants a fiendish race, very impetuous and obstinate deformed in nature as they were unlike to the others in character, of a darker appearance, of vast stature, of exceeding ferocity, having on their heads red coverings instead of helmets, carrying in their hands clubs bristling with iron teeth, which neither helmet nor coat of mail could withstand and they had a carved image of Mahomet for a standard. So great was the multitude of this evil race, that as fast as one party was thrown to the earth, another rushed forward over them. Thus, by their constant attacks, they confounded our men so much, that we doubted which way to turn ourselves for as there was neither security nor rest, we were distressed on all sides, at one time guarding ourselves from sallies of the besieged from the city, at another from the incessant attacks of the enemy from without; and again from the side of the sea where their galleys were lying in wait to convey the Turks into the city as they arrived, or to intercept the succors which were coming to us the Christians. At length, by favor of the Divine mercy, our adversaries were driven back and repulsed.

CHAPTER XXXVI - *How our men were on the point of assaulting the city with three wooden towers; the townsmen offer to surrender; while we are attacked by the enemy below, our machines are set on fire*

Our chiefs contribute mutually to the making of machines for storming the city, and construct three moveable towers of dry wood, of which the making of the first fell to the lot of the Landgrave, the second to the Genoese, and the third to the rest of the army. The huge machines raised with zealous emulation, and being carried up by stories, were urged forwards on wheels, which, assisted by mechanical contrivances, moved easily. To prevent their catching fire, the workmen covered them with tarpaulins and raw hides and that the blow of the petrarice might not injure them, which it does if caught by a softer substance, they suspend twisted ropes in front. And the upper parts of the towers which were much higher than the walls and bulwarks of the city, contained slingers and darters, while the middle story was occupied by men armed with stakes and poles. Each camp had its petrarice, which stood on the side and afforded protection to the towers as they were drawn along, as well as serving to throw down the opposite walls. The townsmen now entirely despairing offered to surrender the city if they might be allowed to depart and take away their property with them. Our people refused, and hastened with all their might to bring the machines they had made against the walls, upon which the townsmen' resisted, and in turn revenge themselves on their besiegers and assaulters; for, on the Saturday after Ascension day, when the machines had been brought nearer the walls, after we had assaulted the city from morn till even, behold the army of the Turks from without came rushing in troops with immense violence upon the trench, to attack from the rear those who were assaulting the city, that they might draw them off if not entirely disperse them. Thus, while our men, held in check on both sides, and having their attention divided, were either defending themselves against the attacks from without, or were engaged in storming the city, and their strength was weakened from having so many objects to contend with, the enemy set fire to our towers, which our utmost endeavors could not extinguish, and being burnt with Greek fire, they were rendered useless. And thus, by an unfortunate accident, our hope of triumph fell,—the more mortifying in the result from being considered so certain at first.

CHAPTER XXXVII - *Of the famine among the citizens and the succour brought in by the galleys*

The besieged were now so sorely pressed from the great want of provisions that they ate up their horses and spared not beasts of other kinds, forgetful of the Mahometan law, while, reduced by hunger to eat forbidden things, they satisfied their ravening appetites. Meanwhile, they turned out the older Christian captives, whom they reckoned useless, having become speechless and decrepit; but they reserved the younger captives, who were hale and fit for work. While the Turks were thus straitened, there arrived three vessels of burthen, whose crews suddenly threw themselves into the city, for fear of meeting the Christians, in such haste that some of them were wrecked, but those that carried provisions were saved. Whereupon the besieged, overcome with excessive joy, as if their wishes had been gratified, testify their deliverance by howling in loud tones to the music of cymbals and pipes; they hoped by these rejoicings to confirm the belief that they had not sustained any loss.

CHAPTER XXXVIII - *How Saladin, having collected the armies of his kingdom together, attacks our men, who by their bold resistance force him to retire in confusion*

Meanwhile, Saladin, having gathered together the forces of all Asia, from the Tigris as far as India, as well as from the parts between the Tigris and Euphrates, and thence to the southern districts, led them forth to war. From Africa too, there came countless tribes; the Nadabarae, Gaetulians, and Numidians, and from the scorching south, the people named Moors or Mauritanians, from the Greek word fiavpog, which means black. Thus two divisions of the globe attacked the third against both of which Europe entered into conflict, the only one of them which acknowledged the name of Christ. Most of these troops served Saladin as stipendiaries so that the money which had been raised was no longer sufficient for their pay. For by common agreement the barbarians decreed that whoever died should leave the third of his property to the defenders of the law. Some, however, served for nothing as a sort of pilgrimage, and instead of performing the ceremonies of the law, went to fight against the Christians. The pouring out, therefore, of these multitudes from all parts, gave the king excessive joy; and falling on our men boldly, he hoped either to carry them all away captive, or to exterminate them with the edge of the sword. And if we read that Darius king of the Persians fought with seven hundred thousand men, we may judge of the multitude on the present occasion for his army could be numbered, but this army none could count. That large plain, stretching from sea to sea, over which they were spread far and wide, would not hold so many thousands; and had the ground been itself much more extensive, it would have been narrow compared with the numbers engaged. The Christians, though pressed by the townsmen on one side and by the enemy on the other, stood their ground manfully and having placed guards at the trenches, repelled the assaults of both. The attack commenced on the Saturday of Pentecost, and continued for eight days, the great slaughter on both sides bearing witness to the fury of the combat. Our men found the holidays no holidays but their resolute valor strengthened them to the confusion of the foe and He who ordained of old the Apostles to prophecy, now inflamed his soldiers to battle. All had strict charge not to go beyond the camp for there was no need to go in search of an enemy, when one was at their doors. And so great was the multitude which came to attack, that darts thrown at random were not without effect nor did any take aim, when the crowded squadrons afforded so many objects to wound. On the eighth day, a blow from a sling killed one of the sultan's sons, whose death put a stop to the attack which had begun, and terrified the hostile army. Very many of them, therefore, returned to their own land in great dread of coming in contact with the Christians, who had resisted so great a multitude so boldly.

CHAPTER XXXIX - *Further of the famine among the citizens and of the succors by the galleys*

Meanwhile, hunger afflicts the townsmen sorely, but the south wind brings them supplies of corn from the sultan in Egypt. The vessels were five and twenty in number of the three largest of these, two were run aground, while attempting to push through between the Tower of Flies and the adjacent rock the third got into port unhurt for our galleys had turned them from their intended course but one of ours, in its hasty pursuit of the enemy, struck on a rock and was dashed to pieces.

CHAPTER XL - *Of the misfortunes of our men, arising from a battle begun without the counsel of their chiefs*

As time wore on, and our army had enjoyed a long repose, the common soldiers, desirous of a change, began to tax the chiefs with sloth and all excited with one wish, each encourages his fellow to battle. Their indignation is excited by the proximity of the heathen camp the greedy are encouraged by the prospect of spoil, and the honor of victory inflames the warlike. They therefore enter into a tumultuous plot, and with eager heat, prepare unanimously for battle, without asking the consent of their chiefs. The latter endeavor, as far as possible, to check the rash daring of the people and the patriarch forbids them under pain of anathema from provoking the enemy and incurring the dangers of a battle, without consulting their chiefs but neither the dissuasions of these, nor the threats of the others, availed for fury overcame counsel, violence reason, and order yielded to multitudes whichever way the vulgar are impelled, they think rashness a virtue, and that to be the best which is the object of their wishes and not weighing the issue of things, they reject him who chide, and despise him who ruleth. Therefore, on St. James's day, a mournful and unpropitious one, the ill-fated crowd of common soldiers burst forth; they go forth in arms, it is true, but they oppose themselves without precaution against the coming danger a fine body of young men, indeed, distinguished for bravery, and that would yield to no victor, had it had a head, or used counsel in its darings, or been as fond of battle as it was of booty. But the army had no leader every one was his own soldier and guide they scarcely paid attention to or followed their proper standards many ran before them, and thought more of the booty than the battle in which they were to perish. The Mahometans, when they saw the crowd coming forth, whether from fear or design, gave way a little, and as they did not gather up their baggage, they left their tents behind, rich with various things. But under the declivity of an adjacent mount they collected their lost courage, and stopped, while they sent spies to discover the object at which our men aimed, and why they had come forth. Tecadin, the sultan's grandson, at that time had pitched his tent opposite the camp of Himbert; he was a man of active spirit and bold in arms, but of exceeding wickedness and implacable cruelty, and he hated above all things the name of Christian. Hither the aforesaid multitude hastened; hither the lust for plunder urges every one, and they, who were eager after the spoil, explored not the ambuscades that lay around. Many glutted their appetite with the abundance of food they met with, and having relinquished their arms lay down in over security, as if they had been invited to a feast. The Turks, having learnt what was going on, soon poured in on all sides, and shouting with a terrible noise, as is their wont, gained an easy victory over a scattered and stupefied foe. No one dreamt of fighting, every one thought of flight but being on foot, laden with arms, and exhausted with thirst and heat, they could not escape when pursued by an active and mounted enemy. In all directions they were routed, and thrown into confusion no quarter was given, nor a captive taken; fury could not satisfy its appetite, and anger recalls the sword, which the weariness of the striker had for a moment laid aside. Wherever fear urged any one, he was sure to meet with death an inevitable fate threatened one and all. The foe and slaughter presented themselves on all sides; numbers were wounded, and four thousand are reckoned to have been slain. Though they heard the tumult, and saw the slaughter, the chiefs pretend to be ignorant of it hard-hearted, inhuman, and impious, certainly they were, who saw their brethren butchered before them, and offered no assistance to them when perishing, whose only crime was the leaving the camp against orders. At length, when others hesitated from sloth, rather than from anger, Ralph de Hauterive, archdeacon of Colchester, came to the assistance of those who were suffering and succored them when on the point of falling. He was a man of handsome form and figure, and merited a twofold laurel for his excellence in both kinds of warfare — being illustrious for his knowledge, and famous in arms. He met with a glorious and happy end, after performing many remarkable actions in the siege in which he was then engaged. The townsmen on seeing the success of their friends, issued out boldly, and went so far as to attack and overthrow some of the nearest tents.

CHAPTER XLI - *Of the ships and succors which came to our men*

After this sad slaughter had been brought about, by which our strength was considerably diminished, fortune smiled more favorably and the west wind setting in brought some vessels laden with soldiers. Meanwhile the barbarian fleet, mixing itself secretly with ours, got forward, and imitating the language and ensigns of the Christians, made a sudden and unexpected approach to the city.

CHAPTER XLII - *What men and warriors of the higher and lower grades of the laity and clergy came to our succour*

When, therefore, our men were utterly purified by the constant fire of tribulation, and the heavy trials which penetrated them to the very soul, the Lord regarded them, and withdrew them from the scourge, for He deserteth not those who hope in Him, and He grieved over them, and brought them powerful allies from the uttermost parts of the earth, illustrious men, mighty in battle, who not only made up for the past valor of the lost army, but also augmented it by numerous additions. Amongst the first that landed was Count Henry of Troyes, count of Champagne, with a powerful body of soldiers. There came, also, many others in succession, whose names are given as they arrived. They were Theobald, Count of Blois, who died within three months after his arrival; next came Count Stephen, the Count of Clairmont, Count of Scalons, Manserius de Garland, Bernard de St. Waleri, John Count of Pontiny, Erard de Castiny, Robert de Buon, Adaunius de Fontaines, Louis de Ascla, Walter d'Arzillieres, Guy de Castellan, with his brother Lovel, Guy de Meisieres, John de Montmirail, John d'Arcy; also the Lord of Camte in Burgundy, Gaubert d'Aspremont, Clarembald de Noyers, the Bishop of Blois, the Bishop of Toulon, the Bishop of Ostia, the Bishop of Mordre (Mordrensis), the Bishop of Brescia, the Bishop of Aste also the Patriarch of Jerusalem, the Archbishop of Caesarea, the Bishop of Nazareth; there were also the bishop elect of Acre, and the Archbishop of Besancon, Baldwin, Archbishop of Canterbury, and Hubert Bishop of Salisbury as well as the Archdeacon of Colchester, Rodolph de Hauterive, of whom we have spoken before, and the Abbot of Scalons, the Abbot of Esterp. There came, also, a priest, who was incessantly active against the enemy, hurling darts from a sling with indefatigable toil.

There came, also, many from Normandy, such as Walkelin de Ferrars, Robert Trussebot, Richard de Vernon with his son, Guilbert de Tillieres with a strong band of warriors, and Ivo de Vipont, Ranulph de Glanville, formerly justiciary of England, Gilbert de Malines, and Hugh de Gorney. Besides these came many from different parts of the earth, whose names have not been enumerated and if we knew them we would not mention them, for fear of wearying our hearers.

CHAPTER XLIII - *How Henry of Champagne was set over the army*

Henry count of Troyes at that time landed with a strong body of soldiers, into whose hands was committed the command of the army, which James d'Avennes and the Landgrave had held hitherto conjointly or by turn; for the Landgrave being in ill-health left the camp on the pretext of returning home;—a man who, after performing many noble actions, to the admiration of all, tarnished the bright glory of his deeds by his pusillanimous return.

CHAPTER XLIV - *How the duke of Suabia came to Acre by the persuasion of the marquis*

At this time, the duke of Suabia, shortly after his father's death, was staying at Antioch with the sons of the emperor, and the chiefs send to him to remain in that quarter, to make war upon the neighboring territory of the barbarians. This was sound and wholesome policy for if he had occupied the enemy by urging the war in many places at one their endeavors would have become distracted, and consequently weaker for individual operations. The marquis, who was charged with this message, failed to execute his instructions faithfully, and by an invidious interpretation of them influenced the duke's mind, for he represented that the chiefs wanted to procure his absence through jealousy, that they might have the glory of taking the city without him. Some asserted that the marquis had received from the sultan sixty thousand byzantines to persuade the duke to depart from the confines of Antioch. The duke, therefore, on arriving at Acre, proved a cause of disagreement, for the French had an old and long-standing quarrel with the Germans, since the kingdom and empire contended for the supremacy.

CHAPTER XLV - *How the marquis, by the advice of the duke, aspired to the kingdom*

Moreover, the marquis, secretly assisting the cause of the duke, to whom he was related by blood, studiously sought his presence, that by his means, if he could, he might obtain the throne. An accident also favorable to his wishes made him indulge more confidently in his hopes, for premature death carried off the queen and the offspring she had conceived from King Guy but in order that this point may be more clearly understood, we will trace the succession of the royal race from its first origin.

CHAPTER - *The genealogy of the kings of Jerusalem, and the cause why the marquis aspired to the throne*

It must be stated that Fulk, father of Geoffrey, count of Anion, who was chosen king of Jerusalem on account of his singular virtues, had two sons, Baldwin and Almaric, by Melesende, the daughter of King Baldwin, his predecessor. Of these the elder ascended the throne, and bearing his grandfather's name, married Theodora, the daughter, emperor of Byzantium, but died without children after he conquest and capture of Askalon. His brother, who succeeded to his valor and throne, compelled Babylon to pay tribute, and by his two marriages had offspring of both sexes. His first wife, Beatrix, whom he married before coming to the throne, was daughter of the Count of Roasia but forasmuch as she was related to him by blood, the marriage was set aside by judgment of the clergy, by a formal divorce. He had, however, two children by her, a daughter named Sybille, and a son called Baldwin, who on his father's death being presented with the crown, although a minor and afflicted with leprosy, miraculously defeated Saladin and sixty thousand Turks, with a small body of soldiers. He, being removed at an early age from the affairs of this world, appointed as his successor his nephew Baldwin, whose mother had married William, the brother of the marquis; but who died while yet a child in his seventh year. But as the boy's father had been dead some time, Guy, who had come to visit the sepulchre, and was sprung from Poitou, married his mother by bill, and in her right assumed the insignia of royalty by her he had four daughters, whose premature death, and that of their mother, caused Guy to be accused, and gave the marquis the hope of reigning. Furthermore, Maria, whom King Almaric had married after divorcing his first wife, was a kinswoman of the Emperor Manuel, and had two daughters one of them died in infancy, but Enfrid of Tours espoused Elizabeth, the second daughter, before she was of a marriageable age but forasmuch as she was heiress to the throne, the marquis determined to remove both, and deprive Enfrid of his wife, as well as Guy of his sceptre.

CHAPTER XLVII - *The wonders which happened during the siege are subjoined*

Meanwhile, according to the various events of war, as has been said, success changing from one side to the other, there occurred manifold incidents not less wonderful than to be wondered at, which seem worthy of our notice.

CHAPTER XLVIII - *How a certain petraria of the enemy by its strength destroyed all our machines, and how it struck one of our men without hurting him*

One of the enemy's petrarice, of which there were a great number in the city, was of an unusual magnitude and form, and as the engineers intended it, able to cast stones of immense weight, the blows of which nothing could resist for it cast stones of incredible size to a great distance, and its blow destroyed everything it struck. When the stones met with no obstacle, they were driven into the ground a foot deep. It struck and shivered in pieces some of our petrarice, or rendered them useless, and either destroyed our other machines, or knocked off the part it touched. In fact there was nothing so solid or compact, of whatever kind or substance that would bear its overwhelming blow, so great was the violence with which it acted. This machine struck one of our men from behind with a stone of enormous size, as he was standing with his face turned away, quite unsuspicious of danger, not supposing that a stone could be sent so far, yet it hurt him not in the least, but, rebounding as from a mountain, fell close by, and the man, when he saw it, was more horrified at the sight than injured by the blow. Who does not see by this the wonderful works of the Lord, and that his mercy is ever ready for those who fight for him? To the praise of his mightiness I will subjoin other of his works.

CHAPTER XLIX - *How a javelin, hurled against one of our men, penetrated his armor, but would not penetrate his breast, where a writing containing the name of God lay*

Furthermore, one of our body-guard, while walking in the ditch outside the city wall, either for the purpose of reconnoitering the weak parts of the wall, or to strike any of the enemy he could see with his sling, stopped at last; he was armed sufficiently like a foot-soldier, with iron headpiece, coat of mail, and a tunic of many folds of linen, difficult of penetration, and artificially worked with the needle, vulgarly called a pour point. A Turk from the wall struck him with a dart from a sling with great force on the breast, so that it penetrated all the aforementioned, the iron armor descending from the head, and the coat of mail and pour point, but it was stopped by a certain writing hanging from his neck on his breast, and fell out blunted and twisted as from an iron plate. Are not the works of God manifest in the dart penetrating many folds of steel, and bounding back blunted from a little scroll? For the man was said to have worn suspended from his breast, the name of God on a scroll, thus proved to be impenetrable to steel. God is a wall of strength to them that hope in him.

CHAPTER L - *How one of our men unarmed, having retired to satisfy the calls of nature, struck down with a stone a Turk attacking him with a lance*

Again, as one of our men was stooping down outside the camp, a Turk rode up to attack him unawares, but the soldier on seeing him advance sideways, and scarcely having done what he came for at the aforesaid ditch, rose up hastily, though unarmed, either to avoid him as he came up, or by an impulse from the Lord to receive him in the best way he could. As the Turk struck at him with the point of his lance, he bent down and escaped the blow by the protection of God. "The horse rode by and passed with scatheless blow." The Turk annoyed at his ill success, prepared to repeat the attack, and brandishing his lance, bore down upon the soldier. What could the latter do, unarmed as he was? On foot, single-handed, and a ready prey for the foe, he called upon God, who is always by his grace present with his people, and seeing a stone by chance ready at hand, lie aimed it at the face of his enemy, which was exposed beneath his helmet, and it struck him on the temple. The Turk fell stunned from his horse, broke his neck, and died; the soldier caught the horse, mounted, and returned to his friends. One who saw the occurrence, related it; and it is well known as a fact in the camp.

CHAPTER LI - *How a woman on the point of death, while our men were filling the city trench with earth, threw herself in instead of earth*

On another occasion, amongst those who were carrying earth to make a mound in the ditch for assaulting the town more easily, was a woman who labored with great diligence and earnestness, and went to and fro unceasingly, and encouraged others unremittingly, in order that the work might be accomplished but her zeal put an end to her life and labors for while a crowd of all sexes and ages were constantly coming and going to complete the work in question, and while the aforesaid woman was occupied in depositing what she had brought, a Turk, who had been lying wait for her, struck her a mortal blow with a dart. As she fell to the ground, writhing with the violence of her pain, she entreated her husband and many others who had come up to assist her, with tears in her eyes, and very urgently, saying, "By your love for me, my dearest lord, by your piety as my husband, and the faith of our marriage contracted of old, permit not my corpse to be removed from this place; but I pray and beseech you, that since I can do nothing more towards the fulfillment of the work, I may deem myself to have done some good, if you will allow my lifeless body to be laid in the trench instead of earth, for it will soon be earth." This she urged with supplications to all the multitude that stood around, and soon after gave up the ghost. Oh! Wonderful faith of the weaker sex! Oh! Zeal of woman, worthy of imitation, for she ceased not, even dead, to help those who labored, and in her death continued to show her zeal in the cause!

CHAPTER LII - *Of the Turk's horse caught in a net*

Again, a common fellow of our camp was spreading his net outside the camp, either for the purpose of driving off the Turks or to catch them if they came on one of them came rushing forward on horseback, and put the man to flight before he had finished what he was about but unable to overtake him, he gave up the pursuit, when he saw him reach the camp, and in his excessive indignation, he began to pluck up the net. But after pulling up some poles by which the net was fixed with cords, his horse's head was accidentally entangled and caught by the net, which he was trying to roll up in a hasty, incautious manner. The horse, being one of great beauty, was indignant at being thus hampered, and in his wild attempts to get free, became more and more entangled. Some of our men seeing this rode down in haste toward him. The Turk, finding his horse entangled, quickly dismounted and fled on foot, and although deprived of his steed, escaped his pursuers, for fear added wings to his feet. His valuable horse, which had broken the net in many parts, was with difficulty disentangled, and became an object of contention, but was given to the man who had fixed the net, as compensation for his loss.

CHAPTER LIII - *Of the Turk's horse that was caught in a foot-trap*

At another time, when, on account of the frequent and sudden sallies of the Turks, our chiefs ordered that foot-traps should be made and buried in the earth to escape being seen, it happened one day, that while some of our young men were exercising by appointment in the plain by throwing darts at a mark, some of the Turks, putting spurs to their horses, suddenly attacked them, upon which our young men, being unarmed and inferior in numbers, retreated to the camp. But one of the pursuers, as if trusting in the activity of his horse, too eagerly out strip the others, when the animal was suddenly stopped in its career by being caught in a foot-trap, and no effort or endeavor of his rider could extricate him. The Turk, preferring the loss of his horse to that of his head, escaped on foot, uninjured, to his own friends. The horse was decreed to be given to him whose instrument caught it, viz. Robert Count.

CHAPTER LIV - *How Ivo de Vipont slays eighty pirates with a handful of men*

On another occasion, as three sailors were conducting Ivo de Vipont with ten companions to Tyre, and had wandered too far from the port, some Turkish pirates, coming out in a galley from an eddy of the sea near the land, bore down upon them; they were about eighty in number, and when the sailors saw them coming near, in their excessive fear they cried out together, "O Lord God, we shall be taken and slaughtered." To whom Ivo de Vipont said, "Why do ye of little faith fear those whom you shall soon see dead. And when the enemy's galley appeared by force of rowing to be on the point of striking the vessel with its beak, Ivo leapt into it and began to cut down the Turks who pressed upon him, with the axe he carried in his hand. His companions, when they saw his work prosper, gaining heart, leapt into the galley also, and either beheaded whomsoever they found, or led them away captives. Thus these men triumphed who placed their hope in God, who knows not how to be conquered, and with whom a counterfeit faith avail not, nor a multitude of warriors, for it matters not with the Lord whether the valor of battle and the glory of victory rest with a few or with many.

CHAPTER LV - *The admiral's genitalia destroyed by the Greek fire with which the enemy proposed to destroy our machines*

Again, when the townsmen beheld a great multitude of our people going, as was their wont, in search of provender for the animals, they sallied out against them under the command of their admiral Bellegeminus, a famous and powerful man, and rushed without care upon them but our men withstood the enemy obstinately, and after many were killed on both sides, drove them back into the city. But the admiral stood his ground a long time, as he was a man of greater bravery than the others while he was doing his best to execute the main object of the attack by cutting to pieces or burning with Greek fire the machines which were ready to move against the walls of the city, and as, while his men fled, he lagged behind to accomplish his purpose, a soldier, coming behind, threw him from his horse, and the vessel in which he carried the Greek fire being broken by the fall, the inextinguishable liquid burnt his genitalia. So that what he had intended for our detriment became his own destruction.

CHAPTER LVI - *How a Turk, while earring the Greek fire, is caught in a net by our men*

On one occasion, some of our fishermen were throwing their nets for fish at no great distance from land,—men who, being devoted to this pursuit, gained a livelihood for themselves and no small relief by selling the fish. It happened one day towards sunset, when the nets were stretched out, that one of our men, sitting on an elevated spot on shore, saw a man swimming at a distance with his head only above water, and on his pointing him out, the aforesaid fishermen closely pursued the swimmer in their boat to ascertain what this strange appearance might be and when they approached nearer they perceived that he was a Turk. He was frightened at their shouts and tried to escape, but they rowed quickly and caught him in their net. The man, being an expert swimmer, had already passed their nets with a load which he carried suspended from his neck, for he had with him in a skin Greek fire, destined for the besieged in the city. In this way the Turks used to send Greek fire to the besieged by skilful swimmers, as they judged it the safest and most secret plan. The fishermen landed with their captive, and told their story to those on shore and then conducted him with the fire he carried through the midst of the army, and after scourging him severely and gibing at him, they sadly mangled, and then decapitated him, and so he had his reward. Thus the Lord showed that he cared for his people for he scatter the counsels of the heathen and of princes, and brought to nothing the plans which the malignity of the enemy imagined.

CHAPTER LVII - *How a Turk, who attempted to defile the cross of Christ, died of a wound with a dart in his bowels*

Again, we think we ought not to pass over the following fact in silence, though irksome of relation and horrible to listen to viz. that the Turks were wont, to the scandal and disgrace of our faith, to take whatever images and pictures representing the mysteries of our religion they could find in the city, bringing them on the walls in sight of the Christians, to scourge and beat them with rods as if they were alive, and spit upon and treat them shamefully in many other ways as the humor took them. One day as some of our men saw a Turk doing this and tossing about a cross with the image of our Savior in a shameful and impious manner, and obscenely giving utterance to blasphemies and impious revilings against our religion, on his proceeding further and attempting to defile the same, a zealous man cast a dart from his sling and killed the Turk, and thus proved to him how man's attempts against the Lord are as nothing.

CHAPTER LVIII - *How a Parthian bowman was shot by a Welch bowman, for not keeping to his agreement*

It chanced, moreover, one day that the slingers and bowmen, and all who were skilled in throwing missiles, frequently challenged one another on both sides, and discharged their weapons for exercise. When the rest had departed from the field in their turns, a Parthian and a Welchman began to aim their arrows at each other in a hostile manner, and discharge them so as to strike with all their might. But the Welchman, aware of his foe's intention, repaid like for like on which the Parthian, making a truce, approached him, and when within hearing, began a parley. "Of what country is you," said he, "and by what name may I be pleased to know you? I see you are a good bowman, and in order that you may be more inclined to tell me, I am a Parthian by nation, brought up from childhood in the art of shooting, and my name is Grammahyr, of good reputation amongst my people for my deeds of renown, and well known for my victories." The Welchman told his name and nation. "Let us prove," said the Parthian, "which is the best bowman, by each taking an arrow, and aiming them against one another from our bows. You shall stand still first, and I will aim an arrow at you, and afterwards you shall shoot in like manner at me." The Welchman agreed. The Parthian having fitted his arrow, and parting his feet as the art requires, with his hands stretched asunder, and his eyes fixed on the mark.

The Welchman, unhurt, demanded the fulfillment of the aforesaid condition. "I will not agree," said the Parthian "but you must stand another shot, and then have two at me." The Welchman replied, "You do not standby your agreement, nor observe the condition you yourself dictated and if you will not stand, although I may delay it for a time, as I may best be able, God will take revenge on you according to His will, for your treachery;" and he had scarce finished speaking, when in the twinkling of an eye he smote the Turk with his arrow in the breast, as he was selecting an arrow from his quiver to suit his purpose, and the weapon, meeting with no obstacle, came out at the back, having pierced the Turk's body upon which he said to the Turk,

"You stood not by your agreement, nor I by my word." Animated by these and the like successes, the Christians thought they should preserve themselves for good fortune by bearing all their misfortunes with more cheerful faith, and more fervent hope.

CHAPTER LIX - *Of the sea-fight between the Turks and, our men, and how, while our men are trying to take the Tower of Flies with towers and machines fixed on the galleys, our machines are destroyed by fire*

Meanwhile the Pisans, and others who were skilled in managing ships, to whom had been entrusted the siege of the city from the sea, had built and fitted on their galleys a machine in the form of a castle, with bulwarks, with a great deal of toil, to overlook the walls, and give the power of throwing in their missiles more effectually. They had also built two ladders, with some steps, whereby they might reach the top of the walls. These machines they covered, as well as the galleys, with raw hides, so that it was judged they would not be affected by iron, or any kind of weapon.

Having all things in readiness, they proceeded to lay siege to the Tower of Flies, and fiercely attacked it with slings and missiles. Those who were in the tower manfully resisted them and being a match for them, both in strength and good fortune, they took immediate revenge on our men for the death of one of their party. And in order to vanquish them or drive them away, nearly two thousand Turks went out from the city against the galleys to give assistance to the besieged in the tower, while they harassed the Pisans from the opposite quarter. Our men being skilful and experienced warriors, moved their machines as conveniently as they could against the aforesaid tower, and immediately strove to cast immense anchors on it, and throw on its defenders whatsoever stones or weapons they had at hand while others were appointed to fight by sea, and no less bravely repelled those who attacked them in that quarter. With the anchors they threw on the tower the defenses were pulled down, and the bucklers and shields crushed to pieces. The tower was assaulted for a long time with wonderful and intolerable violence; one party succeeding the other when tired, in rapid succession and with invincible valor. Darts flew with horrid crash, and ponderous missiles rushed whizzing through the air. The Turks give way for a time, for they were not able to withstand the brunt of the battle; and behold! Our men, having fixed the ladders for scaling the tower, were ready to mount, when the Turks, seeing that it was their last struggle, and that they must resist our ascent with all their might, cast masses of enormous size down to crush our men and throw them from the ladders. They afterwards threw

Greek fire on our castle, which at last caught fire and when those who were in it saw this, they were obliged to descend and retreat. An incalculable slaughter of the Turks, who attacked our men from the sea, was made and although the design of our men was defeated on the side of the tower, those to seaward slew an immense number of the enemy. In the end the machines were destroyed by the devouring fire, together with the turret and the galleys in which they were placed, and the upright ladders. The Turks, overcome with excessive joy, laughed with loud shouts, making a mockery of us, and wagging their heads at our misfortune and the Christians, being disheartened above measure, were not less annoyed by the revilings that were heaped upon them, than by the losses they had sustained. However, their spirits were raised by the constant arrival of strangers, and they were thus strengthened by the increase of their numbers.

CHAPTER LX - *The townsmen, with great loss to themselves, burn the battering ram of the archbishop of Besancon, with Greek fire*

Meanwhile, the archbishop of Besancon had caused to be built, with great labor and much expense, a machine to batter down the walls, covered with iron plates, commonly called a battering ram; because by repeated and frequent blows, after the manner of a ram, it overthrows the most solid walls. Another very strong ram was built by Count Henry and the other princes and heroes, either singly or conjunctively, had caused to be made different kinds of machines. Some prepared sows of different kinds; others poles or whatsoever each fancied, or which came first to hand. A day was then appointed for bringing against the walls the instruments that each had prepared. The archbishop brought his machine, like a ceiled house, to strike the walls; it had in front a very long mast of a ship, with its head covered with iron, which was impelled by many men, and then being drawn back again, was leveled with greater force and thus, by frequent blows, they tried to breach or cast down the city walls. Those who impelled the machine below were secure from all injury that came from above. The Turks defended themselves manfully from the walls, and collected and threw upon it immense heaps of dry wood, to set the machine on fire, while, independently of its being easily assailed by fire, they cast immense masses from the petraria without ceasing. Last of all, they threw on it Greek fire, and the dry wood having caught, the men in it saw it must be inevitably destroyed, and were obliged, by the intolerable heat, to leave it, and continue their attack with what instruments they could lay hold of. The Turks were indefatigable in their efforts to destroy the machine, by throwing down immense masses on it, or consuming it by means of liquid oil. Great was the contest and show of prowess between the Turks and Christians; the latter strove to extricate the battering-ram, the former to resist their attempts. The fire, once lighted, and fed constantly by the Turks, who spared no material for the purpose, reduced the machine to ashes. The Christians retired, grieving at the failure of their efforts while the Turks hastened to and fro, with dances and shouting, and thought their deeds incomparable. But they did not insult our adversities with impunity, for they lost eighty of their number, and amongst them, a certain renowned admiral, at whose command these things were done though they concealed their grief, that their loss might escape our notice. Our chiefs, observing that their exertions had not the success they expected, broken down by their misfortunes, determined to take respite for awhile, and relax their efforts.

CHAPTER LXI - *How a fleet off fifteen ships was sent to the aid of the townsmen of which several perished*

Meanwhile, soon after the feast of St. Michael, a fleet of fifteen ships arrived from Alexandria, glittering in gorgeous array, and a short distance one from another; they arrived towards dusk, and being driven by a violent wind, were unable to slacken their course. Hence, when they saw our army, they dreaded lest we should go forth to meet them, and they could not avoid us but the Christians did not venture, as the night was coming on, and the wind high. The fleet, too, having gathered together, made for the chain, with all speed the three largest ships, of the kind called dromons, came behind; the galleys, which were swifter of motion, went before. They bore down violently into port, and coming into collision with each other, two of them dashed on the rocks, and most of the men on board perished, amidst the shouts and laughter of the Christians, who beheaded some of them that were cast on shore by the fury of the waves. Besides this, they seized upon the largest of the galleys, which was driven by the wind into port, laden with provisions; and having killed the crew, they kept the cargo for themselves. The remainder reached the desired haven, below the chain, in safety and when the townsmen saw them, they went out with numberless lamps, and received them with much pomp into the city, overjoyed at their arrival. Afterwards, their numbers being thus augmented, they turned out of the town those of their men who were less fit for fighting, lest their numbers should consume their provisions and strength and so the time was protracted.

CHAPTER LXII - *How, on our men being set in battle array under the command of Archbishop Baldwin against Saladin-Saladin flies to the mountains*

The common men now murmured at the inactivity of the chiefs, and the continuance of a fruitless blockade, and grew weary of the siege and when the chiefs had considered for some time what had best be done, the result was, that the enemy on the outside should be challenged to a general engagement for if the hostile army gave way, the city would more easily be assaulted and stormed. On the morrow of St. Martin's, therefore, our chiefs led out their troops in order of battle into the plain, in the cold rays of a winters sun and when we saw them come forth, with their various standards, the Templars, the Hospitallers, and the others, their number, valor, and varied costumes, created in us mixed sentiments of admiration, confidence, and pleasure. The clergy claimed no small share of military glory for abbots and prelates led their own troops, and fought manfully for the faith, joyfully contending for the law of God. Among and above the others, the venerable Archbishop Baldwin distinguished himself and although his advanced age might have inclined him to inactivity, the perfection of his virtues made up for the defect of nature. Raising the standard on which was inscribed the name of the glorious martyr Thomas, he found for it a meet and worthy company for two hundred knights and three hundred followers served in the pay of the holy man. He himself, with the duke of Suabia, and Theobald, count of Blois, had charge of the camp and having performed the duties of the patriarch, who was ill in bed, he blessed and gave absolution to the army as it went forth. Nor could the noble bishop of Salisbury endure to be absent from the fray, but he performed the duties of a soldier in the field, a leader in the camp, and a pastor in the church. Towards sunset, when the army had advanced and pitched their tents, the townsmen came into the vacant space, and burst upon the baggage to plunder it but our men received them manfully, and putting them to flight, saved their friends without sustaining any loss. At night, the sultan ordered all his tents and property to be carried to the mountains and what could not be moved in time was burnt. It was the part of a spirit conquered and hesitating, thus declining battle on the plain, to destroy his own property, change his position, and retreat to the mountains. When he found a spot not easy of access, he halted and sent out an overwhelming number of infantry and bowmen to check those who should pursue, that at least he might annoy from above, those whom he feared to engage at close quarters. Our men, therefore, cheated of their battle in the plain, and unable to follow the foe up the precipitous road, returned equally without hurt and without glory.

CHAPTER LXIII - *How the Turks fought with a party of our men, who had gone out to Caiffa for provisions, and were returning, and how they yielded*

After this, hearing that provisions, of which they were much in want, might be procured at Caiffa, the army proceeded in that direction but when they came to a place called Recordana, behold the Turks suddenly rushing down, made a fierce attack on them, taking them for fugitives some of them threw their darts, others pressed on with their spears; one party made loud shouting, another blew their trumpets like horns, to frighten those who were flying. Our men, having pitched their tents in the plain that night, kept quiet till morning and then they saw the Turks in vast numbers surrounding them on all sides. Our men terrified at such a multitude, having taken up their arms, and put themselves in array, went forth in battle array to meet them yet the Turks did not venture to attack, but gave way as our men came on, although their own numbers were countless. Having heard that there were no provisions at Caiffa, as they supposed, for the Turks had carried them all away, our men returned towards Acre in order of battle. The Turks constantly harassed them on the road, but they sustained little loss from their attacks. At a certain river, however, which flows from thence to Acre, near a fountain, there was a severe engagement, and great slaughter of noble steeds, before the armies were separated our army now proceeded on one side of the stream, while the other was occupied by the enemy, who were constantly engaged in throwing missiles, and threatening them without ceasing, as well as harassing them in the rear. They harassed our men much, for the foot followers and bowmen, who occupied the rear of our army, were forced to keep facing about and discharging arrows at their pursuers without intermission.

On the following night they pitched their camps close by the stream, and had very little rest, but much anxiety for they were obliged either to drive off the enemy, who attacked them openly, or watch against hidden ambuscades for it was not so much by constant, as continued, attacks, that the enemy tried to annoy them with injuries, or provoke them with jeers. There was a bridge over the river, which it was necessary for us to pass, but which was occupied by the Turks before our arrival; this they had not had time to break down, as they intended, but closing together, they placed themselves in the middle of it to check our advance but when our men saw that nothing but absolute force would remove them, Godfrey of Lusignan, the king's brother, with five other chosen knights, made a fierce attack upon them, and put them to flight in a moment, and by the same assault threw thirty of them into the river, never more to rise, for they were drowned thus they gained a free passage across the river in spite of all opposition, and returned to the siege of Acre.

CHAPTER LXIV - *With what guiles the marquis espoused the wife of Reinfred, who was yet alive, in order to gain the heirship of the kingdom*

Now the marquis, having for some time aspired to the glory of reigning, on seeing a way open to his wishes, made himself confident of obtaining the kingdom, if he could supplant the wife of Reinfred to this end he strained every effort, and put in practice every art. But adopting an underhand policy, he complained of the condition of the kingdom that the king was not able to manage affairs, that he was reigning without right now his wife was removed, and that another daughter of King Amalric still survived. He first set forth these matters among the people, but he sedulously courted the chiefs also, enticing these with gifts, and binding others by the tie of kindred; and all he either allures by his bland manners, or obliges by his gifts, or gains over by his promises. It was easy for so active a man, surpassing Sinon in devices, Ulysses in eloquence, and Mithridates in variety of tongues, to gain all his wishes, armed as he was with such cunning but forasmuch as the Church forbade the bonds of marriage to be broken asunder, the crafty man found out a new charge to take away the wife of Reinfred; for the chiefs persuaded him that she could be separated from her husband without violation of the law, as having married when too young, and without consent. But Reinfred himself had conceived the Lope of gaining the kingdom in the right of his wife a person more akin to a woman than a man, effeminate in manner and loose in language, and to whom that verse of Virgil applies, "While Nature doubts, if boy or girl be made. You're born, fair boy, to be a pretty jade." For one day, when, at the mandate of the chiefs, Reinfred had brought forward his wife, he lost his bride and his kingdom together by the arts of the marquis. Oh wickedness worthy of the satirist's pen and of tragic declamation! For if we condemn the rape of Helen, the present deed is much more base, and its injustice greater for Helen was stolen, surreptitiously stolen, in the absence of her husband, whereas this one was violently withdrawn in his presence. But that the act might lose the infamy of its wrong, the girl is given into the keeping of a sequestrator, while the judgment of the clergy is sought for a divorce. The marquis, therefore, tampered with the clergy by gifts and wiles; he sounded all those whom he believed agreeable to his purpose and effects, by immense largesses and the fascination of gold, to corrupt their judicial impartiality. The report of so great a wickedness was carried to the ears of the most sacred metropolitan of Canterbury; it arouses his innocence to astonishment, and inflames the anger of the defender of the law. While he performed with due rigor the duties of the patriarch, who, as we said, was sick, the friends of the marquis tried to quash the verdict which was to be given, under the pretext of appeal. Three of his chief favorites were Reginald, lord of Sidon, Pagan, of the castle of Caiffa and Balisantus; and there would have been a fourth, the count of Tripoli, had he not gone away, who would have formed this consummate council of iniquity. For in them, as in an abode of wickedness, were united the treachery of Judas, the cruelty of Nero, the impiety of Herod, and all that the present or olden times regarded as abominable and wicked. Now, Balisantus, on Amalric's death, had married his wife, this damsel's mother; and she, having imbibed from her childhood the lowest Grecian morals, had a husband similar to herself in cruelty, levity, and faithlessness. The marquis wins them both over by presents and promises, to persuade the girl to prefer a complaint, that she had married Reinfred against her will, that she had always opposed it, and that the marriage could not stand, because she had never given her consent. This plot is entirely successful, and the woman easily changes her mind for a female is always variable and changeable, her sex frail, her mind fickle, and she delights in novelty; so she lightly rejects and forgets those whom she knows; the girl is thus easily taught what is bad, and willingly receives evil advice, and so blushed not to say that she was not carried away, but had followed the marquis willingly. Indeed the chiefs themselves, in defiance of justice, used their efforts to bring it about that the marquis should have the kingdom and the damsel. The venerable archbishop of Canterbury seeing that justice and equity were perversely confounded, and that ecclesiastical authority would be rejected; perceiving also that the clergy, with some of the bishops, who had a sounder mind and more fervent zeal, murmured as far as they dared; he pronounced sentence of excommunication on those who had contracted and agreed to this unholy wedlock, and not undeservedly, because he had cohabited with another man's wife, and taken her to his own house and espoused her, by the ministry of the bishop of Beauvais, and because he had a wife in his own country, and another in Constantinople, both of noble birth, young, and beautiful, and suitable to his position; whence the clergy charged him with threefold adultery, and as far as they could, spoke against the act which the holy church deemed impious. Those who favored him tried to excuse themselves on the plea that the marquis had sworn to supply the army, when in much want, with an abundance of provision from Tyre, on condition of their aiding him in the marriage but he had set at nought his oath, and transgressed the sanctity of his honor, for he who is faithless in a little, fears not to commit a greater crime. And while the nuptials were celebrated with great festivity, it happened that some of our men, who were guests at the feast, having gone to a short distance from the spot, were set upon by an ambuscade of the Turks, and some taken, others slain. This was the commencement of misfortunes. Here the Butler of St. Lice was taken, and whether the Turks kept him captive or killed him, was never known afterwards. Twenty men were taken prisoners or slain on this occasion.

CHAPTER LXV - *How the marquis returned to Tyre, and perjured himself, by not assisting our men when in need of provisions*

But the marquis, having gained his wishes, returned to Tyre quickly with his wife and his men and the army was disappointed in their expectation of obtaining through him a supply of provisions. For, on the contrary, either forgetful of this agreement, or ungrateful for what was done for him, he did not send so much as an egg when the army was in danger of starvation but, both perjurer and liar, he would not allow those who wished to sail to Acre with provisions to depart. Therefore, the want of provisions increased daily amongst the besiegers little or nothing was found to purchase, and nothing was brought by ships.

CHAPTER LXVI - *How Baldwin, archbishop of Canterbury, died*

When the archbishop of Canterbury saw what he had before heard, that the army had become altogether dissolute, and given to drinking, women, and dice, it afflicted his spirit, unable to bear such excesses, even to the weariness of life. And because a disease which is general is difficult to cure, when one day the worst reports of this kind reached his ears, knowing that man is charged with the care of things, though the power of creating is God's, he sighed and uttered these words, "Lord God! Now is there need of chastening and correcting with holy grace, that if it please thy mercy that I should be removed from the turmoil of this present life, I have remained long enough in this army." Scarcely fifteen days after these words, as if heard by the Lord, he began to feel cold and stiff, and overcome by a fever, a few days after he slept in the Lord.

CHAPTER LXVII - *Of the bitterness of the famine amongst our men, and the enormous price of provisions which was the cause of their cursing the marquis*

Meanwhile, the want of provisions increased daily, and the middle and lower classes were tormented at first continuously rather than constantly by the approaching famine, the more severely as the marquis prevaricated more shamefully. Nevertheless, he sent provisions secretly to those accomplices and favorers he had won over to join in his illicit and impious transaction. And now the higher ranks of the army obtained hardly sufficient food to sustain life, and the winter was drawing near, a period when they were usually more prodigal and luxurious, formerly abundant in all kinds of food, but now with the change of circumstances threatening want and the hungry stomach, once overloaded, now became satisfied with any food it could procure. The greedy table had consumed their substance, and not satiating the sharp appetite of those who were in search of it, they were worn away by hunger, being without the common necessaries of life and they felt it so much the more severely, as it was the time when they were accustomed to dainties. The heat of the season, too, added to the horrors of the impending famine, and want is always felt more severely by those who have been brought up in affluence. Why need we say more? A moderate measure of wheat, which a man could carry under his arm, was sold for 100 aure, a chicken for twelve sols, and an egg for six deniers. By these examples, the rates of all other kinds of provisions may be imagined. The army then cursed the marquis for withdrawing their means of support, and because through him they stood in danger of starvation.

CHAPTER LXVIII - *How our men, while perishing of famine ate the dead bodies of their horses, with their intestines*

Famine, as we have said, urges to the commission of crimes, and yet pardonable ones, for the Lord created all things for man, and gave them into his hands to be of service to him, that man should not perish while beasts lived they therefore slew valuable horses, and without taking off the skins of some of them, ate horse-flesh with joy; even the intestines were sold for ten sols. And wherever it was known a horse was killed, they crowded to it one before the other to buy or steal, and like birds of prey to a corpse, so the starving soldiers rushed in troops to a dead steed, that they might devour the bodies of those that once carried them and thus the animals who once carried them on their backs were in turn carried themselves the dead horse sold for more than a living one, and the words of the evangelist seemed to apply to them, " Where the body is, there the eagles are gathered together;" saving the mystical interpretation, from the dignity of which we do not wish to derogate.

None of the intestines of the slain horses were rejected, owing to the pressure of the famine, and the most worthless part was valued at a high rate they ate up the head with the intestines, so that after all was consumed, nay, devoured with avidity, they licked their fingers with a relish, that while any thing remained, it might be removed with the tongue rather than wiped away with a napkin. Hence they held the marquis in detestation for depriving them of the means of subsistence, since by his means they had been defrauded of their food, and stood in danger of starvation.

CHAPTER LXIX - *How he who had some food ate it secretly*

In progress of time, the famine increased exceedingly for want of provisions, and if any one had any thing appertaining to food, he hid away secretly for his own use that which was enough for more than once, in order that it might not be taken away from him by force and thus it happened that little was exposed for sale, and whatsoever they had they did not distribute for common use, but the poor man was everywhere in want. Hence their detestation of the marquis for depriving them of the means of subsistence, as by his means they were deprived of food, and stood in danger of starvation.

CHAPTER LXX - *How those who were once delicate ate grass*

Wherever by chance grass was discovered growing, it was greedily devoured by men who once were brought up delicately, men of high rank and the sons of great men; they fed on grass like beasts, that the violence of famine might be extinguished by such food, whence many, led to reason by necessity, planted herbs fit for eating and good for driving away the pangs of hunger; and such as they once despised and believed not fit for human use, the greatness of the famine made now most sweet to the starving. Oh! Then, the voice of the people, cursing the perfidy of the marquis because he cared not for the misery of a starving people.

CHAPTER LXXI - *How they perish from rain and hunger*

Moreover, owing to the great quantity of rain that fell, a certain very severe disease spread among the men; for unusual showers, by their constant and continuous fall, had such an injurious effect upon the soldiers, that, with the excess of the affliction, their limbs becoming swollen, the whole body was affected as with the dropsy, and from the violence of the disease, the teeth of some of them were loosened and fell out. O the lamentations of each of them! O the sorrow of all while those who were safe grieved for the sufferings of their comrades, and day by day saw the funerals of their friends, for every day they performed the rites of a thousand who had perished. Some, however (but they were few), recovered from their disease, and becoming more eager after food, regained health only to suffer the excessive miseries of famine. O, then, the voice of the people, cursing the perfidy of the marquis, for he cared not for the sufferings of the perishing people!

CHAPTER LXXII - *How our starving men fought at the oven*

Wherever it was known that bread was baking at the oven, there was a concourse of the people crying out and saying, "Here is money; we will give what price you please, so that you give us plenty of bread." For each asked to be served first, offering a price in exchange for bread, and each violently struggling to snatch from the others what they had not yet received, and perhaps never would. But as often as it happened that any of the rich bought much bread, then arose mourning, and sorrow, and clamor among the poor, united in one voice of wailing, when they saw that quantity of bread carried away by the rich, which, if distributed in portions, might have done good to the poor as far as it would go. They eagerly offered the price of the bread at the will of the seller but, because any moderate quantity was not enough for so great a multitude, there arose frequent and angry disputes, quarrels, contentions, jealousies, and sometimes fights around the oven which contained the bread, and they contended for it like dogs before they were sure of obtaining it. O, then, the voice of the people, cursing the perfidy of the marquis, for he cared not for the wretchedness of a perishing people!

CHAPTER LXXIII - *How they gnawed and ate up dirty bones which had been already gnawed by dogs*

But who can write or set forth how great their misery was—how great the general suffering, when some were seen from the pressure of famine running about like rabid dogs and snatching up bones that had been gnawed by dogs for three days together, and sucking and licking them when there was nothing on them to be gnawed, not because they did them any good, but because they gratified the imagination with the remembrance of flesh? What need we add to these horrors? The enemy, harassing them by constant attacks from both sides, when they slew them suddenly, were held less terrible than the violence of so great a famine; for the former put an end to their lives and their miseries by the edge of the sword and at once, whereas by the famine they pined away in lengthened torments. Oftentimes, in the sight of all, they whom hunger had stripped of shame, fed upon abominable and filthy things, found by chance, and which cannot be named; yet they deemed them delicious food, though unlawful for man to make use of. O the voice of the people, cursing the perfidy of the marquis, for he cared not for the wretchedness of a perishing people!

CHAPTER LXXIV - *How noblemen also, when they had not wherewith to buy bread, stole it*

From some other instances worth relating, the magnitude of the famine may be estimated for in those who endured it patiently according to the flesh, it may be not undeservedly considered martyrdom, unless perchance by murmuring they diminished the credit which they would thus have received. The pressure of necessity moreover led to the commission of many disgraceful acts and some even of noble extraction, who were on that account ashamed to beg openly, feared not to sin in secret to obtain the subsistence so difficult to get honestly, and were in the habit of stealing bread. Thus it happened that one man was caught in this kind of robbery, and was bound tightly with thongs, in which condition he was placed in custody in the house of the man who had caught him, who was a baker and while the family was very much engaged in domestic matters, by some movement or other, the captive managed to get his hands loose, and as he was placed by chance close by a heap of new loaves, he ate his full unperceived by any one, and then escaping with one loaf in his hand, returned unpunished to his friends; and after telling his story distributed the bread he had in his hand to them to eat. But what was this among so many? Want irritated the appetite, and exasperated rather than quieted hunger. O then the voice of the people, cursing the perfidy of the marquis, because he cared not for the wretchedness of a perishing people!

CHAPTER LXXV - *How many turn apostates from the bitterness of the famine*

What was still worse, some of our men and it cannot be told or heard without great grief, gave way to the severity of the famine, and in paying attention to their corporeal safety incurred the damnation of their souls. For after having overcome a great part of their tribulation, some of our men taking refuge among the Turks, did not hesitate to turn apostates, and to procure for themselves by wicked blasphemies eternal death, that they might enjoy a little longer this mortal life. O pernicious exchange! O crime for which no punishment can suffice! O foolish men like unto senseless beasts while ye fled from the death, which must soon come, you took no care against the death that is without end! For if a just man liveth by faith, perfidy is accounted death, but the conscience of all who act foolishly must be purged. Then they execrate the marquis for breaking his covenant, and imprecate evil on him and mortal woe.

CHAPTER LXXVI - *How two friends buy thirteen beans for a denier*

There were two friends, comrades in misfortune as well as in war, so needy and distressed that the two possessed only one piece of money, commonly called an angevin, and with that only they wished to purchase something to eat but what could they do? It was a mere trifle, and worth little, even if there had been abundance of all sorts of good things and they had nothing else but their armor and clothing. They considered for a long time very thoughtfully what they should buy with that one little piece, and how it could be done to ward off the pressing evil of the day. They at last came to the resolution of buying some beans, since nothing was to be bought of less value with difficulty, therefore, they obtained after much entreaty, thirteen beans for their denier, one of which on returning home they found consumed by maggots, and therefore unfit for eating. Upon this, by mutual agreement, they went a long distance in search of the seller, who consented not without difficulty and after much supplication, to give them a whole bean in exchange. How strange this exchange of such a thing after a long search, and at such a distance! From those beans, which were consumed in a moment, how much benefit do we think could accrue to the hungry? "We judge that must be weighed more by the opinion of the hearer than described by the pen. Then they execrated the marquis for the violation of his covenant, and prayed for evil on him and mortal woe."

CHAPTER LXXVII - *How the famished ate karrubles, and died from drinking wine*

There was exposed for sale a kind of fruit growing on trees; a grain enclosed in a pod like a pea, which the common people called karruble, sweet to the taste, and very pleasant to eat. The hungry were recruited by them, because there was a greater abundance of them than other things, whence the way to buy them was much frequented; for although they were of inferior value, they were something. Of those who lay weak and ate little, either because they had nothing to eat, or because they could not eat, the wine which they drank heated them so much that many were suffocated, either from the violence of the liquor, which was not tempered with food, or from being too weak to support its strength and goodness. There was a tolerable supply of wine for sale, but much wine is not good for the preservation of the body with little food for it is necessary to proportion the one to the other. But inasmuch as the marquis was the cause of the scarcity, they ceased not to curse him and execrate him for the violation of his covenant, and invoked evil on him and mortal woe.

CHAPTER LXXVIII - *How the famished ate flesh during Lent*

Some were driven by the pressure of the famine to eat flesh in the beginning of Lent, on what is commonly called Ash Wednesday,—not because they had plenty of it, but because it was more easily obtained afterwards, however, as the famine slackened, they repented and made proportionate penitence. Above all these things, during the whole of that winter, the charity of all was so cooled by the fear of want of money, that a man did not even share his necessaries with his friend, their little faith leading them to doubt God's love, and to believe that if they shared with others, they themselves would lack the necessaries of life. To such a degree the vice of parsimony, and the concealment of their stores increased, that even they hid what they had, and those that had were thought not to have at all. What did the voice of so many in want then imprecate on the marquis? Who did not think him the cause of so many being in jeopardy?

CHAPTER LXXIX - *The exhortation of the bishop of Salisbury and some others to the rich, to make collections to assist the poor*

The intercourse of the faithful becoming beyond measure checked, and no one taking thought or notice of the poor and needy, the infamy of this want of faith extended itself to all. The bishop of Salisbury was active in showing that nothing was greater than charity, nothing more acceptable to God, nothing more fruitful than to give and to this end he induced all, by his powerful persuasion, to open their hands and distribute to their neighbors, to give to the needy, and support the perishing, lest, if they neglected the wants of others, they should not obtain their own for it is said that he who leads them not when he may, is the cause of death to the anguishing he showed that he was guilty of another man's death, who refused to assist him when he could for we are commanded to give drink to our enemy when thirsty, and to need him when hungry. And the bishops of Nerrona and Faenza in Italy, earnestly assisted in his exhortation. In consequence of the exhortation and urgency of these men, a collection was made for distribution amongst the poor, and so many and so great were the hearts God moved to contribute to the support of the needy, that the hungry were greatly recruited and the substance of the givers, also, by the grace of God cooperating, was not diminished. Then arose fresh joy, then the lips of many blessed the givers, then were benefits multiplied, then it is said that pity was turned gratefully towards them, whilst the powerful yearned with compassion over the afflicted. Among the most active in performing these duties, were Watlin de Ferrars and Robert Trusebot, and not behind them were Henry count of Champagne, Jocelin de Montoirs, as well as the count of Clairmont and the bishop of Salisbury, who was the first promoter of these good deeds.

By the care of these men, aided by the others, every one contributed according to his means to a common fund, that it might be distributed to each as he had need. Thus, those whose hearts were before cold under cover of the ashes of avarice, through God's grace became fervent in deeds of charity, and because they were converted to compassion the Lord regarded and magnified his pity with them, according to his words, "turn unto me and I will turn unto you, saith the Lord."

CHAPTER LXXX - *How a small ship arrived with provisions, and how that which cost a hundred gold pieces one day, was bought for four on the morrow*

For while all were engaged in these works of charity, behold the Lord sent a ship laden with provisions, by which the former scarcity of food was very much alleviated. For so great a want of bread had not existed because there was no corn, but because the sellers asked such a price for it from the buyers, that it could scarcely be obtained for a large sum after much bargaining for what will not avarice do? The aforesaid ship, which was but a small one, had arrived, as I think, on a Saturday and on the morrow, a measure which had been sold hitherto for a hundred pieces of gold, by the bounty of God, the dispenser of all good things, was lowered to four. Meanwhile there arises among the people an unusual hilarity, the avaricious merchants being the only persons who grieved, owing to the decrease of their wonted gain, and with difficulty concealing it. But why need I say more? There is no counsel against the Lord, for he doeth whatsoever he will.

CHAPTER LXXXI - *How, when a Pisan wished to keep his provisions till the morrow, his house and provisions were consumed by fire*

A certain Pisan, a seller of provisions, had kept some corn untouched during the whole year, until he could sell it according to his wishes hereafter, expecting that the famine would increase and if at any time he sold any, he sold it at his own price, as he liked, to those who could not do without it. But God, by his judgment, showed the wickedness of this action, for it happened that the house of that Pisan, filled with wheat, suddenly and violently caught fire. And though very many hastened to extinguish the fire, their efforts were ineffectual, for every thing was destroyed.

CHAPTER LXXXII - *How all vied in giving away meat, and how apenance was enjoined on those who ate what was unlawful*

All therefore being emulously engaged in such works of piety, strove with all their might to distribute alms; while each one in his zeal was eager to outdo his neighbors in bounty, thinking that he was performing an acceptable duty to God, if he could more abundantly administer what was necessary to the needy. Those also, who from necessity fed on flesh during Lent, as we before said, repenting of their guilt, after each had received penitence from the illustrious and venerable bishop of Salisbury, undertook with a vow to perform proportionate satisfaction as was enjoined them.

BOOK II

CHAPTER I - *Of the kings of England and France*

After Easter arrived Philip, king of France, and not long after him, Richard, king of England but in order that the course of their voyage may be more fully known, it seems advisable to commence our history from their first departure from their kingdoms, so that it may be set forth, in the due order of events, until it reaches the period of the siege of Acre.

CHAPTER II - *Of the emulation of the French and the English m taking up the Cross*

When report, then, had spread these events, as we have described, throughout the world, that the cities of the Holy Land were in possession of infidels that the holy relics were scornfully treated and trodden under foot and that the Christians were plundered and despoiled, the empires were moved by the most strenuous exhortation of Pope Gregory VIII and many men of various nations were aroused, and above all, the French and English devoutly took up the sign of the cross, and prepared with all their strength to hurry to the aid of the Holy Land, being incited like David to take vengeance on the Philistines, who were defying, with their Goliath, the oppressed armies of the God of Jerusalem. For the chief pontiff earnestly stimulated all to obtain by these means pardon for their sins, and according to the authority with which he was invested, gave them absolution from the guilt of their past transgressions, if they would devote themselves to the performance of so pious and so necessary a work; proving to them that they would deservedly be the happier for undertaking the mission at once, in fervent zeal and without delay. Yea, their journey would be the more praiseworthy, and their endeavors many times more excellent, in behalf of a place, though desolate, yet rendered holier by the divine mystical promise, and which was consecrated by the nativity, dwelling, and passion of our Lord. Moreover, it was distinguished, by the divine choice, from every other nation and being his dwelling, ought to be snatched from the heathen, of whom the Lord had said, "that they should not enter into His Church." They hastened, therefore, with ready zeal and pious emulation to take the cross at the hands of the clergy; so that the question was, not who should take it up, but who had not already done so. The voice of song was now silenced, the pleasures of eating and luxurious habits were abandoned, the quarrels of disputants quieted; new peace was made between old enemies, causes of litigation were settled by mutual agreement, and for this new ground of quarrel, every one who had cause of dispute, even for longstanding enmity, was reconciled to his neighbor. What need is there to say more? By the inspiration of God, all were of one accord, for one common cause led them to undertake the labor of this pious pilgrimage.

CHAPTER III - *How Henry, king of England, and Philip, King of France, with an immense multitude, took up the cross between Gisors and Trie*

Richard, then count of Poitou, was the first to take up the cross, and an immense multitude with him but they did not set out on their pilgrimage, owing to some delay, occasioned by a dispute between Philip, king of France, and Henry, king of England, the father of Count Richard. An inveterate dispute had excited them to international war, as it had done their ancestors, the French and Normans, from an inexorable and almost uninterrupted feud. The archbishop of the land of Jerusalem, that is of Tyre, was earnest to effect a reconciliation between them, and had fixed the day they were to meet, to take up the cross, at a place between Gisors and Trie. The aforesaid archbishop had come on a mission to animate the faithful, and obtain assistance for the deliverance of the Holy Land, having been specially sent to the king of England, the fame of whose virtues was spread far and wide above all the other kings of the earth, on account of his glory, riches, and the greatness of his power. On that day, after many plans had been proposed, and much spoken on either side, they both came finally to the determination that each of them should take up the cross, and depart from his land, it appearing to each a safe precaution against the one invading the kingdom of the other, while absent, for neither would venture to go unless the other went also. At length, these conditions having been, with some difficulty, agreed on, the two kings exchanged the kiss of peace, and assumed the cross with the blessing of the archbishop, and with them an immense number of both nations, partly from the love of God and for the forgiveness of their sins, partly from respect for their king and so great was the multitude that took up the cross on that day, that the people, from the crush and intolerable heat (for it was summer) nearly fainted. The delay in entering upon their march must be reprehended; it was the work of the enemy of the human race, whose interest it is to foment discord, and excite inexorable enmity, and by whose instigation, the altercation between the kings was revived, and the seeds of discord sown from a very light occasion, that by their diabolical superstition neither was inclined to forego, lest, as it were, his fame and honor should be derogated thereby; as if it were abject and mean to yield obedience to justice and right.

CHAPTER IV - *Henry, king of England, dies*

The death of Henry, king of England, put an end to these dissensions, and the vow of making the crusade, which he had deferred fulfilling while in safety, after a lapse of time, could not be performed, by the intervention of his death. As a vow must be entirely voluntary, so when taken, it must irrefragably be discharged and he who binds himself by a vow is to be condemned for the non-performance of it, as he could not have made it lawfully, but of his own accord and free-will. Now King Henry died on the day of the holy apostles Peter and Paul, in the year of our Lord 1189, and was buried at Fontevrault.

CHAPTER V - *How Richard, count of Poitou, was crowned king of England*

Therefore in the same year, after the death of his father, Richard, count of Poitou, having arranged his affairs in Normandy, in about two months crossed over to England, and on St. Giles's day he was received at Westminster, with a ceremonious procession; and three days afterwards, viz., on the 3rd of September, the day of the ordination of St. Gregory the pope, which was a Sunday, he was solemnly anointed king by the imposition of hands, by Archbishop Baldwin, in virtue of his office, who performed the service, assisted by many of his suffragans. At his coronation were present his brother John, and his mother Eleanor, who, after the death of King Henry, had been, by the command of her son Richard, the new king, released from prison, where she had been ten years and there were also present counts and barons, and an immense crowd of men and soldiers and the kingdom was confirmed to the hands of King Richard. On the 3rd day of September, in the year of our Lord 1189, Richard was anointed king, on a Sunday, with the dominical letter A, viz., in the year after leap year. Many were the conjectures made, because the day above that was marked unlucky in the calendar and in truth it was unlucky, and very much so to the Jews of London, who were destroyed that day, and likewise the Jews settled in other parts of England endured many hardships. Having therefore celebrated the occasion by a festival of three days, and entertained his guests in the royal palace of Westminster, King Richard gratified all, by distributing money, without count or number, to all according to their ranks, thus manifesting his liberality and his great excellence. His generosity, and his virtuous endowments, the ruler of the world should have given to the ancient times for in this period of the world, as it waxes old, such feelings rarely exhibit themselves, and when they do, they are subjects of wonder and astonishment. He had the valor of Hector, the magnanimity of Achilles, and was equal to Alexander, and not inferior to Roland in valor; nay, he outshone many illustrious characters of our own times. The liberality of a Titus was his, and, which is so rarely found in a soldier, he was gifted with the eloquence of Nestor and the prudence of Ulysses and he showed himself pre-eminent in the conclusion and transaction of business, as one whose knowledge was not without active goodwill to aid it, nor his good-will wanting in knowledge. Who, if Richard were accused of presumption, would not readily excuse him, knowing him for a man who never knew defeat, impatient of an injury, and impelled irresistibly to vindicate his rights, though all he did was characterized by innate nobleness of mind. Success made him better fitted for action; fortune ever favors the bold, and though she works her pleasure on whom she will, Richard was never to be overwhelmed with adversity. He was tall of stature, graceful in figure; his hair between red and auburn; his limbs were straight and flexible; his arms rather long, and not to be matched for wielding the sword or for striking with it and his long legs suited the rest of his frame while his appearance was commanding, and his manners and habits suitable and he gained the greatest celebrity, not more from his high birth than from the virtues that adorned him. But why need we take much labor in extolling the fame of so great a man? He needs no superfluous commendation, for he has a sufficient need of praise, which is the sure companion of great actions. He was far superior to all others both in moral goodness, and in strength, and memorable for prowess in battles, and his mighty deeds outshone the most brilliant description we could give of them. Happy, in truth, might he have been deemed had he been without rivals who envied his glorious actions, and whose only cause of enmity was his magnificence, and his being the searcher after virtue rather than the slave of vice.

CHAPTER VI - *How King Richard, having arranged the affairs of his kingdom, celebrated the Nativity of Christ at Liuns, in Normandy, and how, by agreement, he and the king of France met on the feast of St. John the Baptist at Vezelai*

After the coronation-feast was ended, as we before said, King Richard arose in his father's stead, and, after having received the oath of allegiance from the nobles, as was the custom, in the form of homage, and each having submitted to his sovereignty, he left London and went round his country and afterwards he set out on a pilgrimage to St. Edmund, whose festival was at hand; thence he went to Canterbury, and at his command some bishoprics, which, having become vacant, had been kept so by the king his father, were filled up, and, with the approval of the king, the following were installed bishops: Richard the treasurer, of London; Godfrey de Luci, of Winchester; Hubert Walter, of Salisbury, William de Longchamp, of Ely, whom the king also made his chancellor and justiciary of all England. In like manner, also, the king caused bishops to be ordained to the vacant bishoprics in his other territories. Having prepared every thing necessary for his journey, and having set the kingdom of England in order as far as time permitted, he returned to Normandy without delay, and kept the festival of the Nativity of Our Lord at Liuns for his intention of setting out upon his journey and the fulfillment of his vow made him unceasingly anxious, as he judged delay to be dangerous, whilst it was of consequence to commence the journey which was due wherefore he wrote to the king of France that he was quite ready to set out, and urged that he should be ready also, showing by his fathers example that delay was hurtful when every thing was prepared. Therefore, in the year of our Lord 1190, with the dominical letter G, the kings met at Dreux to confer about the arrangement of their journey. After many had communicated their opinions, and while the conference was going on, there suddenly arrived a messenger with the news that the queen of France was dead. The king, smitten by the bitterness of this news, was greatly cast down, so that he almost thought of laying aside his premeditated journey; and to augment this bereavement, news was brought that William, king of Apulia, was likewise dead. Overwhelmed by these adverse occurrences, and utterly overcome by the belief that they predicted ill, they abstained from the transaction of the business, and the fire of their zeal in a measure grew lukewarm. However, by the favor of the inspiration of God, who guide the footsteps or man, and in whose hands are the hearts of kings, to prevent the ruin of a work planned with so much toil and solemnly arranged, and the turning into condemnation and disgrace what had been disposed for the attainment of good, they recovered their strength, and were animated to proceed and set out, and not to grow lukewarm by unpardonable slothfulness. Now they bad agreed together to set out on the Nativity of St. John the Baptist, in order that the kings, together with their men, should meet on the eighth day at Yezelay. Whereupon Philip, king of France, setting out from the city of Paris, which is the capital of France, with a large quantity of provisions, shortly afterwards marched by the chapel of St. Denis, to whose prayers and merits he commended himself, and thus commenced his journey accompanied by a very large multitude. There also set out with him on his journey, the duke of Burgundy and the count of Flanders. Who can relate the progress of each with their forces? You might meet them on all sides flocking together and assembling from different parts, and joining together in one army, amidst pious tears while those who went forward with their friends or kinsmen, regarded them with a look of love, and on their departure were unable to restrain the tears from bursting forth, as devotion or sorrow affected them.

CHAPTER VII - *How King Richard, being at Tours, commanded his fleet to proceed and go round Spain by the Straits, and wait for him at Messina*

King Richard was at Tours with a chosen body of soldiers. Both the city and suburbs were so crowded with the multitude of men that they inconvenienced each other from the crowd and the narrowness of the streets and roads. Therefore, by the command of the king, the royal fleet, being collected together, was ordered to proceed in order, being in number a hundred and eight, not including the ships that followed afterwards. Thus the royal fleet, having been set forward on its voyage by the command of the king, with a fair wind and in close company, reached the destined port of Messina, after having safely escaped the dangerous sandbanks, and the perils of the terrible rocks, the stormy straits of Africa, and all the dangers of the ocean. Here they awaited the arrival of the king, according to his command, who was inarching with his army by land. When the king departed from Tours with his forces, the inhabitants of the land were terrified by the appearance of so great a multitude. Who could relate the numbers of those who accompanied him, the variety of their arms, the trains of nobles and chosen bands of combatants? Or who could describe the troops of infantry and their bodies of slingers, which those who saw as they advanced in order, from their inmost hearts, and with pious zeal forcing out the tears, equally mourned and congratulated their lord the new king, who thus, at the commencement of his reign, without having tasted the sweets of rest, so devotedly and so speedily left all pleasures, and, as if chosen by the Lord, he undertook a work of so great goodness, so arduous and so necessary, and a journey so commendable. O the miserable sighs for those that left them! O the groans of those who embraced at parting and the good wishes for those who were going away! O the eyes heavy with tears, and the mutual sobs interrupting the words of the speakers amidst the kisses of those who were dear to them, not yet satisfied with the conversation of those who were leaving them; and although they grieved, those who were setting out feigned equanimity by the gravity of their countenances, and separated from each other, after long conversations, as if choking for utterance, and often interchanging a farewell, staid a little longer, and repeated it to gain delay and to appear about to say something more and at last, tearing themselves from the voices of those that cheered them, they bounded forward and extricated themselves from the hands of those who would detain them.

CHAPTER VIII - *How the two kings, according to agreement, met at Vezelai*

Thus, in the first year of his coronation, Richard, king of England, set out from Tours on his journey. From Tours he marched to Luti, then to Mount Richard after that to Celles, thence to Chapelles, thence to Dama, thence to Vitiliaeum, that is, Vezelai, where the two kings and their forces were to meet. And because the people of both nations were reckoned to be incalculably numerous, the mountains, far and wide, were spread with pavilions and tents, and the surface of the earth around was covered, so that the level of the sowed fields which were occupied, presented to the beholder the appearance of a city, with its effect heightened by a most imposing variety of pavilions, and by the different colors that distinguished them. There you might see the martial youth of different nations equipped for war, which appeared able to subdue the whole length of the earth, and to overcome the countries of all the world, and to penetrate the retreat of different tribes, and judge no place too hard or no enemy too fierce to conquer and that they would never yield to wrong while they could aid and assist each other by the help of their valor. That army, boasting in its immense numbers, well protected by the defense of their arms, and glowing with ardour, was scattered by the intervention of disputes, and overthrown by internal discord, which, if combined with military discipline and good-will, would have remained invincible to all without and thus, by the violation of the ties of fellowship, it met with a heavier downfall, whilst it was distracted by its own friends for a house divided against itself is made desolate.

CHAPTER IX - *How the two kings entered into a treaty at Vezelai, and agreed to wait for each other at Messina, and how they arrived together at Lyons on the Rhone*

There the two kings made a treaty for their mutual security, and for preserving good faith with each other in every respect, and for inquiring into all things according to the rights of war, with a view to their equal division. Besides that, it was agreed that he who should arrive first at Messina was to wait for the other to follow after which, each of their friends who had followed them so far on their pilgrimage should return home. The two kings set forward with their men, and arranged the manner of their march, holding frequent intercourse with great magnificence, and paying each other mutual honor and being also of one accord, the mighty army, during the progress of their march, performed their duties without complaint or dissension—nay, with joy and alacrity. And as they thus passed along cities and villages with a mighty equipment and clash of arms, the inhabitants, observing the multitude, and marking the distinctions of the men by the place of each nation in the march, and noticing their discipline, exclaimed, "O heaven! What meaneth so great a multitude of men, and so mighty an army? Who can resist their valor? O noble soldiery in the flower of their youth! O young men, happy in so much beauty! Were your parents affected with sorrow at your departure? What land gave birth to youths of so distinguished a mien, or produced such fine young soldiers? And who are the rulers of so mighty a multitude that govern with their word such brave legions?" Uttering these words, and such like, and following with good wishes those that passed, they paid the most marked attention to the people of different nations and those who were fatigued by the march, by testifying all the devotion in their power. Thus the army proceeding in order by separate divisions, went joyfully from Vezelai to St. Leonard of Curbeny, thence to Mulins, afterwards to Mount Escot, then to Tulnis, near St. Mary de Bois, thence to Belivi, afterwards to the village of Furaca, and thence to Lyons on the Rhone; there they stopped some days, owing to the difficulty of crossing the river from its rapidity and unknown depth so that the army which had come in the interim might cross over, and wait the arrival of those who were to follow. Having at length crossed the river, the two kings pitched their pavilions on the other side in the meadows as many of the army as it could contain lodged in the town the others in the fields in the suburbs. There you might see people of different nations, distinguished by their proper places and by the forms of their arms, in countless numbers for they were reckoned to exceed a hundred thousand, and recruits had not yet ceased to flock in. Afterwards, the king of England followed up his show of friendship and honor to the king of France, on his departure with all his troops for Genoa. For the king of France had engaged the Genoese, who were good seamen to carry him over the gulf. For they had agreed, as has been afore said, that whichever first put in at Messina in Sicily, should await the arrival of the other.

CHAPTER X - *How, after the departure of the king of France to Genoa, the bridge over the Rhone gave wag from the pressure of the crowd, and how King Richard embarked at Marseilles and crossed over to Messina*

While the crowd of pilgrims, who came in constantly from all quarters, was incautiously hastening to cross the bridge over the Rhone, a part of it gave way under their weight, with those who were on it, and, as it was of considerable elevation, about a hundred men fell into the water, which was very violent, and its course rapid, and owing to its depth, it was difficult for any who had fallen in to get out alive. But they who fell in cried out loudly, and implored assistance and, wonderful to relate, though exhausted, they all escaped save two, who were drowned, and experienced death of the body, though they live spiritually in Christ, in whose service they were. Those who came behind were embarrassed by their numbers, as each sought his own way or means of crossing the Rhone but they were thrown into despair by the breaking down of the bridge, which seemed to cut off their hopes of reaching the other side. On learning this, King Richard, whose constancy was never shaken, relieved their anxiety by causing a bridge to be made, by collecting as quickly as possible a number of boats together, such as the urgent necessity of the case should suggest and so they crossed over, after some delay and difficulty. This accident caused a delay of three days to the king and his army: one part then proceeded to the nearest port, Marseilles; part went to Venice; part to Genoa, or Barlata, or Brundisium and very many set out for Messina, the port where the two kings were to meet. Three days afterwards, the king departed, and on the same day the bridge was broken up. From Lyons we crossed by Vicaria near Alba Ripa, thence to Mount Galonte, afterwards to St. Bernard of Rumaux, then by Valence, afterwards by Ariola, after that to Valois, thence to St. Paul of Provence; we afterwards passed through Mount Drague and Orange, and then crossing Mount Sorgre, we came to Dompas, near Avignon, then by Tenaiz, then by Salus and Marignan near the sea, and thence to Marseilles, where we stayed three weeks; then we embarked the day after the Assumption of the Blessed Virgin Mary, in the first year of King Richard's coronation, and passed between two islands, of which Sardinia, one of them, was on our right, Corsica, the other, on our left here there is a great strait of the sea. We then passed between two burning mountains, one called Yulcano, the other Strango, and by Farus, a very perilous stream, and then arrived at the city of Messina, where the fleet of King Richard lay, which he sent forward, as we have said before.

CHAPTER XI - *Of the city of Messina, and of the queen, sister to King Richard, and of her dowry from Tancred*

You must know that the city of Messina is filled with abundance of good things; its situation is pleasant and very agreeable; it lies on the confines of Sicily and Rasa, which was said to have been given to the famous Agoland, for his services. Thus the city of Messina stands the first in Sicily for affluence and wealth; but its inhabitants are a wicked and cruel race. Their king, Tancred, was very rich in every kind of wealth, which his predecessors, from the time of Robert Guiscard, had amassed. At the same time, the queen of Apulia, having lost her husband, William, was staying at Palermo; for King William had died without an heir, and his queen with her dowry was in ward of the same King Tancred, who had succeeded King William on the throne. This dowager queen was sister to Richard, king of England, who taking up her cause, forced King Tancred to give condign satisfaction, over and above the dowry that was due to her.

CHAPTER XII - *Of the injuries which the Griffons at Messina did to our men before the arrival of King Richard*

The noble fleet of the king of England, as we have said before, waited here the arrival of their sovereign,—a fleet wonderful for its numbers, complement, and the splendor of its array, and the like of which none was ever seen fitted out with such labor, and so numerous, besides the various classes of men that belonged to it, stationed on the shore in pavilions and tents of different forms; for they kept apart from the city, until the arrival of King Richard, on account of the overbearing insolence of its citizens. For this wicked people, commonly called Griffons, many of whom are of Saracen extraction, hostile to our men, annoyed them by repeated insults, by pointing their fingers into their eyes, and calling them stinking dogs, and mocking them in many other ways, privately killing some of them, and throwing others into the sewers, of which crime many of them were afterwards convicted. In this manner they upbraided our men, and showed their hatred by doing them every ill turn they dared and if our men attempted to resist, or retaliate, they threatened to drive them entirely from their city, being strangers, and no match for them in numbers or strength but the citizens acted in this without foresight, for they forgot that their king was coming.

CHAPTER XIII - *With what show, first the king of France, then the king of England, arrived in Messina*

It is a general custom, that when any particular king or prince of the earth, conspicuous for his glory, might, and authority, comes forth in public, his appearance of power shall not fall short of that with which he is actually invested, —nay, it is but right and becoming that the greatness of a king should be shown in his display and the homage which is paid him for a common proverb says, "Such as I see you are, I esteem you." Moreover the general style and manner is taken from the disposition of the chief. When, therefore, the king of France, of so high renown, whose edict so many princes and nations obeyed, was known to be entering the port of Messina, the natives, of every age and sex, rushed forth to see so famous a king ; but he, content with a single ship, as if to avoid the sight of men, entered the port of the citadel privately, while those who awaited him along the shore conceived this to be a proof of his weakness, and spoke upbraidingly of him as one not likely to be the performer of any great actions who thus slunk from the eye of man and being frustrated in their hopes of seeing him, they returned indignant to their homes. But when the report was spread of the arrival of the noble-minded king of England, the people rushed out eagerly to behold him, crowding along the shore and seating themselves wherever they were likely to catch a glimpse of him. And lo! They beheld the sea in the distance covered with innumerable galleys and the sound of trumpets and clarions, loud and shrill, strike upon the ear! Then, as they approached nearer, they saw the galleys as they were impelled onward, laden and adorned with arms of all kinds; their pennons and standards floating in countless numbers in the breeze in good order and on the tops of their spears; the prow of the galleys distinguished from each other by the variety of the paintings, with shields glittering in the sun, and you might behold the sea boiling from the number of oarsmen who plied it, and the ears of the spectators rang with the peals of the instruments commonly called trumpets, and their delight was aroused by the approach of the varied crowd, when to the magnificent king, accompanied by the crowd of obedient galleys, standing on a prow more elevated and ornamental than the others, as if to see what he had not seen before, or to be seen by the crowds that densely thronged the shore, lands in a splendid dress, where the sailors whom he had sent before him, and others of his equipage, receive him with congratulations, and bring forward the chargers and horses which had been committed to their care for transportation, that he and his suite might mount. The native crowd round him on all sides, mixed with his own men, and followed him to his hostel. The common people conversed with each other in admiration of his great glory and agreed that he was worthy of empire, and deserved to be set over nations and kingdoms, "for the fame of him which we had before heard fell far short of the truth when we saw him." Meanwhile the trumpets blew, and their sounds being harmoniously blended, there arose a kind of discordant concord of notes, whilst the sameness of the sounds being continued, the one followed the other in mutual succession, and the notes which had been lowered were again resounded.

CHAPTER XIV - *What injuries our men suffered at Messina at the hands of the Lombards*

"When the Griffons saw the kings land in such strength, their arrogance was in part checked, for they perceived that they were their inferiors in valor and appearance; but the Lombards ceased not contumaciously to menace and revile our men and to provoke them by insults, threatening even to attack our camp, to slay us and plunder our goods. They were excited by jealousy on account of their wives, with whom some of our men had talked, more for the purpose of irritating their husbands than with the intention of seducing them. From this quarrel and through envy, the Lombards were aroused, together with the commune of the city, and were always hostile to us as far as they could, chiefly because they had learnt from their ancestors that they had been subdued by us of yore whence they did them as much annoyance as they could, at the same time heightening the battlements of their towers, and deepening the fosses that surrounded them. To irritate our men still more, they provoked them by repeated revilings and insulted them with contumelies.

CHAPTER XV - *How, owing to a loaf of bread which was sold by a woman a fight took place between us and the Lombards*

By chance one day it happened that one of our men was bargaining with a woman about a new loaf which she offered for sale and while they were conversing together and he threatened to have the loaf weighed, the woman, because he would not give her the price she asked, flew into a great passion and insulted him with contumelious and wicked language, and scarcely restrained her hands from striking him or tearing his hair. Immediately a concourse of the citizens flocked together at the noise of the abusive woman, who seized hold of the man and beat him unmercifully and after tearing out his hair and injuring him in many other ways, they trod him under foot and left him for dead. When complaint was made, King Richard begged for peace and friendship, asserting that he had come in peace, and that he had set out merely to perform a pilgrimage and he desisted not from praying for peace, until each party, having given a promise to that effect, returned quietly to their abodes.

CHAPTER XVI - *How the Lombards attacked King Richard's men, and how King Richard besieged, assaulted, and stormed the city, and raised his standard on the towers, which gave umbrage to the king of France, who was preparing to assist the Lombards*

But by means of that old enemy of the human race, whose part it is to disturb peace and excite sedition, the dispute was renewed on the morrow, so that a more destructive altercation arose between the citizens and the pilgrims. Meanwhile the two kings had a conference with the justiciaries of Sicily and the chief citizens, to treat of peace and security when behold, a cry arose that the natives were already slaying the men of the king of England; which when the king minded not, chiefly because the Lombards asserted that it was not true, there came a second messenger announcing that the natives had attacked the pilgrims. The Lombards, who had been in the same conflict, persuading him that it was not so, thought to circumvent the king by falsehood when a third messenger rushed in headlong, exclaiming that such peace was not to be approved of when the sword was actually hanging over their necks. Then the king, hastening without delay from the said conference, mounted on horseback, and went out with the design of putting a stop to the quarrel and making peace between the wranglers. There were two Lombards, very cunning and deceitful, at whose instigation the mob of the city had been excited against the pilgrims; who, to conceal their craft by a lie, asserted that they had come thence, and that no harm had been done their names were Jordan Luppin and Margarit. When King Richard arrived at the spot, the two parties were already at blows, and strove no longer with words, but with fists and bludgeons and the Lombards now inflamed with rage, instead of yielding to the king's endeavors to separate the combatants, attacked him with contumelious and profane railings; whereupon he, irritated by their mockeries, took up arms, and besieged them in their city. The French, meanwhile, doubtful what their lord the king would do, ran about in search of him here and there; when they saw him come hastily from the place of conference and enter the palace in which he was lodged. There was a general commotion in the city; every one seized upon what came to hand, and they talked boastingly of defending themselves to the last. The Lombards went to the king of France to implore his aid and assistance, offering to give themselves and their property into his power and will, if he would relieve their city from the assaults of the king of England, and take it into his own subjection. The king of France immediately took up arms, and as we were told by one who knew the truth, answered that he would rather assist the Lombards than the men of the king of England, although he was bound to him by his oath, and had pledged his honor to give him aid and to be faithful to him everywhere. The gates of the city being closed and guards placed along the battlements, there arose a clamor, tumult, and commotion from the assaulters without; while those within ran to arms and seized whatever weapons fury supplied them with to defend themselves. The French having joined themselves with the Lombards, they were animated with one purpose, and acted together as one body. But those without knew not that their associates had thus become their adversaries. Some Lombards had gone out before the gates of the city were shut, to attack the hostel of Hugh le Brun, and obstinately persevered in fighting. The king of England, hearing of it, turned his course thither, and when they saw him coming, they took hastily to flight and were scattered in a moment, like sheep before wolves; after which, their attacks and revilings ceased. The king pursued them as far as a postern of the city, which they made for, not daring to look at, much less resist, him, though the king is said to have had only twenty men when he first attacked them. He slew some of them, however, as they entered the postern. The Lombards, now seeing that the attack had become serious, and that they were besieged in earnest, resisted with all their might, and occupying the battlements of the walls, they hurled down stones and javelins from bows and slings like showers of rain and impeded their assailants in every way they could, either to put an end to their assaults, or cause them to be less formidable; and thus at the commencement of their impetuous defense, they did much hurt to our men, killing some, bruising others, wounding and shattering the limbs of many; for by the shower of darts, javelins, and stones that were thrown at us, we lost, besides others, three knights, Peter Tireprete, and Matthew de Saulcy, and Radulph de Roverei. Indeed, if they had had the true faith of Christ in them, and a due regard for justice, they might have made a great slaughter of our men, and might have conquered by their numbers but their arrogance and dishonesty deservedly proved hurtful to them, who had wrought such injury without a cause for the number of the citizens and others who defended the city was said to exceed fifty thousand. You might there see men making most valorous attacks to force an entrance, some showering darts, and others assaulting the gates while our galleys from seaward occupied the port opposite the palace, and blockaded the city but the king of France hindered them from entering the port, and some were destroyed in the attempt. But, on the land side, where the king of England was, a man remarkable for his skill in arms, the attack was closely pressed some essayed to cut the fastenings of the gates, and not succeeding, they ascended a high hill, close by the city, and by means of a postern, which King Richard, on the second day of his arrival, when going round the walls to reconnoiter with two companions, had observed to be neglected by the citizens, they forced an entrance with great boldness and violence, and having broken down the gates, they admitted the rest of the army into the city. Then they slew or made captive all citizens they met who resisted them, and entered the city in a body and many, as well

Lombards as our men fell in that conflict. For the citizens, not daring to oppose us as we were now entering and occupying the city, threw down darts from the tops of houses and battlements of towers, and tried in every manner they could to annoy us from the solers, in which they had taken refuge. But our men now marched through the captured city as victors, preceded by King Richard, who was the first in every attack by his own daring example he at once gave courage to his own men, and carried dismay amongst the foe. About ten thousand men marched in after him, and plundered the whole city. There you might hear horrible clamors, in a variety of confused tones, on the one side, of our men, urging on the pursuit, on the other, of the flying Lombards, screaming for fear, while they redoubled their blows, and mowed down those who met them with their swords, like corn. When our men entered the houses, the Lombards threw themselves from the house-tops and the solers, rather than fall into the hands of their enemies; conscious that by their own inhospitality they had forfeited all claim to mercy. The city was now subdued by force, and no one appeared to make further resistance; what need we say more? King Richard captured Messina by one assault, in less time than a priest could chant the main service. Many more of the citizens would have fallen, had not King Richard, with an impulse of generosity, ordered their lives to be spared. But who could reckon the sum of money which the citizens lost? All the gold and silver, and whatsoever precious thing was found became the property of the victors. They also set fire to, and burnt to ashes, the enemy's galleys, lest they should escape, and recover strength to resist. The victors also carried off their noblest women. And long after this action had been performed, the French suddenly beheld the ensigns and standards of King Richard floating above the walls of the city at which the king of France was so mortified, that he conceived that hatred against King Richard which lasted during his life, and afterwards led him to the unjust invasion of Normandy.

CHAPTER XVII - *How the king of France being displeased that the standards of the king of England only should be placed on the city walls, King Richard, humbling himself, allowed the standards of both to be placed there together*

The king of France, jealous of the successes of the king of England, and mis liking his high spirit, very much grieved that he should not have the glory which the other had gained by the force of his own greatness for, contrary to the conditions of mutual agreement, and while the army was in the greatest danger, and a great slaughter going on before his eyes, he proffered not a helping hand to the king of England against an obstinate foe, as he was bound by the treaty of alliance. Nay, he resisted as much as he could, and kept him a long time from occupying the entrance of the city where he himself abode. The city being taken, as we said before, and the banners of King Richard planted on the walls, the king of France, by the advice of his council, sent orders to King Richard to take down his standards, and substitute those of France, as an acknowledgment of his superiority. King Richard, indignant at this command, considering what previously occurred, and bearing in mind the rights of their fellowship, sent no answer, lest he should seem to surrender his right, and the victory should be ascribed not only to one who had been inactive, but to a perjured adversary. At the intercession of mediators however, the anger of King Richard was at length appeased an end was put to their wrangling, and yielding to the soothings of his friends, with some difficulty, he, who was held invincible, being overcome by his foes, gave way to the request of the king of France, viz., that he should deliver into his custody the towers he had taken, and place in them guards of both nations, until they should learn the sentiments of King Tancred as to what had been done and he who remained angry and obdurate to threats and boastings was moved by prayers and soothing. The standards of both were, therefore, raised above the walls of the city, until he should try the consistency of the king of France, and proved his friendship.

CHAPTER XVIII - *How messengers were sent to King Tancred to demand satisfaction and the restoration of the queen's dowry, and how the king of France sends secretly a contrary message*

It was therefore decreed by common counsel that King Richard should send messengers to Tancred, king of Sicily, to require satisfaction for the enormous outrage committed by his people, and to ascertain his intentions in regard to what had occurred. Moreover, King Richard commanded King Tancred to give his sister, the queen of Sicily, a sufficient dowry, and the portion of the king her husband's treasure which belonged to her by right, as well as the table of gold, which ought to be equally shared with the wife of him who had possessed it. The duke of Burgundy and Robert de Sabloel, and some others, whose names are lost, were the messengers appointed for this business. Meanwhile, the king of France weighing in his mind the greatness of King Richard, and repining from envy began to raise a question about the plunder of the city, demanding his portion, according to the covenant they had entered into. Giving vent, therefore, to arrogant and contumelious speeches about these things, because King Richard sternly refused his demand, he ceased not to irritate his spirit to passion by sly insinuations and opprobrious taunts and he hesitated not to transgress the terras of the covenant which had been entered into between them, and to show the hollowness of his friendship. Whereupon King Richard, more from indignation than from any other feeling, determined to reject his friendship, and ordered his ships to be ready to depart with all their baggage for he had rather, under the guidance and direction of the Lord, proceed alone with his own men to the accomplishment of his pilgrimage, than have any dealings with an envious man according to the common proverb, "It is better to be alone than to have a bad companion." When, however, this was known to the king of France, the latter procured, by means of mediators, the renewal of their broken friendship and their association as before, with the condition that every thing which was gained hereafter should be equally divided.

CHAPTER XIX - *How King Tancred made an ambiguous reply, on which the king of England was inflamed with anger and how the Lombards refused his men provisions*

Meanwhile the messengers, in discharge of the business of their mission, inquired the sentiments of King Tancred on the matters in question. But the king replied in ambiguous terms, asserting that he would give satisfaction to the kings by advice of the nobles of the land in proper time, place, and manner, upon all the subjects specified. It was reported that the king of France had by letter exhorted King Tancred not to yield to the demands of the king of England, but to show himself firm in defending his right in every thing, with the assurance that he would not take part with King Richard against him, but would be faithful to him. If such a message was sent, there was an evidence of it something like the proverb; for King Tancred loaded the messengers of the king of France with presents, while he did not give those of the king of England so much as an egg. Therefore the messengers returned, and when they had reported their answer to the kings, King Richard replied, "There is no need of much talking or long speeches since King Tancred will not give satisfaction of his own accord, I will endeavor and labor my utmost to correct his faults myself." These quarrels restored the courage of the natives, who, incited by the king of France, endeavored to injure King Richard and his men as much as they could, and prohibited the supplying of provisions necessary for so great an army; and ordered that nothing should be exposed for sale, in order that they might thus be compelled to submit themselves to the power of the natives.

CHAPTER XX - *Of the construction of Mategriffin, and of the discord between the two kings*

King Richard had expended great labor and diligence in erecting a castle, to which he gave the name of Mategriffin at which the Griffons were very much exasperated, because this erection they saw was intended for their destruction. The building was now completed on the hill, close by the city, and very convenient for retreat. The army would have suffered much from want of provisions, which were forbidden to be exposed for sale, had they not used those which were brought by the fleet as provision against future wants. The enemy, therefore, did what harm and injury they could to our soldiers; they placed guards over the city by night and the army in their turn defended themselves from their attacks by keeping watch. Moreover, discord again took possession of the minds of the kings, and the king of France openly showed himself a favorer of the enemies of King Richard. But the great majority of the nobles were earnest for the renewal of peace, visiting at one time the palace, at another Mategriffin, to try and pacify their anger but their labor and endeavors were in vain, for each accused the other, and offered to prove that the other was the aggressor, and neither of them would yield to the other's will the king of France, unwilling to commit himself to the power of an inferior, and so derogate from his own dignity and King Richard, fearful that the acknowledgment of subjection might lessen the glory of his own deeds.

CHAPTER XXII - *How King Tancred made peace with King Richard, by giving him 40,000 ounces of gold as a dowry for the queen and the marriage of Arthur and how the two kings and the citizens made peace*

Thus matters fluctuated, when King Tancred considering that danger might arise from further discord, and perceiving that King Richard would not desist from his purpose until he had obtained what he wished, sent messengers of noble birth to offer peace, and beg for reconciliation, asserting — very appositely for persuading him—that he was unwilling, as far as lay in him, to bear the ill-will of so great a man, to the danger of his own people; that he was willing to purchase his alliance with money, and that he would give the queen, sister of King Richard, 20,000 ounces of gold for her dowry, and 20,000 ounces more as a marriage portion for a daughter of his own, a damsel of talent and beauty, to become the wife of his nephew, Arthur of Brittany, if he chose. King Richard, at the earnest request of the messengers on both sides, agreed, and the affair was concluded; the money, viz. 40,000 ounces of gold, was paid, and his sister, the queen, delivered up altogether to her brother s care. And thus, after peace had been agreed upon, and confirmed in writing, all controversy ceased entirely. So when King Richard saw that satisfaction had been given him, as he required, he ordered the money which had been received from King Tancred to be equally divided, and also the money which had been given as a dowry for his sister he divided in like manner, although he was not bound to do so but he did it from mere liberality, which redounded to his glory and praise, and relieved him in part from the hatred of his adversaries. Finally, by the advice of Walter, archbishop of Rouen, all who should not restore entire whatever silver or gold had been plundered from the city, were laid under an anathema. All things having thus been restored, and to outward appearance peace established, the citizens rejoiced in their safety, and the pilgrims in their tranquility; the condition of the city was thus rendered secure, and penal laws made against the disturbers of the peace. The citizens had free intercourse with the pilgrims, without either quarrelling or giving offence all rejoiced exceedingly and henceforth provisions, for both man and horse, were exposed for sale, at a very reasonable price. The friendship of the kings was also renewed, and by the intervention of justice, universal goodwill was restored. But though in outward appearance the king of France dissembled his feelings, the rivalry which had been once engendered continued immortal in his mind, and throwing a veil over his envy at the illustrious deeds of King Richard, he concealed the cunning of the fox beneath an unmoved exterior.

CHAPTER XXII - *How King Tancred and King Richard meet at the city of Fatina*

Meanwhile, King Tancred, who was residing at that time at Palermo, not a little astonished at the fame of the magnificence and glory of King Richard's deeds, sent ambassadors of noble birth to invite him to an interview at the city of Fatina. He very much desired to behold the face of the man whom he much admired for the report of his magnanimity and valor. Now the city of Fatina was situated midway between Messina and Palermo, and King Richard assenting, went to meet him at the appointed place, with a splendid company of his nobles. And when they had met according to appointment, each was exceedingly rejoiced at the arrival of the other, and strove to show every mutual civility, and they entered into a treaty of friendship by which they bound themselves to preserve peace between each other, and having exchanged gifts of royal magnificence, they concluded the ceremony in a becoming manner, and separated, King Tancred returning to Palermo, and King Richard to Messina.

CHAPTER XXIII - *How King Richard bestows most ample gifts on his soldiers and others who had been impoverished by his stay there*

Meanwhile, the soldiers, who had been at great expense during the summer while the aforesaid troubles and disturbances were going on, liked not so long, so idle, and so useless a delay. For they considered that their brethren in Christ were constantly engaged in contests at the siege of Acre, and that they had already spent the greater part of their substance, and had even been compelled to restore what they acquired by plundering the captured city. King Richard, being moved by the prevalence of complaints of this kind, with royal munificence bestowed gifts on all that needed it, beyond their expectation, so that each one was most sufficiently enriched according to his rank. The knights were amply relieved by these gifts, whether of gold or silver, or any other kind and even noble women of Palestine, who had been deprived of their inheritance and exiled, both widows and virgins, were bountifully enriched. King Richard thus obtained the gratitude and favor of all, for he gave the foot-soldiers and attendants of inferior rank a hundred sols at least. The king of France, also allured by his example, bestowed very many gifts on his own men. Hence fresh joy reigned among the people, and those who had been broken down by sorrow were raised up by such generous magnificence.

CHAPTER XXIV - *Of the great feast given by King Richard at Mategriffin on Christmas Day to which he invited the king of France and all his people, and of his splendid gifts*

The great festival of Christmas was at hand, kept with the greater solemnity as it was the more needful for the redemption of the human race. In honor of this festival, King Richard invited, with all respect, the king of France to dinner, and by the public crier called upon every soul to pass that day with him in joy and gladness. At his courteous request, the king of France came with an innumerable band of nobles, and a crowd of others. He labors not much who compels a willing person and we cannot suppose many were absent from King Richard's feast. They were, therefore, received with honor into the castle of Mategriffin, which he had built against the will of the natives, and where every one sat down according to his rank. Who could count the variety of dishes which were brought in, or the different kinds of cups, or the crowds of servants in splendid attire which, if any one wishes to do, let him measure in his mind the magnanimity of King Richard, and then he can understand the kind of feast which would be prepared. You might have seen there nothing unbecoming or inapposite—nothing which was not of value and commendable for the dishes and platters on which they were served were of no other material or substance than gold or silver, and all the vessels were of wrought gold or silver, with images of men and beasts worked thereon with the chisel or the file, and adorned with precious stones. Moreover, their joyous countenances were conspicuous above all, and gave grace to the festival and the guests were entertained with the cheerfulness of the entertainers over and above the variety and abundance of meat and drink. After the feast was at an end, King Richard set before the king of France the most beautiful cups, and gave him his choice in honor of the occasion, and gave to each of the nobles presents according to his rank; for like Titus, with whose hand he lavished his wealth, he thought that the day.

CHAPTER XXV - *How the Pisans and the Genoese attack the guards of King Richard's fleet*

It happened at that time that some Pisans and Genoese, heated with wine, and disturbed by some cause or other, attacked the guards of King Richard's fleet in a hostile manner, and from the vehement nature of their assault a great number were killed on both sides. On the morrow, as if grieving that they had not wrought their full malice the day before, they returned to the attack, and while they were fiercely engaged, King Richard came upon them hastily, and with difficulty restraining the combatants, forced them to separate.

CHAPTER XXVI - *Of the arrival of Queen Eleanor and Berengaria, the future wife of King Richard, and of the departure, first, of the king of France, and then of the king of England, for the Holy Land*

Therefore, in the year of our Lord 1191, with the dominical letter E, after the stormy months of the more idle season of winter, when brighter days were coming on, the people, who were wearied with slothful delay, hailed with joy the arrival of the season for navigation for the kings had stayed in the city of Messina from the feast of St. Michael until after Lent. They therefore held a conference about the transportation of their men, alleging the inconvenience of further delay, both on account of the presence of fine weather, and because their means would fail if spent in useless idleness, and because their friends at Acre were suffering from want of them, and they were grieved at having given them such tardy help. While, therefore, each was preparing to proceed on his journey, couriers arrived who informed Richard that his mother Eleanor was hastening after him, and having completed her journey, was close at hand and that she was bringing with her the noble damsel, daughter of the king of Navarre, named Berengaria, the intended wife of King Richard. A long time previous, while yet count of Poitou, he had been charmed by the graces of the damsel and her high birth, and felt a passion for her on which account her father, the king of Navarre, had committed her to the care of King Richard's mother to be carried to him, in order that he might marry her before crossing the sea as he intended. All rejoiced at their coming. Meanwhile the king of France, having made ready with all his equipment, taking advantage of a favorable wind, set out with all his fleet, on the Saturday after the Annunciation of the Blessed Virgin Mary and King Richard accompanied him some way in his galleys, with his noblest peers. But he himself was not ready to cross the sea, for he had not yet collected all his transport ships and he thought that they were not sufficiently provisioned moreover, he had heard that his mother was coming with the illustrious Berengaria. When, therefore, he had let the king of France go on his voyage in peace, crossing past the Faro he came to Risa, where he heard that the queen his mother and Berengaria were, and having taken them on board with great joy, he returned to Messina where having stayed a short time, he let his mother depart, and committed to her the care of his kingdom, together with Walter, archbishop of Rouen, as we have said before, a man of great virtue. And with them returned Guilbert de Gascuil, by whose treachery the king of France afterwards gained possession of the celebrated castle of Gisors, situated in a very strong position on the confines of France and Normandy, which had been committed to his safekeeping. But King Richard retained with him the aforesaid damsel, whom he was about to marry. Queen Eleanor returned by Bourges, and thence to Salerna, and thus to Normandy. But King Richard, having furnished himself with every thing necessary for the voyage, prepared, according to agreement, to follow after the king of France as quickly as he could and appointed Robert de Torneham to conduct and take care of the fleet. He sent forward his betrothed, with his sister the dowager queen of Sicily, in advance, in one of the ships which are commonly called dromons, keeping a course direct to the east; he had also placed some knights on board and a numerous retinue of servants, for their comfort and safekeeping. These kinds of vessels are slower than others, on account of their burthen, but of stronger make. The multitude of the galleys remained immoveable, until the king, having dined, on account of the annoyances which had happened, bade farewell, with all his army, to the natives, and was on the point of setting out and committing himself to favorable winds and the waves of the sea. Then the whole multitude of ships was launched into the sea, impelled by numerous oarsmen. The city of Messina might justly boast that so great a fleet had never in past ages quitted those shores and that they never will see there such a one again. Therefore, on the seventeenth day after the departure of the king of France, i. e. on the Wednesday after Palm Sunday, King Richard followed with a numerous fleet of ships, and passing amid the Faro with a fair breeze, some by sailing, some by rowing, they came out into the deep,—the dromons, however, keeping them in the rear as Richard had planned, in order that, as far as it was possible to avoid it, they should not part company, unless they were accidentally separated by the tides while the galleys purposely relaxed their speed and kept pace with the ships of burthen, to guard their multitude and protect the weaker.

CHAPTER XXVII - *Of the winds that were at one time calm, at another agitating the sea, and the dangers which King Richard sustained as far as Crete, and from Crete to Rhodes*

The wind all at once began to fall gradually, so that the fleet was compelled to remain motionless at anchor between Calabria and Mount Gibello but on the morrow, i. e. the day of the Lord's Supper, He who withdraws and sends forth the winds from his treasuries, sent us a wind which continued the whole day, not too strong, but impelling the fleet at a moderate speed but after that it abated altogether on the following night. But on Holy Friday, a contrary wind arising drove it back to the left, and the sea being very much agitated thereby, boiled up from the very depths, while the waves beat together, and the storm increased the roar of the dashing waves, and the ships creaking with the violence of the wind, struck all with no small terror, and from the excessive fury of the latter, all management of the ships was at an end for no pilot could steer them while tossing to and fro in such a manner. They were borne hither and thither their line was broken, and they went different ways. The crews committed themselves to the guidance of the Lord, despairing of earthly aid but as far as human weakness permitted, we determined to bear all things with patience, under the eye of our Savior, who on that day had suffered so undeserved a death for our sakes. And as the ships were tossed to and fro, and dispersed divers ways, men's stomachs began to feel a qualm, and were affected by a violent nausea and this feeling of sickness made them almost insensible to the dangers around but towards evening, it grew by degrees calm, and the fury of the winds and waves abated. A favorable wind now springing up, according to our wishes, and the sailors having recovered their strength and confidence, we strove to keep a direct course for our voyage. King Richard, unmoved amid this state of confusion, never ceased to animate those who were dispirited, and bid them take courage, and hope for better fortune; moreover he had as usual a very large wax-light in a lantern, hoisted aloft in his ship to give light to the rest of the fleet and direct them in their way. He had on board most experienced sailors, who did every thing which human art could do to oppose the fury of the winds. All, therefore, as far as they could, followed the light burning in the king's ship. The king remained stationary some time to collect his fleet, which congregated together by seeing the light, so that the king resembled a hen gathering together her chickens. After that, we started with a favorable wind, and sailed along, without obstacle or injury, on the Saturday of the Passover, as well as on the day of the festival, and until the following Wednesday. That day we came in sight of Crete, where the king put in to repose and collect his fleet. When the ships had come together, twenty five were found missing, at which the king was much grieved. Among the steep mountains of this island of Crete, is one raised above the others, like a lofty summit, which is called the Camel, which sailors acquainted with those seas say is exactly midway between Messina in Sicily, and Acre in Palestine. On the morrow, being Thursday, the king and all his army entered their ships when the wind began to rise stronger, and though favorable, was very vehement in impelling us forward, for we moved rapidly along, with sails swelled out and mast slightly bent, not unlike the flight of birds. The wind, which slackened not all night, at dawn of day drove our fleet violently upon the island of Rhodes there was no port, and the surf stretched along the shore; however, we enjoyed there our rest the better for having wished for it so earnestly, from that day until the following Monday, when we put in at Rhodes. Rhodes was anciently a very large city, not unlike Rome though its extent can scarcely be estimated, there are so many ruins of houses and portions of fallen towers still standing, and such wonderful remains of walls and buildings of admirable workmanship. There are also a few monasteries still remaining out of so many ancient edifices, for the most part deserted though formerly inhabited by such numerous societies of monks. The site of so great a city, though by time laid waste, proves the former existence of a large population but very few inhabitants were found there now who could sell us food. But as the king was indisposed, we tarried there a few days, during which he waited the arrival of the ships that had wandered out of their course and lost us, and the galleys which followed him. He made inquiries also about that cruel tyrant, emperor of Cyprus, who was wont to detain the pilgrims who put in at his port.

CHAPTER XXVIII - *Of the departure of King Richard from Rhodes, through the gulf, and of the arrival of the queen at Cyprus*

Having spent ten days at Rhodes, which is a very fertile and productive island, they went on board, and set out on their voyage on the 1st of May. They were borne on their course into that most dangerous place, called the Gulf of Satalia. There is a mighty strife of currents formed by the junction of four seas, struggled violently together, each dashing against and resisting the other. We were on the point of entering it, when low as if apprehensive of our safety a contrary current carried us back to the place from whence we had started. But in a short time, the wind, which in those parts is constantly shifting, drove us from behind back again into the gulf, with the more danger from its increased violence. Fearing the effects of its fury, we did all we could to guard against the dangers of the place, and pass over the waves that boiled and foamed around. The royal ship was always in advance, and when the king lifted his eyes, he saw beneath a calm sky, a very large ship of the sort called a buss (buza) bearing down, which was returning from Jerusalem. The king, therefore, speedily sent men to inquire for intelligence concerning the siege of Acre, from those who were in the ship who replied that the king of France had already arrived at Acre in safety, and was diligently employed in making machines, until the arrival of the king of England. The king of France had put into the port of Acre on the Saturday of Easter week, and was applying all his energies to the taking of the city. He had therefore caused petrariseto be erected, and placed near the tower Maledictum, as well as other machines for throwing down the walls, for the king of France lay on the side near to that tower. By means of filling up and treading in the trenches, and bringing machines and petrarioe for casting stones, the wall was in part broken down but not long afterwards, the machines were attacked and burnt to ashes by the exertions of the Turks. When King Richard heard all these things from the aforesaid sailors, the buss passed on its way, and he made all his arrangements in high spirits and as the wind was not fair, he beat about, and toiled much to master its uncertainty but the fleet, from the adverse gales, and the rising and falling of the waves, was forced back, and driven into the open sea. However, the buss from Lyons, in which the queens were, first put into the port of the city of Limozin, in the island of Cyprus though they did not come to the land, but dropped their anchors at some distance out at sea.

CHAPTER XXIX - *Of the many misfortunes which befel the Holy Land, especially through the emperor of Cyprus*

With what expiation do we deem the Holy Land to have been punished, or with what scourge smitten, or of what crime guilty, that so many adversaries should have resisted its succour, whereby assistance should have been so long deferred? Nay, it began to be believed that the cause of its redemption being so long delayed was the wickedness of its defenders and it is very evident by many proofs that the Divine aid was withheld in consequence of the iniquity of its inhabitants whence also it happened that the excellent soldiers of France, who were looked forward to as brave allies, were unseasonably taken away in the midst. For why need we speak of the death of the illustrious emperor of Germany, whose end sullied the glory of his former reign or who could relate the grief felt for the death of the once rich and glorious Henry, king of England? By his money, the city of Tyre was preserved, and by his wisdom and prudence it was hoped that the Holy Land would be recovered Lastly, what might we say of the decease of William, king of Sicily, who after he had made all the necessary preparations for his pilgrimage, and had oftentimes sent the wished-for aid, was cut off by sudden death, and closed his career? All these, and many other misfortunes, impeded the recovery of the Holy Land, and each of them was more than enough to injure the cause. But there was one thing above all others, we mean that which concerned the island of Cyprus, from which the land of Jerusalem used annually to gain no small profit but now, after shaking off the yoke of subjection, it disdained to give it any thing, by the direction of the tyrant of the island, who had usurped the imperial power. Most wicked of all bad men, and surpassing Judas in treachery and Guenelon in treason, he wantonly persecuted all who professed the Christian religion. He was said to be a friend of Saladin, and it was reported that they had drunk each other's blood, as a sign and testimony of mutual treaty, as if by the mingling of blood outwardly, they might become kinsmen in reality. This, too, was afterwards evident by certain proofs for the tyrant, gaining confidence by this step, and setting at nought the subjection which he owed, falsely usurped the name of emperor, and he was accustomed to seize upon every one who put into the island of his own accord, or was driven thereto by the violence of the wind, that he might extract a ransom from the rich, and force the poor to become slaves. When, therefore, he learnt that a strange fleet had arrived, he determined, according to his custom, to seize upon all who were on board, and, having plundered them of their money, to keep them captives.

CHAPTER XXX - *Of the shipwreck and misfortune of some of our men, and of their capture and imprisonment also of the attack they made and the victory they gained over the islanders of Cyprus*

On the vigil of St. Mark the Evangelist, a little before sunset, dark clouds covered the horizon, and the spirit of the storm rushed forth, and the violence of the wind disturbed the waters; some of our ships which had been dispersed by the shifting of the winds, while attempting to reach the island of Cyprus before his arrival, were driven by adverse waves and wind on the rocks and though the sailors used their utmost efforts to resist the wind that assailed them, three of the king's ships filled and went to pieces, and some of those on board were drowned but some who had by chance caught hold of the timbers of the ship, were by this means, and not without the greatest toil, from the tossing of the waves, cast on shore naked and penniless. Amongst those who were drowned was Roger, surnamed Mai us Catulus, the king's signet-bearer, and the signet was lost. But on the body being cast on shore by the tide, a man found the signet on him, and brought it to the army for sale and thus it was redeemed, and restored to the king. As to the sailors who were cast on shore, the inhabitants, under the garb of peace, hailed their coming with joy; and, as if to recruit them, introduced them into a certain fort close by and all those who put to shore in safety, the Griffons stripped of their arms, and conducted to the same place, asserting that if they entered in arms, they might appear to be spies, or to have intentions of attacking the island, and they would wait until they ascertained the will of the emperor. But our nobles compassionating the shipwrecked men who were detained in custody, sent them clothing and other necessaries. Also Stephen de Turnham, the king's steward and treasurer, sent them abundance of provisions, which, as they were brought to the entrance of the fort for the captives, were plundered by the Griffons and guards of the city. However they pacified them with specious language, and did not yet show their enmity openly, but they would not set them at liberty until the emperor had been informed of what had happened; meanwhile, they promised with crafty words to supply them with every thing necessary. They then convened the nobles of the land, and entered into counsel to keep captive as many of the pilgrims as they could by stratagem, and then slay them which when it became known to our men, they shut themselves up of their own accord in the fort, with the intention of defending themselves, and some of them were killed by the natives. Thus, considering that danger really threatened them, they chose to stand the hazard of a battle, rather than die of starvation by falling into the hands of the infidel persecutors of Christians. Therefore, when they had come forth from the fort and reached a certain plain, the natives began to surround and kill them but though unarmed, they resisted as much as they could, and effected not less slaughter than their adversaries, though they had only three bows to defend themselves with, which they had kept concealed from the natives. There was amongst them one Roger de Hardecurt, who, having found a mare and mounted her, rode down the crowd that opposed him and also William du Bois, a Norman, and a most skilful archer, scattered first these, then those, by casting darts and arrows at them incessantly. The soldiers who were yet on board, seeing this, came hastily with their arms to their succour and the Griffons, with their bows and slings, hindered them as much as they could from landing but by the protection of the Lord they sallied from their ships and came into port unhurt. At last, after the Griffons had been dispersed and were giving way, the pilgrims, coming out of the aforesaid fort, and defending themselves, came in the rear, and made their way to the port, where they found our men, who had disembarked from their ships, fighting with all their might against the Griffons who opposed them. Having thus formed a junction, they dispersed the Griffons, and gained the port of Limozin, in which was the buss of the two queens that had put in before the arrival of King Richard, as has been said before but owing to their ignorance of the state of the island, and from dread of the cruelty and treachery of the emperor, they had not disembarked.

CHAPTER XXXI - *Of the arrival of King Richard at Cyprus*

On the same day, towards evening, on which the pilgrims had made their exit from the aforesaid port, viz. on a Thursday, the emperor of Cyprus, who had been informed of their arrival, came to the city; and when the pilgrims made complaint of the injuries they had received, the emperor promised every kind of satisfaction, and agreed to restore the money taken from the shipwrecked men and they also obtained entrance and egress into and from the city of Limozin, on condition of a mutual exchange of four men as hostages. Meanwhile, the emperor gave orders that the warriors of all his empire should be assembled, and a mighty army formed. The day after his arrival, the emperor sent a crafty message to the two queens, bidding them put to shore for greater security, and go about as they pleased without fear of molestation or ill-treatment from his people and on their refusing, he sent them the next day, under pretence of paying them respect, bread and ram's flesh and wine from the vineyards of Cyprus, which are said to have no match for quality throughout the world. On the third day, also, he tried to circumvent and beguile them, by bland and deceptive messages, and on the other hand they were in a great state of perplexity, lest the emperor should make them prisoners, if they should listen to him, or else, if they obstinately refused, they must fear some violence for as yet nothing was known of the expected arrival of the king, or the good condition of his fleet; but they kept him in suspense by returning an ambiguous answer, saying, that on the morrow they would place themselves at his disposal. In expectation of the fulfillment of this promise, the emperor kept quiet; and while the queens were agitated by intense anxiety, and were questioning and conversing with each other, that same day, being Sunday, behold there appeared in the distance, like crows, on the foaming summit of the curling waters, two vessels, driven forwards and sailing swiftly towards them. And while the queens, and those with them, were in doubt as to what they were, some more ships were espied coming on, and directly after the whole fleet was seen, bearing down with rapid course to the port and conjecturing that it was the king's fleet, they were so much the more rejoiced that it had come to their succour, when they were despairing of their desolate position. And thus King Richard arrived by the guidance of the Lord, after many dangers overcome, in the port of Cyprus. Therefore, on the festival of St. John before the Latin Gate (May 6), King Richard put into the port of Limozin, with all his fleet, but did not go on shore.

CHAPTER XXXII - *How King Richard with his forces, routed the emperor with his forces, first by sea and then by land*

When the king learnt in what danger the shipwrecked men had been, and how they were plundered of their property, and all that had happened in the interim, he was exceedingly angry and on the morrow, being Monday, he sent two knights to the emperor, to ask satisfaction of him, in a peaceful manner, for the injuries received, and the money he had plundered, at his will. The emperor was very indignant at this demand, and just as though he himself had been the injured man, burst out into abusive language, saying, "Prunt, Sire," and declaring he had nothing to do with a king boasting, as he did, for the assumption of imperial authority, and wholly confiding in impunity from Heaven, he acted just as it pleased him. When the ambassadors brought back his answer, the king, irritated at the emperor s arrogance, his abusive reply, and the loss his own men had sustained, shouted out aloud, "To arms!" a command his men immediately obeyed. Therefore the king, having armed himself, proceeded, in the boats of the "Esneckars," with his soldiers, to seize on the port ; but the emperor, with a large army, surrounded it, and resisted their landing, and they blocked up the entrance to the port with every kind of bar and obstacle, taking the doors and windows from the houses, casks with hoops, benches and ladders, and long pieces of wood, placed crosswise; also, bucklers and shields, old galleys, abandoned vessels, dirty from being laid up, and every description of utensil, to prevent their coining on shore;—in a word, every thing portable of wood or stone that could be found in the city of Limozin, the Griffons piled upon the shore to oppose the assailants. Moreover, the emperor and his troops marched up and down the beach. Oh! How splendidly was the emperors host equipped! They had on costly armor, and very valuable and many colored garments, and rode on war-horses that champed the foaming bit, and beautiful mules; they marched to and fro, ready for battle, their numberless pennons and gorgeous banners floating in the breeze, to keep off those that were advancing, or to give them battle. As our men were endeavoring to reach the shore, they tried to frighten them by horrible shoutings, like growling dogs, and abused them as if they had been curs, and told them they were hastening after what it was impossible to accomplish. They also had some slingers and archers and five galleys on the shore, well armed, and filled with young men skilled in sea fights. Our troops, who were making for the port to seize upon it, blocked up as it was, seemed no match for the enemy, because they were exposed in small boats, and were also much fatigued by long tossing about on the sea, and besides, they were foot soldiers, burdened with their proper arms; the natives, on the contrary, were in their own country, and could do every thing at pleasure. So when our men approached in their boats, in order, they determined on coining to close quarters to drive off the slingers and archers in the galleys, and against them our archers and slingers directed their attacks and the Griffons, after losing a great many of their men, gave way, for they could not withstand the brunt of the battle. And when the arrows flew thickly, three or four at a time leaped out of the galleys into the sea, and dived under water, where they perished by knocking against each other in their attempts to seek refuge in flight. The galleys, therefore, being captured, and our boats come to shore, our slingers and archers, gaining courage by success, sent a shower of arrows, like rain, at those who were guarding the landing-place. The Griffons not able to stand the charge, retreated from the beach to firmer ground, while their arbalesters and ours kept constantly throwing darts, so that the sky was darkened, and the calmness of day seemed to grow into night from the shower of arrows, while the whole city swarmed with men, and the neighborhood was filled with a multitude of men plying their engines. It was a long time doubtful on which side the victory lay, or which party was superior for our troops, though they strove with all their strength, did not make progress. The king, perceiving that his men were not daring enough to get out of their boats, and make for the shore, leaped first from his barge into the water, and boldly attacked the Griffons and then our soldiers, imitating his example, eagerly sought to put the enemy to flight and having made an impression on their troops, forced them to give way. Then you might see a shower of flying darts, and the Greeks cut down and you might hear the murmurs of the combatants, the groans of the dying, and the yells of the retreating. Then, also, our men in a body, mowing down the Greeks as they fled in confusion, drove them first into the city and from thence to the plains beyond. The king, pushing on in pursuit of the emperor, found a common horse, upon which he speedily vaulted by the aid of a lance, placed behind the saddle, and rode on with cords for stirrups. The king thus hastily pressed after the emperor, crying out, "My lord the emperor, I challenge you to single combat;" but, as though he were deaf, he fled swiftly away. The king, having thus taken the city, caused the two queens to be landed from the buss and lodged in Limozin, where, after the fatigues and perils of their voyage, they recruited themselves in security.

CHAPTER XXXIII - *Further of the fight between the king and the emperor, and of the victory of the king and the flight of the emperor to Nicosia*

The same night the king lodged in his pavilion, and caused his horses to be landed by the Esneckars. But the emperor, not thinking he had any horses, feared him the less, and passed the night encamped within a distance of two leagues. On the morrow, about two o'clock, the king mounted his horse, and discovered some Greeks standing not far off in an olive-yard with their gorgeous banners, and on their taking to flight, he pursued them. But forasmuch as our horses had been injured by being tossed about on the sea, standing for a whole month, our men spared them and went at a moderate pace, until they saw the army of the emperor, which had spent the night in a valley, and then they stopped in their pursuit. The Greeks, crying out with a horrible clamor, began to insult our men; on which the emperor, aroused from his sleep, mounted his horse, and marched with his men towards ours gradually, as far as a neighboring hill, where he took his station to overlook the engagement. The Greeks making use only of their bows and slings cried out that our men were immoveable. Then there came to the king a certain clerk, by name Hugo de Mara, in arms, and said to the king, "My lord the king, it appears to be a wise plan to decline for a time so large and so powerful a multitude." To whom the king answered, "Sir clerk as for our profession, you had better employ yourself in writing, and leave war to us, and take good care to keep out of the crowd." Others likewise dissuaded the king from fighting against so mighty a host indeed he had not with him at that time more than fifty men but taking courage from the enemy's wavering, he put spurs to his horse, and was suddenly carried against the enemy, and piercing through their line, scattered them, and attacking first one and then the other, he instantly dispersed them. For when their army perceived that their adversaries were collecting together, their valor gave way, and they took to flight those who had swift and nimble horses escaped, but the foot-soldiers and common people, who were less fitted for flight, were slain in all directions without distinction, and could not fly further, on account of the arrival of the king. And while the emperor was encouraging and animating his men to fight, the king coming suddenly upon him at full speed, knocked him off his horse with his lance but he quickly procured another, and escaped in the crowd some of his companions, however, were lost. Oh! How many noble horses might you have seen slain there, and coats of mail, and helmets, and swords, and lances, and pennons fallen down, and standards of various shapes, and the bodies of dead men weltering in their blood, and some yet breathing their last, in countless numbers. The emperor, perceiving the boldness of our men, and the flight of his own, and not forgetting his spurs which he saw were the only thing that remained, fled with the utmost swiftness to the mountains. The king struck down his banner-bearer, and gave orders that the splendid and beautiful banner should be kept for him. Then our horsemen pursued the fugitives as fast as they could for two miles; after which, coming back at a moderate pace, they quietly returned. The people then turning to the booty took much spoil, viz. arms, and costly woven vestments, and the tent of the emperor, with all the vessels of gold and silver which were found therein, and all his splendid apparel and household stuff: besides coats of mail, helmets, choice swords horses and mules, and also very much plunder in sheep and cattle, and goats, noble mares and mules, swine, fowls, and hens; and they also found choice wines and provisions of all sorts, and carried off a host of captives so that from the immense quantity of plunder they became fastidious—in a word, every mind was satiated with booty, nor would they regard any thing that was precious when offered them, for they were amply laden. After these things were done, the king proclaimed an edict by herald that whoever of the inhabitants was disposed for peace, might go and return as they liked without harm from his men, and enjoy perfect liberty but that whoever held the king as an enemy, should take care not to fall into his hands, or those of the army, for he would certainly treat him as a foe, and that he would prove himself such as they stood to him. By these means the emperor lost very many of his men, who constantly deserted him. At last he betook himself to a very strong fort called Nicosia, in confusion and sorrow at having failed in his intentions.

CHAPTER XXXIV - *Of the arrival of King Guy at Cyprus*

On the following Saturday three galleys bore in sight, and all doubted what they could mean, or whence they came. The king, always prompt, not to say venturous, embarked in a small vessel impelled with oars, and went to meet them and inquire who the comers were and whence they came and on their answering that it was Guy de Lusignan, the king returned quickly and ordered supper to be immediately prepared for the guests that were coming. And when King Guy landed, he received him with the greatest respect, and entertained him most cordially. King Guy had come to King Richard to ask his advice and assistance against the king of France, who had planned that the marquis, of whom we have before spoken, should be made king of Jerusalem, and Guy be deposed. Then King Richard welcomed him kindly, and honored him with gifts, because he was poor and destitute of means for he gave him two thousand marks of silver and twenty cups of the value of a hundred and five marks, of which two were of the purest gold.

CHAPTER XXXV - *Of the nuptials of King Richard and Berengariay and of the arrival of the king's galleys*

On the morrow, viz. on the Sunday, which was the festival of St. Pancras, the marriage of King Richard and Berengaria, the daughter of the king of Navarre, was solemnized at Limozin she was a damsel of the greatest prudence and most accomplished manners, and there she was crowned queen. There were present at the ceremony the archbishop, and the bishop of Evreux, and the bishop of Baneria, and many other chiefs and nobles. The king was glorious on this happy occasion, and cheerful to all, and showed himself very jocose and affable. The nuptials having been solemnly celebrated in a royal manner, one day all the king's galleys, which had been anxiously looked for, arrived in port they were equipped and defended with splendid armories, and no one ever saw better or safer ships; and he added to them the five galleys which he had taken from the emperor. The king had thus forty armed galleys and sixty others of a very good quality.

CHAPTER XXXVI - *Of the conference and the manner of making peace between the king and the emperor*

The king, elated with success, thought that fortune smiled upon him he therefore exhorted his soldiers to expedition, and commanded them to get every thing in readiness, lest the emperor should make a sudden attack upon them and he caused watches to be kept, and appointed sentinels to guard the army. The king proposed with his army to pursue the emperor wherever he was, and so take him by force or induce him to surrender; but by the mediation and earnest request of the masters of the Hospitallers of Jerusalem, it was determined that a conference should be held between the king and the emperor, who greatly lamented the loss of his men, and that he had been forced to fly in a shameful manner to Nicosia from the face of the king and he feared pursuit the more, because the natives detested him, and he could not, therefore, trust to their assistance. Wherefore, having called together as many as he could, the king proceeded to a very large plain, between the sea and the highway, close by the city of Limozin. He was mounted on a Spanish charger, of high mettle, of large size and elegant shape, with high shoulder and pointed ears; his neck was long and slender, and his thighs faultless; his feet were broad, and his limbs so perfectly marked, that a painter could not have imitated them with perfect accuracy. As if preparing himself for a swifter movement, he disdained to be checked by his golden curb, and by the alternate change of his feet he seemed at one time to move forward on his hind, at another on his fore legs. The king bounded into his saddle glittering with gold spangles interspersed with red, while on the hinder part two small lions of gold were turned towards each other, with their mouths open, and one pointed to the other on each of the fore legs, as if stretched out to devour. The king's feet were decorated with golden spurs, and he was clothed in a vest of rose-colored stuff, ornamented with rows of crescents of solid silver, like orbs of the sun shining in thick profusion. The king thus appareled rode forward, girded with a sword of proved metal with a handle of gold and a woven belt, and the mouth of the scabbard was fastened with silver on his head he wore a hat of scarlet, ornamented with the shapes of various birds and beasts worked with the hand, and sown in with or fray-work by the needle. He carried a staff in his hand, and the manner of his bearing it proved him to be a soldier of the highest order, and afforded the greatest gratification to all who saw him. After many proposals from both sides, between the king and the emperor, the emperor offered to swear fidelity to him in every thing, and that he would send five hundred knights to the land of Jerusalem, for the service of God, to be at the disposal and command of King Richard; and in addition to all these things, in order that he might fully satisfy the king and leave no doubt on his mind, he offered to place all his castles and forts in the hands of the king's guards, and he gave besides three thousand five hundred marks as satisfaction to those who had lost their money, or had it plundered and if the king, according to the agreement between them, should think that he and his men fought faithfully, the emperor should have his territory with his castles and forts restored to him; the friendship between them remaining the same as heretofore. And when the king referred this offer to his friends for examination, to see whether there was any thing derogatory to the king's honor by such an agreement, and whether all were satisfied with it, they answered that it was in every respect to the king's honor, and that they were perfectly satisfied with it. And after the king had heard this, the emperor immediately aware to observe faithfully all the aforesaid conditions to the king and having exchanged the kiss of peace, they made an alliance in the manner described. The king, returning from the conference, which had been broken up, immediately sent to the emperor his pavilion, which he had captured in the aforesaid battle, as a pledge of peace and friendship; he sent, besides, the vessels which had been plundered from it, and the emperor caused tents to be erected forthwith on the spot where the abovementioned conference took place.

CHAPTER XXXVII - *Of the flight of the emperor by night through Famagusta as far as Candosia, and of the capture of Nicosia*

On the following night, at the suggestion of a treacherous knight named Pain de Caiffa, the emperor, trusting to the darkness, fled away with all speed on a valuable and favorite horse, for the knight told him that King Richard intended to seize upon him that night, and throw him in chains and the emperor, frightened thereat, escaped to his city of Famagusta, leaving behind him his tents and chargers, and all his household stuff. On hearing which, King Richard commenced a pursuit after him, with his galleys, accusing him of perjury and the violation of his word, and he entrusted to King Guy the conduct of his army by land to Famagusta, where he arrived on the third day, and found it deserted, for the emperor, convinced that it would not be safe for him to stand a siege, concealed himself in the woods, where access was difficult, that, if our men should venture to pass through, he might attack them from an ambuscade. The king, on arriving at Famagusta, gave orders that the ports of the sea should be most strictly watched by his galleys, in order that he might take the emperor prisoner, if he attempted to escape. And, after staying there three days, there came as ambassadors, the bishop of Beauvais, and Drogo de Mirle, a nobleman of high renown, to exhort him to cross the sea without delay, and to assure him that the king of France would not proceed to the assault of Acre before his arrival and they added words of rebuke, that he had neglected necessary matters, and expended his endeavors on vain duties, and was presumptuously persecuting innocence Christians, when so many thousand Saracens were to be attacked in the land adjoining, for whom, even his valor, although so mighty, would be no match on trial. To this message, the king replied in angry terms, by no means suitable for insertion here but their labor was in vain, although they used every argument to dissuade him from his purpose, for he was busy enough in attacking and pursuing the Greeks as they deserved, as it appeared to be of the greatest consequence to subdue an island so necessary to the land of Jerusalem. Paying no attention to the messengers, he advanced to Nicosia, whither each had brought the provisions necessary for himself, as it was a desert place; they moved forward in order of battle, for they had learnt that the emperor intended to lie in ambush 'for them. The king marched in the rear, to guard against attacks, when on a sudden, the emperor burst from his hiding-place, and assailed them with about seven hundred Greeks. Their arbalesters exerted all their ability to throw their darts against the foremost of our men but not even thus did our troops suffer themselves to be broken, for they kept together in good order, while the emperor advancing on the flank to reconnoiter, bore down upon them pell-mell, with a view either to break up our lines, or to find out and shoot the king and when he found that the king was in the rear, he shot two poisoned arrows at him, which inflamed the king to a pitch of anger, and putting spurs to his horse, he bore down on the emperor, with the intention of striking him with his lance but the emperor evaded him, and fled as swiftly as possible to his aforesaid fort of Candaira, in exceeding dismay and confusion, because he had not succeeded according to his wishes; and the king did not pursue him far, for he doubted of taking him ; for he had a bay horse of such swiftness and perseverance in running, that no one ever saw his match for speed. Then the king marched towards Nicosia, with his army, and an immense booty of noble horses and men, which had been taken in the encounter and the citizens of Nicosia came forth in a body, to congratulate him, and admitted him as if he had been their lord and the king received them in peace, and caused their beards to be shaved in token of their change of masters. The emperor, on hearing this, in his fury, caused them to seize upon every one of our men that they could, and they plucked out their eyes, or cut off their noses, or mutilated their arms or legs, to satisfy his revenge and soothe his grief. The king exacted homage of the Greek nobles, who appeared to throw off the emperor's yoke with joy and feeling himself somewhat afflicted with sickness, he tarried there to rest and recruit himself.

CHAPTER XXXVIII - *Of the capture of the three forts, in one of which was the emperor's daughter and treasure*

With the army, which had been divided into three parts by the king, King Guy laid siege to the three forts, Cherimes, Didimus, and Butphenens; the two first he quickly gained possession of; for, with the help of a guide who knew the ways and the places of difficult access, the army, approaching the fort of Cherimes by land and by sea, assaulted it instantly; and they who were in it, not expecting any aid, surrendered the fort, in which were found the emperors daughter, and his treasure. When the emperor heard of his loss, he was so overwhelmed with grief, that it nearly drove him mad. King Guy, having hoisted the banners of King Richard on the battlements of the fort, proceeded to attack the second fort, called Didimus, very strong by situation, and exposed to attack on no side; and those who were shut up therein prepared to defend themselves, and for some days kept throwing stones and darts at the besiegers, until they were commanded by the emperor to give it up and in it the king placed the emperor's daughter, to prevent her being recaptured. From thence King Guy returned to the army at Nicosia, where King Richard, as has been afore said, lay sick and immediately on his recovery, he attacked and stormed the fort of Bufferentum, which had hitherto been deemed impregnable.

CHAPTER XXXIX - *How the emperor came from Candaira to Nicosia, and prostrating himself at the feet of King Richard, surrendered Cyprus to his power*

O mighty wealth of the emperor land, rich in every good thing! O forts, most strong by position that was given up, which could never have been stormed by the machines of any enemy, unless obtained by treachery or famine! The emperor considering that he was pressed by misfortune enough ; that his daughter, on whom his life hung, had been taken captive and that his forts had been either seized upon or surrendered, and his people alienated from him and that he was only tolerated, not beloved by his men; perceiving also, that there was no hope of resistance left, he determined that, although a foe, he would sue for peace and mercy. He therefore sent ambassadors to King Richard, to plead his cause and in order to incline Richard to feel kindness for him, he followed them in sad attire, and with a dejected countenance and coming into the presence of King Richard, he fell on his knees in humiliation before him, saying that he submitted himself entirely to his mercy, and that he had neither territory nor fort left but that he would consider him lord of every thing else, if only he would not throw him into iron chains. The king, moved with pity, raised him up, and made him sit beside him ; he also had his daughter brought to him, and when he saw her, he was wonderfully overjoyed, and embracing her most affectionately, covered her with kisses, while the tears started from his eyes. This took place on the Friday after the feast of St. Augustine, and before Pentecost. And the king threw the emperor not into iron chains, but silver ones.

CHAPTER XL - *How, after that the king had subjugated Cyprus and set it in order, he made preparations for his voyage, and sent his army to Limozin*

Thus the king gained possession of Cyprus in fifteen days and gave it to his men to inhabit. He found all the towers fortified, and the forts filled with much treasure and various riches, in golden cups, and vases, and plates also in silver jars, and caldrons, and casks of a large size; with saddles, bits, and spurs of gold; and a large quantity of precious stones, of great value. He also found robes of scarlet and woven cloths, of beautiful pattern, and very costly. Why need we say more? Whatever different kinds of wealth Croesus is said to have possessed, King Richard found that the emperor had amassed and being necessary for his expedition, he took possession of them as if they had been prepared for him; for it is scarcely possible that means should fail the man who is rich in courage, or abundance attend on one who is poor in spirit. Having done all these things, King Richard sent back his army to the city of Limozin, where the queens were, and the domestics, with the baggage and he gave them orders to give their whole attention to the repair of the fleet, for crossing the sea. He committed the emperor to the custody of King Guy, and his young little daughter he delivered to his queen, to bring her up and educate her.

CHAPTER XLI - *How, while the fleet of King Richard was sailing towards Acre, a very large Saracen ship bore in sight and how the king immediately attacked it, and took it*

Having concluded these operations, the king gave his attention to the immediate crossing of the sea, and when they had placed the baggage on board, a favorable wind blowing, the fleet set sail from the shore and the queens moved forward in company with the king in person. The king had left in Cyprus brave and diligent men to secure a supply of necessary provisions hereafter; viz. wheat, corn, and barley meat and live stock of various kinds, which abound in that island.

By this time a report was spread that Acre was on the point of being taken, and when the king heard it, he sighed deeply and said, "May God defer the taking of Acre till I come, after it has been so long besieged, and therefore the triumph will be the more glorious with the assistance of God." Then getting ready with all speed, he went on board one of his largest and swiftest galleys, at Famagusta and as was his wont, he moved forward in advance, impatient of delay, while the other ships followed in his wake as quickly as they could, and well prepared, for there is no power that might not justly have dreaded their hostility. As they ploughed across the sea, the holy land of Jerusalem was descried for the first time, the fort called Margat being the first spot that met the eye; afterwards Tortuosa, situated on the sea-shore; then Tripolis, Nephyn, and Bocion. And soon after appeared the lofty tower of Gibelath. Lastly, on this side of Sidon, opposite Baruth, there bore in sight a vessel filled with Saracens, chosen from all the Pagan empire and destined by Saladin for the assistance of the besieged in Acre. They were not able to obtain a speedy entrance into the port, because of the Christian army that menaced them, and so were waiting a favorable moment for entering the port by surprise. The king, observing the ship, recalled Peter des Barres, commander of one of his galleys, and ordered him to row quickly, and inquire who commanded the vessel. And when they answered that it belonged to the king of France, the king in his eager haste approached it; but it had no mark of being French, neither did it bear any Christian symbol or standard; and on looking at it near, the king began to wonder at its immense size and compact make, for it was crowned with three tall masts, and its sides were marked with streaks of red and yellow, and it was well furnished in all manner of equipments, so that nothing could exceed them, and it was abundantly supplied with all kinds of provisions. One of those on board said, that while at Baruth, he saw the vessel laden with all these things; viz. one hundred camel-loads of arms, slings, bows, darts, and arrows it had also on board seven Saracen admirals, and eighty chosen Turks, besides a quantity of all kinds of provisions, exceeding computation. They had also on board a large quantity of Greek fire, in bottles, and two hundred most deadly serpents for the destruction of the Christians. Others were therefore sent to obtain more exact information who they were, and when, instead of their former answer, they replied that they were Genoese, bound for Tyre, our men began to doubt the truth at this change of reply one of our galleymen persisted that they were Saracens, and on the king's questioning him, he said, "I give you leave to cut off my head, or hang me on a tree, if I do not prove these men to be Saracens. Now let a galley be sent quickly after them, for they are making away, and let no kind of salute be given them by us, and in this way we shall have certain proof what their intention is, and how far they are to be believed." At the king's command, therefore, a galley was went at full speed after them and on reaching their ship, and rowing by its side without giving a salute, they began to throw darts and arrows at our men. On seeing this, the king ordered the ship to be attacked forthwith, and after casting a shower of darts against each other, the ship relaxed in its speed, for the wind carried it but slowly along. Though our galleymen rowed repeatedly round the ship, to scrutinize the vessel, they could find no point of attack it appeared so solid and so compact, and of such strong materials; and it was defended by a guard of warriors, who kept throwing darts at them. Our men, therefore, relished not the darts, nor the great height of the ship, for it was enough to strive against a foe on equal ground, whereas a dart thrown from above always tells upon those below, since its iron point falls downwards. Hence, their ardour relaxed, but the spirit of the king increased, and he exclaimed aloud, "Will you allow the ship to get away untouched and uninjured? Shame upon you are you grown cowards from sloth, after so many triumphs? The whole world knows that you engaged in the service of the Cross, and you will have to undergo the severest punishment, if you permit an enemy to escape while he lives, and is thrown in your way." Our men, therefore, making a virtue of necessity, plunged eagerly into the water under the ship's side, and bound the rudder with ropes to turn and retard its progress, and some, catching hold of the cables, leapt on board the ship. The Turks receiving them manfully cut them to pieces as they came on board, and lopping off the head of this one, and the hands of that, and the arms of another, cast their bodies into the sea. Our men seeing this, and glowing with anger, gained fresh courage from the thirst for vengeance, and crossing over the bulwarks of the vessel, attacked the Turks in a body with great fierceness, who, though giving way a little, made an obstinate resistance. The Turks gathering boldness from despair, used all their efforts to repel those who threatened them, cutting off the arms, hands, and even heads of our men but they, after a mighty struggle, drove the Turks back as far as the prow of the ship, while from the interior others rushed upon our men in a body, preparing to die bravely or repel the foe; they were the choice youth of the Turks, fitted for war, and suitably armed. The battle lasted a long time, and many fell on both sides but at last, the Turks, pressing boldly on our men, drove them back, though they resisted with all their might, and forced them from the ship. Upon which our men retired to their galleys, and surrounding the vessel of all sides, tried to find a easier mode of attacking it. The king seeing the danger his men were in, and that while the ship was uninjured it would not be easy to take the Turks with the arms and provisions therein, commanded that each of the galleys should attack the ship with its spur, i.e. its iron beak. Then the galleys drawing back, were borne by rapid strokes of the oar against the ship's sides to pierce them, and thus the vessel was instantly broken, and becoming pervious to the waves, began to sink. When the Turks saw it, they leapt into the sea to die, and our men killed some of them and drowned the rest. The king kept thirty-five alive, namely, the admirals and men who were skilled in making machines, but the rest perished, the arms were abandoned, and the serpents sunk and scattered about by the waves of the sea. If that ship had arrived safely at the siege of Acre, the Christians would never have taken the city; but by the care of God it was converted into the destruction of the infidels, and the aid of the Christians, who hoped in Him, by means of King Richard, who by His help prospered in war. The Saracens saw from a distance on the heights what had happened, and sorrowfully carried the news to Saladin, who, on hearing it, seized and plucked out his beard in anger and fury, and afterwards broke out into these words with a sigh, "O God! have I lost Acre, and my dear and chosen soldiers, in whom I had so much confidence? I am overwhelmed by so bitter a loss." When they who saw it told the tidings to the Saracenic army, there arose long and loud wailings, and bitter lamentations for their misfortune, and they cut off the tresses of their hair, and rent their garments, and cursed the hour and the fate of the stars, by which they had come to Syria. For in the above-mentioned ship they had lost all their choice youth, in whom they trusted.

BOOK III

CHAPTER I – *Of the serial of King Richard at Acre*

Thus, after his success by sea, King Richard hastened with joy and alacrity and with all his suite, towards Acre, whither his eager wishes carried him; and the next night, with the aid of a prosperous gale, the fleet anchored off Tyre. In the morning they weighed anchor, and hoisted sail, and soon afterwards passed Candalion, of which we have before spoken and going by Casella Ymbrici, the high tower of Acre came in sight, and then, by little and little, the other fortifications of the city. Around it the besiegers lay in countless multitudes, chosen from every nation throughout Christendom and under the face of heaven, and well fitted for the labors and fatigues of war; for the city had now been besieged a long time, and had been afflicted by constant toil and tribulation, by the pressure of famine, and every kind of adversity, as we have before described. Moreover, beyond the besiegers, was seen the Turkish army, not in a compact body, but covering the mountains and valleys, hills and plains, with tents, the colors of whose various forms were reflected by the sun. They saw, also, the pavilion of Saladin, and his brother Safahadin's tent, and that of Kahadin, the mainstay of Paganism; he was watching the parts to seaward, and planning constant and vigorous attacks upon the Christians. King Richard beheld and computed all their army and when he arrived in port, the king of France and a whole army of natives, and the princes, chiefs, and nobles, came forth to meet him and welcome him with joy and exultation, for they had eagerly longed for his arrival.

CHAPTER II - *Of the joy, songs, and processions which took place on account of King Richard's arrival*

On the Saturday before the festival of the blessed apostle Barnabas, in the Pentecost week, King Richard landed at Acre with his retinue, and the earth was shaken by the acclamations of the exulting Christians. The people testified their joy by shouts of welcome and the clang of trumpets; the day was kept as a jubilee, and universal gladness reigned around, on account of the arrival of the king, long wished for by all nations. The Turks, on the other hand, were terrified and cast down by his coming, for they perceived that all egress and return would be at an end, in consequence of the multitude of the king's galleys. The two kings conducted each other from the port, and paid one another the most obsequious attention. Then King Richard retired to the tent previously prepared for him, and forthwith entered into arrangements about the siege for it was his most anxious care to find out by what means, artifice, and machines, they could capture the city without loss of time. No pen can sufficiently describe the joy of the people on the king's arrival, nor tongue detail it; the very calmness of the night was thought to smile upon them with a purer air; the trumpets clanged, horns sounded, and the shrill intonations of the pipe, and the deeper notes of the timbrel and harp, struck upon the ear; and soothing symphonies were heard like various voices blended in one and there was not a man who did not, after his own fashion, indulge in joy and praise; either singing popular ballads to testify the gladness of his heart, or reciting the deeds of the ancients, stimulating by their example the spirit of the moderns. Some drank wine from costly cups, to the health of the singers while others mixing together, high and low, passed the night in constant dances. And their joy was heightened by the subjugation of the island of Cyprus by King Richard; a place so useful and necessary to them, and one which would be of the utmost service to the army. As a further proof of the exultation of their hearts, and to illumine the darkness of the night, wax torches and flaming lights sparkled in profusion, so that night seemed to be usurped by the brightness of day, and the Turks thought the whole valley was on fire.

CHAPTER III - *How the Pisans gave themselves up to King Richard, and how the Turks challenged us to battle*

The Pisans, admiring the glory and magnificence of King Richard, came before him and did him homage, and took the oath of allegiance that they submitted voluntarily to his authority and service. But the cunning Turks envied the honor paid him, and some of them, either to feign the assumption of fresh boldness on his arrival, or to provoke a speedy encounter, one Sunday morning exposed themselves to attack outside our camp, wandering up and down as if for the sake of exercise, and throwing their darts at random; and at times they seemed to threaten to cross the ditch in numbers, and annoyed our men, irritating them to a contest unceasingly.

CHAPTER IV - *Of the gifts of the two kings to their needy soldiers, and of the sickness of*

King Richard

By the conjunction of the retinues of the two kings, an immense army of Christians was formed with the king of France, who had arrived on the octaves of Easter, there came the count of Flanders, the count of St. Paul, William de Garlande, William des Barres, Drogo d'Amiens, William de Mirle, and the count of Perche and with them also came the marquis, of whom we have before spoken, and who aspired to be king of Jerusalem. But why should we enumerate them singly? There was not a man of influence or renown in France who came not, then or afterwards, to the siege of Acre. And on the following day of Pentecost, King Richard arrived with an army, the flower of war, and upon learning that the king of France had gained the good-will and favor of all, by giving to each of his soldiers three aurei a month,—not to be outdone or equaled in generosity, he proclaimed by mouth of herald, that whosoever was in his service, no matter of what nation, should receive four statute aurei a month for his pay. By these means, his generosity was extolled by all, for he outshone every one else in merit and favors, as he outdid them in gifts and magnificence. "When," exclaimed they, "will the first attack take place, by a man whom we have expected so long and anxiously? A man, by far the first of kings, and the most skilled in war throughout Christendom? Now let the will of God be done, for the hope of all rests on King Richard." But after some days' sojourn, the king was afflicted with a severe illness, to which the common people gave the name of Arnoldia, which is produced by change of climate working on the constitution. But for all that, he caused petrarise and mangonels to be raised, and a fort in front of the city gates and spared no pains to expedite the construction of machines.

CHAPTER V - *How, while King Richard was sick, the king of France assaulted Acre vigorously and how the Turks, upon Saladin attacking our trenches without, made a vigorous resistance, and set the king's machines on fire, upon which the king fell sick*

The king of France, not liking the delay in commencing the attack, sent word to King Richard, that a favorable opportunity now offered itself and he also warned, by voice of herald, the army to prepare for an assault. But King Richard had signified his inability hitherto to attend to his duty, both on account of indisposition, and because his men were not yet come though he hoped that they would arrive in the next fleet of ships, and would bring with them materials for the construction of machines. The king of France not thinking fit to desist, on that account, from his purpose, commanded an assault to be proclaimed, by voice of herald, throughout the army. Therefore, on the Monday after the feast of the Nativity of St. John the Baptist, the king of

France, having erected his machines, gave orders to his men to arm. Then might have been seen a countless multitude of armed men, worthily equipped and so many coats of scale armor, gleaming helmets, and noble chargers; with pennons and banners of various workmanship, and soldiers of tried valor and courage, as never had been seen before. Having placed men to defend the trenches against the threatened attack of Saladin from without, the army approached the walls of the city, and commenced a most vigorous assault, by casting darts and stones from arbalests and machines, without ceasing. When the Turks who were shut up in the city saw this, they raised a tumultuous clamor, and shouted to the skies; so that it resembled the crash in the air caused by thunder and lightning for some had this sole duty—to beat basins and platters to strike timbrels and by other means, to make signal to Saladin and the army without in order that they might come to their succour, according to agreement. And when the Turks from without saw and heard this, they gathered in a body and collecting every material within their reach to fill up the ditch, they essayed to cross over, and attack our men, but failed in effecting their object. For Godfrey of Lusignan, a man of the most approved valor, opposed them, and drove them back from the barricades, which they had already seized upon, above our men and he slew ten of them with an axe he carried in his hand, in a most glorious manner and none he smote escaped; nay, he took some alive for such was his courage and activity, that no one since the time of those famous soldiers, Roland and Oliver, could lay claim to such distinction, from the mouth of all, as himself. Our men regained the barricades, but with much labor and difficulty for the Turks kept pouring in, and by their obstinate persistence made the issue a long time doubtful. So severe and insupportable was the struggle, and so horrible the clamor of the conflict, that the men who were making the assault on the city, and were intent on filling up the trenches, were forced to retire, and give up the attempt, for they were not able to carry on the assault, and at the same time defend their camp from the Turks without. And many of the French perished by the darts cast from the arbalests, the throwing of stones, and the pouring on them of Greek fire and there was great mourning and lamentation amongst the people. O! With what earnestness had we expected the arrival of the kings! How fallen were our hopes! They had come, and we profited not nay, we suffered a severer loss than usual and those we expected came to no purpose. Our men of France having laid aside their arms, the Turks began to revile them shamefully and reproached them with not being able to accomplish what they had begun; moreover, they threw Greek fire on the machines and other warlike instruments of the king of France, which had been made with such care, and destroyed them. Whence the king of France, overcome by fury and anger, sunk into a state of languid sickness, from sorrow, it was said and, from confusion and discouragement, mounted not on horseback.

CHAPTER VI - *How, in consequence of the illness of the two kings, the army was closely pressed and how they were comforted by the arrival of the Nectars*

Thus the army pined away from excessive grief and discouragement at the sickness of the two kings for they had not a chief or leader to fight the battles of the Lord. To add to the public grief, the count of Flanders died immaturely. The arrival of the Nectars (Esneckars) in some measure consoled the army, amidst the distress which these circumstances occasioned. There came, after a tranquil voyage, very many bishops and princes, each accompanied by his own retinue, to the aid of the Christians, whose names were, the bishop of Eneverria, Roger de Toony, and many brothers and kinsmen surnamed de Cornebu ; Robert de Newbury, Jordan de Humez, the chamberlain of Tancarville, Robert, earl of Leicester; Gerard de Talebor, Radulph Taisson; also the knights named of Torole; the viscount of Castle Dim, Bertram de Verdun, Roger de Hardencort, and the knights of Praels; Garin fitz Gerold, and those of Mara, Henry fitz Nicholas; Ernald de Magnaville, the Stutevilles, William Martel, William Maler, William Bloez, Godard de Loreora, Roger de Satya, Andrew de Chavenguy, Hugo le Brun, Geoffrey de Rancona, Radulph de Mauleon, William cles Rocques, Geoffrey de Lancelles; Hugh de Fierte, who was in Cyprus when it was taken, and afterwards came to Acre. The two kings were sick, but the Lord reserved them to succour the Christians, and to recover the city.

CHAPTER VII - *How the petrarice of the two kings, and those of the army of the faithful, attacked the tower Maledictum, and shook down and destroyed a great part of the wall*

The king of France first recovered from his sickness, and turned his attention to the construction of machines and petrarise, suitable for attacks, and which he determined to ply night and day, and he had one of superior quality, to which they gave the name of "Bad Neighbor." The Turks also had one they called "Bad Kinsman," which by its violent casts, often broke "Bad Neighbor" in pieces; but the king of France rebuilt it, until by constant blows, he broke down part of the principal city wall, and shook the tower Maledictum. On one side, the petraria of the duke of Burgundy plied on the other that of the Templars did severe execution; while that of the Hospitallers never ceased to cast terror amongst the Turks. Besides these, there was one petraria, erected at the common expense, which they were in the habit of calling the "petraria of God."

Near it, there constantly preached a priest, a man of great probity, who collected money to restore it at their joint expense, and to hire persons to bring stones for casting. By means of this engine, a part of the wall of the tower Maledictum was at length shaken down, for about two poles' length. The count of Flanders had a very choice petraria of large size, which after his death, King Richard possessed; besides a smaller one, equally good. These two were plied incessantly, close by a gate the Turks used to frequent, until part of the tower was knocked down. In addition to these two, King Richard had constructed two others of choice workmanship and material, which would strike a place at an incalculable distance. He had also built one put together very compactly, which the people called "Berefred," with steps to mount it, fitting most tightly to it; covered with raw hides and ropes, and having layers of most solid wood, not to be destroyed by any blows, nor open to injury from the pouring thereon of Greek fire, or any other material. He also prepared two mangonels, one of which was of such violence and rapidity that what it hurled, reached the inner rows of the city market-place. These engines were plied day and night, and it is well known that a stone sent from one of them killed twelve men with its blow; the stone was afterwards carried to Saladin for inspection and King Richard had brought it from Messina, which city he had taken. Such stones and flinty pieces of rock, of the smoothest kind, nothing could withstand but they either shattered in pieces the object they struck, or ground it to powder. The king was confined to his bed by a severe attack of fever, which discouraged him for he saw the Turks constantly challenging our men, and pressing on them importunately, and he was prevented by sickness from meeting them, and he was more tormented by the importunate attack of the Turks than by the severity of the fever that scorched him.

CHAPTER VIII - *How the Turks burnt with Greek fire all the machines and the cat and cercleia belonging to the king of France, when assaulting the city*

The city of Acre, from its strong position, and its being defended by the choicest men of the Turks, appeared difficult to be taken by assault. The French had hitherto spent their labor in vain in constructing machines and engines for breaking down the walls, with the greatest care; for whatever they erected, at a great expense, the Turks destroyed with Greek fire or some devouring conflagration. Amongst other machines and engines which the king of France had erected for breaking down the walls, he had prepared one, with great labor, to be used for scaling it, which they called "a cat;" because like a cat it crept up and adhered to the wall. He had also another, made of strong hurdle twigs, put together not compactly, which they used to call a "cercleia," and under its covering of hides the king of France used to sit, and employ himself in throwing darts from a sling; he would thus watch the approach of the Turks, above on the walls, by the battlements and then hit them unawares. But it happened one day that the French were eagerly pressing forward to apply their cat to the walls, when, behold the Turks let down upon it a heap of the driest wood, and threw upon it a quantity of Greek fire, as well as upon the hurdle they had constructed with such toil, and then aimed a petraria in that direction, and all having forthwith caught fire, they broke them in pieces by the blows from their petraria. Upon this, the king of France was enraged beyond measure, and began to curse all those who were under his command and rated them shamefully for not exacting condign vengeance of the Saracens, who had done them such injuries. In the heat of his passion, and when the day was drawing in, he published an edict, by voice of herald that an assault should be made upon the city on the morrow.

CHAPTER IX - *How, while the French army was undermining the city walls, the Christians within the trenches vigorously repelled the Turks, who had fiercely attacked them from without*

In the morning, therefore, all armed themselves, and some of the bravest soldiers chosen from the whole army were posted at the trenches towards the exterior, against the repeated annoyances and sudden attacks of the Saracens; for Saladin had vaunted that on that day he would cross the trenches in force, and prove his valor in humbling to the dust the army of the Christians. But he kept not his word, and came not though his army, under the command of Kahadin, his vizier, came in a body to the trenches and attempted to cross them but the French were not slow to resist, and endeavored to drive them off. The slaughter on both sides was great and the Turks dismounting, advanced on foot with greater ease, and having joined battle, fought most obstinately with swords, hand to hand, and with poignards and two-edged axes, and some of them used clubs bristling with very sharp teeth. Their strokes on the one hand, and cries on the other, were terrific, and many were slain on both sides. The Turks pressed on, and the Christians drove them back the one the most obstinate, the others the most valiant of men but they effected this with so much the more difficulty, as the numbers of the Turks who pushed on was the greater, and both melted with twofold heat, as it was now summer. Those who directed their attacks against the city tried by every means in their power to batter down or undermine the walls, or else to surmount them with scaling-ladders. The Turks who were shut up in the city, dreading the spirit of our men, hoisted a signal to the Turks of Saladin's army without, and intimated to them, either to make an attack, for the purpose of removing the French from the walls, or to give them instant succour. The Turks from without pressed on obstinately, when Kahadin learnt this, and driving our men back with all their might, violently filled the ditch but the Christians, notwithstanding, resisted, and opposed their attacks, so that by God's aid our men stood as an impenetrable wall, and the enemy was repulsed. Meanwhile, the men employed by the king of France to undermine the wall, advanced so far as to remove the foundations, and they filled the space thus dug out with logs of wood, and set them on fire these ignited the piles of wood forming the foundations of the wall, which sunk clown gradually, with a slight inclination, and without falling altogether. A large number of Christians hastened to that part, in order to enter and drive back the Turkish army. O! how many banners might then be seen there, and piles of wood, of different shapes, and on the other hand the Turks throwing Greek fire on the one side were the French applying ladders to the wall, that was but partially thrown down, and trying to cross over whilst the Turks were also mounting with ladders on the other side to defend the breach which had been made in it.

CHAPTER X - *How Alberic Clements was slain by the Turks whilst scaling the walls*

There happened a wonderful event, not to be passed over in silence. There was a man of renown for his tried valor and excellence, named Alberic Clements, who, when he saw the French toiling to very little purpose, exerted his strength in the vehemence of his ardour, exclaiming, "This day I will perish, or, if it please God, I will enter into the city of Acre." With these words, he boldly mounted the ladder and as he reached the top of the wall, the Turks fell on him from all sides and killed him. The French were on the point of following him, but were overwhelmed by the pressure of numbers which the ladder could not hold and some were bruised to death, and others dragged out much injured. The Turks shouted with the greatest joy and applause when they saw the accident, for it was a very severe misfortune. They surrounded and overcame Alberic Clements, who was left alone on the top of the wall, and pierced him with innumerable wounds. He thus verified what he had before said, that he would die a martyr if he was unable to render his friends assistance by entering Acre. The French were much discouraged by his loss, and ceasing the assault, gave themselves up to lamentation and mourning on account of his death, for he was a man of rank and influence and great valor.

CHAPTER XI - *How the French from without undermine the tower Maledic turn while*

Not long after, the French miners, by their perseverance, undermined the tower Maledictum, and supported it by placing beams of wood underneath. The Turks also digging in the same direction, had reached the same part of the foundations on which they entered into a mutual treaty of peace, that the Turks should depart uninjured; and some of the Christians whom they held captive, were by agreement, in like manner, set at liberty. On discovering this, the Turks were very much chagrined, and stopped up the passages by which they had gone out.

CHAPTER XII - *How King Richard, though still sick, assaulted the city with his men, slew many by a sling with his own hand, and threw down one of the towers by means of his miners and petrarice*

King Richard was not yet fully recovered from his sickness nevertheless, anxious for action, and strenuously intent upon taking the city, he made arrangements that his men should assault the city, in the hope that under Divine Providence he should succeed. For this purpose, he caused to be made a hurdle, commonly called a circleia, put together firmly with a complication of interweaving, and made with the most subtle workmanship. This king intended to be used for crossing over the trench outside the city. Under it he placed his most experienced arbalesters and he caused himself to be carried thither on a silken bed, to honor the Saracens with his presence, and animate his men to fight and from it, by using his arbalest, in which he was skilled, he slew many with darts and arrows. His sappers also carried a mine under the tower, at which a petraria was directed; and having made a breach, they filled it with logs of wood, and set them on fire; when, by the addition of frequent blows from the petraria, the tower fell suddenly to the ground with a crash.

CHAPTER XIII - *How the Turks vigorously repelled King Richard's men who were assaulting the city, and how King Richard slew with his arbalest one who had on the armor of Alberic Clements*

Perceiving, therefore, how difficult success was, that he had a most warlike enemy to contend with, and that there was need of all his strength for the attack, the king thought it best to incite the minds of his younger soldiers by rewards, rather than to urge them by severe orders for whom will not the love of gain draw on? He therefore ordered the herald to proclaim a reward of two aurei, afterwards three, and then four, to whoever should overthrow a petraria from the walls and for each stone displaced from the wall, he promised a reward of four aurei. Then you might see the young men bound forward, and soldiers of great valor press on emulously to draw stones from the wall, as eager for glory as for gain, and persisting in their efforts amidst the darts of the enemy. Very many of them failed in their undertaking, while others were driven back by fear of death; for the Turks from above vigorously repelled them, and neither shields nor arms availed to protect them. The height of the wall was very great, as well as its thickness but the men of valor, overcoming all difficulties, extracted very many stones from the solid wall; and when the Turks rushed upon them in a body, and tried to cast them down, they strove to repel them, but, having forgot their arms, they exposed themselves to the darts, in an almost unarmed condition. One of the Turks, vaunting in the armor of the aforesaid Alberic Clements, which he had put on, was showing himself, to the annoyance of our men, on the highest part of the wall, in a boastful manner but King Richard inflicted on him a deadly wound, piercing him through the heart with a cast of his arbalest; the Turks, grieving at his far, ran together in crowds to avenge his death, and to assuage the bitterness of their grief by the fierceness of their onslaught. They boldly exposed themselves, as if they feared not that the darts and missiles would strike them, and repelled and pressed on our men like madmen,—never were there braver warriors of any creed on earth and the memory of their actions excites at once our respect and astonishment. In the hottest of the combat, however close the armor fitted, or whether the coat of mail was twofold, it availed little to resist the darts from their arbalests. Nevertheless, the Turks kept mining from within, so that our men were obliged to retreat and the enemy raised a loud shout, as if they had gained their purpose.

CHAPTER XIV - *How our esquires and the Pisans boldly scaled the tower, which had been shaken, for the purpose of entering the city and hew the Turks repelled them with spirit, both with arms and Greek fire*

At last the aforesaid tower was thrown down by the constant blows of our petraria and the pulling away of stones and when King Richard's men had ceased from undermining, and the assaults were discontinued, our esquires eager for praise and victory, and fitted and equipped for war, armed themselves. Among them were the retainers of the earl of Leicester, and those of Andrew de Cavegin and Hugo Brun; there also came, most nobly arrayed, the bishop of Salisbury, and very many others. It was about tierce, i. e. the hour of dinner, when the men of valor and the most excellent esquires, prepared to attack the aforesaid tower, and forthwith boldly mounted it. The sentinels of the Turks on seeing them began to shout, and the whole city, being roused, took up arms with all haste, and ran to oppose them; and the Turks pressed in dense numbers upon the squires, who were nimbly making their way. While our men tried to enter the city, and the Turks to drive them back, they met in a body and fought hand to hand on both sides, right hand met right hand, and swords flashed against swords; some seized hold of each other, others struck each other,—some were driven back, and others fell. Our men were few in numbers; the multitude of the Turks increased constantly, and by throwing Greek fire, they forced our men, who could not withstand it, to retire and descend from the tower some of them were killed by the enemy and afterwards burnt to ashes by this destructive conflagration. Then the Pisans, either thirsting for praise or revenge, mounted the tower in full force; but the Turks again attacked them like madmen, and although the Pisans made a bold resistance, they were compelled to retire and abandon the tower. For there never was seen any thing like that race of Turks for efficiency in war. The capture of the city would, however, have been accomplished on that day, had the battle been fought with the whole combined army, and on a prudent plan but the greater part of the army was at dinner at the time, and the attempt was a presumptuous one, and therefore did not succeed.

CHAPTER XV - *A commendation of the Turks in the city, who sent Mestoc and Caracois in despair to our kings, in order to obtain a respite until they should consult Saladin, but they returned fruitlessly*

What can we say of this race of unbelievers who thus defended their city? They must be admired for their valor in war, and were the honor of their whole nation and had they been of the right faith, they would not have had their superiors as men throughout the world. Yet they dreaded our men, not without reason, for they saw the choicest soldiers from the ranks of all Christendom come to destroy them their walls in part broken down, in part shattered, the greater portion of their army mutilated, some killed, and others weakened by their wounds. There were still remaining in the city 6,000 Turks, with Mestoc and Caracois, their chiefs, but they despaired of succour. They perceived that the Christian army was very much dejected at the death of Alberic Clements, and their sons and kinsmen, who had fallen in battle, and that they were determined either to die bravely or gain the mastery over the Turks, and that they thought a middle course dishonorable. Under these circumstances, by common counsel and assent, the besieged begged a truce in order to inform Saladin of their condition, and to ascertain how far he would afford them security according to the manner of barbarous nations, by either sending them speedy help, or giving them leave to depart from the city with honor. To obtain this object, two of the most noble of the Saracens and of Paganism, Mestoc and Caracois, came to our kings with the promise that if Saladin did not send them speedy assistance, they would give up the city, on the condition that all the besieged Turks should be permitted to depart in freedom, with their arms and property, and go whithersoever they liked. And on the king of France and nearly all the French giving their assent to this condition at the conference, King Richard absolutely refused his, and said, it was not to be consented to, that after so long and laborious a siege, they should enter a deserted city only. On his pleasure being known, Caracois and Mestoc returned to the city without effecting their object. And Saladin, when he learnt that ambassadors had been sent by the besieged, commanded them to persevere and defend their city with as much courage as that which they had hitherto shown, promising that most ample assistance should soon come to them without a doubt; for he declared to the ambassadors who waited upon him, that he would certainly persevere, and as he was expecting a large body of soldiers from Babylon, they would soon come in ships and galleys for he had given orders to Muleina to be with him, without fail, in eight days and if they did not come according to agreement, he promised, with an oath, to procure for them as honorable a peace as he could from the Christians, and the liberty to depart. On hearing these things, the ambassadors returned to the city, and, repeating the promises of Saladin, persuaded the townsmen to resist, while they looked forward with anxiety for the promised assistance.

CHAPTER XVI - *How, while our men were courageously assaulting the city, some of the Turks in despair escaped out of it*

Meanwhile, the petrarise of the Christians never ceased, day and night, to shake the walls and when the Turks saw this, they were smitten with wonder, astonishment, terror, and confusion and many, yielding to their fears, threw themselves down from the walls by night, and without waiting for the promised aid, very many sought, with supplications, the sacrament of baptism and Christianity. There was little doubt, and with good reason as to their merits, that they presumptuously asked the boon more from the pressure of urgent fear than from any divine inspiration but there are different steps by which men arrive at salvation. It was now well known to Salad in, by means of messengers, who passed backwards and forwards, that to persevere any longer in defending the city, was dangerous, as it could not be kept from the Christians.

CHAPTER XVII - *How the besieged entered into treaty with the Christians by the advice of Saladin*

Saladin, perceiving the danger of delay, at length determined to yield to the entreaties of the besieged he was, moreover, persuaded by his admirals, and satraps, and his influential courtiers, who held many friends and kinsmen amongst the besieged. The latter alleged also, that he was bound to them by his promise made on the Mahometan law, that he would procure for them an honorable capitulation at the last moment, lest, perchance, made prisoners at discretion, they should be exterminated or put to an ignominious death, and thus the law of Mahomet, which had been strictly observed by their ancestors, be effaced by its dependence on him and nevertheless, very much would be derogated from his name and excellence if the worshippers of Mahomet should fall into the hands of the Christians. They also begged to remind Saladin of the fact, that they, a chosen race of Turks, in obedience to his commands, had been cooped up in the city, and withstood a siege for so long a time; they reminded him too that they had not seen their wives and children for three years, during which period the siege had lasted; and they said, it would be better to surrender the city, than that people of such merit should be destroyed. The princes persuading the sultan to this effect that their latter condition might not be worse than their former one; he assented to their making peace on the best terms they could, and they drew up a statement of what appeared to them the most proper terms of treaty. On the messengers bringing back the resolution of Saladin and his satraps, the besieged were filled with great joy and forthwith, the principal men of the city went to the kings, and through their interpreters, offered to surrender unconditionally the city of Acre, the Cross, and two hundred and fifty noble Christian captives and when they perceived this did not satisfy them, they offered two thousand noble Christian captives, and five hundred of inferior rank, whom Saladin would bring together from all parts of his kingdom, if they would let the Turks depart from their city, with their shirts only, leaving behind them their arms and property and, as a ransom for themselves, they would give two hundred thousand Saracenic talents. As security for the performance of these conditions, they offered to deliver up, as hostages, all the men of noble or high rank in the city. After the two kings had considered with the wisest of the chiefs, the opinion of all was for accepting the offer, and consenting to the conditions that on taking the oath for security, and subscribing the terms of peace, they might quit the city, without carrying any thing with them, having first given up the hostages.

CHAPTER XVIII - *How, on giving hostages for the delivery of the Cross, money, and captives within a month, the Turks marched out of the city and the Christians entered it and how the two kings divided every thing equally between them*

Thus, on the Friday after the Translation of St. Benedict the principal and noblest of the admirals were given and received as hostages, and the space of one month fixed for the delivery of the Cross, and the collecting together of the captives. And when it was rumored abroad that the city was to be given up, the common people, in their folly, were inflamed with fury, but the wiser portion rejoiced at gaining so profitably, and without danger, what they had been so long a time unable to obtain. Then was it proclaimed and prohibited, by voice of herald, that any one should molest the Turks by word or deed, or provoke them by abuse, or that missiles should any longer be cast for the destruction of the walls or of the Turks who might be seen on the battlements. And when the day came that the Turks, so renowned for their courage and valor, most active in the exercise of war, and famous for their magnificence, appeared on the walls ready to leave the city, the Christians went forth to look at them, and were struck with admiration when they remembered the deeds they had done. They were also astonished at the cheerful countenances of those who were thus driven almost penniless from their city,—their demeanor unchanged by adversity and those who but now had been compelled by extreme necessity to own themselves conquered, and betake themselves to supplication, bore no marks of care, as they came forth, nor any signs of dejection at the loss of all they possessed—not even in the firmness of their countenances, for they seemed to be conquerors by their courageous bearing; but the form of superstitious idolatry, and the miserable error of sinfulness, threw a stain upon their warlike glories. At last, when all the Turks had departed, the Christians, with the two kings at their head, entered the city without opposition, through the open gates, with dances, and joy, and loud vociferations, glorifying God, and giving Him thanks, because He had magnified His mercy to them, and had visited them, and redeemed His people. Then the banners, and various standards of the two kings, were raised on the walls and towers, and the city was equally divided between them. They also made a proportionate division of the arms and provisions they found and the whole number of captives, being reckoned, was divided by lot. The noble Caracois, and a large number, fell to the lot of the king of France and King Richard had for his portion Mestoc and the remainder. Moreover, the king of France had for his share the noble palace of the Templars, with all its appurtenances and King Richard had the royal palace, to which he sent the queens, with their damsels and handmaids; thus each obtained his portion in peace. The army was distributed through the city, and after the protracted contest of so long a siege, gave themselves indulgence, and refreshed themselves with the rest they needed. The night following our entrance, Saladin, through fear of us, retired from the place in which he was posted, and occupied a most distant mountain.

CHAPTER XIX - *How vilely and shamefully the Turks, when in possession of the city, had treated our sacred things*

From the day on which the Saracens first got possession of the city of Acre, to that on which it was restored, was a space of four years. It was restored, as has been said on the morrow of St. Benedict. The state of the churches within the city was not beheld without horror, and it is not without grief that we relate the unseemly things that had been perpetrated within them. For who could behold, without tears, the countenances of the holy images of the crucifixion of the Son of God, and of many saints, defiled or disfigured in one way or another? Who would not shudder at the horrible sight of altars overthrown, and crucifixes cast to the earth3 and beaten in contempt by that insulting and impious nation, the Turks, and their own Mahometan rites exhibited in holy places—all the relics of man's redemption and the Christian religion effaced, and the corruption of the Mahometan superstition introduced?

CHAPTER XX - *Of the quarrel between the two kings on account of the Marquis and King Guy, and, of their reconciliation*

After this a great discord arose between the two kings, on account of the aforesaid marquis whom the king of France favoured, and to whom he had determined to give his share of all that fell to his lot, present or future, in the Holy Land. But King Richard, who compassionated the distress of King Guy, would not consent to this grant, for he thought that all and every thing belonged to Guy. On this point the kings were at variance for some time until, by the mediation of the chiefs and leaders of the people, they were reconciled, on the condition that, as the marquis was heir by marriage to the throne, he should have the government of Tyre, i.e. Tyre, Sidon, and Baruth, with the title of count, as a recompense for the assistance he had given during the siege, and that Godfrey of Lusignan should be count of Joppa, i.e. Joppa and Askalon, as a recompense for his services, being brother to King Guy. And if King Guy died first, the marquis should receive his crown, although he had married in so unlawful a manner the heiress to the throne, as we have before said but that if the marquis and his wife should happen to die while

King Richard was in those parts, it should be left to him to dispose of the kingdom at his pleasure. On these conditions, the disputants were one and all pacified.

CHAPTER XXI - *How, after the city was restored, the king of France, amidst the wonder, disapproval, and execrations of all, prepared to return home*

Affairs being in this position, at the end of the month of July, within which the Turks had promised to restore the holy cross, and receive back their hostages, a rumor spread amongst the army, that the king of France, on whom the hope of the people rested, intended to return home, and was making active preparations for his journey. Oh how wicked and how in suiting a proceeding, while as yet so much work remained on hand, to wish to go away, when his duty was to rule so large a multitude of people, and when his presence was so necessary to encourage the Christians to so pious a work, and to provide for the progress of so arduous an undertaking! O why did he come so long a way, with so much toil, if he intended to return almost immediately! O wonderful performance of his vow, by merely entering the Holy Land, and contending against the Turks with such small triumph! But why need we say more? The king of France alleged sickness as the cause of his return and said that he had performed his vow as far as he was able; most of all, because he was well and sound when he took up the cross with King Henry between Trie and Gisors. But in making this assertion, he produced no one by whose evidence it could be confirmed. It must not be denied, at the same time, that the king of France expended much labor and money in the Holy Land for the assaulting of the city, and that he afforded aid and assistance to very many, and that by the influence of his presence, he procured the more speedy execution and consummation of so great a work in the capture of the city, as the most powerful of Christian kings, and of the highest dignity, should have done whence, by how much the greater in valor and surpassing in excellence, by so much the more he was held bound to recover a land so cast down and destitute of aid, against which the heathen had come to pollute it for, according to St. Gregory, when gifts are increased, the reasons for them increase also, and to whom much is given, of the same much will be required. But when the inflexible determination of the king of France to return became known to all, and his refusal to yield to the murmurs of his men, or their supplications to remain, the French would have renounced their subjection to him, if it could have been done, and would have loathed his dominion and they imprecated on him every kind of adversity and misfortune that could fall to the lot of man in this life. But for all that, the king of France hastened his voyage as much as possible, and left in his stead the duke of Burgundy, with a large number of men. Moreover, he begged King Richard to supply him with two galleys, and the king readily gave him two of his best how ungrateful he was for this service, was afterwards seen.

CHAPTER XXII - *How the king of France swore to King Richard that he would observe peace towards his subjects and his territories until the latter returned home*

King Richard was of opinion that the king of France should enter into a covenant for the preservation of their mutual security for they, like their fathers, regarded each other with mistrust, under the veil of friendship, which even in the following generation never expelled fear. King Richard was therefore anxious with this uneasy feeling and required an oath from the king of France to keep his faith not to do injury to his men or territory knowingly or purposely, while he, King Richard, remained in a foreign land; but if on any occasion any thing that should appear reprehensible went unpunished, King Richard on his return should have forty days' notice before the king of France should proceed to obtain redress. The king of France took the oath which was required faithfully to observe all these conditions, and gave the duke of Burgundy and Count Henry as hostages, and five or more others, whose names are lost. How faithfully he stood to his covenant and oath is very well known to all the world for he had no sooner reached his own country, than he set it in commotion and threw Normandy into confusion. What need we say more? The king of France, having taken leave, retired from his army at Acre, and instead of blessings, he received wishes of misfortune and execrations from all.

CHAPTER XXIII - *How, on the King of France retiring with his hostages and the Marquis to Tyre, the duke of Burgundy and many others of the French remained with King Richard*

On St. Peter's day the king of France embarked and sailed for Tyre, but he left the greater part of his army with King Richard and with him he took that infamous marquis and Caracois and the other hostages that had fallen to his lot and he reckoned that he would receive for their ransom a hundred thousand aurei or more, which would support his army till Easter. But on the term expiring for ransoming the hostages, the Turks paid no attention to it, and most of them perished for it was very evident that they would not give an egg or a farthing to release them and by their means nothing at all was gained, nor any portion of provisions found in the city; which caused the French to remember the more frequently that they received no other remuneration from the king of France. On this account there arose frequent wrangling and murmuring amongst them, until King Richard, at the request of the duke of Burgundy, lent him, over and above his hostages, five thousand marks of silver to support his men.

BOOK IV

CHAPTER I - *How King Richard bestows gifts on his soldiers, and repairs the walls of Acre*

King Richard, therefore, perceiving that the consummation of the business and the progress of affairs, together with the labor and expense, devolved upon him chiefly, made most ample largesses of gold and silver to the French and to all the others of every nation, by means of which they might abundantly recruit themselves and redeem what they had put in pledge. On the king of France returning home with haste as aforesaid, King Richard turned his attention to the repair of the walls to a greater height and perfection than before they were thrown down and he himself walked about, exhorting the workmen and masons, as if his whole intention was to strive for the recovery of God's inheritance.

CHAPTER II - *How Saladin stood not to his covenant for restoring our Lord's cross and paging the money and neglected his men, who were hostages*

He therefore awaited the term which had been agreed upon between the Turks and himself as aforesaid, and turned his attention to the packing up of the petraria and mangonels for transportation. For when the time had expired which had been fixed by the Turks for the restoration of the cross and the ransom of the hostages, after waiting three weeks, according to the conditions, to see if Saladin would stand to his word and covenant, the king looked upon him as a transgressor, as Saladin appeared to have no care about it and perhaps this was by the dispensation of God, that something more advantageous might be obtained. But the Saracens asked further time to fulfill their promise and make search for the cross. Then you might hear the Christians inquiring for news, and when the cross was coming but God was unwilling that it should be restored for those by whom it was promised, but preferred rather that they should perish. One would exclaim, "The cross is coming I" another, that he had seen it in the Saracen army; but each speaker was deceived, for Saladin had not taken any steps to restore the cross;

nay, he neglected the hostages who were bound for it, for he hoped, by means of it, to obtain much more advantageous terms. Meanwhile, he sent constant presents and messengers to King Richard to gain delay by artful and deceptive words, though he fulfilled none of his promises, but tried to keep the king's mind in suspense by crafty and ambiguous messages.

CHAPTER III - *How the king of England sent twice to Tyre, before he could obtain the hostages of Saladin from the Marquis, and how he himself refused to return*

In the meantime messages were sent to Tyre to command the marquis to return to the army, and bring with him the hostages which had been committed to his charge, in order to get the ransom for them,—viz., the share of the payment which belonged to the king of France. With the message were sent the bishop of Salisbury, Earl Robert, and Peter de Pratellis, a very eminent soldier. To these three messengers the marquis answered indignantly, that he dared not venture into King Richard's presence: moreover, he boasted that if the true cross was ever recovered, he was to receive the half of it for the king of France and that until this was accomplished he would not resign the hostages. On ascertaining the obstinate determination of the marquis, the messengers tried to prevail upon him with soft speeches, offering to leave one of themselves as an hostage to secure his safe journey to and from King Richard but they did not succeed in persuading him—nay, he refused with an oath to come. They therefore returned unsuccessful and empty handed, and excited the kings anger by telling him the whole matter. At his request the duke of Burgundy, Drogo d'Amiens, and Robert de Quincey, were sent on a second embassy to request the said marquis to come with them to the army, as his presence seemed necessary to the progress of the business, especially as he aspired to the kingdom, the acquisition of which he was preventing and that he should grant those who were bringing provisions a free passage from Tyre, for (according to his former conduct) he had hitherto hindered them ; and on their arrival at Tyre, they set forth their zeal in behalf of King Richard, and urged him to come to their aid in Syria, the dominion of which he aspired to obtain. But he replied arrogantly, protesting that he would not come, but would maintain the government of his own city. When they answered each of his assertions, by contrary arguments, the matter was with difficulty brought to this point that the messengers should take back with them the Saracen hostages to King Richard but they could, by no method or persuasion, prevail on the marquis to turn from his obstinate and wicked intentions.

CHAPTER IV - *How the hostages of Saladin were slain by our men*

When it became clearly evident to King Richard that a longer period had elapsed than had been fixed, and that Saladin was obdurate, and would not give himself trouble to ransom the hostages, he called together a council of the chiefs of the people, by whom it was resolved that the hostages should all be hanged, except a few nobles of the higher class, who might ransom themselves, or be exchanged for some Christian captives. King Richard, aspiring to destroy the Turks root and branch, and to punish their wanton arrogance, as well as to abolish the law of Mahomet, and to vindicate the Christian religion, on the Friday after the Assumption of the Blessed Virgin Mary, ordered 2,700 of the Turkish hostages to be led forth from the city, and hanged his soldiers marched forward with delight to fulfill his commands, and to retaliate, with the assent of the Divine Grace, by taking revenge upon those who had destroyed so many of the Christians with missiles from bows and arbalests.

CHAPTER V - *How King Richard ordered his army to move by land and by sea towards Ashalon*

When evening approached, it was proclaimed by mouth of herald, that the armor should march on the morrow, and cross the river of Acre in the name of the Lord—the dispenser of all good things—in order that they should proceed to Askalon and conquer the maritime districts. It was also ordered that the ships should take on board, for the army, ten days' provisions—viz., biscuits, meal, meat, and wine, and whatever else appeared necessary. The sailors were strictly enjoined to keep sailing along shore, with the barges and smacks, which carried the provisions as well as armed men and thus the forces advanced in two divisions, one by sea the other by land for otherwise it was not possible to keep possession of the country so completely occupied by the Turks.

CHAPTER VI - *How many of our chiefs had died in a year and a half at the siege of Acre*

It must be known, that during the two winters and one summer, and up to the middle of the autumn, when the Turks were hanged, as they deserved to be in the sight of God and man, in return for the destruction of our churches and slaughter of our men, many of the Christians who were engaged in the siege of Acre at a great sacrifice had died. The multitude of those who perished in so great an army appears to exceed computation but the sum total of the chiefs, as a certain writer has estimated it, omitting the others which he says he has no means of reckoning, is as follows:—We lost in the army six archbishops and patriarchs, twelve bishops, forty counts, and five hundred men of noble rank also a vast number of priests, clergy, and others, which cannot be accurately counted.

CHAPTER VII - *How King Richard compelled the French to quit Acre and how he fixed his own tent outside the city*

After the Turks were hanged, King Richard, having recovered his health, went out from the city with all his retinue, and ordered his tents to be pitched in the plain outside, and compelled all his soldiers, who were not willing, to quit the city thus the army took up their quarters on the aforesaid plain, to be ready for setting out on its march of the French some he allured by soft words, others by entreaties, and many by money, to leave the place, and some he forced out violently. King Richard thereupon appointed a large number of guards to lodge about his pavilion in their tents and awnings, for his protection, as the Turks were making constant irruptions, and all day coming up and rushing out on them unawares, and it was the king's custom to be the first to go forth to attack and punish them, as far as the divine favor would allow him.

CHAPTER VIII - *How the count of Hungary and the king's marshal, having put the Turks to flight who had attacked our men, were captured by them*

It happened one day that our camp was put into commotion by the Turks, who were attacking our men, as was their custom, and making a disturbance. Our men immediately ran to arms, the king and his cavalry went forth, and also the count of Hungary, and very many Hungarians with him, who, having put the Turks to flight, pursued them further than they ought to have done for some of our men, although they behaved themselves most nobly, were taken captive on the spot and disgracefully treated. The count of Hungary, a man of tried valor and renown, was taken prisoner by the Turks and carried off, as well as a man of Poitou, named Hugh, King Richard's marshal. The king fought recklessly, careless of his own person, and strove with all his might to rescue Hugh, his marshal but he was hurried away too rapidly and carried off. Oh how uncertain is the fate of war! Those who were but now victors are often vanquished, and the vanquished becomes as suddenly victor it was fated for those who had put the enemy to flight to perish themselves, for the pursuers were now captured by the pursued, and that which was ascribed to their glory now proved their folly, and the deed of valor became the cause of danger. In short, the Turks were not loaded with armor like our men but from their light movements distressed us so much the more severely, for they were for the most part unarmed, carrying only a bow, or a mace, bristling with sharp teeth, a scimitar, a light spear with an iron head, and a dagger suspended lightly and when put to flight with greater force, they fled away on horseback with the utmost rapidity, for they have not their equals for agility throughout the world for it is their custom to turn if they see their pursuers stop;—like the fly, which, if you drive it away, will go, but when you cease, it will return as long as you pursue, it will fly, but it reappears the moment you desist so likewise the Turks, when you desist from the pursuit they will pursue you if you attack them, they will fly away so when the king put them to flight, they fled without stopping; when he was disposed to return, they threatened from the rear, sometimes not with impunity, and sometimes to the injury of our men.

CHAPTER IX - *How our army, being abandoned to pleasures, could scarcely be forced to quit the city and cross the river of Acre, while the Turks infested them on all sides*

King Richard was resting in his tents, waiting for the army to come out of the city, but they came out slowly and peevishly, as if they did it against their will and the numbers of the army did not increase, but the city was crowded with an immense multitude. The whole army, including those who were yet in the city, was computed at 300,000 men. The people were too much given up to sloth and luxury, for the city was filled with pleasures, viz.—the choicest wines and fairest damsels, and the men became dissolute by indulging in them; so that the city was defiled by the luxury of the sons of folly and the gluttony of its inhabitants, who made wiser faces blush at their shamelessness and, in order to blot out this contamination, it was ordained by the council that no woman should quit the city or go with the army, except the washerwomen, on foot, who would not be a burthen to them, nor an occasion for sin. Therefore, on the morning of the aforementioned day, the soldiers armed themselves, and were arranged in becoming order. The king was in the rear of the army to check the Turks, who threatened annoyance; but the duty was a slight one. From the time that impious race saw our army in motion they poured down from the mountains in scattered bands, like rushing waters, and dispersed themselves in numbers of twenty or thirty, to find out the best opportunity of harassing us. For they were exceedingly grieved at the deaths of their parents and kinsmen, whose slaughtered bodies they saw strewn about as aforesaid and they therefore pressed upon our army continuously, and harassed it as much as they could. But, with the assistance of the Divine Grace, the Turks succeeded not as they wished for our army passed over the river of Acre unhurt, and again pitched their tents on the other side the stream until on Friday, being the vigil of St. Bartholomew, they were all assembled together and on the following Monday, two years had elapsed since the Christians first laid siege to Acre.

CHAPTER X - *How our army, departing from the city in battle array, boldly repulsed the Turks, who attacked them in force the standard is here described*

On the morrow, therefore, of St. Bartholomew, being Sunday, the army was drawn up, early in the morning, to advance along the sea-coast, in the name of the Lord. Oh! What fine soldiers they were! You might there see a chosen company of virtuous and brave youth, whose equals it would have been difficult to meet with, bright armor and pennons, with their glittering emblazonry; banners of various forms; lances, with gleaming points shining helmets, and coats of mail an army well regulated in the camp, and terrible to the foe! King Richard commanded the van, and kept the foremost guard. The Normans defended the standard, which we do not consider it irrelevant here to describe. It was formed of a long beam, like the mast of a ship made of most solid ceiled work, on four wheels put together with joints, bound with iron, and to all appearance no sword or axe could cut or fire injure it. A chosen body of soldiers was generally appointed to guard it, especially in a combat on the plains, lest, by any hostile attack, it should be broken or thrown down for if it fell by any accident, the army would be dispersed and put into confusion. For they are dismayed when it does not appear, and think that their general must be overcome by faint-heartedness when they do not see his standard flying; for no people have strength to resist the enemy if their chief is in alarm from the fall of his standard but whilst it remains erect they have a certain refuge. Near it the weak are strengthened the wounded soldiers, even those of rank and celebrity, who fall in the battle, are carried to it, and it is called "Standard" from its standing a most compact signal to the army. It is very properly drawn on wheels, for it is advanced when the enemy yields, and drawn back if they press on, according to the state of the battle. It was surrounded by the Normans and English.

The duke of Burgundy and the French brought up the rear and by their tardy movements and long delay incurred severe loss. The army marched along the sea-shore, which was on its right, and the Turks watched its movements from the heights on the left. On a sudden the clouds grew dark, and the sky was troubled, when the army arrived at some narrow roads impassable for the provision-wagons; here, owing to the narrowness of the way, the order of march was thrown into confusion, and they advanced in extended line, and without discipline. The Saracens, observing this, poured down suddenly on the pack-horses and loaded wagons, slew both horses and men in a moment, and plundered a great deal of the baggage, boldly charging and dispersing those who opposed them as far as the sea-shore. Then there took place a fierce and obstinate conflict each fought for his life. Here a Turk cut off the right hand of Everard, one of the bishop of Salisbury's men, as he held his sword; the man, without changing countenance in the least, with his left hand boldly took the sword, and closing with the Turks, who were pressing on him, defended himself courageously from them all. By this time the rear was put into great confusion, and John Fitz-Luke, alarmed at this mishap, put spurs to his horse, and went to tell King Richard, who was ignorant of what had taken place. On hearing it, he rode at full gallop to their assistance, cutting down the Turks, right and left, like lightning, with his sword. And quickly, as of yore the Philistines fled from Maccabeus, so were the Turks now routed, and so did they fly from the face of King Richard, and make for the mountains but some of them remained amongst us, having lost their heads. In that conflict one of the French, William de Bartis, who had been at variance with King Richard from some old grudge, by his extraordinary good conduct was reconciled and restored to the king's former favor. The sultan was not far off with the whole strength of his army, but owing to the aforesaid repulse, the Turks, despairing of success, refrained from attacking our men any more, but watched them from the heights. Our troops, being restored to order, proceeded on their march as far as a river which they by chance met with, and cisterns, the excellence of which being ascertained, they pitched their tents, and rested there on a spacious plain, where they had seen that Saladin had fixed his camp before, and they judged that he had a very large army by the extent of the trodden ground. On the first day there our army fared thus, and by God's providence they were warned to be more cautious, after having experienced how much loss they might escape if properly on their guard another time.

CHAPTER XI - *How our army arrived at Cayphas from the river of Acre*

Saladin and the Turks, always on the watch to do us harm, had seized upon some passes between the rugged mountains, by which our army was to proceed and they intended to kill, seize, or disperse us as we issued forth in an extended line but when our army had advanced cautiously from the aforesaid river, and by slow march, as far as Cayphas, they pitched their tents there, and waited for the mass of the army who were following. They posted themselves between the town of Cayphas and the sea, and remained there two days, looking into and arranging their baggage, and they threw away what they thought they could dispense with, only retaining what was absolutely necessary, for the common soldiers marched on foot, and were much distressed by the weight of their baggage and provisions so that in the aforesaid battle they suffered much from fatigue and thirst.

CHAPTER XII - *How our army kept along the maritime parts, where they were wounded by the under wood, and met with wild beasts and how they left Cayphas by way of Capernaum, and reached the passes*

On a Wednesday, which was the third day after stopping at Cayphas, the army moved forward in order, the Templars leading the van, and the Hospitallers closing the rear, both of whom by their high bearing gave evidence of great valor. That day the army moved forward with more than wonted caution, and stopped after a long march, impeded by the thickets and the tall and luxuriant herbage, which struck them in the face, especially the foot-soldiers. In these maritime parts there were also numbers of beasts of the forest, who leapt up between their feet from the long grass and thick copses, and many were caught, not by design, but coming in their way by chance. When the king had proceeded as far as Capernaum, which the Saracens had razed to the ground, he dismounted, and took some food, the army, meanwhile, waiting those who chose took food, and immediately after proceeded on their march to the house called M of the narrow ways," because the road there becomes narrow; there they halted and pitched their tents. It was the custom of the army each night before lying down to rest, to depute some one to stand in the middle of the camp, and cry out with a loud voice, "Help! help! For the holy sepulchre! The rest of the army took it up, and repeated the words and stretching their hands to heaven, amid a profusion of tears, prayed for the mercy and assistance of God in the cause. Then the herald himself repeated the words in a loud voice, "Help! help! For the holy sepulchre I" and every one repeated it after him a second time, and so likewise a third time, with contrition of heart and abundant weeping. For who would not weep at such a moment, when the very mention of its having been done would extract tears from the auditors? The army appeared to be much refreshed by crying out in this fashion.

CHAPTER XIII - *How the tarrentes afflicted our people with their venomous stings*

As each night came round, a sort of reptile attacked us, commonly called tarrentes, which creep on the ground, and have most venomous stings. As the day comes on, they are harmless; but on the approach of night, they used their stings most pertinaciously, and those they stung were instantly swelled with the venom, and tortured with pain. The more noble and wealthy of those who were attacked applied theoretical ointment on the stings, and the antidote proved efficacious to remove the pain. At last, the more observant, perceiving that the reptiles were frightened away by loud sounds, raised a great noise at their approach by beating and clashing their helmets and shields together; also by beating against their seats, poles, casks, flagons, basins, platters, caldrons, and whatever household ware they could lay hands on to make a sufficient sound and by these sounds they drove away the reptiles. The army remained two days at the abovementioned station, where there was plenty of room for their camp, and waited there until the ships arrived which they were expecting namely, barges and galleys, laden with provisions, of which they were in need; for these vessels were sailing in connection with the army along the shore, and carried theirs.

CHAPTER XIV - *How our men marched from the house of the narrow ways to Merla, and thence to Casarea and the Dead River, The Turks, attacking them, were defeated*

The army advanced, using all precaution against the Turks, who kept on their flank, to a town called Merla, where the king had spent one of the previous nights there he had determined that he would lead the van himself the next day, on account of the obstacles in the way, and because the Templars kept guard in the rear for the Turks continually threatened them in a body on the flank. On that day the king, putting spurs to his horse, charged them furiously, and would have reaped great glory, had it not been for the backwardness of some, which retarded his success for, when King Richard pursued the Turks to a distance, some of his men suddenly halted, for which they were rebuked in the evening. If the king's companions had followed up their pursuit of the Turks, they would have gained a splendid victory; for the king drove all before him. The army had a very difficult march along the sea-shore on account of the great heat for it was summer time, and they marched a long day's journey. Many of them, overcome by the fatigue of the march, dropped down dead, and were buried where they died but the king, from compassion, caused many to be transported in galleys and ships, when they were overcome by the fatigue of the march or sickness, or any other cause, to their destination. The army, after accomplishing its march with much difficulty, arrived that day at Caesarea. The Turks had been there before them, and broken down part of the towers and walls, and destroyed the city as much as possible but on the approach of our army they fled. There the army pitched their tents, and passed the night by the side of a river close to the city, called the river of Crocodiles, because the crocodiles once devoured two soldiers while bathing therein. The circuit of the city of Caesarea is very great, and the buildings are of wonderful workmanship. Our Savior with his disciples often visited it, and worked miracles there. It was here the king had charged his ships to meet the army. Meanwhile the king caused it to be proclaimed by voice of herald in the city of Acre, that those who had remained behind from slothfulness should embark on board the ships which he had sent and come to the army, for the love of God, and to promote the success of the Christian cause, and to perform their vow of pilgrimage more fully. In obedience to his mandate, many came to Caesarea with the fleet, which was amply laden with provisions and he arranged that the ships should advance from that place in attendance on the army. A large number of ships here came together, and when the king had divided the army into squadrons, they set out one day about nine o'clock, at a slow pace, on account of the Turks, who continually harassed them when they left their stations, and, coming up to them as close as they dared, caused them all the molestation and annoyance in their power. They troubled us more than usual on this day, but by the help of God we escaped unhurt, having cut off the head of one of their admirals, a man of the greatest courage, and renowned for his valor he was said to have such strength that no one could throw him from his horse, or even dare to attack him and he carried a lance heavier than two of ours, to which he gave the name of alas estog. The Turks were overcome with grief and lamentation at his fall, so that they cut off their horses' tails, and, had they been permitted, would have carried off the corpse of their chief. After that the army arrived at a river called the Dead River, which the Saracens had previously covered over, in order that, not being seen, our men might endanger their lives by falling into it but by the providence of God they were preserved from danger, and, the river having been uncovered, our men drank thereof, and passed the night there.

CHAPTER XV - *How on quitting the Dead River, our army, before they arrived at the Salt River, were much harassed by the Turks, who slew many of our men and horses*

On the third day the army advanced slowly from the Dead River, through a country of a most desolate character, and destitute of every thing for they were compelled to march through a mountainous country, because they were unable to go by the sea-side, which was choked up by the luxuriant growth of the grass and the army on its march kept itself in closer companies than usual. The Templars on that day had charge of the rear, and they lost so many horses by the attacks of the Turks that they were almost reduced to despair. The count of St. Paul also lost many horses for he himself opposed the Turks with great valor, when they attacked and made incursions against us so that by his exertions the rest got off" in safety, and thus he earned the thanks and favor of the whole army. On that day the king was wounded in the side by a dart while he was driving the Turks but this slight hurt only incited him to attack them more vehemently; for the smarting of the wound made him more eager for vengeance, and during the whole of the day he fought against them and drove them back. The Turks, on the other hand, obstinately annoyed our men, and, keeping by the side of our army, did them all the injury they could, by throwing darts and arrows, which flew like hail. Alas! How many horses fell transfixed with darts how many died afterwards of the wounds which they received! There was such a stream of darts and arrows that you could not find four feet of ground, where the army passed, free from them. This terrible tempest continued all day, until at night-fall the Turks returned to their tents and dwellings. Our people also stopped near what was called the Salt River, and passed the night there they arrived there on the Tuesday after the festival of St. Giles, and tarried there two days. Here there was a great throng on account of the horses who died from their wounds for the people were so eager to purchase the horse-flesh that they even had recourse to blows. The king, on hearing this, proclaimed by herald that he would give a live horse to whoever would distribute his dead one to the best men in his service who needed it and thus they ate horse-flesh as if it was venison, and they reckoned it most savory, for hunger served in the place of seasoning.

CHAPTER XVI - *How our army marched from the Salt River, through the forest of Assur, in safety, to the river Rochetailie*

On the third day, about nine o'clock, our army marched in battle array from the Salt River; for there was a rumor that the Turks were lying in ambush for them in the forest of Assur, and that they intended to set the wood on fire to prevent our troops from crossing it. But our men, advancing in order, passed the place where the ambuscade was said to be, unmolested and on quitting the wood, they came to a large plain that ran along it, and there they pitched their tents, near the river commonly called Rochetailie. Here they sent spies to reconnoiter, who brought back news that the Turks were awaiting their approach in countless numbers for their multitudes covered the whole face of the earth around, and were estimated at 300,000 men, while the Christians were only 100,000 strong. The Christian army arrived at the river Rochetailie on the Thursday before the Nativity of the blessed Virgin Mary, and tarried there until the morrow.

CHAPTER XVII - *How our army, on advancing from the river Rochetailie towards*

Assur, prepared for battle with the Turks, whom they had vowed to attack on that day with all their might

On the Saturday, the eve of the Nativity of the blessed Virgin Mary, at earliest dawn, our men armed themselves with great care to receive the Turks, who were known to have preceded their march, and whose insolence nothing but a battle could check. The enemy had ranged themselves in order, drawing gradually nearer and nearer and our men also took the utmost care to place themselves in as good order as possible. King Richard, who was most experienced in military affairs, arranged the army in squadrons, and directed who should march in front, and who in the rear. He divided the army into twelve companies, and these again into five divisions, marshaled according as the men ranked in military discipline and none could be found more warlike, if they had only had confidence in God, who is the giver of all good things. On that day, the Templars formed the first rank, and after them came in due order the Bretons and men of Anjou; then followed King Guy, with the men of Poictou and in the fourth line were the Normans and English, who had the care of the royal standard and last of all, marched the Hospitallers: this line was composed of chosen warriors, divided into companies. They kept together so closely, that an apple, if thrown, would not have fallen to the ground, without touching a man or a horse and the army stretched from the army of the Saracens to the sea-shore. There you might have seen their most appropriate distinctions—standards, and ensigns of various forms, and hardy soldiers, fresh, and full of spirits, and well fitted for war. There was the earl of Leicester, Hugh de Gurnay, William de Borriz, Walkin de Ferrars, Roger de Toony, James d'Avennes, Robert count of Druell, the bishop of Beauvais, and William des Barres his brother, William de Garlande, Drogo de Mirle, and many of his kinsmen. Henry count of Champagne kept guard on the mountains side, maintaining a constant look-out on the flank: the foot-soldiers, bowmen and arbalesters, were on the outside, and the rear of the army was closed by the pack-horses and wagons, which carried provisions and other things, and journeyed along between the army and the sea, to avoid an attack from the enemy. This was the order of the army, as it advanced gradually, to prevent separation for the less close the line of battle, the less effective was it for resistance. King Richard and the duke of Burgundy, with a chosen retinue of warriors, rode up and down, narrowly watching the position and manner of the Turks, to correct any thing in their own troops, if they saw occasion for they had need, at that moment, of the utmost circumspection.

CHAPTER XVIII - *How our armies were much harassed by the Turks, who attacked them incessantly on all sides, and especially in the rear, wounding and cutting them down; and our men would have yielded under the weight of the battle in despair, had not the grace of God assisted them, when they were just on the point of giving way*

It was now nearly nine o'clock, when there appeared a large body of the Turks, 10,000 strong, coming down upon us at full charge, and throwing darts and arrows, as fast as they could, while they mingled their voices in one horrible yell. There followed after them an infernal race of men, of black color, and bearing a suitable appellation, expressive of their blackness. With them also were the Saracens, who live in the desert, called Bedouins: they are a savage race of men, blacker than soot; they fight on foot, and carry a bow, quiver, and round shield, and are a light and active race. These men dauntlessly attacked our army. Beyond them might be seen the well-arranged phalanxes of the Turks, with ensigns fixed to their lances, and standards and banners of separate distinctions. Their army was divided into troops, and the troops into companies and their numbers seemed to exceed twenty thousand. They came on with irresistible charge, on horses swifter than eagles and urged on like lightning to attack our men and as they advanced, they raised a cloud of dust, so that the sky was darkened. In front came certain of their admirals, as it was their duty, with clarions and trumpets; some had horns, others had pipes and timbrels, gongs, cymbals, and other instruments, producing a horrible noise and clamor. The earth vibrated from the loud and discordant sounds, so that the crash of thunder could not be heard amidst the tumultuous noise of horns and trumpets. They did this to excite their spirit and courage, for the more violent the clamor became, the bolder were they for the fray. Thus the impious Turks threatened us both on the side towards the sea and from the side of the land and for the space of two miles, not so much earth as could be taken up in one's hand could be seen, on account of the hostile Turks who covered it. Oh! how obstinately they pressed on, and continued their stubborn attacks, so that our men suffered severe loss of their horses, which were killed by their darts and arrows! Oh! how useful to us on that day were our arbalesters and bowmen, who closed the extremities of the lines, and did their best to repel the obstinate Turks. The enemy came rushing down, like a torrent, to the attack and many of our arbalesters, unable to sustain the weight of their terrible and calamitous charge, threw away their arms, and fearing lest they should be shut out, took refuge, in crowds, behind the dense lines of the army yielding, through fear of death, to sufferings which they could not support. Those whom shame forbade to yield, or the hope of an immortal crown sustained, were animated with greater boldness and courage to persevere in the contest, and fought with indefatigable valor face to face against the Turks, whilst they at the same time receded step by step, and so secured their retreat. The whole of that day, on account of the Turks pressing them closely from behind, they faced about and went on skirmishing, rather than proceeding on their march. Oh! how great was the strait they were in on that day! How great was their tribulation when some were affected with fears, and no one had such confidence or spirit as not to wish, at that moment, he had finished his pilgrimage, and had returned home instead of standing with trembling heart the chances of a doubtful battle. In truth, our people, so few in number, were hemmed in by the multitudes of the Saracens, that they had no means of escape, if they tried neither did they seem to have valor sufficient to withstand so many foes,—nay, they were shut in, like a flock of sheep in the jaws of wolves, with nothing but the sky above, and the enemy all around them. O Lord God! What feelings agitated that weak flock of Christ straitened by such a perplexity whom the enemy pressed with such unabating vigor, as if they would pass them through a sieve. What army was ever assailed by so mighty a force? There you might have seen our troopers, having lost their chargers, marching on foot with the footmen, or casting missiles from arbalests, or arrows from bows, against the enemy, and repelling their attacks in the best manner they were able. The Turks, skilled in the bow, pressed unceasingly upon them it rained darts the air was filled with the shower of arrows, and the brightness of the sun was obscured by the multitude of missiles, as if it had been darkened by a fall of winters hail or snow. Our horses were pierced by the darts and arrows, which were so numerous that the whole face of the earth around was covered with them, and if any one wished to gather them up, he might take twenty of them in his hand at a time. The Turks pressed with such boldness that they nearly crushed the Hospitallers on which the latter sent word to King Richard that they could not sustain the violence of the enemy's attack, unless he would allow their knights to advance at full charge against them. This the king dissuaded them from doing, but advised them to keep in a close body they therefore persevered and kept together, though scarcely able to breathe for the pressure. By these means they were able to proceed on their way, though the heat happened to be very great on that day so that they labored under two disadvantages,—the hot weather and the attacks of the enemy. These approved martyrs of Christ sweated in the contest and he who could have seen them closed up in a narrow space, so patient under the heat and toil of the day and the attacks of the enemy, who exhorted each other to destroy the Christians could not doubt in his mind that it augured ill to our success from their straitened and perilous position, hemmed in, as they were, by so large a multitude for the enemy thundered at their backs as if with mallets, so that having no room to use their bows, they fought hand to hand with swords, lances, and clubs and the blows of the Turks, echoing from their metal armor, resounded as if they had been struck upon an anvil. They were now tormented with the heat, and no rest was allowed them. The battle fell heavily on the extreme line of the Hospitallers; the more so, as they were unable to resist, but moved forward with patience under their wounds, returning not even a word for the blows which fell upon them, and advancing on their way, because they were not able to bear the weight of the contest. Then they pressed on for safety upon the centre of the army which was in front of them, to avoid the fury of the enemy, who harassed them in the rear. Was it wonderful that no one could withstand so continuous an attack, when he could not even return one blow to the numbers who pressed on him? The strength of all Paganism had gathered together from Damascus and Persia, from the Mediterranean to the East there was not left in the uttermost recesses of the earth one man of fame or power, one nation of valor, or one bold soldier, whom the Sultan had not summoned to his aid, either by entreaty, by money, or by authority, to crush the Christian race for he presumed to hope he could blot them from the face of the earth ; but his hopes were vain, for their numbers were sufficient, through the assistance of God, to effect their purpose. The flower of the chosen youth and soldiers of Christendom had indeed assembled together and were united in one body, like ears of corn on their stalks, from every region of the earth and if they had been utterly crushed and destroyed, there is no doubt that there were none left to make resistance.

CHAPTER XIX - *The battle continued, and the wonderful victory of the Christians*

A cloud of dust obscured the air as our men marched on and, in addition to the heat, they had an enemy pressing them in the rear, insolent, and rendered obstinate by the instigation of the devil. Still the Christians proved good men, and, secure in their unconquerable spirit, kept constantly advancing, while the Turks threatened them without ceasing in the rear but their blows fell harmless upon the defensive armor, and this caused the Turks to slacken in courage at the failure of their attempts, and they began to murmur in whispers of disappointment, crying out in their rage, "that our people were of iron, and would yield to no blow." Then the Turks, about twenty thousand strong, rushed again upon our men pellmell, annoying them in every possible manner when, as if almost overcome by their savage fury, brother Gamier de Napes, one of the

Hospitallers, suddenly exclaimed, with a loud voice, "excellent St. George will you leave us to be thus put to confusion? The whole of Christendom is now on the point of perishing, because it fears to return a blow against this impious race." Upon this, the master of the Hospitallers went to the king, and said to him, "My lord the king, we are violently pressed by the enemy, and are in danger of eternal infamy, as if we did not dare to return their blows; we are each of us losing our horses one after another, and why should we bear with them any further?" To whom the king replied, "Good master, it is you who must sustain their attack no one can be everywhere at once." On the master returning, the Turks again made a fierce attack on them from the rear, and there was not a prince or count amongst them but blushed with shame, and they said to each other, "Why do we not charge them at full gallop? Alas! alas! We shall for ever deserve to be called cowards, a thing which never happened to us before, for never has such a disgrace befallen so great an army even from the unbelievers. Unless we defend ourselves by immediately charging the enemy, we shall gain everlasting scandal and so much the greater the longer we delay to fight." O, how blind is human fate! On what slippery points it stands! Alas, on how uncertain wheels doth it advance, and with what ambiguous success doth it unfold the course of human things! A countless multitude of the Turks would have perished, if the aforesaid attempt had been orderly conducted but to punish us for our sins, as it is believed, the potters wheel produces a paltry vessel instead of the grand design which he had conceived. For while they were treating of this point, and had come to the same decision about charging the enemy, two knights, who were impatient of delay, put every thing in confusion. It had been resolved by common consent that the sounding of six trumpets in three different parts of the army should be a signal for a charge, viz., two in front, two in the rear, and two in the middle, to distinguish the sounds from those of the Saracens, and to mark the distance of each. If these orders had been attended to, the Turks would have been utterly discomfited but from the too great haste of the aforesaid knights, the success of the affair was marred. They rushed at full gallop upon the Turks, and each of them prostrated his man by piercing him with his lance. One of them was the marshal of the Hospitallers the other was Baldwin de Carreo, a good and brave man, and the companion of King Richard, who had brought him in his retinue. When the other Christians observed these two running forward, and heard them calling, with a clear voice, on St. George for aid, they charged the Turks in a body with all their strength then the Hospitallers, who had been distressed all day by their close array, following the two soldiers, charged the enemy in troops, so that the van of the army became the rear from their position in the attack, and the Hospitallers, who had been the last, were the first to charge. The count of Champagne also burst forward with his chosen company, and James d'Avennes with his kinsmen, and also Robert count of Dreux, the bishop of Beauvais, and his brother, as well as the earl of Leicester, who made a fierce charge on the left towards the sea. Why need we name each? Those who were in the first line of the rear made a united and furious charge after them the men of Poictou, the Bretons, and the men of Anjou, rushed swiftly onward, and then came the rest of the army in a body each troop showed its valor, and boldly closed with the Turks, transfixing them with their lances, and casting them to the ground. The sky grew black with the dust which was raised in the confusion of that encounter. The Turks, who had purposely dismounted from their horses in order to take better aim at our men with their darts and arrows, were slain on all sides in that charge, for on being prostrated by the horse soldiers they were beheaded by the foot-men. King Richard, on seeing his army in motion and in encounter with the Turks, flew rapidly on his horse at full speed through the Hospitallers who had led the charge, and to whom he was bringing assistance with all his retinue, and broke into the Turkish infantry, who were astonished at his blows and those of his men, and gave way to the right and to the left. Then might be seen numbers prostrated on the ground, horses without their riders in crowds, the wounded lamenting with groans their hard fate, and others drawing their last breath, weltering in their gore, and many lay headless, whilst their lifeless forms were trodden under foot both by friend and foe. Oh how different are the speculations of those who meditate amidst the columns of the cloister from the fearful exercise of war! There the king, the fierce, the extraordinary king, cut down the Turks in every direction, and none could escape the force of his arm, for wherever he turned, brandishing his sword, he carved a wide path for himself; and as he advanced and gave repeated strokes with his sword, cutting them down like a reaper with his sickle, the rest, warned by the sight of the dying, gave him more ample space, for the corpses of the dead Turks which lay on the face of the earth extended over half a mile. In fine, the Turks were cut down, the saddles emptied of their riders, and the dust which was raised by the conflict of the combatants, proved very hurtful to our men, for on becoming fatigued from slaying so many, when they were retiring to take fresh air, they could not recognize each other on account of the thick dust, and struck their blows indiscriminately to the right and to the left so that, unable to distinguish friend from foe, they took their own men for enemies, and cut them down without mercy. Thus the Christians pressed hard upon the Turks, the latter gave way before them but for a long time the battle was doubtful they still exchanged blows, and either party strove for the victory : on both sides were seen some retreating, covered with wounds, while others fell slain to the ground. Oh, how many banners and standards of various forms, and pennons and many colored ensigns, might then be seen torn and fallen to the earth swords of proved steel, and lances made of cane with iron heads, Turkish bows, and maces bristling with sharp teeth, darts and arrows, covering the ground, and missiles enough to load twenty wagons or more! There lay the headless trunks of the Turks who had perished, whilst others retained their courage for a time until our men increased in strength, when some of them concealed themselves in the copses, some climbed up trees, and, being shot with arrows, fell with fearful groan to the earth; others, abandoning their horses, betook themselves by slippery foot-paths to the seaside, and tumbled headlong into the waves from the precipitous cliffs that were five poles in height. The rest of the enemy were repulsed in so wonderful a manner, that for the space of two miles nothing could be seen but fugitives, although they had before been so obstinate and fierce, and puffed up with pride: but by God's grace their pride was humbled, and they continued still to fly; for when our men ceased the pursuit, fear alone added wings to their feet. Our army had been ranged in divisions when they attacked the Turks; the Normans and English also, who had the care of the standard, came up slowly towards the troops which were fighting with the Turks,—for it was very difficult to disperse the enemy's strength, and they stopped at a short distance therefrom, that all might have a rallying point. On the conclusion of the slaughter, our men paused but the fugitives, to the number of twenty thousand, when they saw this, immediately recovering their courage, and armed with maces, charged the hindmost of those who were retiring, and rescued some from our men who had just struck them down. Oh how dreadfully were our men then pressed for the darts and arrows, thrown at them as they were falling back, broke the heads, arms, and other limbs of our horsemen, so that they bent, stunned, to their saddle-bows; but having quickly regained their spirits and resumed their strength, and thirsting for vengeance with greater eagerness, like a lioness when her whelps are stolen, they charged the enemy, and broke through them like a net. Then you might have seen the horses with their saddles displaced; and the Turks, who had but just now fled, returning, and pressing upon our people with the utmost fury every cast of their darts would have told, had our men kept marching, and not stood still in a compact immovable body. The commander of the Turks was an admiral, by name Tekedmus, a kinsman of the sultan, having a banner with a remarkable device; namely, that of a pair of breeches carved thereon, a symbol well known to his men. He was a most cruel persecutor, and a persevering enemy of the Christians; and he had under his command seven hundred chosen Turks of great valor, of the household troops of Saladin, each of whose companies bore a yellow banner with pennons of a different color. These men, coming at full charge, with clamor and haughty bearing, attacked our men who were turning off" from them towards the standard, cutting at them, and piercing them severely, so that even the firmness of our chiefs wavered under the weight of the pressure yet our men remained immovable, compelled to repel force by force, and the conflict grew thicker, the blows were redoubled, and the battle raged fiercer than before : the one side labored to crush, the other to repel both exerted their strength, and although our men were by far the fewest in numbers, they made havoc of great multitudes of the enemy and that portion of the army which thus toiled in the battle could not return to the standard with ease, on account of the immense mass which pressed upon them so severely for thus hemmed in they began to flag in courage, and but few dared to renew the attack of the enemy. In truth, the Turks were furious in the assault, and greatly distressed our men, whose blood poured forth in a stream beneath their blows. On perceiving them reel and give way, William de Barris, a renowned knight, breaking through the ranks, charged the Turks with his men; and such was the vigor of the onset that some fell by the edge of his sword, while others only saved themselves by rapid flight. For all that, the king, mounted on a bay Cyprian steed, which had not its match, bounded forward in the direction of the mountains, and scattered those he met on all sides for the enemy fled from his sword and gave way, while helmets tottered beneath it, and sparks flew forth from its strokes. So great was the fury of his onset, and so many and deadly his blows, that day, in his conflict with the Turks, that in a short space of time the enemy were all scattered, and allowed our army to proceed and thus our men, having suffered somewhat, at last returned to the standard, and proceeded in their march as far as Arsur, and there they pitched their tents outside its walls. While they were thus engaged, a large body of the Turks made an attack on the extreme rear of our army. On hearing the noise of the assailants, King Richard, encouraging his men to battle, rushed at full speed, with only fifteen companions, against the Turks, crying out, with a loud voice, "Aid us, O God and the Holy Sepulchre!" and this he exclaimed a second and a third time; and when our men heard it, they made haste to follow him, and attacked, routed, and put them to flight pursuing them as far as Arsur, whence they had first come out, cutting them down and subduing them.

Many of the Turks fell there also. The king returned thence, from the slaughter of the fugitives, to his camp and the men, overcome with the fatigues and exertions of the day, rested quietly that night. Whoever was greedy of gain, and wished to plunder the booty, returned to the place of battle, and loaded himself to his heart's desire and those who returned from thence reported that they had counted thirty-two Turkish chiefs who were found slain on that day, and whom they supposed to be men of great influence and power, from the splendor of their armor and the costliness of their apparel. The Turks also made search for them to carry them away, as being of the most importance and besides these the Turks carried off seven thousand mangled bodies of those who were next in rank, besides of the wounded, who went off in straggling parties and when their strength failed, lay about the fields and died. But by the protection of God we did not lose a tenth nor a hundredth part so many as fell in the Turkish army. Oh the disasters of that day! Oh the trials of the warriors for the tribulations of the just are many. Oh mournful calamity and bitter distress! How great must have been the blackness of our sins to require so fiery an ordeal to purify it for if we had striven to overcome this urgent necessity by pious long suffering, and without a murmur, the sense of our obligations would have been deeper.

CHAPTER XX - *How the admirable tonight James was slain in the second encounter*

But we had to mourn greatly the loss of James d'Avennes, who was overpowered by the numbers of the Turks for he was thrown by a grievous fall of his horse, while bravely fighting and the Turks, gathering round him, after much labor, put him to death. But before breathing his last, he slew fifteen of the Turks, according to the report of those who were sent to bring his body to the camp, and who found so many Turkish soldiers lying dead around him. There were also found dead along with him three of his kinsmen, to whom some of our men did not give the assistance which they ought but, shame to say, deserted them in their struggle against the attack of the Turks, on which account the count of Dreux and others who were present obtained the infamy and detestation which they deserved. Alas for the manifold calamities of war! How loud were the groans and sighs of our soldiers on that night for the absence of James d'Avennes, the excellent soldier and renowned warrior for they augured his fall, as they did not see him and his kinsmen with the rest, and the whole army was afflicted by his irreparable loss. On the Saturday before the Nativity of the Blessed Virgin Mary, the aforesaid battle was fought and on the Sunday following, it was decreed that a search should be made for the body, in order that it might be buried. Therefore, the Hospitallers and knights of the Temple armed themselves, and took with them many of the Turcopoli and others, and, on arriving on the field of battle, they made anxious search, and at last found the body, its face covered with clotted blood, so that it was difficult of recognition until it was washed with water, for it was dyed in gore and swollen with wounds, and very unlike his former self. Thus, having decently wrapped up the body, they bore it back to Arsur, whence a great multitude of the soldiers came forth to meet it and all lamented the death of so great a man, for they called to mind his prowess, bounty, and the many virtues that adorned him, and King Richard and King Guy assisted at his funeral, where a solemn mass was celebrated, with large offerings, in the church of our Lady the Queen of Heaven, whose nativity it was. After the mass, the funeral rites were solemnly performed, and the nobles, taking his body in their arms, buried it in a grave, erecting a mound thereon and there was great wailing, weeping, and lamentation for his death. When the obsequies were ended, the clergy solemnly performed the service for the day, being that of the Blessed Virgin Mary.

CHAPTER XXI - *Of the rout of the Turks, who first turned their backs and then fled, and how they left all their baggage about the fields a prey to the Christians*

Now the emirs and nobles of the Saracens, to whom Saladin had given great territories and riches, had been induced, by his deceitful words and high-flown language, to believe, that on that day, with the aid of Mahomet, he would utterly extirpate the Christians but the oracle of Mahomet deceived them, and their insolent boasting was repressed. For according to the report of those who saw it, you might trace the flight of the Turks through the mountains, on the day of battle, by the booty that was thrown aside, the dead horses and camels lying along the way, as they had fallen, and laden with heavy baggage; for the Turkish bowmen had fled from the face of the Christians, and retreated with all that was left them and on the day of battle, the more anxiously they hastened their flight, the more surely they failed, and perished, leaving behind them an immense quantity of spoil. Such was the vigor of our men's last attack, that if the enemy had remained a little longer, and had not taken to flight, they would never again have been in fighting order, and the land would have been left for the Christians to occupy.

CHAPTER XXII - *Saladin reproaches and derides his men, who excuse themselves by praising King Richard and his troops, beyond all they had ever seen*

The sultan, hearing that his choice troops, in whom he had placed so much confidence, were routed in this manner by the Christians, was filled with anger and excitement and calling together his admirals, he said to them, "Are these the deeds of my brave troops, once so boastful, and whom I have so loaded with gifts? Lo! the Christians traverse the whole country at their pleasure, for there is no one to oppose them. Where now are all their vaunts, those swords and spears with which they threatened to do such execution where is that prowess which they promised to put forth against the Christians, to overthrow them utterly? They have fought the battle which they desired, but where is the victory they promised? They are degenerated from those noble ancestors who performed such exploits against the Christians, and whose memory will endure for ever. It is a disgrace to our nation, the most warlike in the world, thus to become as nothing in comparison with their glorious ancestors." The admirals held down their heads at these words but one of them, named Sanscuns, of Aleppo, returned this answer:—"Most sacred Sultan, saving your majesty, this charge is unjust, for we fought with all our strength against the Franks, and did our best to destroy them we met their fiercest attacks, but it was of no avail; they are armed in impenetrable armor which no weapon can pierce, so that all our blows fell as it were upon a rock of flint. And, further, there is one among their number superior to any man we have ever seen he always charges before the rest, slaying and destroying our men he is the first in every enterprise, and is a most brave and excellent soldier; no one can resist him or escape out of his hands they call him Melech Ric. Such a king as he seems born to command the whole earth what then could we do more against so formidable an enemy?"

CHAPTER XXIII - *How Saladin destroyed all the fortresses, except Jerusalem, Crack, and Darum*

Saladin, in the heat of his indignation, called to him his brother Saphadin. "It is my wish," said he, "to try what reliance can be placed on my men in this extremity go and destroy without delay the walls of Ascalon and Guadres, but deliver Darum into the custody of my people, to insure safety to those who pass that way. But destroy also Galatia, Blancheward, Joppa, the castles of Plans, Maen, St. George, Ramula, Belmont, Toron, the castle of Ernald, Beauverie, and Mirabel : destroy, in short, all the mountain fortresses; spare neither city, castle, nor fort, except Crach and Jerusalem." Saphadin obeyed these commands, and destroyed all these fortresses without delay.

CHAPTER XXIV - *The Turks with 15,000 men attack our men on the river Arsur, but without success*

Meanwhile, a powerful Saracen prince, named Gaysac, urged Saladin to send scouts into the plains of Ramula to reconnoiter the movements of the Franks. "For I hope," added he, "if I have stanch troops, to be able to cut off the greater part of them, and to draw them into the narrow passes, that few of them shall be able to escape us." By his advice, Saladin ordered thirty of his principal admirals, each at the head of five hundred men, to occupy the banks of the river Arsur. Here, therefore, they kept guard, to prevent the Franks from passing. On Monday, the morrow of the Nativity of the Blessed Virgin, and the third day after the battle before mentioned, King Richard marched with his army to the Arsur. The Templars were in the rear, and marched with much order and circumspection, to guard against sudden attacks of the enemy but they reached the river without opposition. The Turks now, having kept close in their ambuscade, when the Christians came up, assailed the foremost of them with their javelins and arrows, but failing of success, retreated, and our men encamped that night on the Arsur. In the morning our infantry, who could hardly maintain the march, advanced with the quarter masters to Joppa, which they found so entirely dismantled, that the army could not find lodgings in it. They therefore encamped in an olive-garden on the left side of the town, about three weeks after they left Acre.

CHAPTER XXV - *How our ships brought us provisions from Acre to Joppa*

The army remained outside the walls of Joppa, and refreshed themselves with abundance of fruits, figs, grapes, pomegranates, and citrons, produced by the country round when to the fleet of King Richard, with other vessels, which accompanied the army and went to and fro between Joppa and Acre, brought us necessaries, much to the annoyance of the Turks, because they could not prevent them.

CHAPTER XXVI - *How King Richard advised to save Ascalon from the Turks, who were dismantling it out by the sinister counsels of the French they preferred to repair to Joppa, and indulged themselves there in vice and luxury*

Saladin, meanwhile, had destroyed the walls of Ascalon. This intelligence was brought by some common soldiers, who escaped, whilst it was in progress but our people could hardly believe that Saladin had done this in despair, as if so powerful a prince could not or did not dare defend them. To ascertain the truth, King Richard, by advice of his nobles, sent Geoffrey de Lusignan, William de Stagno, and others, in a strong galley to sail to Ascalon, and bring back word how matters stood. This commission they faithfully discharged, and reported that all they had heard was true. King Richard, therefore, and his nobles now deliberated whether they should march to save Ascalon, or proceed at once to Jerusalem many opinions were given, and the king gave his own, in the presence of the duke of Burgundy and others, in these words "It seems to me," said he, "that our difference of opinion may be not only useless, but dangerous to the army. The Turks who are dismantling Ascalon, dare not meet us in the field. I think we should endeavor to save Ascalon, as a protection to the pilgrims who pass that way." The French violently opposed this opinion, and recommended rather that Joppa should be restored, because it furnished a shorter and easier route for pilgrims going to Jerusalem. The acclamations of the multitude seconded the opinion of the French. Foolish counsel fatal obstinacy of those indolent men! By providing for their immediate comfort, and to avoid labor and expense, they did what they would afterwards repent of for if they had then saved Ascalon from the Turks, the whole land would soon have been clear of them. But the cry of the people prevailed, a collection was made, and they immediately began to rebuild the towers, and to clear out the moat of Joppa. The army remained there long enjoying ease and pleasure; their sins grew daily upon them women came to them from Acre, to stir up their passions and multiply their misdeeds the whole people became corrupted, the zeal of pilgrimage waxed cold, and all their works of devotion were neglected.

CHAPTER XXVII - *How the people returned to Acre, where they spent their time in taverns, and were led back by King Richard to Joppa, where they remained seven weeks*

It was now the end of September, and Joppa partly rebuilt, when the army, issuing from the suburbs, encamped before the fortress of Habacuc; too small an army, alas for many of them had withdrawn to Acre, where they spent their time in the taverns. King Richard, seeing their idleness and debauchery, sent King Guy to bring them back to the army at Joppa, but very few of them returned, and King Richard was obliged himself to sail to Joppa, where he urged them by exhortations of their duty as pilgrims, and by these means induced many of them to return to Joppa. He also conducted back with him the queens and their females. They now remained seven weeks at Joppa, to assemble and make ready the army, so that when they came together, they formed a much more numerous and efficient body than before.

CHAPTER XXVIII - *How King Richard went out unadvisedly with only a small escort, and would have been taken by the Turks, if William de Pratelles had not pretended to be the king, and so secured Richard's escape*

About this time King Richard went out hawking with a small escort, and intending, if he saw any small body of Turks, to fall upon them. Fatigued with his ride, he fell asleep, and a body of Turks rushed suddenly upon him to make him prisoner. The king, awakened at the noise, had hardly time to mount his bay Cyprian horse, and his attendants were still getting on their horses also, when the Turks came upon them and tried to take him but the king, drawing his sword, rushed upon them, and they, pretending flight, drew him after them to a place where there was another body of Turks in ambush. These started up with speed and surrounded the king to make him prisoner. The king defended himself bravely, and the enemy drew back, though he would still have been captured if the Turks had known who he was. But in the midst of the conflict one of the king's companions, William de Pratelles, called out in the Saracenic language, that he was the "melech," i. e. the king and the Turks, believing what he said, led him off captive to their own army. In this skirmish were slain Regnier de Marum, a brave knight, but almost unarmed, his nephew Walter, and Alan and Luke du Stable. At the news of this action our army was alarmed, and seizing their arms, came at full gallop to find the king and when they met him returning safe, he faced about and with them pursued the Turks, who had carried off William de Pratelles, thinking they had got the king. They could not, however, overtake the fugitives, and King Richard, reserved by the divine hand for greater things, returned to the camp, to the great joy of his soldiers, who thanked God for his preservation, but grieved for William de Pratelles, who loyally redeemed the king at the price of his own liberty. Some of the king's friends now reproved him for his temerity, and entreated him not to wander abroad alone, and expose himself to be taken by the ambuscades of the Turks, who were especially eager to make him prisoner but on all occasions to take with him some brave soldiers, and not to trust to his own strength against such numbers. But, notwithstanding these admonitions on the part of his best friends, the king's nature still broke out in all expeditions he was the first to advance, and the last to retreat, and he never failed, either by his own valor or the divine aid, to bring back numbers of captives, or if they resisted, to put them to the sword.

CHAPTER XXIX - *King Richard and his army rebuild the forts of Plans and Maen, and repel the Turks who attack them*

The army seemed now by rest to have recovered their vigor, and a royal order was issued for them to march and rebuild the fortress of Plans, which was necessary for the safety of the pilgrims who passed that way. The king therefore left a garrison in Joppa, with orders that none should leave it besides merchants bringing provisions. The care of the town was deputed to the bishop of Evreux, the count of Chalons, Hugh Ribole, and others. On Wednesday, the feast of

All Saints, King Richard was riding in the plains of Ramula, and seeing by chance some Turkish scouts, he attacked them bravely, and put them all to the rout, slaying some of them, and cutting off the head of a noble Turkish admiral the rest took to flight. The next day was the eve of All Saints, and the army, after a short march, encamped between the forts of Plans and Maen. The Turkish army was then at Ramula, whence they frequently sallied to attack us. The army remained fifteen days or more where they were, during which time the king repaired the fort of Maen, and the Templars rebuilt the fort of Plans, notwithstanding the attacks of the Turks, who one day assailed them with an immense multitude of foot and a thousand cavalry ; but the king mounting his horse in haste, and the whole army being roused, the Turks fled, losing twenty in slain, and sixteen taken prisoners. All the king's attempts to overtake the others were ineffectual he pursued them till he came in sight of Ramula, and then led back his troops to the camp.

CHAPTER XXX - *Of the wonderful victory of King Richard and his men, in defending their men-at-arms who were for aging*

On the sixth day after the feast of All Saints, namely, on the day of St. Leonard's, the esquires and men-at-arms went out to get fodder for their horses and beasts of burthen. The Templars were guarding the esquires whilst they dispersed to find fresh herbage, a duty which sometimes cost them dear, when they acted without much caution. Whilst the Templars were thus engaged, about four thousand Turkish cavalry rushed upon them from Bombrac, in four divisions, and in an instant the Templars were surrounded by a multitude of Turks, which was continually increasing. Acting with promptitude according to the emergency, they dismounted, and, standing back to back with their faces to the enemy, defended themselves bravely. Three of them were slain in a moment, but they still fought bravely, and a fierce conflict ensued, as the Turks assailed them with the utmost fierceness, and tried to take them all prisoners. On a sudden, news of what was going on having been conveyed to the camp, Andrew de Chamgui galloped up to the rescue with fifteen knights in his train, and, attacking the Turks, liberated the Templars from their dangerous position. Andrew bore himself like a brave knight on that day, as well as his companions bore witness but the Turks were continually receiving reinforcements, and sometimes attacked, sometimes retreated, and the battle still raged, until King Richard, who was busy in rebuilding Maen, heard of the tumult, and sent the count de St. Paul and the earl of Leicester to assist the Templars. With them, also, went William de Cagen and Otho de Pransinges, and the party soon heard the cries of the men at-arms for assistance. Then the king, exhorting the counts to get ready, seized his arms, and followed them as fast as he was able. As the counts were galloping onwards, about four thousand Turks sprang up in four bodies, from the neighborhood of a certain river, and half of them attacked the Templars, whilst the others assailed the two counts. The count of St. Paul then made an unworthy proposition to the earl of Leicester, that only one of them should fight with the enemy, whilst the other should stand by to assist whenever it might be necessary. The earl of Leicester chose to attack the enemy, not liking to stand by and do nothing. He at once, therefore, charged the enemy, and rescued from their hands two of our men whom they had made prisoners, and by his achievements on that day added greatly to his former reputation. The conflict was raging fiercely when the king came up, and as his retinue was very small, some of his men said to him, "My lord, we do not think it prudent or possible, with our small body, to resist this great multitude, nor shall we be able to save our men who are fighting with the Turks. It is better to let them perish, than to expose your person and all Christendom to certain danger, whilst we have the power of escaping." The king changed color with indignation at these words. "What!" said he, "if I neglect to aid my men whom I sent forward with a promise to follow them, I shall never again deserve to be called a king." He said no more, but spurring his horse, dashed into the middle of the Turks, overthrowing them on both sides of him, and brandishing his sword, carved his way to and fro among the thickest ranks, slaying and maiming every one he came near. Amongst others, he slew a Turkish admiral, named Aralchais, whom chance threw in his way. In short, the enemies were put to the sword or took to flight, and our men returned with several prisoners to the camp. This success was gained without any help from the French. The same day three Turks, from fear of death perhaps, renounced their superstitions, and embracing Christianity, submitted to King Richard.

CHAPTER XXXI - *How Saladhi amused King Richard by false promises, and thereby gained time to destroy certain fortresses*

The two castles before mentioned were now partly restored, and King Richard, perceiving that his troops not only hated the Turks, but had less fear of them than before, because they had always, with God's help, defeated them, even when superior in numbers, now sent a distinguished embassy to Saladin and Saphadin his brother, to demand the surrender of the kingdom of Syria, with all that belonged to it, such as the leprous king had last possessed it. He demanded also tribute from Babylon, as the kings, his predecessors, had received it, together with all the privileges and dues which had at any time before belonged to the kingdom of Jerusalem. The ambassadors unfolded their message before Saladin, who would not, however, acquiesce in the demand. "Your king," said he, "makes an unreasonable claim, and we cannot, with regard to the honor of Paganism, consent to it but I will offer to your king, through my brother Saphadin, to give up to him the whole land of Jerusalem, from Jordan to the sea, without tribute or hindrance, on condition that the city of Ascalon shall never be rebuilt, either by the Christians or the Saracens. When Saphadin came with this message to the king, Richard, who had just been bled, would not converse with him on that day but Stephen de Torneham, by the king's order, supplied him with every kind of delicacy for his table, and entertained him in the valley between the castles of the Temple and of Jehoshaphat. The next day Saphadin sent a present of seven camels and a rich tent, and coming into the king's presence, delivered Saladin's message upon which Richard, considering the disturbances and uncertainties of war, determined to have patience for a time, that he might the better make provision for the future but, alas! he showed too little prudence in not foreseeing the deceit with which they sought to protract the time until the cities, castles, and fortresses of that country were destroyed. In short, Saphadin so cunningly beguiled the too credulous king that one would have thought they had contracted a mutual familiarity for the king received Saphadin's gifts, and messengers were daily passing with presents to the king, much to the annoyance of his friends, who blamed him for contracting friendship with the Gentiles. But Saphadin pleaded that he wished to make peace between them, and the king thought he was adopting a wise policy, by which the bounds of Christianity would be enlarged, and a creditable peace concluded, particularly since the departure of the French king, from whom he feared treachery, for he had always found his friendship hollow and deceitful. When, however, the king discovered that the promises of Saphadin were mere words, and likely to produce no result, particularly in the matter of Fort Erach of Mount Royal, of which, according to the understood conditions, the king demanded the demolition, but the Turks would not consent to it, he at once broke off the negotiations. This failure of the treaty becoming known, the enemy was soon again to be seen on our flanks, and King Richard was again in the field to meet them and by way of wiping out the former charges which had been made against him, he brought every day numbers of Turkish heads, to prove that his zeal had not slackened in the cause of Christianity. The difficulties thrown in his way, and accusations made against him, had arisen from those who sought to obtain his money for it is rare to find persons not actuated by the desire of gain.

CHAPTER XXXII - *Of the annoyance which our men experienced from the rains and the enemy, whilst they encamped between St. George and Ramula, and in the town of Ramula itself*

When the two forts were repaired and garrisoned, Richard moved his army towards Ramula which caused Saladin to order Ramula to be dismantled, because he did not dare meet the king in the field. He then withdrew with his troops towards Darum, because he had most confidence in the mountainous districts. Our troops then encamped between St. George and Ramula, where they remained twenty-two days waiting for reinforcements and provisions. There also we endured severe attacks from the enemy, and the heavy rains drove the king of Jerusalem and our people to remove into St. George and Ramula the count of St. Paul went to the Castle of the Baths. We stopped in Ramula seven weeks, not however in ease, for we had a rough beginning, though it was afterwards made amends for by a more pleasant termination. The Turks would not allow us the least repose, but continually attacked us with their javelins. On the eve of St. Thomas the Apostle, King Richard had sallied forth with a small retinue towards a fort called Whitecastle, on some enterprise against the Turks, but foreboding something wrong, by inspiration as is thought from heaven, he returned to the camp. The same hour he was told that Saladin had a little before sent a body of three hundred of his choicest troops to Whitecastle, where Richard was going. The same day also King Guy went to Acre whither he was followed the next day by Stephen de Torneham. In the middle of the night of the Holy Innocents, the Hospitallers and Templars left the camp, and returned in the morning with two hundred oxen, which they had driven off from the mountains near Jerusalem.

CHAPTER XXXIII - *Of the glorious victory gained by the earl of Leicester against the Turks, when our men at last came to his assistance*

The noble earl of Leicester, one day, followed by a few men only, endeavored to drive off a large body of Turks who were passing by with much arrogance and boasting. The enemy fled with precipitation and was followed by three of the swiftest knights in the ears train by this act of imprudence they placed themselves in the power of the Turks, who turned back and made them prisoners. The earl, seeing this, spurred his horse and rode into the midst of more than a hundred Turks, to rescue the knights. His men, following him, pursued the enemy over a river, when a fresh force of about five hundred Turkish cavalry charged them with bows and lances of reed, and cutting off the retreat of the earl and his small party, essayed to make him prisoner.

Already was Garin Fitz-Gerald dismounted and severely beaten with the iron maces. A fierce struggle took place. Drogo de Fontenille Putrell and Robert Nigel were unhorsed, and the Turks made such exertions to seize the earl that at last they struck v formed such brave deeds. So many of the best soldiers sallied from the camp to assist him, that not one of them was slain, but they repulsed the Turks and pursued them, until, fatigued with their exertions, they returned quietly to the camp.

CHAPTER XXXIV - *Of the annoyances which our soldiers experienced from the rain and the attacks of the enemy as they marched by Betenoble towards Jerusalem*

In the mean time it became known to Saladin that our men were preparing to attack Jerusalem, and were only two miles distant from him but, not thinking it safe to fight with the Christians, he gave orders to destroy Darum, its walls and towers, and retreated himself to Jerusalem. The Turks, also, in general left the plains and withdrew to the mountains. In consequence of this, our men were commanded by voice of herald to move towards the foot of the mountains and, when all the arrangements were completed, they marched towards a castle called Betenoble. Then the rain and hail began to beat upon our men, and killed many of their beasts of burthen the storm was so violent that it tore up the pegs of the tents, drowned the horses, and spoiled all their biscuit and bacon. The armor and coats of mail, also, were so rusted, that the greatest labor was necessary to restore them to their former brightness their clothes were dissolved by the wet, and the men themselves suffered from the unwonted severity of the climate. Under all these sufferings, their only consolation arose from their zeal in the service of God, and a desire to finish their pilgrimage. To this end each contributed his share of provisions for the siege, and they came together with joy prepared for any pilgrimage. Even those who were sick in bed at Joppa, were carried in litters, so great was their wish to see Jerusalem. A large number of them, also, were influenced by a desire to see our Lord's tomb, and this was their only hope under their great sufferings. But the Turks, paying no regard to these convoys of the sick, lay in wait for them and killed both them and their bearers, looking on them all as enemies alike. But, surely, these are all to be accounted martyrs, and there is this consolation for them, that though the Turks slew them with evil intentions, yet they suffered but for a moment, and gained the reward of a long service.

CHAPTER XXXV - *How the army prepare with joy to march on Jerusalem, neglecting the advice of the Templars and other wise men who dissuaded them*

The army now rejoiced that they should soon set eyes on our Lord's sepulchre; and all began to brighten up their armor, their helmets and their swords, that there might not be a single spot to spoil their brightness. In short, all were most eager for the enterprise, and boasted that not all the power or assaults of the hostile Saracens should prevent them from accomplishing their plighted vow. But the wiser ones did not acquiesce in these views for the Templars, Hospitallers, and Pisans, who had sharper eyes on the future condition of that land, dissuaded King Richard from marching at present to Jerusalem, lest, whilst they were besieging Saladin and the garrison of that city, the Turkish army, which was without among the mountains, might attack our men by surprise, and so place them between the attacks of the garrison from within, and the Turkish army from without and even if they should take the city, it would be necessary to garrison it with some of their bravest troops, which could hardly be done, in consequence

of the people's eagerness to complete their pilgrimage and return each to his own home, for they were now all tired out with the privations and disturbances which they had suffered. For these reasons, they advised that the siege should be delayed, and the army be kept together, because their vow would not have been accomplished for if they could once fulfill their pledge, the army would at once be dissolved. But the advice of the Templars was not listened to.

CHAPTER XXXVI - *How King Richard, concealing his troops near the Castle of the Baths, surprised and slew the Turks on his march towards Jerusalem*

It was now the beginning of a new year, A.D. 1192, being leap-year, and having D for its Dominical letter. On the third day after our Lord's circumcision, the army bent on their march, were assailed by a multitude of Turks who had lain in ambush during the night near the fort des Plans among the bushes on the line of their route. The two foremost of our men were instantly slain but God had already prepared to avenge their death, for King Richard had been apprised of the amsbuscade, and advanced with all speed in the morning, hoping to rescue the advanced guard. But the Turks who had beheaded them, recognizing the king's banner, took to flight, being about a hundred in number, of whom seven were either killed or taken prisoners by the king in the pursuit. Eighty of the Turks fled towards Mirabel, and were speedily overtaken by the king, who, seated on his bay horse, a charger of incomparable swiftness, slew two of them before any of their friends could assist them. In this skirmish were Geoffrey de Lusignan and some others, who either slew or made prisoners twenty Turks, and if they had pursued them further, there is no doubt that they would have taken many more.

BOOK V

CHAPTER I - *By the advice of the Templars, though much against the inclinations of the army, the march to Jerusalem was abandoned until the walls of Ascalon should first be rebuilt*

In the year 1192, not many days after the feast of the Epiphany, the councilors of the army, joining with them some of the more discreet of the natives again consulted about the march to Jerusalem. The Hospitallers, Templars, and Pisans, urged, as before, that the city of Ascalon should first be rebuilt as a check on the Turkish convoys between Babylonia and Jerusalem. To this the majority of the council gave their assent, that Ascalon should be rebuilt to check the arrogance and impede the free passage of the Turks in those parts. When the decision became known the army was much dejected, conceiving that their hopes of seeing the Lord's sepulchre would altogether be frustrated. Their former hilarity altogether disappeared, and was succeeded by despair at what they had just heard. They uttered imprecations on the authors of this counsel as destroyers of all their most ardent wishes. If, however, they had known the penury and destitution of those who dwelt in Jerusalem, they would have derived some little consolation from the tribulation of the enemy. For the Turks in Jerusalem were enduring many severe sufferings from the hail and snow, which, melting in the mountains, caused a flood of water to descend upon the city, either drowning their cattle, or causing them to perish afterwards from the cold. So great were their sufferings from the state of the weather, that if the Christians had known of them they might certainly have taken the city though they could not long have kept it, for the people would have returned home after fulfilling their vow of pilgrimage, and there could not have been a sufficient garrison left to defend it.

CHAPTER II - *Of the despondency of the army at the abandonment of their enterprise, and of their return to Ramula*

The feast of St. Hilary was now at hand, and so great was the disaffection and sorrow of the army that many of them abandoned their pilgrimage, cursing the day in which they were born to suffer such a disappointment. Some of them also were so worn down by their sufferings and by want that they with difficulty could bear up against it. Their horses and beasts of burden, also, affected by the cold and rain, were unable to proceed through the mud, but fell famished and knocked up beneath their loads. The drivers, in bitterness of spirit, raised their hands in anguish to heaven, and uttered imprecations approaching even to blasphemy. It was impossible to conceive as ever lot, even in the worst of criminals, than that which our men now suffered. Their brave deeds, their prowess in war, were now succeeded by grief and despair of mind, in addition to their bodily sufferings and whilst all were in this state, the weak and sick would have been in danger of perishing, if it had not been for the care of King Richard, who sent out messengers on all sides to collect them together and bring them to Ramula, where the whole army soon assembled, not long after they had left it.

CHAPTER III - *Of the tribulation and anguish which our men endured between Ramula and Ascalon, from the dangers of the roads and the state of the weather, and how many of the French left the army*

Whilst our men remained at Ramula, many of them, either to avoid the painful march, or from indignation and obstinacy, deserted from the army, thereby considerably diminishing its numbers. The greater part of the French departed out of indignation; some of them went to enjoy their ease at Joppa, others retired to Acre, where there were plenty of provisions. Some joined the marquis at Tyre, as he had often urged them to do others, with the duke of Burgundy, from anger and indignation turned aside to the fort des Plans, where they remained eight days. King Richard, angry at the situation in which things were, proceeded with his nephew, Henry Count of Champagne, and the army thus reduced in its numbers, towards Ibelin; but they found the roads so muddy that it was necessary to halt there, that the army might have rest for their misery, both mental and bodily, was so great that no pen can write, nor tongue tell it. At dawn of day the men with the tents were sent forwards, and the rest of the army followed the sufferings of the day before were nothing to those which they now endured from fatigue, rain, hail, and floods, so that it might be thought all heaven had conspired to destroy them. The ground, too, was muddy and soft beneath them, and the horses and men had the greatest difficulty to maintain their footing: some of them sunk, never to rise again. Who can tell the calamities of that day? The bravest of the soldiers shed tears like rain, and were wearied even of their very existence for the severity of their sufferings. When the beasts of burden fell, the provisions which they carried were either spoiled by the mud, or dissolved in the water. In this manner, cursing the day on which they were born, and beating their breasts with their hands, they reached Ascalon, which they found so dismantled by the Saracens that they could scarcely enter through its gates for the heaps of stones. This day was the 20th of January, and they encamped for the night, every man as well as he was able.

CHAPTER IV - *How the army suffered at Ascalon from the weather and want of provisions*

The city of Ascalon lies on the coast of the Grecian sea, and, if it had a good harbor, could hardly find an equal for its situation and the fertility of the adjoining country. It has indeed a port, but one so difficult of access, owing to the stormy weather in which the army reached it, that for eight days no vessel could enter it; so that our troops and their horses, who were greatly in want of provisions, could get nothing for eight days, except what they had brought with them; for it was not safe, on account of the Turks, to forage for provisions in the neighboring country. At last, when the weather became more favorable, some ships entered the harbor with provisions: but the storm again came on, and the army began again to be in want for some barges and galleys, loaded with provisions, perished on the voyage with all their crews the snakes also, belonging to the king and others, were broken by the storm and the king made long vessels out of their materials, vainly imagining that they would serve to cross the sea.

CHAPTER V - *Saladin, hearing of the return and dispersal of our army, sends his men to their homes until May*

Saladin, hearing that our troops were dispersed along the sea- coast, and in part broken up, dismissed his troops to return to their homes, and attend to their domestic affairs, with orders to assemble again in the month of May. The Turks, who had now for four years been serving laboriously in the Sultan's army, now gladly return to see their wives and families. There their admirals and princes, men of renown, recapitulated their adventures, and the disastrous campaigns which they had gone through men who before had always came off victorious, and got abundance of spoil from all their former wars; but now, on the contrary, they had suffered both in their own property and by the deaths of their relations slain in the battles which they had fought. They, in particular, grieved for the fate of those princes, admirals, and others, who had been slain by King Richard, as before related, in the siege of Acre, when Saladin failed in his promise to redeem them. For this reason they had conceived bitter anger against Saladin, and now left his army for a time with groans and lamentations.

CHAPTER VI - *King Richard persuades as many of the French as he can to return, and, by common consent, they rebuild Ascalon*

The month of January was now ended, and the sky was becoming brighter. The king, annoyed at the dispersal of the army, sent messengers to persuade the French to return and so strengthen the army that they might be in a condition for further deliberations. "For," said he, "it is desirable that all the army should be together when we deliberate, for division will only weaken us, and expose us to the attacks of our enemies." The French by these arguments were led to promise that they would rejoin the army until Easter, on condition that they should have leave to depart and safe conduct at that time, if they should wish it. The king, seeing that it was necessary to use forbearance, assented to these conditions, and the army was thus reunited. It was now agreed by all to rebuild Ascalon but the princes and nobles were so exhausted, that they found their means insufficient for the purpose. They, nevertheless, began the work as well as they could, and dividing it out amongst them, they dug to the foundations of one of the chief gates, until they came to solid masonry, and removed the rubbish that was lying on the top. All engaged in the work: princes, nobles, knights, esquires, and retainers, might be seen tossing the stones from hand to hand. There was no distinction made between clerks and laymen; nobles and plebeians, princes and their attendants, all worked alike, so that they were even themselves astonished at their own progress. Masons were then brought, the work went on with double vigor, and the walls rose rapidly. Fifty-three of the highest and strongest towers, besides other smaller ones, had been leveled with the ground. Five of these towers had received names from their founders; according to tradition, the first and most powerful, was Ham, the son of Noah, who had thirty two sons: these all reigned after him, and built Ascalon, with the help of the people whom they invited together from all the country under their dominion and to gain their favor, and a lasting name to themselves, the females built the tower which is called the tower of the "maidens." In the same way the soldiers built the tower of the "shields" the "Bloody tower" was so called because founded by certain criminals, who, by this work, are said to have saved their lives from the punishment due to their crimes the fourth tower was erected by the admirals, and is therefore called the "Admirals' tower" the fifth, called the " Bedouins' tower," was constructed by the race of men bearing that name. Such are the five principal towers of Ascalon, named from their founders. When skilful masons were employed upon it, the work advanced more rapidly. The king, as in all other matters, was conspicuous in promoting the work and by joining therein with his own hands, encouraging the men, and distributing to each their allotted tasks, he rendered great service. For, at his exhortation, each of the nobles and chiefs undertook the completion of his share in proportion to his means and if any one desisted from the work for want of money, the king, more exalted still in heart than in outward dignity, gave to them from his own purse as he knew each had need. And such was his approval and encouragement of the workmen, such his diligence and expenditure, that three-fourths of the city of Ascalon were said to have been rebuilt by his means.

CHAPTER VII - *How King Richard rescued from the Turks at Darum 12,000 Christian captives, who were on their way to Babylon*

Meanwhile Saladin had made preparations for sending 12,000 Christians, French, and natives of the Holy Land, captives to Babylon and his servants had brought them as far as Darum, and were spending the night there, with the intention of setting forward on their journey on the morrow when it happened, by the dispensation of God, that they were rescued by King Richard from slavery. For one day the king chanced to be out, with a chosen body of soldiers, reconnoitering the fortress of Darum, to ascertain how he could take it for there was a passage there too convenient for the Turks, who brought provisions from Babylon to Jerusalem. The Turks, who had arrived just before sunset, recognizing the king by his banner, became frightened for their lives, and consulting their own safety, let themselves quickly into the tower of the fort, leaving their captives outside and these persons, on seeing this, took refuge with all speed in a church close by. The king, coming up, released them without a moment's delay, and let them go away uninjured whilst he and his men slew many Turks, who happened to fall in their way. Then the king took many valuable horses, and captured twenty of the Turkish chiefs alive. Who can doubt but that the king's coming, which turned out so advantageous to those captives, was ordained of God? Had he not come and rescued them, there is no doubt they would have been condemned to perpetual slavery.

CHAPTER VIII - *How King Richard sent an order to the marquis and was not obeyed*

After performing these exploits, King Richard sent messengers to the marquis, whom we have so often already mentioned, as he had done many times before, bidding him come to Ascalon to join in the campaign for the kingdom to which he aspired and this he charged him to do by the oath which he had taken to the king of France, who was a pledge for his fidelity but the base marquis replied, with a perverse sneer, that he would on no account stir unless King Richard first gave him a meeting. They afterwards held a conference by appointment at the fort of Ymbric.

CHAPTER IX - *How the duke of Burgundy, who had been recalled by King Richard to Ascalon, again left him, and retired to Acre, because the king would not lend him money*

While, therefore, the king and his army were diligently engaged in the restoration of the walls of Ascalon, a quarrel took place between King Richard and the duke of Burgundy; for the provisions, being for the most part consumed, and the substance of each man almost brought to nothing, the French began to importune the duke of Burgundy for the pay which was owing to them, alleging that if they were not paid, they could not serve any longer in the camp. The duke, not being able to meet their pressing demands, thought it best to ask King Richard to supply him with a large sum of money. For, on a former occasion, as before said, the king, at the duke's request, lent the French an immense sum of money at Acre, which was to be repaid out of the ransom money from the captives but this had turned out to be nothing, as the captives had paid no other ransom than their heads; wherefore King Richard refused his application. It was owing to this and other causes of disagreement, that the duke left Ascalon and for all his inability to pay them, the French set out hastily with him towards Acre.

CHAPTER X - *How the Pisans at Acre, who favored King Guy, fought with the Genoese, who sided with the marquis and the French, and how they threw the duke of Burgundy from his horse, and compelled him and the marquis to flee to Tyre and how they sent for King Richard, who made peace between them*

On their arrival at Acre, the French found the Pisans and Genoese engaged in a fierce conflict with each other. For the Pisans, from mere generosity, and a sense of the justice of his cause, were favorers of King Guy, while the Genoese were on the side of the marquis—chiefly on account of the oath of fidelity by which he was bound to the king of France. Hence arose discords which ended in bloodshed and mutual attacks, as in a civil war, at Acre; and the whole city was in a state of confusion. On approaching the city the French heard a great uproar, and the noise of the people, exhorting each other to fight upon which they, and the duke of Burgundy, in full armor, hastened to give succour to the Genoese, who were elated to an insolent pitch by their arrival. For all that, the Pisans, irritated when they saw them coming, went forth boldly to meet them; for their appearance was that of men disposed to fight. Falling upon the duke of Burgundy, who seemed to be their leader, they surrounded him, and having pierced his horse with a lance, threw him to the ground they then retreated to the city, and closed and bolted the gates, as a precaution against any unforeseen accidents which might happen. For they had heard that the Genoese had sent to the marquis to ask him to come as quickly as possible, and seize the city of Acre, which they promised to deliver over to him. The Pisans, therefore, took every precaution against this faction, for their own safety and that of the city. The marquis, without a moment's delay, came to Acre in his galleys, with a large number of armed men, in the hope of seizing on the city unawares and on their arrival, the Pisans attacked them manfully with petrarise and mangonels and confiding in their own valor, and the justice of their cause, they resisted their adversaries for three days, and fought bravely with them, until they sent a message to King Richard to inform him of the state of affairs, and bid him come with all speed. The king was then at Caesarea, on his way to the conference with the marquis, when the messengers arrived, and set forth the whole matter, and asked of him on the part of the Pisans, to come quickly and preserve the city they then returned to Acre under favor of the darkness of the night. The marquis, on hearing that King Richard was close at hand, returned hastily to Tyre, as if conscious that the king's coming betokened ill to himself. For all his haste, the duke of Burgundy and the French reached Tyre first. But King Richard, on learning the confused state of things on his arrival at Acre, took upon himself to arrange everything on the day after Ash Wednesday, as if he were the only man left in the place and having called the people together, he persuaded them, with most convincing arguments, that nothing was more commendable, amongst comrades, than friendship, nothing pleasanter than good fellowship, or sweeter than peace and concord, or more lasting than unity and, on the contrary, that nothing was more dangerous to the continuance of peace, or more pernicious than ill-will, for it loosened the bonds of affection in fine, that whatever was bound by mutual charity, and strengthened by the graceful ties of friendship, was always dissolved by the fermentations of envy. By means of such arguments, King Richard reconciled the Genoese and Pisans, and caused them to unite in harmony and concord, and reestablished their former good understanding.

CHAPTER XI - *How King Richard held a conference with the marquis at the castle of Ymbric, and admonished him to return and join the army and how, on his refusing, he disinherited him of the lands and revenues which had been promised to him*

King Richard, having pacified them in this manner, sent a messenger to the marquis to return to the conference at Ymbric, and try if they could, with the help of the divine grace, come to an amicable understanding about the arrangement of affairs, in order that the government of the kingdom might be the better administered by their joint efforts. They therefore met, and held a long conference, but to little purpose. The marquis brought forward, as a pretext for not performing his duty, the retirement of the duke of Burgundy and the French and returning to Tyre, concealed himself in his wife's chambers, away from camps and war. King Richard, perceiving that the duke of Burgundy and the marquis, as well as the French, had now voluntarily absented themselves from the army, and reflecting deeply on the terms of peace which had been agreed upon, hesitated for a long time in his mind what it was best to do under the circumstances, and took into his counsel the leaders and more discreet men of the army, to ascertain what they thought most expedient and they, after carefully weighing the merits of the whole matter, adjudged that the marquis had forfeited his claim to the kingdom which had been promised him, and that, in consequence of his doubtful and prevaricating conduct, he should be deprived of all his revenues. In consequence of this decision, great discord arose between the nobles of the French and King Richard, and especially between him and the marquis; who, as he had often done before, importuned all the French to quit Ascalon, and come to him at Tyre thus throwing the kingdom and country into such a state of confusion, that King Richard, fully aware of his treachery, remained in Acre from the day after Ash Wednesday until the Tuesday before Easter. For it is the part of a prudent man to take precautions even against an humble foe.

CHAPTER XII - *How, while King Richard was at Acre, our men at Joppa and Ascalon made an expedition and brought back an immense booty and how King Richard knighted Saphadin's son*

On the third day, before Palm Sunday, a number of young men at Joppa went on an expedition as far as Mirabel and carried off a large booty of cattle from the Saracens, thirty of whom they killed, and brought back fifty alive, besides an immense spoil. A moiety of it was given to the count, who was governor of the city; the other moiety was sold for eight thousand Saracenic bezants, of good money. Likewise, on the morrow, which was the Saturday before Palm Sunday, all those at Ascalon who had horses made an expedition, and scoured the whole country, as we were told by those who were present, as far as Egypt, four miles beyond Darum and having collected a large number of cattle, horses, and mares, also twenty asses, thirty camels, and seventy sheep, and other cattle, they formed in a body and returned with all speed to Ascalon, bringing back also with them 200 Saracens, with their wives and children. On Palm

Sunday, King Richard, amid much splendor, girded with the belt of knighthood the son of Saphadin, who had been sent to him for that purpose.

CHAPTER XIII - *How the duke of Burgundy and the marquis, from envy at the successes of King Richard, recalled the French, who were with him at Ascalon and Joppa*

Meanwhile, the duke of Burgundy and the marquis, inflamed with envy, which is always jealous of the virtues of a superior, sent ambassadors from Tyre to Ascalon, to charge the residue of the French who remained to come to them at Tyre as quickly as possible, and join in their new schemes and designs, and that they should act together in common concert, in accordance with their former oath of allegiance to the king of France. Then the treachery and premeditated faithlessness with which the marquis had, from the first, himself entered into treaty with the king of France, became manifest which was, that the marquis should join the French to his party, in order to expedite the accomplishment of his own plans. Hence he strove to withdraw the French, as if they were bound to his service, in order that King Richard might be the less able to carry on the war.

CHAPTER XIV - *How King Richard returned to Ascalon, and how 700 of the French soldiers, in obedience to the commands of the duke of Burgundy and the marquis, left the king and went to Tyre*

On the Tuesday before Easter, King Richard returned to the army at Ascalon, exceedingly sorrowful and disturbed. On the morrow, i. e. Wednesday, the leaders of the French requested of the king to furnish them, according to agreement, with an escort and safe conduct and the king consenting, assigned to them the Templars, to conduct them on their journey, as well as the Hospitallers, and Count Henry of Champagne, and many others, as their comrades. The king also, anxious to omit no proper mark of attention, escorted them on their way in person while he entreated them, with tears and soothing words, to stay a little longer with him, and that they should be provided for at his expense if they would succour the Holy Land in its desolation, to the utmost of their power. This, however, they absolutely refused, so he let them go away, and returned to Ascalon; whence he sent messengers at full speed to Acre, to charge the garrison not to admit the French within the city to lodge, but yet not to offer them any insult or annoyance, from which offence might be taken, or an occasion of dispute so when the French arrived there, they stationed themselves outside the city.

CHAPTER XV - *How Saladin, hearing of the departure of the French, summoned his*

Thus on the clay of our Lord's Supper the army was dejected at the departure of the French, for it lost no small portion of its strength thereby, as 700 French knights had left, men of tried valor and great activity, and the people were in consequence thrown into much tribulation. But the Turks were rejoiced on hearing what had taken place and Saladin, when he was told of it, sent messengers on horseback to carry letters, addressed to all the admirals and people throughout his dominions, charging them by edict to lay aside every occupation, and come to the land of Jerusalem with all speed. "The French," he said, "have, from ill will, departed, and left the land almost without a defender, and the strength of the war and the power of the Christian army are fallen wherefore we trust that in a short time we shall gain possession of Acre and Tyre, the chief cities of the land." The Turks returned at the command of the Soldan, but with less readiness, and in smaller bodies than before for they had not forgotten the past in comparison, however, with our paucity of numbers, they exceeded us greatly in strength.

CHAPTER XVI - *How fire from heaven, as usual, lighted the lamp at the Holy Sepulchre, in the sight of Saladin and how he had it extinguished three times, and how it was three times relighted*

On Easter Eve, Saladin, with his retinue, paid a visit to the Holy Sepulchre of our Lord, to assure himself of the truth of a certain fact, namely, the coming down from Heaven of fire, once a year, to light the lamp. After he had watched for some time, with great attention, the devotion and contrition of many Christian captives, who were praying for the mercy of God, he and all the other Turks suddenly saw the divine fire descend, and light the lamp, so that they were vehemently moved, while the Christians rejoiced, and with loud voices praised the mighty works of God. But the Saracens disbelieved this manifest and wonderful miracle, though they witnessed it with their own eyes, and asserted that it was a fraudulent contrivance. To assure himself of this, Saladin ordered the lamp to be extinguished; which, however, was instantly rekindled by the divine power: and when the infidel ordered it to be extinguished a second time it was lighted a second time and so likewise a third time. God is all-patient. Of what use is it to fight against the invincible Power? There is no counsel against God, nor is there any one who can resist his will. Saladin, wondering at this miraculous vision, and the faith and devotion of the Christians, and exceedingly moved, asserted by the spirit of prophecy, that he should either die or lose possession of the city of Jerusalem. And his prophecy was fulfilled for he died the Lent following.

CHAPTER XVII - *How King Richard celebrated Easter Sunday at Ascalon*

King Richard celebrated the feast of Easter, which fell on the fifth of April, at Ascalon, with great magnificence and he supplied all who needed with abundance of meat and drink. For he caused his pavilions to be pitched in the meadows outside the city, and provided in abundance every necessary for his people to celebrate the occasion with splendor. Nothing, however, was there to be seen more glorious than the ready good-will with which these bounties were dispensed, for courage in action always goes hand in hand with liberality and where nobleness of heart harmonizes with deeds of renown,— "The stingy mind suits not the bounteous hand

But rather checks its givings; let each gift

Be eVer attended with a generous heart."

CHAPTER XVIII - *How the rebuilding of Ascalon is completed at the king's expense*

On Easter Monday, King Richard returned with diligence to the work which he had commenced, and continued with all eagerness the rebuilding of the city walls, and familiarly urged the rest to proceed in the work so that by his care and cooperation it was all accomplished at his own expense, and without the contributions of the French, who had departed, and who ought by right to have shared in the burden.

CHAPTER XIX - *How King Richard set out to reconnoiter Gaza and Darum*

On Easter Tuesday, the king set out with a few followers to reconnoiter Gaza. On the Wednesday he set out to make a close survey of Darum, walking round, and trying to ascertain the best point of assault. But the Turks shut themselves up in Darum, and threw out many missiles from bows and arbalists with much abuse at the king and his men, as if the place were impregnable. When the king had fully surveyed it, he returned to Ascalon.

CHAPTER XX - *How the French, who were recalled to Tyre, amused themselves only in luxury and taverns*

After the French had departed, as aforesaid, those who had been charged by the king to conduct them as far as Acre returned to the camp at Ascalon but the French, arriving at Tyre, gave themselves up to all kinds of amusements, which we may think worth while here to mention. The very men who were supposed to have been led by their devotion to succour the Holy Land, now left the camp and abandoned themselves to amatory and effeminate songs and debaucheries, for, as was told by those who saw them, they delighted in dancing-women and their luxurious apparel bespoke their effeminacy, for the sleeves of their garments were fastened with gold chains, and they wantonly exposed their waists, which were confined with embroidered belts and they kept back with their arms their cloaks, which were fastened so as to prevent a wrinkle being seen in their garments and that which was once intended to cover their back, was now forced into the service of other parts of the body, for their bellies, not their backs, were covered by their cloaks and around their necks they wore collars glittering with jewels, and on their heads garlands interwoven with flowers of every hue they carried goblets, not falchions, in their hands, and after spending whole nights in drinking and carousing, they went, heated with wine, to the houses of prostitutes, and if by chance they were preoccupied, and the door closed against them, they pulled it down, giving utterance to language and oaths which horrified those who heard them, as is well known from the habits of the French. In a word, their external condition proved their inward levity. Shame on the French for indulging in such excesses! We do not assert that all were guilty of this folly, for there were some who were much concerned at their dissolute habits, and sorry for their discord with King Richard.

CHAPTER XXI - *How the discord which arose between the Christians, who were now come to the Holy Land, never occurred amongst the ancients*

The great King Charlemagne, famous for his deeds and the subjugation of so many kingdoms to his authority, when he set out for the conquest of Spain is said never to have suffered a quarrel to occur in his army. Such was the case also when he made his expedition against Saxony, where he performed so many exploits and utterly subdued the famous Wercelin. Likewise, when he went from Rome to give battle to that powerful warrior, Aguland, who had landed at Pisa, a city of Calabria, with a large body of Saracens, which would have been invincible but for the divine aid, no discord ever took place in his army. So also, in the land of Jerusalem, shattered by so many wars, during which so much slaughter of the enemy was made, and so many battles were successfully fought, wherever of yore we read of famous deeds of arms being carried on, there was no quarrel to divide the army who served under one general, no factious ill-will to disunite the people of different nations who formed it, nor did jealousy distract those who were under the guidance of one prince, nor was reviling or insulting language heard of amongst them,—nay, they showed each other every honor and kindness, and they were called one people on account of their unity, amongst whom no contention could last long. This was the reason why the French prevailed in those days over all foreigners, and so likewise should we moderns imitate with advantage the example of the ancients.

CHAPTER XXII - *How the prior of Hereford was sent to the Holy Land*

When Easter was over, and the season for crossing the sea came on, the prior of Hereford, an English priory came with a message for King Richard which put the whole army in commotion. The prior brought letters from William, bishop of Ely, the king's chancellor, informing him that he and the others whom King Richard had deputed to govern the country in his absence, had been insolently expelled from the fortresses of the kingdom, and some of their party killed in the riots; also, that by the agency of the king's brother, Earl John, the chancellor, had been driven from England that there was no more money in the king's treasury or any where else, except what was with difficulty kept concealed in the churches. In addition to this, the prior said that the same chancellor, priest, and bishop, had been forced to fly to Normandy, after much annoyance and ill treatment; and that the said earl rigorously exacted from the earls and nobles of the land the oath of allegiance, with homage, and the custody of the castles. He had also arbitrarily laid hands on the king's yearly revenues, namely, those of the exchequer. "And," said the prior, "if your majesty does not take speedy counsel on these matters, and return home with all haste and avenge our wrongs on the insurgents, it will fare worse, and you will not be able to recover your kingdom without the hazard of a war." The king was exceedingly astonished at what he heard, and turning it over in his mind for a long time, said but little, for he thought it incredible and a piece of wickedness exceeding belief. Where is the man who, when his wealth is plundered, bears it patiently? "Who endures wrongs without a murmur? Fear, in its anxiety, gives all things, however uncertain, an appearance of probability and when a confused state of affairs comes to the knowledge of others, they are themselves disturbed, and their minds are apt to be alarmed lest every thing should turn out disordered. The discord of princes is seldom to be allayed but if King Richard should be obliged to return home, probably not a man would remain in the Holy Land, as there was jealousy and strife between the people of Tyre and Ascalon, and without a doubt the Turks would have possession of the land for ever.

CHAPTER XXIII - *How the army, on hearing the secret news brought by the king's messenger, took counsel to choose a king for themselves and how the people preferred the marquis to King Guy*

On the morrow, the king having called together the leaders of the army, laid before them the news which he had heard, fully explaining the words of the prior, and at the same time declaring that he must, of necessity, return home directly, but promised to furnish to the campaign in the Holy Land three hundred knights and two thousand chosen foot soldiers, at his own expense. He then inquired who would return with him, and who would stay behind? He would compel no one to do either, but left it entirely to their own choice. Having taken counsel, in common, on this point, they made the following reply to the king's inquiries:—That as the land was suffering from the discord of certain parties, and the issue of events was still uncertain, especially as King Guy had not yet effected his purpose of recovering the kingdom, they thought it absolutely necessary that a new king should be appointed, to whom all should pay allegiance, and to whose care the land should be entrusted, that he might fight the battles of the people; one, in fine, whom the army could follow and obey and if this should not be settled before the king's departure, that they would, one and all, depart from the land, for they should not otherwise be able to guard it against the enemy. On the king inquiring, in reply to this, which of the two they would rather have for king, King Guy, or the marquis, the whole army, high and low, entreated, on their bended knees, that the marquis should be elevated to the sovereignty, as much better able to defend the country than any other they could choose. The king, listening to their petition, censured them in gentle terms for their fickleness, for they had before this often detracted from the character and good qualities of the marquis.

CHAPTER XXIV - *How King Richard, to satisfy the people, sent for the marquis, though known to be seditious and in league with Saladin*

King Richard, when he had weighed well the petition of the people for choosing the marquis as their king, gave his assent, and appointed noble men to go to Tyre, and bring back the marquis with all due honor. On the king's giving his consent, a general decree was unanimously issued for the election of the marquis, and certain men of high rank, viz., Henry Count of Champagne, Otho de Transinges, and William de Cague, were sent by sea with a retinue, to impart the good news to the marquis at Tyre but, as the proverb says, "There is many a slip 'twixt the cup and the lip" for God proved the marquis to be unworthy of the kingdom and as a further evidence of his judgment of him, we may add this:—that after the departure of the French, King Richard had asked the marquis, as he had often done before, for the aid which was required to recover the kingdom, as we have already said, but he refused it obstinately, so that blame must deservedly be imputed to him and over and above this, he was diligently plotting against the honor of the king's crown, and the army at Ascalon, by entering into a treaty of peace with Saladin, on the conditions that he should come to him and swear to observe concord hereafter, and that the Christians should have a share of the city of Jerusalem and that he should have the fortress of Baruth, and Sidon, and half the land on this side the river Jordan. To these terms Saladin readily assented in spite of his brother, who opposed them and, as we heard afterwards, constantly persuaded Saladin to agree to no conditions of peace with any of the Christians without the consent of King Richard. "There is not a better man than he in Christendom," said Saphadin "nor has he his match for probity and I will neither advise, nor assent to the confirmation of peace, unless with his consent and privity." By these means the infamous design was abandoned, and the treason failed of success. The existence of this plot was clearly proved afterwards for during the time that ambassadors were going to and fro, between Saladin and the marquis, to arrange and negotiate the matter, Stephen de Tornehan happened to meet them coming out of Jerusalem from the presence of Saladin. They were men notorious for infamy of character; one of them was called Baban of Ibelin, the other, Reginald of Sidon but we pass them by, for all their anxious endeavors and zeal came to nought, like dust, which a man scatters against the wind.

CHAPTER XXV - *How the marquis, on hearing that he had been chosen king, was elated with great joy, as well as his friends and how the latter prepared armor for themselves, and every thing necessary for his coronation*

The ambassadors, who had been sent to fetch the marquis, arriving at Tyre, set forth to him how he had been unanimously chosen king by the whole army, and with the consent of King Richard and that the crown of the kingdom had been granted to him, if he would come with his army and perform the duties thereof, vigorously and bravely, against the Turks, and apply himself to the government of the kingdom of Jerusalem in all other matters as his own. On hearing this, it is said, that the marquis, in the excessive joy of his heart, stretched forth his hand to heaven, and prayed thus: "Lord God! who has created me, and infused life into my body; who art a just and merciful King; I pray Thee, O Lord, if thou think me deserving of the government of Thy kingdom, grant me to see myself crowned but if Thou judge otherwise, consent not thou to my promotion!" When it became well known throughout the city of Tyre that the marquis was to be crowned king, so great was the joy of the people, that they got in readiness whatever they had, and used their utmost diligence to prepare for celebrating his coronation. They borrowed money to buy robes and armor, for they wished to make the most splendid appearance possible in the service of one so magnificent, who had been raised to so high a dignity. Men were now to be seen cleaning their armor, polishing their rusty arms, sharpening their swords, and rubbing their lances soldiers and boys engaged in sham battles, and maintaining the appearance of a real conflict of combatants, boasting at the same time of the future destruction of the Turks and, in fact, they were a brave people, had they not been without the Divine aid. Thus they indulged in joy, the more unreasonable, for being so intemperate, according to the proverb—"We should not rejoice too much, nor grieve too much," for all excess is reprehensible.

CHAPTER XXVI - *How the marquis was stabbed with two poniards, by two young men, assassins, sent by the old man (senior) of Musse*

Meanwhile, Count Henry, after executing his embassy, turned off with his companions to Acre, to equip themselves in becoming attire for the coronation, and were on the point of returning to Ascalon, when the marquis was overtaken by sudden death at Tyre. For it happened one day that he was returning, in a very cheerful and pleasant humor, from an entertainment given by the bishop of Beauvais, at which he had been a guest, and had reached the custom-house of the city, when two young men, assassins, without cloaks, suddenly rushed upon him, and having drawn two poniards, which they carried in their hands, stabbed him to the heart, and ran off at full speed. The marquis instantly fell from his horse, and rolled dying on the ground: one of the murderers was slain directly, but the second took shelter in a church; notwithstanding which he was captured, and condemned to be dragged through the city until life should be extinct. One of them was closely questioned before expiring, at whose instigation, and for what reason, they had done the deed, when he confessed that they had been sent along time before to perpetrate the crime, and that they had done it by the command of their superior, whom they were bound to obey. This turned out to be true for these very young men had been some time in the service of the marquis, waiting for a favorable opportunity to complete the deed. The old man of Musse had sent them over to assassinate the marquis, whom he thought worthy of death, within a certain space of time; for every one the old man judged deserving of death, he caused to be assassinated in the same manner. The old man of Musse, according to hereditary custom, brought up a large number of noble boys in his palace, causing them to be taught every kind of learning and accomplishment, and to be instructed in various languages, until they could converse in them without the aid of an interpreter, in any nation of the known world. Cruelty of the greatest degree was also inculcated with profound secrecy and the pupils were carefully and anxiously trained to follow it up. When they reach the age of puberty, the senior calls them to him, and enjoins on them, for the remission of their sins, to slay some great man, whom he mentions by name and for this purpose he gives to each of them a poniard, of terrible length and sharpness. From their devoted obedience, they never hesitate to set out, as they are commanded nor do they pause until they have reached the prince, or tyrant, who has been pointed out to them and they remain in his service until they find a favorable opportunity for accomplishing their purpose for by so doing they believe they shall gain the favor of heaven. Of this sect were the persons who slew the marquis.

Now while he was breathing his last, the attendants who were about him took him up in their arms and carried him to the palace, mourning and weeping inconsolably; the more so, as their joy had been, but now, so great. He enjoined his wife to attend carefully to the preservation of the city of Tyre, and to resign it to no one, save King Richard, or to whomsoever the kingdom should fall by right of heirship. Immediately afterwards he expired, and was buried in the Hospital, amidst great mourning and lamentation. Thus the former state of excitement and public joy was cut short and the dominion so long desired, but not yet secured, vanished. The cheering hopes of that desolate land were destroyed, and intense grief suspended the former gladness.

CHAPTER XXVII - *How the French, from envy, accused King Richard, of the marquis's death*

In the confusion which now prevailed amongst the people, the tares which an enemy had sown sprung up and corrupted the wheat. For it was whispered by certain of the French, who sought to veil their own wickedness by such a falsehood, and they infused it into the minds of all the people, that King Richard had vilely brought about the death of the marquis, and that he had hired these men from the Assassins for that purpose. Oh, infamous and malicious envy that always carps at virtue, hates what is good, and endeavors to blacken the splendor which it cannot extinguish! Nor were they content with defaming the character of King Richard in those quarters, but also sent a warning to the king of France, to be on his guard against the satellites of the old man of Musse detailing the manner in which the marquis died, and stating that King Richard had directed four of these ministers of superstition against himself. What did not they deserve who fabricated such misrepresentations, by means of which so many nations are believed to have been confounded, and so many provinces shaken! The infamous authors thought, by the invention of this malicious slander, to add to their own strength, and perhaps palliate their own wickedness.

CHAPTER XXVIII - *How Count Henry was chosen Icing at Tyre, and how messengers were sent to report this and the assassination of the marquis to King Richard*

After the marquis was buried, the French, who lived in tents outside the city, to the number of about 10,000, met together, and after a long discussion, sent orders to the wife of the marquis, bidding her to place the city in their charge, without delay or opposition, for the service of the king of France. But the queen replied, that when King Richard came to see her, she would give it up to him, and to no one else, for such were the commands of her dying lord, as there was no one who had labored so much to rescue the Holy Land from the hands of the Turks, and restore it to its former freedom and that the kingdom ought to be given to the bravest man, to dispose of it as he thought fit. The French were exceedingly indignant at this reply, and while they were striving to obtain possession of the city, Count Henry, astonished at what he heard had taken place, came unexpectedly to Tyre; and when the people saw him amongst them, they forthwith chose him as their prince, as if he had been sent by God and began with much earnestness to entreat him to accept the crown of the kingdom, without excuse or hesitation, and to marry the widow of the marquis, as the kingdom was hers by right of inheritance. To this he replied, that he would act according to the advice of his uncle, King Richard, respecting the settlement of the business, to which it had pleased the Lord to call him; and immediately, ambassadors were sent to announce to King Richard the solemn election of Count Henry by all the people and the horrible assassination of the marquis.

CHAPTER XXIX - *Of the great zeal with which King Richard fought, slew, and made captives of the Turks*

Meanwhile, before the messengers from Tyre to King Richard reached their destination, the fair season sat in, after the cold winter months and King Richard began again to attack the Turks, with indefatigable ardour, as before. For there never was a man like him, nor one whom the Turks feared so much; no one had ever before injured them in like manner, falling upon them almost single-handed, and bringing back the heads of his foes, sometimes ten in a day, sometimes twelve, or twenty, or thirty, according as they happened to fall in his way and besides all this, he would also bring home captives every day in large numbers. There never was a man in the times of the Christians who destroyed so many Saracens single-handed.

CHAPTER XXX - *How Mestoc was ransomed, and how some of our men-alarms, while out foraging, were captured by the Turks*

On the Thursday before the feast of Saint Alphage, Mestoc, who, as aforesaid, was taken with many others in the city of Acre, was ransomed and released. Shortly after this, some of our men-at-arms and servants, who had gone out in search of fodder for the beasts of burden, while proceeding incautiously too far, were set upon by an ambuscade of the Saracens and many were killed and made captives, as well as a large number of horses.

CHAPTER XXXI - *Of the fight between King Richard and a boar that he met, and of the king's boldness in the contest*

On the Wednesday before the feast of St. Mark the evangelist, the king and his army set out to Gadida to protect the city, but found no one there, for the enemy had taken to flight when they heard of his coming. On their way back, the king attacked a fierce boar, which, hearing the noise of the party passing by, had come out and stood in the way. The fierce animal, foaming at the mouth with rage, and with his shaggy hair bristling up, and his ears erect, seemed to be collecting all his strength and fury to receive or make an attack. He did not move from his place when the king shouted; nay, when the king made a circuit round him, he also turned himself in his astonishment round in a circle, and kept in the same place which he had first occupied. The king now making use of his lance for a hunting spear, moved on to pierce him and the boar, turning a little to one side, prepared to meet him. The animal was of enormous size, and terrible aspect, and the lance which was boldly thrust against his broad breast broke in two, from not being strong enough to bear the pressure of both, as they were closing with each other. The boar, now rendered furious by his wound, rushed with all his might upon the king, who had not an inch of room, or a moment of time to turn away; so putting spurs to his horse, he fairly leapt over the animal, unharmed, though the boar tore away the hinder trappings of his horse but the activity of the latter frustrated the blow; and the part of the lance which was fixed in the animal's breast prevented him from coming to closer quarters. They then make a simultaneous attack on each other, and the boar made a rapid movement, as if to close with the king but he, brandishing his sword, smote him with it as he passed, and stunned him with the blow then wheeled round his horse, and cutting the boar's sinews, he consigned the animal to the care of his huntsmen.

CHAPTER XXXII - *Of the capture of some Turks by our men*

On the Tuesday before the feast of St. Philip and St. James, Roger de Glanville set out with his soldiers, from Whitecastle, and passing, in force, before the gates of Jerusalem, intercepted some Saracens, whom he put in chains, and brought back captives. On the following Wednesday, King Richard fell in with some Saracens also, between Whitecastle and Gaza, and slaying some, made prisoners of five of them, whom he sent to Ascalon.

CHAPTER XXXIII - *Likewise of the capture of some Turks by King Richard at Furbia, and by the Templars at Darum*

While the king was passing the night after the day of the blessed apostles St. Philip and St. James with a few followers at Furbia, the Turks, early in the morning, came upon them by surprise, thinking either to capture or destroy them but the king was the first to leap from his bed, and seizing only his shield and sword, took seven of the Turks captive, and slew four; the rest fled from before him,, Afterwards he sent out the Templars and Turcopoles, as far as the fortress of Darum, to explore the country, and they found twenty Saracens, who had come out from the fort, sowing barley these they seized, and sent to Ascalon.

CHAPTER XXXIV - *How the aforesaid messengers arrived from Tyre, and how, on their announcing the death of the marquis, and the election of Count Henry, King Richard was rejoiced at the said election, and granted the count all he asked for and how he sent for the French*

In those days, while King Richard was engaged on the plains of Ramula, in pursuit of the flying Turks, the messengers, who had been sent from Tyre, came to him, and informed him of the state of affairs there of the death of the marquis, and the choice of Count Henry to be his successor but that the latter would not venture to accept the kingdom without the king's consent and advice. King Richard hearing of the death of the marquis, was for a long time silent, with astonishment, at his violent and untimely end but he was exceedingly rejoiced at the election of his nephew, and the regal honors so solemnly conferred upon him for he knew that his own people desired it much. "Wherefore," said he, "as the marquis, by the inexorable decrees of fate, has ceased to exist, it is of no use to indulge in sorrow mourning will avail nothing to the spirit of the departed! I congratulate you on the election of Count Henry and I am very desirous, if it be the will of God, that he should be invested with the government of the kingdom as soon as we have obtained entire possession of the Holy Land but concerning his marrying the widow of the marquis, I have no advice to give, for the marquis seized upon her unlawfully while her husband was alive, and committed adultery by his intercourse with her; let Count Henry take the kingdom, and the city of Acre, with all its appurtenances, Tyre and Joppa, and the whole of the land, if it so please God, for ever. Tell him also, in my name, to set out for the campaign as quickly as possible, and bring the French with him for I purpose to take Darum in spite of all the opposition of the Turks.

CHAPTER XXXV - *How on the return of the messengers from King Richard, and their announcing his pleasure, the count was married to the marquis's widow, to the great jog of all, and how Tyre and other fortresses were given up to the count*

After receiving the instructions of King Richard, the ambassadors returned to Tyre to the count, their future king, and reported the message entrusted to them. Then the joy and exultation of all was revived, and the principal persons persuaded the count to marry the marquis's widow, who was heiress to the kingdom but he refused, lest he should offend King Richard. Upon this, the French, and the nobles of the kingdom, urged him to it, alleging that his position would be strengthened thereby and by their influence, the lady came of her own accord to offer him the keys of the city. This was done at the instance of the French, who were for hurrying on the matter. The marriage was solemnized in the church in the presence of the clergy and laity. Those who persuaded the count to this step were not supposed to have had much difficulty for there is no trouble in persuading a willing man. The nuptials were solemnized with royal magnificence, and all were rejoiced at the accomplishment of the affair, which was wished for by every one; the French exulted, and the Normans were equally joyful, for the count was a nephew of both the kings of France and England and by this union happier times were hoped for, and a return of those who differed to peace and concord. On the completion of his nuptials, the count immediately sent persons to assume the government of Acre, Joppa, and other cities and forts, in his name and to take possession of all his dominions, which they were to hold under him as their lord. He then published an edict, calling on all to get ready for the expedition against Darum.

CHAPTER XXXVI - *With what joy Count Henry was received at Acre on his way, with the duke of Burgundy and his army, to aid King Richard*

Having, therefore, left fit persons to guard the city of Tyre, and the rest of the land, Count Henry, in company with the duke of Burgundy, moved forward his army towards Acre, in order to hasten the campaign and provide what was necessary; and he also brought his wife with him, as he could not yet endure to be without her. When the count's coming was known to the people of Acre, they came out, with dances, to meet and applaud their new lord and crowding round him, they accompanied him into the city, which was adorned on every side like a temple, with curtains and silken cloths burning censers were filled with frankincense, and carried about the roads and streets and women led the dance with joy and exultation. Why need we enter into detail? An immense number of people, calculated at 60,000, went forth in full armor to meet the count, and testify their joy and regard for him. The clergy led him by the hand into the church before the altar, and offered him the Holy Cross, and other relics, to kiss. The count himself, and several others, made many precious offerings there after which he was conducted to the royal palace, where he ordered a banquet to be prepared, and every one, according to his means, strove to do honor to their new lord.

CHAPTER XXXVII - *How King Richard, moved with pity, gave to King Guy the island of Cyprus as a reward for his prowess in war, and to console him for the loss of his kingdom*

But since it is hardly possible for one man to rise without another's downfall, so that the loss of the one turns to the advantage of the other, King Guy was now deprived of the kingdom, in the acquisition of which Count Henry gloried, and for which he had fought so many battles. He now dwelt therein like a private man, not because he was undeserving of the kingdom, for there was not another king to be found of more royal habits or character than he, but for this only reason, that he was simple-minded and unversed in political intrigue instead of being esteemed the more on this account, as he should have been, he was considered the more contemptible. He was a soldier of great prowess, and conducted the siege of Acre, when occupied by the Turks, with the greatest vigor and perseverance but owing to the increasing numbers of the enemy on the side towards the sea, be could not storm the city, which two kings afterwards with difficulty gained possession of. Ought, then, the simplicity of his character to have injured him in obtaining his rights? For such was the perversity of the age, that he whoever was known to be most inhuman in his actions was thought worthy of greater honor and glory and thus while craftiness gained respect, piety sunk into disrepute, because prudence is the reigning virtue of the present age. Thus, then, Guy became a king without a kingdom, until King Richard, moved with pity for him and his well-known probity, gave him the unconditional sovereignty of the island of Cyprus, although the Templars had previously bought it of him and thus the condition of purchase by the Templars being set aside, Guy was made emperor of Cyprus.

CHAPTER XXXVIII - *How messengers arrived frequently from England, and how the news they brought made King Richard doubtful what to do*

At the time that the marquis was assassinated at Tyre as aforesaid, many messengers arrived from England, soliciting the king to return some of them said that every thing was safe, others that England was on the point of being taken from him; some begged him to return home, while others used all their endeavors to persuade him to accomplish his pilgrimage in the land which he had come to and thus their different assertions disturbed his mind, and made him doubtful to which he should lean. But he measured the spirit of the king of France by his former experience, for, according to the proverb, "He who has a bad man for his neighbor, is sure to find something wrong in the morning."

CHAPTER XXXIX - *How King Richard, without the aid of the French, and with his own army alone, took Darum by storm in four days, and captured 300 Turks therein*

In the meantime, while Count Henry and the French at Acre were proceeding to the siege of the fort of Darum, King Richard, who hated delay, started with his men from Ascalon, and sent his stone-engines, which had been placed piecemeal on board the ships, to proceed thither by sea. The king deputed men to guard the city, and hired others, at the most lavish price, to keep a good look-out by day towards the neighboring forts, and a careful watch by night to prevent the Turks from carrying supplies as before to Darum, or whatever might be wanted by the army at Jerusalem, or from any longer having a safe retreat to Darum, whence they frequently planned ambuscades against our men. Then the king, with his own soldiers only, set out armed for the fort of Darum, and arriving there on a Sunday, he pitched his tent and those of his followers at a short distance from it. Owing to the paucity of our men, it was doubted which part of the fort they should attack, as they were unable entirely to surround it for if our small numbers were scattered, they would not be able to storm the tower, or withstand the attack of the Turks; wherefore they retired in a body towards a village situated in a plain, where they drew up. The Turks, on seeing so small an army, came forth from the castle, as if to solicit and challenge them to battle, and then retired again, and having barred their gates very strongly, prepared to defend themselves. Immediately afterwards, the king's stone engines arrived in his ships, which being disjointed, and in different pieces, the king, his princes, and nobles, carried on their shoulders from the shore, not without much sweating, as we ourselves saw, for nearly a mile. At last, when the engines were put together, and men placed to work them, the king took upon himself to manage one of them, and with it to attack the principal tower of the fort, the Normans had the second, and the men of Poictou the third and all of them were put in motion for the destruction of the fort. The Turks saw that utter destruction was close at hand but for all that, they endeavored to defend themselves manfully. King Richard caused his engines to be plied day and night. Darum had seventeen strong and compact towers, one of which was higher and stronger than the others, and externally it was surrounded by a deep ditch, which was built on one side of layers of paving stones, and a natural rock hung over the other. And now cowardly fears came upon the unbelieving race, lest they should not be able to defend themselves effectually, or even to escape with their lives. On the morrow, the king caused the sappers to carry a mine very cleverly underground, in order to break up the pavement, and make a hollow in the wall and the stone-engines, being plied in common, broke in pieces, by their frequent blows, one of the enemy's mangonels, erected on the principal tower, at which the enemy were very much discouraged. At first the Turks drove back our men with stones and darts, which fell in dense showers from their slings and bows but our slingers, to the great destruction of our foes, wherever they saw any one exposed to their attack on the battlements, threw missiles at him, and wounded and killed so many of them, that the enemy scarcely dared to move for fear and their condition began now to be far from enviable, when on a sudden, one of the gates of the fort was broken down, set on fire, and utterly destroyed by the blows of the king's stone engines. The Turks, now driven to desperation, by this continuous and harassing attack, were not able to make a longer defense, and many were killed, while others lay wounded on the ground. It was now clear that King Richard was invincible in every operation he commenced and that by undermining the towers, and plying his engines, he was sure to succeed. Three, therefore, of the Saracens came from the fort to the king, and sued for peace, offering to surrender the fort, and every thing belonging to it, on condition that they should be allowed to go away with their lives but the king refused, and told them to defend themselves to the utmost of their power. They returned therefore to the fort, and the king's engine was kept constantly at work and directly afterwards, a tower, which had been weakened by a subterranean passage, made by the king's miners, after repeated blows, fell to the ground with a dreadful crash. The Turks in escaping from the ruins became mingled with our men, who pursued them with slaughter, till they took refuge in the principal tower, having first performed the horrible act of cutting the sinews of their horses, to prevent their being of service to the enemy. The Turks now fled, and our men boldly approached the fort. The first who entered it were Seguin Borret, and his armor bearer, named Ospiard; the third was Peter of Gascony, and after him, many others, whose names are lost. The banner of Stephen de Longchamp was the first that was raised above the walls; the second was that of the earl of Leicester and the third, that of Andrew de Chavegui; the fourth was that of Raimund, son of the prince and then the Genoese and Pisans raised on the wall their standards of various forms. Thus the banners of our men were raised, and those of the Turks thrown down. And now the Turks might be seen flying towards the tower, or falling to the earth, smitten with the sword or transfixed with darts, before they could reach it; all whom our men found still standing their ground on the battlements, they hurled down to the earth below. Sixty Turks were killed in different parts of the fort. Those who had taken refuge in the tower, seeing the slaughter of their troops, and that their place of refuge would be demolished (for, at the instance of the king, men were already setting to work to overthrow it), and that there was no longer any safety in opposing the king, in their extremity, on the Friday before Pentecost, gave themselves up to the royal clemency to be slaves for ever; especially as one of their most powerful admirals, by name Caisac, to whose care the fort had been entrusted, had failed in his promise to give them succour. The fort of Darum being thus taken, nearly forty Christian captives were found there in chains, and were now set at liberty. On the following Saturday night, King Richard caused his men to keep guard over the Turks who still survived in the tower, until the morning and on the Whitsuntide eve he ordered them to come down therefrom, having their hands tied behind their backs with thongs, so that their limbs became stiff. Their number amounted to 300, besides boys and women. Thus King Richard, with his own soldiers, gained possession of the fort of Darum with great credit, after assaulting it for four days; for our men were very desirous of accomplishing this without the French, in order that they might gain the greater glory.

CHAPTER XL - *How King Richard gave Count Henri the for of Darum on his arrival there, and returned to Furbia*

Thus Darum was taken but meanwhile Count Henry, with the French, and the Duke of Burgundy, were coming in great haste, that they might be present at its capture, but it was already taken. The king received the count on his arrival with special manifestations of joy and leading him to the fort, gave it over to him, in the presence of all, as the first fruits of the kingdom, which he was to obtain, with the appurtenances thereof, present and future. All remained in the fort of Darum on the great day of the feast of Pentecost. On the Monday after, they placed some of the count's men as guards in the fort, and set out for Ascalon, passing through the midst of Gaza, till they came to Furbia. Here the king tarried three days, but the rest set out for Ascalon, where the French solemnized the festival of Pentecost.

CHAPTER XLI - *How King Richard, on hearing that Caisac, the admiral, was fortifying the castle of Figs with 1,000 Turks, went thither to storm it, and how the enemy fled at his approach*

One of the king's spies, in returning to Furbia, from the direction of the castle of Figs, reported that a thousand Saracens, or more, were with the chieftain, Caisac, posted in that fort, and were actively engaged in fortifying it against the Christians, in case they should come to attack it. On hearing this, King Richard started thither immediately, and the army followed him. At nightfall, they stopped at the fort of Reeds, or the "Cane-brake of starlings" and at dawn of day set out for the castle of Figs, as they had proposed, but they found no one there save two Turks, whom they took away captive with them, for the Turks had leveled the gates of the fort to the ground, and fled rapidly away on hearing of the approach of King Richard and his army. They were also not a little frightened at the capture of the fort, and the men who were found therein and mindful of their loss, took precautions lest they should themselves fall into a like predicament. Our men, therefore, finding the fort deserted, mounted the highest of the battlements, and took a survey around, to see if any enemy was in sight, that they might attack him but not finding any one to fight with, they returned to the house of starlings to spend the night.

CHAPTER XLII - *How on hearing the news of the disturbed state of his kingdom, through the intrigues of Earl John, his brother, King Richard was much moved, and declared his wish to return home*

While Richard was at this place, there arrived a messenger from England, a clergyman, by name John de Alencon, to inform the king of the disturbed state of England, owing to Earl John, his brother, who would not listen to the persuasions of his mother the queen, nor to those of any other person, but was led on by his own will, and the frequent solicitations of the king of France and he assured the king that unless the infamous treason was put a stop to by some means or other, England stood in danger of being alienated from the dominion of King Richard. The king was troubled at hearing this news, and reflected in his mind, for a long time, what would be the best course to adopt; at last he confessed that he must return home, if he would not have his native land, and the kingdom of his fathers, wrested from him. As the report of the king's intention was not made public, some said he was going away others said that he would remain, and not allow uncertain reports to call him away from the accomplishment of so pious an undertaking an act which would neither promote the recovery of the Holy Land, nor redound to his own honor.

CHAPTER XLIII - *How the whole army unanimously agreed that Jerusalem should be besieged, whether King Richard should return home directly or not*

While people differed in opinion as to the departure of King Richard, all the leaders and officers of the army, English, French, Normans, men of Poictou, Maine, and Anjou, met together, and agreed with each other, that whether King Richard returned or not, they would proceed to the siege of Jerusalem, and that nothing should prevent them. When this was known in the army, the people were filled with exceeding joy, and all, rich and poor, high and low, rejoiced in common and there was not a man in the army but evinced by outward signs the most immoderate joy each in his own peculiar manner; wherefore they made a brilliant illumination, and danced and sang nearly all the night; and thus They passed the livelong night in wakeful glee. The king was the only one troubled with care from what he had heard, and he fell into a long train of thought, until, overcome with the weight of it, he threw himself, in an angry mood, upon his bed. It was now the beginning of June, and the whole army was animated with the desire of setting out for Jerusalem.

CHAPTER XLIV - *How the flies called cincenelles stung the soldiers in the face, at Ibelin, so that they looked like lepers*

The king and the army started from the Brake of Starlings, and proceeded through the plains to Ibelin, of the Hospitallers, by Hebron, near the valley, where Anna, the mother of the Virgin Mary, is said to have been born. Here, the army made a halt, exceedingly rejoiced at the prospect of proceeding towards Jerusalem. And here the men were beset with swarms of small insects, which flew about like sparks of fire, and were called cincenelles. The whole region round swarmed with them, and they annoyed the pilgrims horribly, with their sharp stings in the hands, neck, throat, forehead, and face, and in whatever part of the person happened to be exposed their stings were immediately followed by burning and swelling, and those who were stung looked like lepers. They could scarcely keep off their troublesome attacks with veils thrown over the face and neck. But they were in high spirits, and thought they should bear these annoyances with patience for they were all pledged to advance to the siege of Jerusalem, and the king was the only one troubled at the news which he had received from England.

CHAPTER XLV - *How one of King Richard's chaplains addressed him, and dissuaded him, by every argument in his power, from returning home*

One day a chaplain from Poictou, named William, saw the king sitting alone in his tent, with his eyes fixed on the ground, in meditation, and he felt grieved for him, for he knew that he was exasperated at the news brought from England but he did not venture to come up to him, to lighten his mind of the cares which oppressed him; so he regarded him with a respectful look, and shed tears, but without uttering a word. When the king saw by his manner that the man was desirous of addressing him, he called him, and thus spoke to him: "Sir Chaplain, I pray you, by your allegiance to me, tell me, without delay or dissimulation, what is the cause of your weeping, and if the occasion of your distress has any reference to me." The chaplain, with eyes swollen with tears and humble voice, replied, "I will not speak before I know that your highness will not be angered with me for what I say." The king, with an oath, gave him free leave to speak. Upon which, the chaplain, taking confidence, thus began: "My lord the king, I weep on account of the ill repute in which you stand with the army, because you intend to return home, and especially amongst those who are the most solicitous for your honor but may God forbid that you be turned from the recovery of this desolated land, by doubtful or uncertain reports, for we believe it would tend to your eternal disgrace let not then the glory of a most splendid enterprise be overcast by a hasty retreat nor let it be charged against you hereafter, that you returned home in idleness, while your enterprise was still unfinished. How unlike will the end be to the beginning, if you thus derogate from your former glory! I pray you to take heed, lest your glory, so well earned at first, fade and tarnish in the end! My lord the king, remember what God hath done for you, and how he hath prospered all your acts, to be recorded by immortal fame. Never did king of your age perform so many or such glorious deeds! Remember, O king, that even when you were but count of Poictou, you never had a neighbor for a foe, whatever might be his valor or courage, but he was subdued and conquered by your might. Remember, O king, the multitudes of Brabacons whom you so often routed and dispersed, with a small band of soldiers. O king, remember how gloriously you raised the siege of Hautefort, when the count of St. Giles besieged it how you drove him off, and put him to ignominious flight king, remember how you obtained possession of your kingdom, peacefully and quietly, without opposition, or need of shield or helmet. O king, remember how many and mighty nations you have subdued, how bravely you captured the city of Messina, and how nobly you behaved yourself when the Greeks ventured to provoke and make war against you, and how you crushed them, and the divine mercy rescued you out of their hands, whilst they were confounded and destroyed. Remember, O king, the qualities with which God has endowed you, according to the riches of his grace, when you subdued the island of Cyprus, which no one had dared to attack before, and which you subjugated in the short period of fifteen days which you were only able to do by the assistance of God himself. Remember how you then captured the emperor and that ship of extraordinary size, which could not put into the port of Acre by reason of a contrary wind, you met and overwhelmed her with the eighty armed Turks, and cast into the waves of the sea the serpents which were therein. Remember, my lord the king, the siege of Acre, to the capture of which you arrived in good season, and which was surrendered when you assaulted it. Remember how you then fell ill of the sickness called arnalia, and how you suffered much, but, by the mercy of God, recovered when so many princes died of the same complaint. O king, remember that land which God hath committed to your care, and whose eye is turned to you only, for the king of France has departed, like a coward king, remember the Christian captives whom you released from the bonds with which the Turks had fettered them, in the fort of Darum, and to whose succour you were sent by God. How deeply should you reflect on the numberless triumphs with which God has honored you, and the successes with which he has magnified you, so that there is not a king or prince who can venture to resist you. Has it also escaped your memory that you have lately captured the fort of Darum in four days? And what shall we think of that hour, when you were lying asleep incautiously, and were nearly seized by the wicked infidels, had not God aroused you, and rescued you from their hands? Why need I detail the foes whom you have subdued throughout the world, the cities that have fallen before you, and the successful issues of all your undertakings? Remember, that when you came hither from the western world, you were everywhere victorious, and your enemies lay in chains at your feet; for before your face, In vain Antseus rose refreshed from earth, Or Hydra's heads were multiplied. And now the sultan trembles at your name, the hearts of the people of Babylon are astonished, and the Turk is struck with awe. Need I say more? All agree in declaring that you are the father, the champion, and the defender of Christianity, and if you desert them, it is the same as if you gave them up to be destroyed by the enemy. O king, continue to be their chief, bravely as you have begun; succour this people, for their hope is entirely in you: you are their natural protector, and may you, with the aid of Christ, still continue to prosper!"

CHAPTER XLVI - *How King Richard caused it to he proclaimed, by voice of herald, throughout the army, that he would not return until after Easter*

The king attended to the words of the chaplain, and deliberated within himself some time in silence. He had held his peace while the chaplain was speaking, and they also who were sitting with him in his tent had listened with the utmost attention. The king's heart was changed by this address, and his intention was confirmed as to the certainty of the course which he should pursue and therefore, he and his army returned at three o'clock on the morrow to Ascalon, and stopped in the orchards outside the city, while every one supposed that he was on the point of returning home, and that in reality he was hastening his departure. But the king had changed his purpose by the inspiration of God, through the agency of the chaplain; and he told Count Henry, the duke of Burgundy, and others of the nobles, that he would not leave before Easter for the solicitations of any messenger, or any reports or complaints whatever. On the fourth of June, therefore, in Trinity week, he summoned Philip, his herald, and commanded him to proclaim throughout the army, that the king would not depart from the Holy Land before Easter and that all should equip themselves according to their means, and prepare for the siege of Jerusalem.

CHAPTER XLVII - *How the army was rejoiced on hearing the king's determination, and how they prepared for the siege of Jerusalem*

When the army heard the words of the herald, they were as delighted as a bird at dawn of day, and all immediately set themselves in readiness, packing up their luggage, and preparing for the march. Then, with hands lifted up to heaven, they prayed thus: "O God, we adore and thank thee that we shall soon see thy city of Jerusalem, in which the Turks have dwelt so long! O how blessed are our expectations, after this long delay! How deserved have been the sufferings and tribulations of each of us! The much longed-for sight of thy city will recompense us for all!" These and the like prayers were offered up by each their only care and anxiety being now to proceed on their march. Moreover, the crowd of the lower class of people, made active by hope, took the provision baggage on their shoulders, asserting that they were fully able to carry a month's supply, so eager were they to proceed to Jerusalem for there is nothing the mind of a willing man cannot overcome, if he only has the inclination and zeal in the service of God softens the hardships of his toil.

CHAPTER XLVIII - *How King Richard and the army set out from Ascalon towards Jerusalem, and arrived at the White Custody and how two of our men died from the bite of serpents*

While, therefore, each was getting ready for the campaign, every thing that happened seemed to be done in harmony with their intentions. The king and army, therefore, who were encamped outside the city, being now thoroughly prepared for the march, set out from Ascalon on Sunday, the octave of the holy Trinity, towards Jerusalem at dawn of day. A chosen people, and nobly arrayed, were they who now issued forth, advancing slow on account of the heat. The richer classes supplied with lowly generosity the poor pilgrims who were on foot with means of conveyance—horses, and every kind beast of burden, to carry them while the light-armed and robust young soldiers followed spontaneously behind them on the march. Then might you have seen many a banner and pennon of various forms floating in the breeze many a mother's son, people of various nations, arms of various shape, and helmets with crests, brilliant with jewels, and shining mails, and shields, emblazoned with lions or flying dragons in gold; mules and horses, eager to move at full speed, and burning with indignation at being held in by the foaming bit many a lance with its sharp point glittering; the air sparkling with the gleaming of swords, and so many soldiers, choice men, good and true, who, in my opinion, were quite sufficient to crush or withstand the Turkish host, or even a much larger number than they could show. They made such progress on their march, that after crossing a river of sweet water, they arrived at the White Custody, and having pitched their tents in the plain outside, they spent the night there. On the first night of their stay, a soldier and his arm bearer died from the bites of two serpents, within a small space of ground; and may God, in whose service they were taken, give their souls absolution. The army tarried in that place two days.

CHAPTER XLIX - *How the king and his army arrived in three days at Betenoble from the White Custody, and there waited for the arrival of the people one month*

On the third day, i. e. the ninth of June, the army arrived at "Turon of the Soldiers," without obstacle or misfortune. On that night, our men captured fourteen Parthian who had come down from the mountains to plunder. On the morrow, after dinner, the army moved forward, the king going first, with his own private soldiers, as far as the castle of Arnald, where he ordered his tent to be pitched on the right and higher side of the castle. On the morrow, the French arrived, and the whole army set out for Betenoble, where they stayed some time in expectation of Count Henry, whom King Richard had sent to Acre to fetch the people who were living there in idleness; wherefore, it was necessary for the army to stay a whole month or more at the foot of the mountain, which the pilgrims are obliged to cross in going to and returning from the Holy

City. While in the valley, we saw many things happen which we do not think we ought to pass over in silence. On the morrow of St. Barnabas, which was Friday, the king was informed by a spy that the Turks were on the mountains, lying in ambush for those who should pass by, and at earliest dawn he set out in search of them, and coming to the fountain of Emaus, he caught them unawares, slew twenty, put the others to flight, and captured Saladin's herald, who was accustomed to proclaim his edicts;—he was the only one King Richard saved alive. He also took three camels, and horses, mules, and beautiful Turcomans and also two mules laden with costly silken coverings, and different species of aloes, and other things. The rest of the Saracens he pursued over the mountains, routing and slaying them, until he came to a valley, where, after piercing one of the enemy, and casting him dying from his horse, he looked up and beheld in the distance the city of Jerusalem.

CHAPTER L - *How the Turks in Jerusalem, on hearing that King Richard was coming fled away in terror, and how Saladin prepared for flight*

When, therefore, news was brought by the fugitive Turks to those who dwelt in Jerusalem, that King Richard was approaching, they were struck with terror, and there is no doubt that had the king and his army moved forward at this critical juncture of their panic, the Turks would have abandoned Jerusalem, and let the Christians take undisputed possession of it for the Saracens one and all had left it and fled, and not a man who could defend it even ventured to remain in the city; nor was any one deterred by the threats of the sultan, or allured by the hope of reward for all that the sultan himself demanded was to be supplied with his swiftest charger, that he might flee from the face of King Richard, whose arrival he dared not await.

CHAPTER LI - *How, while the French were at Betenoble, they would have been routed in a conflict with 200 Turks, had not the bishop of Salisbury come to their succour*

On the same day on which the king was thus employed, two hundred Saracens came down from the mountains to the plain opposite the tents of the French, and threw the whole army into confusion before they could be put to flight. They had killed two of our guards, who had gone some distance in search of fodder for the beasts of burden at whose cry, the French rushed forth with the Templars and Hospitallers, but the Turks defended themselves manfully at the foot of the mountain, and boldly returned their blows, refusing to fight with, our men on level ground, but turning to resist as soon as they reached the declivity of the mountain; they also unhorsed one of our knights, from which the French obtained no small disgrace. On this occasion a knight would have performed an act of memorable valor, had he not transgressed the rule of his order, and his exploit was ascribed more to rashness than real courage. He was an Hospitaller, byname Robert de Bruges, who, having passed the royal standard, spurred with violence the valuable charger on which he sat, and in his eagerness to close with the enemy, issuing from the ranks, contrary to discipline, charged the Turks alone, before the others came up in order and urging at full speed against a Turk who was most splendidly armed, he pierced him through his coat of mail and body with such force, that the lance came out at his back. The Turk fell to the ground, but his body was not left behind and then our men made a simultaneous charge upon the enemy. After this, Gervier, the master of the Hospitallers, commanded Robert to dismount, and attend to the discipline of his order; Robert obeyed his commands, and dismounting, returned on foot, and waited patiently until some nobles and men of influence prayed Gervier, the master, on their knees, to forgive him, and remit his transgression, warning him not to behave in like manner for the future. Both sides now labored in the contest with doubtful success. The heavens resounded with the shouts of war; the earth was moist with blood swords rung as they clashed together, shields rattled, and each side was agitated by equal fury. Our men, fatigued by the weight of the battle, began to waver, when, by divine providence, the count of Perche, hearing the noise of the combat, came up yet he showed himself but a timid man, and the French would have been routed on that day, had not the bishop of Salisbury, hearing the tumult, come quickly to their succour.

CHAPTER LII - *How, while the army was staying at Betenoble, a large number of our men, who had the charge of the caravans from Joppa, were vilely treated and most roughly beaten by the Turks, and how they were rescued by the earl of Leicester*

On the seventeenth of June, i.e. on St. Botolph's day, being Wednesday, our caravan was on its way from Joppa to the army, laden with provisions and other necessaries. Ferric of Vienna was deputed to conduct it, in the place of Count Henry, who should have protected the rear, but who had been sent to Acre. Ferric had that day asked Baldwin de Carron and Clarenbald de Mont Chablon, to take charge of the caravan, lest the people should straggle too widely, or be incautiously separated ; but they nevertheless fell into this error, and paid the penalty of their negligence. These were Manassier de Lisle, Richard de Erques, Theoderic Philip, and some comrades of Baldwin de Carron, Otho, and many squires, with their relations and friends, who proved their friendship in the hour of need. The foremost of our men moved quickly forwards, but the hindmost followed with a slow and unwilling pace when suddenly, not far from Ramula, the Turkish horse from the mountains, bursting from their ambush, rushed upon the latter at full speed, and endeavored to get before them they therefore penetrated and passed through the horses, which formed the hindmost of the caravan. There Baldwin de Carron was thrown from his horse but brandishing his drawn sword and multiplying his blows in all directions, he proved inaccessible to the enemy. In that encounter Richard Torques and Theodoric were thrown from their horses, but Baldwin fought with great courage until his men brought him a horse, and helped him to mount it. There was then a very severe conflict, and honorable to both sides drawn swords flashing, the one side attacking, and the other defending themselves most bravely horses wandering up and down without riders the Turks rushing about, and our men fighting stoutly. As often as the Turks felled a man to the ground, our men closed round him, and raising him up, helped him to mount his horse, each assisting one another. But our men fought at great odds, for they were very few compared with the hosts of the enemy, and each contended separately with the foe, and was hid as it were by the multitude of his adversaries whence it was not to be wondered that the enemy's numbers excluded our men for whenever one of our bravest men was thrown from his horse, he was overpowered by numbers, and the horses were wounded and much weakened by the showers of darts that were thrown at them. Moreover Baldwin was soon after thrown a second time from his horse, and he immediately commanded one of his men-at-arms to dismount from the horse on which he sat, and himself mounted on it, immediately after which, the man, who had behaved himself with great prowess, had his head cut off. Our men now stood on the defensive, and Philip, the comrade of Baldwin, who behaved himself with great distinction, was taken prisoner, and with him the Turks took another man-at-arms of great prowess, and killed the brother of Richard. The timid would dread a renewal of such a combat. Baldwin and his comrades fought with their swords and defended themselves with all their might. But Clarembald de Mont Chablon deserted his men, and took to flight as soon as he saw the numbers of the Turks increase. Then the conflict was renewed with fresh vigor, and Baldwin was a third time thrown from his horse, and so beaten with clubs, as almost to be rendered lifeless; the blood flowed in streams from his nose and ears, whilst his sword was blunted from constant use, and was unserviceable from its point being broken. Then Baldwin, on finding himself surrounded by a dense mass of Turks, cried out to Manassier de Lisle, a knight of great prowess, and who crushed all he met:—"Manassier," said he, "do you then desert me?" On hearing this, Manassier flew with all speed to rescue him from the Turks but the enemy was so many, that these two could do nothing against them, though they fought bravely for a long time against overwhelming numbers until Manassier was thrown from his horse, and when he was on the ground they beat him cruelly with their iron maces, made rough with teeth, and, standing round, they so mangled him, that they broke off his leg, bone and all, from his body and thus Baldwin and Manassier were being destroyed by the enemy, while their own men were ignorant of their fate. But, at this moment, God sent the valiant earl of Leicester, who had been ignorant of their danger, to rescue and protect them. The earl, on his arrival, dashed at the enemy and cast the first man he encountered from his horse upon which, Auscun, the comrade of Stephen de Longchamps, cut off his head, and hurled it to a distance. Stephen also behaved himself manfully, and our people increasing in numbers, the enemy were routed, and fled with speed to the mountains, except those whom our men overtook. Those of our army who were wounded were placed carefully on horses, and carried to the army. Thus then we have thought that day's action worthy of mention, on account of the brave deeds of the earl of Leicester, who put the Turks to flight, killed some, and captured others.

CHAPTER LIII - *How, while Richard was at Betenote, the Syrian bishop of St. George gave him a piece of the Lord's Cross*

A certain Syrian bishop of St. George, who had been a tributary to Saladin for himself and his flock, when, after the destruction of the country, the Saracens first came to Jerusalem, brought a piece of the Holy Cross to King Richard. He was accompanied by a large number of men and women, belonging to his own people, and gave the piece of the Cross to the king.

CHAPTER LIV - *Likewise, how while King Richard was there, an abbat came to him, and told him he had hidden apiece of the Holy Cross in a certain spot and how the king went thither with the abbat, and found it, and. how the people worshipped it*

It also happened, on the third day before the feast of St. John the Baptist, i.e. St. Alban's day, that while the army was staying there, they were much comforted by news which was brought to the king for a devout man, the abbat of St. Elie, whose countenance bespoke holiness, with long beard and head of snow, came to the king, and told him, that a long time ago he had concealed a piece of the Holy Cross, in order to preserve it, until the Holy Land should be rescued from the infidels, and restored entirely to its former state and that he alone knew of this hidden treasure, and that he had often been pressed hard by Saladin, who had tried to make him discover the Cross, by the most searching inquiries but that he had always baffled his questioners by ambiguous replies, and deluded them with false statements and that on account of his contumacy, Saladin had ordered him to be bound but he persisted in asserting that he had lost the piece of the Cross during the taking of the city of Jerusalem and had thus deluded him, notwithstanding his anxiety to find it. The king, hearing this, set out immediately, with the abbat and a great number of people, to the place of which the abbat had spoken and having taken up the piece of the Holy Cross with humble veneration, they returned to the army and together with the people, they kissed the Cross with much piety and contrition.

BOOK VI

CHAPTER I - *How when the French were desirous of proceeding to Jerusalem, King Richard would not agree, without the advice of the Templars, Hospitallers, and natives of the country*

When the army had worshipped the Cross for a long time, in their exceeding great joy, the lower order and common people complained, and said, "O Lord God, what shall we do? Shall we still proceed to Jerusalem? What more shall we undertake? Shall we be able to hold out until we have accomplished our pilgrimage?" Thus loud murmurs and complaints arose amongst the people. On which account, the king and the leaders of the army assembled together, to consider whether it was expedient to proceed to the siege of Jerusalem or not. The French earnestly entreated, and even exhorted the king to proceed; but he replied, that it could not be done. "For," said the king, "you will not see me acting as the guide and leader of the people in this matter for I might incur disgrace thereby, as it would be the height of imprudence now to press on this enterprise. If it please you to proceed to Jerusalem, I will not desert you; I will be your comrade, but not your commander; I will follow, not lead you. Does not Saladin know all that goes on in our camp and do you think that our weak condition has escaped his notice? He is aware of our precise strength, and that we are so distant from the sea-coast, that if the enemy was to come down with force from the mountains to the plains of Ramula, to watch the roads, and block up the passage, against those who convey our provisions, the consequences would be most disastrous to the besiegers. When too late, we should repent, and pay the penalty of our foolhardy enterprise. Moreover, the walls of Jerusalem, to which we propose to lay siege, are, as we hear, very great in circuit and were we to attempt to blockade it with our troops, few as they now are, and proportionally divided, their number would not be sufficient to carry on the siege, or to protect those who brought in the supplies, in case the Turks should attack them; nay, they would, one and all, be utterly destroyed to a certainty, if they had none to relieve them. Should I, therefore, undertake this hazardous enterprise, and should any misfortune befall when I was general (which God forbid), I alone should be blamed for my blind infatuation and should alone be responsible for the danger, were I, in these circumstances, to conduct the troops to the siege of Jerusalem. But there is no doubt, and I am well aware, that there are persons here at present, as well as in France, who have long wished, and very much desired, that I should exert my utmost efforts in this matter, without due and proper caution and that I should perform daring acts, which might justly be questioned, and bring infamy on my hitherto spotless name. Wherefore, in so hazardous an undertaking, with such doubtful issue, I should deem it wrong to rush rashly forward, without great precaution. Moreover, we, and our people, are ignorant of the locality of this region, of the roads and defiles; which, if we were better acquainted with, we should be able to proceed with greater safety until we attained, with joy and triumph, the long-desired success. But I am of opinion that the best course to pursue, is to ask the advice of the natives of the soil, who long to recover their lands and former possessions, and endeavor to ascertain from them what they deem best to be done, as they are fully acquainted with the nature of the roads. I think also we should consult the Templars and Hospitallers, and take their judgment and opinion, as to whether we should proceed, first, to the siege of Jerusalem, or to Babylon, or Baruth, or Damascus and thus our army will not continue, as now, to be divided into parties, from diversity of opinion.

CHAPTER II - *How it was agreed by common consent that twenty discreet men should be appointed, and that all should abide by their opinion and how the king assented and the French opposed it*

It was therefore agreed, by the king's recommendation, and by common consent, that twenty trusty men should be sworn, and that all should follow their advice, without further opposition. There were chosen five of the Templars, five of the French nobles, five of the Hospitallers, and five of the natives of Syria. These twenty met together, and after conferring for some time on the aforesaid matter, they gave it as their decided opinion, that it was the most eligible plan to proceed direct to the siege of Babylon. On hearing this, the French stoutly opposed it, and protested that they would march nowhere else but to the siege of Jerusalem. The king, on hearing of the obstinacy and defection of the French, was troubled thereat, and remarked: "If the French will accede to our plan, and agree to proceed to the siege of Babylon, according to their oath of obedience, I will give them my fleet, which lies at Acre, fully equipped, to carry their provisions and necessaries, and the army can then march along the coast with confidence. I will also conduct thither, at my own charge, 700 knights, and 2,000 of their followers, in the name of the Lord and if any one has need of the assistance of my money or means, he may be assured that he shall be supplied according to his wants and if any one doubts my doing this, I will march with my own soldiers only, and without other help." Then he immediately ordered that inquiries should be made at the tents of the Hospitallers, which were contiguous to his own, what they could supply for the completion of the siege, and how many men they could furnish. The chiefs also came there, and agreed to make an ample contribution towards the expenses of the siege, though they had very little in their pockets. But at that doubtful and critical juncture, they seemed too eager to undertake so venturous an enterprise, with even less precaution than they evinced in commencing the siege of Jerusalem, from which the jurors had so earnestly dissuaded them.

CHAPTER III - *How, while the army was at Betenoble, Bernard, the king's spy, brought news of the approach of so one very large caravans from Babylon, and how king Richard sent out men to capture, and Saladin sent on the other hand to guard them*

While therefore they were anxiously inquiring what each ought to contribute towards the expenses of the siege, there arrived Bernard, a spy of King Richard's, and two others, all of whom were natives of the country, and came from the neighborhood of Babylon. They were attired in the Turkish costume, and differed in nowise from the Saracens, and it was their business to report to King Richard the condition of the enemy. No one spoke the Turkish language with greater ease, and King Richard had given to each of the three 100 marks of silver for his services. They signified to the king that he should set out, with all his men, as quickly as possible, to intercept the caravans, which were coming from Babylon, and to which they promised to conduct him. The king, delighted at what he heard, charged the duke of Burgundy to join him immediately in the enterprise, and bring the French to assist and they agreed to go, on condition that they should receive the third part of the booty, to which the king assented. Then about 500 soldiers instantly set out, well armed, and the king took with him a thousand hired serving-men. At evening they pursued their march, the king preceding them, and advancing all night, by the light of a splendid moon, they arrived at Galatia. There they rested a short time, and sent to Ascalon for provisions. Meanwhile, they carefully prepared their arms, until the servants, who had been sent for the provisions, arrived. But our men had no sooner started, as we have said, to capture the caravans, than a spy informed Saladin, at Jerusalem, that he had seen King Richard set out, with his people, in great haste, to intercept his caravans and thus the secret of our expedition was revealed. Saladin then hastily sent off 500 chosen Turks, who, on joining with the others that were entrusted with the protection of the caravans, formed a body of 2,000 horsemen, besides a numerous company of foot-soldiers.

CHAPTER IV - *How King Richard fought bravely with the Turks, and took a caravan full of costly things, of inestimable value, camels, dromedaries, horses, and asses*

Whilst King Richard and his people were staying at Galatia, a spy informed the king, that one of the aforesaid caravans was passing by a round cistern, and advised him to proceed at once and capture it, recommending that he should keep back his troops; "for" said he, "whoever shall capture that caravan, will gain an immense booty." But as the spy was a native of the country, the king did not think he ought to place implicit confidence in his sole assertion. Therefore, the king straightway sent a Bedouin and two cautious Turcopolite servants, to inquire into the truth of the matter and ascertain its accuracy and he caused them to be clothed after the fashion of Bedouins, to look like Saracens. These men set out by night across the hills, which were covered with watch-towers, and descended to the valley, by turns, until they saw some Saracens on the higher ground, who were themselves spies, and lying in wait for those who might cross the mountains and when our Bedouin approached, with stealthy steps, to reconnoiter them, the Saracens asked him, who they were, whence they came, and whither they were going? The Bedouin, beckoning the other two to be silent, lest the Saracens should recognize them by their speech, answered," that they were returning from the neighborhood of Ascalon, whither they had gone for the sake of plunder" but one of the Saracens said to him, "You are come to look out for us, and you belong to the king of England." The Bedouin answered, "that he lied," and then proceeded hastily in the direction of the caravan, followed for some time by the Saracens, with their bows and lances, until they ceased in their pursuit from weariness. They, however, strongly suspected that they were of their own country, and not belonging to the enemy. Our spies, therefore, having ascertained the truth, as to the before mentioned caravans returned with all speed to the king, and told him that he might easily capture the caravans if he would make haste. On learning this, the king, after refreshing his horses with provender, set out with his men, and they walked during the following night until they came to the place where the caravan and its guards were resting a short distance from it they halted, armed themselves, and formed into companies; the king being in the front rank, and the French in the rear. The king forbade, by mouth of herald, any one from turning to plunder and commanded, that all should endeavor, by their utmost means, to break and destroy the Turkish lines. When, therefore, day arrived, and they were engaged in forming their ranks, another spy came up at full speed and informed the king that the caravan was preparing to hasten forwards at dawn of day, for the king's intention to attack it had become known to its guards. On hearing this, the king sent forward the lightest of his slingers and bowmen to retard their march and by feigning to challenge them to battle, keep them in check until he and his troops should come up. In this manner the Turks were harassed and delayed by these attacks whilst our army approached in battle array. When the Turks perceived them, they immediately began to ascend a certain mountain, in order that the higher ground might afford them a firmer position but their bearing was less arrogant than usual. Then the Turks, making a fierce onset, threw their darts and arrows like hail, upon our ranks: the caravan, meanwhile, standing motionless. King Richard now having placed his army in two divisions, suddenly charged the Turks, and with his followers, penetrated and routed the foremost rank. Such was the fury of his onset that they fell to the ground almost without a blow and he pressed so hard upon the fugitives, that there were none left to make further resistance, except that several of those who fled turned back and shot their arrows behind them. Thus all of them took to flight, like hares before the hounds, and were routed in every direction, while the caravan stood at the mercy of the pursuers, who slew all they met with so that the enemy lay dead in heaps upon the sand. Those who were thrown from their horses by our knights were put to death by their squires. There might be seen horses with their saddles twisted round; the conquered were miserably destroyed, and the king's men fought nobly. The French, too, fought with the utmost spirit, like men accustomed to battle. The king was conspicuous above all the rest by his royal bearing, surpassing all of them he was mounted on a tall charger, and charged the enemy singly; his ashen lance gave way from his repeated blows, and was shivered in pieces but drawing his sword instantly, and brandishing it, he pressed upon the fugitives, and mowed them down, sweeping away the hindmost, and subduing the foremost; thus he thundered on, cutting and hewing every one he came up with no kind of armor could resist his blows, for the edge of his sword cut open the heads from the top to the teeth thus waving it to and fro, he scared away the routed Turks, as a wolf, when he pursues the flying sheep. While the king was thus scattering the fugitives, who were flying with all their speed over the mountains, some of them despairing of escape from his persevering pursuit, for he had come up with the foremost, turned aside out of their road, and returned to our nearly deserted camp, hoping to effect something against the guards in the king's absence, for their courage failed them when he was in sight, and not without reason, for the life or death of the enemy was always in his hands. About thirty, therefore, of the fugitives came round upon our men by a circuitous route, and made a violent charge on Roger de Toony, whose horse they killed under him and they were near capturing himself, but he was rescued from their hands by one of his comrades, Jakel of Maine, who however was also thrown from his horse but Roger stoutly defended him on foot, and succeeded in rescuing him. Meanwhile, our men-at-arms came up, and the earl of Leicester, who attacked them to the right and left, also Gilbert Malemain, with four companions, Alexander Arsi, and others, to the number of about twenty; Stephen de Longchamp also generously offered his services to Roger de Toony, in the midst of the hostile Turks, and supplied him with a horse to mount. Then the slaughter was renewed swords flashed in the air; and the ground was covered with blood; arms rung and clashed together; bodies were torn limb from limb; heads, arms, feet, and hands, and other limbs, lay scattered about and our men were interrupted as they walked along by the bodies of the enemy, which lay along the fields in great numbers and caused them to stumble at every step. The men of Poictou and Anjou, together with the French and Normans, distinguished themselves in the battle but King Richard, the flower of valor, and the crown of chivalry bore away the prize from all and any praise that I could give him would fall far short of his merits. The slaughter of the Turks was greater than our ancestors had ever seen and such was their confusion and dismay in the encounter, that a boy might have killed ten of them, or, in fact, as many of them as came in his way. By this defeat the pride of the Turks was entirely cast down, and their boldness effectually repressed; whilst the caravan, with all its riches, became the spoil of the victors. Its guards surrendered to our soldiers themselves, their beasts of burden, and sumpter horses and stretching forth their hands in supplication, they implored for mercy, on condition only that their lives should be spared. They led the yoked horses and camels by the halter, and offered them to our men, and they brought mules loaded with spices of different kinds, and of great value; gold and silver; cloaks of silk; purple and scarlet robes, and variously-ornamented apparel, besides weapons of divers forms; coats of mail, commonly called gasiganz; costly cushions, pavilions, tents, biscuit, bread, barley, grain, meal, and a large quantity of conserves and medicines; basins, bladders, chess-boards; silver dishes and candlesticks; pepper, cinnamon, sugar, and wax and other valuables of choice and various kinds; an immense sum of money, and an incalculable quantity of goods, such as had never before (as we have said) been taken at one and the same time, in any former battle.

CHAPTER V - *How many camels and dromedaries were taken, and how many Turks were slain*

The slaughter of the infidels being finished, and the caravan captured, our army was harassed with new toils in gathering together the runaway camels and dromedaries, by which the whole army was thrown into confusion, for they avoided the pursuit of our horses with such great fleetness, that no other kind of animal appeared to be of so active and swift a nature. These animals appeared slothful and tardy until the pursuers were within a short distance, and then they moved at full speed. At last, by one means or another, 4,700 camels and dromedaries were collected together, though the number is not quite certain. They took so many mules of both sexes, and laden asses, that they could not reckon the number, for they appeared more abundant than the number of men could possibly require. Moreover, the number of Turkish horsemen who were that day slain, exceeded 1,700, besides very many foot soldiers, who were trodden to death in the melee.

CHAPTER VI - *How while King Richard was returning with his spoil to Betenoble whence he had started, Count Henry from Acre met him with the army for which he had been sent*

Having accomplished all these things, and prepared the baggage for returning, the king and his army set out, laden with spoil, at an easy pace, and reached Bethaven, which was only four miles distant from Joppa. There they shared the plunder, and then proceeded on the second day to Ramula. Here Count Henry came up with the troops, and the people he had brought with him from Acre, and thence they all set out for Betenoble, from which place they had started. Here the universal joy was renewed, and all knocked together in astonishment at the numbers of beasts of burden with which the army was accompanied. On arriving, the noble king distributed the camels, which were larger than any that had ever been seen there, as well to the soldiers, who had remained to protect the

camp, as to those who had joined in the expedition, in equal proportions. In this respect, he graciously imitated the example of that renowned warrior, King David, who gave an equal share of the spoil to the soldiers who went forth to battle, and to those who remained in the camp and he also divided the asses amongst his serving men. By these means the army was supplied with so plentiful a number of camels and other beasts of burden that it was with difficulty they were kept together. The flesh of the young camels they stuffed with lard and roasted for the table, and they found it very white and palatable.

CHAPTER VII - *How the people murmured at being prohibited, however reasonably and prudently from going to Jerusalem*

Shortly after the distribution of the plunder, the people grew discontented, and complained that the beasts of burden consumed too much barley and provender, and that on this account the price of grain was become higher. Besides this, there arose much complaint and sorrowing amongst the people, because it was not thought expedient to proceed to the siege of Jerusalem, as they wished, owing to the opposition of the twenty counselors aforesaid, who had given their reasons for deciding to the contrary. They thought it a difficult and impossible enterprise, from the want of water, which the men and cattle could not do without, especially as the festival of St. John was close at hand a time when, from the increasing heat of the summer, all things were naturally dry, particularly around Jerusalem, which is situated in the mountains. Besides this, the Turks had blocked up all the cisterns, so that not a drop of drinkable water could be found within two miles of the city, and it would be unsafe to go in search of it to a distance when the siege had once begun and the small stream of Siloe, which runs down at the foot of the Mount of Olives, would not be sufficient for the army. These were the reasons why the counselors dissuaded the king from the siege of Jerusalem at that time, and when it became known to the army that they were not to proceed thither, but were on the point of turning away from that city, they cursed this delay in the hopes they had conceived, and asserted that they only wished to live until Jerusalem and the Holy Land and Cross were once more in the possession of the Christians alone. But God, who is the just judge of men's feelings, govern time and actions and to his mercy and kindness is if to be ascribed that he chastens sinners, and punishes them for all the inventions of their hearts.

CHAPTER VIII - *Of the jealousies and discords of the French, and how they separated themselves from the rest of the army, and how Henry, duke of Burgundy, composed a satirical poem against King Richard*

We must not wonder that the pilgrims who were thus harassed without any good result, grieved at the failure of their wishes, for discord grew rife amongst them nor that the vacillating character of the French, which distinguished them from all other nations, should have been here displayed. For at evening, when the army advanced on their march, the French separated themselves from the rest, and took up a distinct position, as if they disdained their company. They were not, however, content with separating only, but they fell to quarrelling among themselves, and gave utterance to ironical pests and abusive language, each vaunting his own superior prowess, while they disparaged that of the others. Above all, Henry, duke of Burgundy, whether instigated by a spirit of arrogance, or influenced by envy and jealousy, composed and caused to be recited in public, a song, which if he had any sense of shame, he would never have allowed to be published; and those songs were sung not only by men but by immodest women. By which means, they showed the real character of those who indulged in such indecent folly, and the nature of their hearts was sufficiently manifest from this fact, for the stream is clear or turbid according as is its source. On this composition becoming current amongst the soldiers, King Richard was much annoyed, but he thought that a similar effusion would be the best mode of revenging himself on the authors, and he had not much difficulty in composing it, as there was abundance of materials; why then should he hesitate to reply to such a false and scurrilous composition? Moreover, the king's high honor was so evident in all his actions, that his rivals, who could not equal him, assailed him with foul and gratuitous aspersions. For they were not like the pilgrims of yore who besieged and captured Antioch, and whose famous deeds and victories are still recited in song. Such were Boemund, Tancred, and Godfrey of Bouillon, and other princes of high renown, who gained so many triumphs and whose exploits are like food in the mouths of their narrators. Men, who because their hearts were true to the service of God, received from the Lord the reward of their labors, who magnified them by giving them an immortal name, which posterity should regard with the deepest veneration.

CHAPTER IX - *Of the return of the army from Betenoble to Joppa*

The army remained in this state for some days after the capture of the caravan, and was in great sorrow and distress in consequence of the check put on their progress to visit the Holy Sepulchre at Jerusalem, from which they were only four miles distant. The dejection which their return caused was never before equaled in a people of the like valor. Our men, on setting out on their march, were attacked by the Turks from the mountains, and some of our camp-followers were slain, though they were repulsed by our horsemen, from not having good horses. The army afterwards arrived at a place between Saint George and Ramula, where they spent the night, the French posting themselves on the left, the king and his men on the right. Next day they proceeded on their march in separate divisions, and arrived at night at a castle midway; this was on the 6th of July. Here some in disgust deserted the army, on account of the tediousness and penury to which they were exposed in the expedition these went to Joppa.

CHAPTER X - *How Saladin, learning the discord and departure of the Christians, collected an immense army*

When the state and intention of the Christians were made known to Saladin, his hopes revived, and his joy was unbounded. He immediately sent messengers bearing dispatches, sealed with his own ring, to the admirals, princes, satraps, and prefects of his dominions, informing them of the internal discord which had broken up the Christian army and forced them to retire and that whoever wished to serve in his pay, should come forthwith to Jerusalem. So large a number knocked thither in consequence, that the cavalry was estimated at 20,000 strong, besides a countless multitude of foot soldiers.

CHAPTER XI - *How King Richard, seeing the defection of his men, sought to obtain the truce which had been first offered him, but in vain and how in consequence he destroyed Darum and fortified Ascalon, and then returned to Acre by way of Joppa*

Meanwhile our men moved off by degrees, and many went to Joppa. The king, perceiving his inability to check them on account of the diversity of opinion which prevailed, thought the best line of policy was to send to Saphadin at this juncture, and agree to the truce, which had been before offered between him and Saladin, in the plains of Ramula, for a certain period, in order that he might have time to return from his own country. But Saladin, who knew well the condition of our army, and that it was daily growing weaker and weaker, absolutely refused, unless Ascalon was razed to the ground. The king, learning Saladin's answer, was not at all discomposed; nay, he gave immediate orders to the Templars, Hospitallers, and others, to the number of three hundred, to mount their horses and proceed to the destruction of Fort Darum;

and he set guards to watch over and fortify Ascalon as strongly as possible. They hastened to obey the king's orders, and leveled Darum with the ground. The army then returned in dejected mood as far as Joppa, and thence the king and the rest proceeded in all haste to Acre, but many remained from ill health and weakness at Joppa. Thus the army returned to Acre, broken up, with a heavy heart, for God did not as yet judge them worthy of the higher bounties of his grace.

CHAPTER XII - *Of the great army with which Saladin came to Joppa*

When Saladin heard that the men of Joppa were without the presence of King Richard to protect them, he ordered his army should proceed thither, in the hope that he would easily take the city during the king's absence. He therefore led an immense army having 20,000 horse in that direction and he had with him the powerful admiral of Bala, and the son of Arcisus, together with about one hundred and six admirals, and an immense multitude of infantry from the mountains, who covered the face of the earth like locusts, The army, leaving Jerusalem, descended into the plains of Ramula, rushing on in troops and squadrons as if impelled by the furies to the utter destruction of the Christians.

CHAPTER XIII - *How Saladin assaulted Joppa so vigorously that he would have taken it, if the townsmen had not asked for a cessation of arms until the next day*

On the same Sunday, next preceding the feast of St. Peter ad vinculo, being the same day on which King Richard came with his army to Acre, Saladin advanced with his troops to assault Joppa. On the Monday following they began to attack the castle but the citizens issuing forth into the suburbs, resisted them the whole day, and prevented them from approaching the town. Tuesday and Wednesday also passed away in the same manner nor was it till Thursday, that the Turks, ashamed of being baffled by so few, made a great exertion, and formed the siege at once. By the command of Saladin, four powerful petrarice were erected, and two mangonels of great efficiency for casting missiles. The besieged were about 5,000 in number, and they now began to be afflicted at their desperate condition, and to call out upon the Lord to save them. They also turned their thoughts towards the king of England, and to wish that he had not gone to Acre, leaving them there to be destroyed. Meanwhile, the Turks pressed on the siege and it would have melted any one to tears to have seen the distracted state of the townspeople, who offered the bravest resistance, though they were overwhelmed with a thousand cares at once in the defense of their city. The petrarise and mangonels played without intermission; though the latter instruments were worked the most successfully. At last, by the exertions of the Turks, the gate leading to Jerusalem was broken open on the Friday by the frequent strokes of their petrariae, and the wall on the right-hand side was shattered, about two poles in width. The conflict was then fierce, whilst the besieged resisted the entrance of the Turks, who at length, however, became so reinforced by numbers, that the Christians were driven back, and followed even as far as the citadel of the fortress. What a terrific slaughter then took place! The Turks put to death without mercy all those whom they found in the houses sick and lying in their beds. Some of our people fled down to the seashore and escaped; whilst the enemy plundered every thing; and knocking out the heads of the casks which they found in the houses, let the wine run about the streets. Some of them, however, attacked the principal tower of the fortress ; and others pursued those who fled down to the seaside. Numbers of the hindmost were cut off; and Alberic of Alheims, whose duty it was to defend the town, fled on board ship to escape being slain but his companions reproaching him for his cowardice, recalled him to a sense of duty, and absolutely forced him into one of the towers where, seeing nothing but danger on every side surrounding him, he exclaimed, "Here then we shall devote our lives to God's service;" for it was the only thing that remained for him to do. The Turks now fiercely assaulted the tower, and the arrows flew like hail, so as to darken the sky the besieged knew not which part first to defend, and so the attack lasted the whole day; and the besieged would certainly have at length yielded to its violence, if by God's good pleasure the newly-elected patriarch had not been present and he proved himself, at that moment, a man whom no fear of death could vanquish, nor any danger terrify. This man, instigated by the necessity of the case, proposed to Saladin and his brother to grant them a respite from the attack until the next day, on condition, that if before three o'clock, they should not receive assistance, each of those who were in the tower, should pay Saladin ten bezants of gold, every woman five, and every child three bezants, in return for the respite which he had granted them and that the patriarch, with others of the nobles, should be given up to Saladin to be kept in chains as hostages, until the hour agreed on should arrive. Saladin assented and when the guarantee was completed for observing the conditions of the truce, the following hostages were given over to Saladin: the patriarch, Alberic of Rheims, Theobald of Treves, Augustin of London, Osbert Waldin, and Henry de St. John, besides others, whose names we do not remember, all of whom were carried off prisoners to Damascus for the besieged had now conceived hopes of obtaining succour from the king, for which, indeed, they had already sent, the moment they first saw Saladin approaching.

CHAPTER XIV - *How King Richard, though on the point of embarking to return home, and refused aid by the French, no sooner heard of the message from Joptpa, than he proceeded thither immediately by sea, having first sent on his troops by land*

Meanwhile King Richard was busily engaged in preparing to leave Acre for his own country, and his ships were all but ready he had also obtained consent and a blessing from the Templars and Hospitallers, and had sent forward seven of his galleys, with troops to dislodge the enemy from Baruth, by which he would pass and the expedition had succeeded, for the enemy fled in alarm. The king was in his tent, talking with his officers about embarking for their homes on the morrow, when, to the messengers from Joppa entered, and tearing their garments, related to the king how the enemy had taken Joppa, all but the citadel, in which the remnant were besieged, and unless he should render them speedy assistance, they would all be involved in one common fate, according to the conditions which had been entered into with Saladin. The king, hearing of the danger to which the besieged were exposed, and pitying their condition, interrupted the messengers: "As God lives," said he, "I will be with them, and give them all the assistance in my power!" The words were hardly out of his mouth, before a proclamation was made that the army should be got ready. But the French would not vouchsafe even to honor the king with an answer, exclaiming proudly that they should never again march under his command and in this they were not disappointed, for they never again marched under anybody's command, for in a short time they all miserably perished. Meanwhile, however, the soldiers of all nations, whose hearts God had touched, and the sufferings of their fellow-creatures excited to compassion, hastened to set out with the king namely, the Templars, the Hospitallers, and several other valiant knights, all of whom marched by land to Caesarea but the noble king trusting for his safety to his own valor, embarked on board his fleet of galleys, which were equipped with every thing that could be necessary. With him was the earl of Leicester, Andrew de Chaveguy, Roger de Satheya, Jordan de Humez, Ralph de Mauleon, Achus de Fay, and the knights of Pratelles, companions of the king, together with many others of illustrious names, besides Genoese and Pisans. Those who went by land to Caesarea, halted there some time for fear of an ambuscade, which they heard had been laid by Saladin for all such as should pass that way; and there was no better way for them to go by, on account of the son of Arcisus, who guarded the maritime district between Caesarea and Arsur and besides this, a contrary wind arose, which detained the king's ships three days at Cayphas, where they had put in. The king, vexed at this delay, exclaimed aloud, "Lord God, why dost thou detain us here consider, I pray thee, the urgency of the case, and the devoutness of our wishes." No sooner had he prayed thus, than God caused a favorable wind to spring up, which wafted his fleet before it into the harbor of Joppa, in the midst of the night of Friday, immediately preceding the Saturday on which they had agreed to surrender, and all of them would have been given over to destruction. Alas, for the perfidy of that wicked race! Early on the morning of that clay, which was the day of St. Peter ad vincula, the besieged were importuned by the Turks to fulfill the conditions of the truce. They accordingly began at the ninth hour to pay in part the bezants which they had promised when the wicked Turks, behaving worse than brute beasts, and with no feeling of humanity about them, cut off the heads of those who paid them the money and thus seven of them had already perished, and their heads were thrown into a ditch. But those in the town who were still alive, discovering the treachery, were struck with terror, and began to send forth cries of lamentation and distress. Seeing certain death before them, they bent their knees, and confessed their sins to one another, thinking no longer of their lives which were doomed, but of their souls; whilst to delay their fate for some few moments longer,—for who is there that does not fear death?—they fled up the fortress as far they were able, and there awaited the stroke of martyrdom, shedding tears, and supplicating the mercy of the Almighty, who at length was appeased, and deigned to listen to their petition their deliverer was already come, his fleet was riding in the harbor, and his soldiers were eager to land for their rescue!

CHAPTER XV - *Of the fierce conflict by which the king recovered the castle of Joppa, and liberated the besieged*

The Turks, discovering the arrival of the king's fleet, sallied down to the seaside with sword and shield, and sent forth showers of arrows the shore was so thronged with their multitude that there was hardly a foot of ground to spare. Neither did they confine themselves to acting on the defensive, for they shot their arrows at the crews of the ships, and the cavalry spurred their horses into the sea to prevent the kings men from landing. The king, gathering his ships together, consulted with his officers what was the best step to take. "Shall we," said he, "push on against this rabble multitude who occupy the shore, or shall we value our lives more than the lives of those poor fellows who are exposed to destruction for want of our assistance?" Some of them replied that further attempts were useless, for it was by no means certain that any one remained alive to be saved, and how could they land in the face of so large a multitude? The king looked around thoughtfully, and at that moment saw a priest plunge into the water and swim towards the royal galley. When he was received on board, he addressed the king with palpitating heart and spirits almost failing him. "Most noble king, the remnant of our people, waiting for your arrival, are exposed like sheep to be slain, unless the divine grace shall bring you to their rescue." "Are any of them still alive, then?" asked the king, "and if so, where are they?" "There are still some of them alive," said the priest," and hemmed in and at the last extremity in front of yonder tower." "Please God, then," replied the king, "by whose guidance we have come, we will die with our brave brothers in arms, and a curse light on him who hesitates." The word was forthwith given, the galleys were pushed to land the king dashed forward into the waves with his thighs unprotected by armor, and up to his middle in the water; he soon gained firm footing on the dry strand behind him followed Geoffrey du Bois and Peter de Pratelles, and in the rear came all the others rushing through the waves. The Turks stood to defend the shore, which was covered with their numerous troops. The king, with an arbalest which he held in his hand, drove them back right and left his companions pressed upon the recoiling enemy, whose courage quailed when they saw it was the king, and they no longer dared to meet him, The king brandished his fierce sword, which allowed them no time to resist, but they yield before his fiery blows, and are driven in confusion with blood and havoc by the king's men until the shore was entirely cleared of them. They then brought together beams, poles, and wood, from the old ships and galleys to make a barricade and the king placed there some knights, servants, and arbalesters, to keep guard and to dislodge the Turks, who, seeing that they could no longer oppose our troops, dispersed themselves on the shore with cries and bowlings in one general flight. The king then, by a winding chair, which he had remarked in the house of the Templars, was the first to enter the town, where he found more than 3,000 of the Turks turning over every thing in the houses, and carrying away the spoil. The brave king had no sooner entered the town, than he caused his banners to be hoisted on an eminence, that they might be seen by the Christians in the tower, who taking courage at the sight, rushed forth in arms from the tower to meet the king, and at the report thereof the Turks were thrown into confusion. The king, meanwhile, with brandished sword, still pursued and slaughtered the enemy, who were thus enclosed between the two bodies of the Christians, and filled the streets with their slain. "Why need I say more? All were slain, except such as took to flight in time; and thus those who had before been victorious were now defeated and received condign punishment, whilst the king still continued the pursuit, showing no mercy to the enemies of Christ's Cross, whom God had given into his hands for there never was a man on earth who so abominated cowardice as he.

CHAPTER XVI - *Of the severe conflicts by which the Icing made Saladin raise the siege, and fixed his own tents where those of Saladin had been*

But the king had only three horses with him and what were three among so many? If we examine the deeds of the ancients, and all the records left us by former historians, we shall find that there never was a man who so distinguished himself in battle as King Richard did this day. When the Turks leaving the town saw his banners floating in the air, a cry was raised on right and left as he sallied forth upon them, and no hail-storm or tempest ever so densely concealed the sky, as it was then darkened by the flying arrows of the Turks. Saladin, hearing of the king's arrival and of his brilliant contest with the Turks, of whom he had slain all who opposed him, was seized with sudden fear, and like that timid animal, the hare, put spurs to his horse and fled from, before his face. The king, with his men, still continued the pursuit, slaying and destroying, whilst his arbalesters made such havoc of the horses that for two miles the traces of their flight were visible. He now therefore pitched his tent in the same place where those of Saladin had been, and thus by the divine grace so small a body of men had defeated this large army of the Turks. Saladin called together his admirals and thus addressed them: "Has he then beaten all of us ? Has the Christian army returned from Acre to slaughter and defeat us thus? By what superior disposition have they been able to accomplish this? In infantry, as well as cavalry, our army was decidedly superior." To these words, one of those perverse ones who were present, conscious of the state of our army, replied: "My lord, it is not as you think; they have neither horses nor beasts of burden of any kind, except three horses only, which their wonderful king found in Joppa. I think, however, that the king himself could easily be surprised, for he lies almost alone in his tent, and fully worn out with fatigue. Whoever seizes him will at once put an end to our labors and to the whole campaign." It was then given out among the Turks what a reproach it was to them, and lasting scandal, that so large an army and so many thousands of the Turks had been defeated by so small an army, and that Joppa had been recovered from them by force of arms. In this manner they murmured to one another at what had taken place, and trembled with confusion.

CHAPTER XVII - *How the Christians acted in the matter of the swine which the Turks had killed*

Now the execrable Turks, who were surprised in Joppa, had made an immense slaughter of those who were too weak to resist, and in particular had killed a large number of swine, in fact, all they could find for it is against the law of Mahomet to eat them; wherefore they naturally abominate swine as unclean, because swine are said to have devoured Mahomet. The Turks, therefore, in contempt of the Christians, had collected into one mass the bodies of the swine, together with the bodies of the Christians, whom they had slain. But the corpses of the Christians were now buried in peace, whilst those of the Turks were in their turn cast out to rot with those of the swine.

CHAPTER XVIII - *Of the rebuilding of the walls of Joppa*

On the next day, being Sunday, the king diligently set to work to repair the walls of Joppa, and continued his exertions on Monday and Tuesday, that some protection at least might be furnished by them such as it was, though the repairs were made without either lime or cement but this could not be avoided, for an immense army of Turks was close at hand.

CHAPTER XIX - *How certain men called Menelones and Cordivi boasted that they would surprise the king, asleep or otherwise, unawares*

Meanwhile a certain depraved set of men among the Saracens, called Menelones of Aleppo and Cordivi, an active race, met together to consult what should be done in the existing state of things. They spoke of the scandal which lay against them, that so small an army, without horses, had driven them out of Joppa and they reproached themselves with cowardice and shameful laziness, and arrogantly made a compact among themselves that they would seize King Richard in his tent, and bring him before Saladin, from whom they would receive a most munificent reward.

CHAPTER XX - *How Count Henry arrived at Joppa from Caesarea, and of the number of his soldiers*

In the mean time Count Henry came in a galley with his followers from Caesarea, where the rest of our army was detained, on account of the ambuscades of the Turks, who lay in wait at all the roads, bridges, and wells, so that the king could not, on this emergency, bring with him out of all his army more than fifty-five knights, with a strong body of infantry, arbalesters, and retainers besides, about two thousand Genoese and Pisans and others whilst of horses he had no more than fifteen, whether good or bad.

CHAPTER XXI - *How the aforesaid Menelones and Cordivi would have surprised the king in tent, as they had boasted, if a certain Genoese had not perceived them, and awakened the king*

Meanwhile the Menelones and Cordivi aforesaid prepared themselves in the middle of the night to surprise the king, and sallied forth armed, by the light of the moon, conversing with one another about the object which they had in hand. hateful race of unbelievers they are anxiously bent upon seizing Christ's steadfast soldier, while he is asleep they rush on in numbers to seize him, unarmed and apprehensive of no danger. They were now not far from his tent, and were preparing to lay hands on him, when, to the God of mercy, who never neglects those who trust in Him, and acts in a wonderful manner even towards those who know him not, sent the spirit of discord among the aforesaid Cordivi and Menelones. The Cordivi said, "You shall go in on foot, to take the king and his followers, whilst we will remain on horseback to prevent their escaping into the castle." But the Menelones replied, "Nay, it is your place to go in on foot, because our rank is higher than yours: we are content with the service which is our duty but this service on foot belongs to you rather than us." Whilst thus the two parties were contending which of them were the greatest, their continued dispute caused much delay, and when at last they came to a decision how their nefarious attempt should be achieved, the dawn of day appeared, viz. the Wednesday next following the feast of St. Peter ad vinculo. But now, by the providence of God, who had decreed that his holy champion should not be seized whilst asleep by the infidels, a certain Genoese was led by the divine impulse to go out early in the morning into the fields, where he was alarmed at the noise of men and horses advancing, and returned speedily, but just had time to see helmets reflecting back the light which now fell upon them. He immediately rushed with speed into the camp, calling out "To arms! to arms!" The king was awakened by the noise, and leaping startled from his bed, put on his impenetrable coat of mail, and summoned his men to the rescue.

CHAPTER XXII - *Of the marvelous bravery of the king in this never-to-be forgotten skirmish*

God of all virtues lives there a man who would not be shaken by such a sudden alarm? The enemy rush unawares, armed against unarmed, many against few, for our men had no time to arm, or even to dress themselves. The king himself therefore, and many others with him, on the urgency of the moment, proceeded without their crushes to the fight, some even without their breeches, and they armed themselves in the best manner they could, though they were going to fight the whole day. Whilst our men were thus arming in haste, the Turks drew near, and the king mounted his horse, with only ten other knights, whose names are as follows: Count Henry, the earl of Leicester, Bartholomew de Mortimer, Ralph de Mauleon, Andrew de Chavegui, Gerald de Finival, Roger de Sacy, William de Aetang, Hugh de Villeneuve, a brave retainer, and Henry le Tyois, the king's standard-bearer. These alone had horses, and some even of those they had were base and impotent horses, unused to arms: the common men were skillfully drawn out in ranks and troops, with each a captain to command them. The knights were posted nearer to the sea, having the church of St. Nicholas on the left, because the Turks had directed their principal attack on that quarter, and the Pisans and Genoese were posted beyond the suburban gardens, having other troops mingled with them. O who could fully relate the terrible attacks of the infidels? The Turks at first rushed on with horrid yells, hurling their javelins and shooting their arrows. Our men prepared themselves as they best could, to receive their furious attack, each fixing his right knee in the ground, that so they might the better hold together, and maintain their position; whilst there, the thighs of their left legs were bent, and their left hands held their shields or bucklers; stretched out before them in their right hands they held their lances, of which the lower ends were fixed in the ground, and their iron heads pointed threateningly towards the enemy. Between every two of the men who were thus covered with their shields, the king, versed in arms, placed an arbalester, and another behind him to stretch the arbalest as quickly as possible, so that the man in front might discharge his shot whilst the other was loading. This was found to be of much benefit to our men, and did much harm to the enemy. Thus every thing was prepared as well as the shortness of the time allowed, and our little army was drawn up in order. The king ran along the ranks, and exhorted every man to be firm and not to flinch. "Courage, my brave men," said he, "and let not the attack of the enemy disturb you. Bear up against the frowns of fortune, and you will rise above them. Every thing may be borne by brave men; adversity sheds a light upon the virtues of mankind, as certainly as prosperity casts over them a shade; there is no room for flight, for the enemy surround us, and to attempt to flee is to provoke certain death. Be brave, therefore, and let the urgency of the case sharpen up your valor brave men should either conquer nobly, or gloriously die. Martyrdom is a boon which we should receive with willing mind: but before we die, let us whilst still alive do what may avenge our deaths, giving thanks to God that it has been our lot to die martyrs. This will be the end of our labors, the termination of our life, and of our battles." These words were hardly spoken, when the hostile army rushed with ferocity upon them, in seven troops, each of which contained about a thousand horse. Our men received their attack with their right feet planted firm against the sand, and remained immovable. Their lances formed a wall against the enemy, who would assuredly have broken through, if our men had in the least degree given way. The first line of the Turks, perceiving, as they advanced, that our men stood immovable, recoiled a little, when our cross-bowmen plied them with a shower of missiles, slaying large numbers of men and horses. Another line of Turks at once came on in like manner, and were again encountered and driven back. In this way the Turks came on like a whirlwind, again and again, making the appearance of an attack, that our men might be induced to give way, and when they were close up, they turned their horses off in another direction. The king and his knights, who were on horseback, perceiving this, put spurs to their horses, and charged into the middle of the enemy, upsetting them right and left, and piercing a large number through the body with their lances at last they pulled up their horses, because they found that they had penetrated entirely through the Turkish lines. The king now looking about him saw the noble earl of Leicester fallen from his horse, and fighting bravely on foot. No sooner did he see this than he rushed to his rescue, snatched him out of the hands of the enemy, and replaced him on his horse. What a terrible combat was then waged a multitude of Turks advanced, and used every exertion to destroy our small army vexed at our success, they rushed towards the royal standard of the lion, for they would rather have slain the king than a thousand others. In the midst of the melee the king saw Ralph de Mauleon dragged off prisoner by the Turks, and spurring his horse to speed, in a moment released him from their hands, and restored him to the army; for the king was a very giant in the battle, and was everywhere in the field,—now here, now there, wherever the attacks of the Turks raged the hottest. So bravely did lie fight, that there was no one, however gallant, that would not readily and deservedly yield to him the preeminence. On that day he performed the most gallant deeds on the furious army of the Turks, and slew numbers with his sword, which shone like lightning some of them were cloven in two from their helmet to their teeth, whilst others lost their heads, arms, and other members, which were lopped off at a single blow. While the king was thus laboring with incredible exertions in the fight, a Turk advanced towards him, mounted on a foaming steed. He had been sent by Saphadin of Archadia, brother to Saladin, a liberal and munificent man, if he had not rejected the Christian faith. This man now sent to the king, as a token of his well-known honorable character, two noble horses, requesting him earnestly to accept them, and make use of them, and if he returned safe and sound out of that battle, to remember the gift and recompense it in any manner he pleased. The king readily received the present, and afterwards nobly recompensed the giver. Such is bravery, cognizable even in an enemy; since a Turk who was our bitter foe, thus honored the king for his distinguished valor. The king, especially at such a moment of need, protested that he would have taken any number of horses equally good from any one, even more a foe than Saphadin, so necessary were they to him at that moment. Fierce now raged the fight, when such numbers attacked so few the whole earth was covered with the javelins and arrows of the unbelievers; they threw them several at a time against our men, of whom many were wounded. Thus the weight of the battle fell heavier upon us than before, and the galley-men withdrew in the galleys which brought them, and so in their anxiety to be safe, they sacrificed their character for bravery. Meanwhile a shout was raised by the Turks, as they strove who should first occupy the town, hoping to slay those of our men whom they should find within. The king, hearing the clamor, taking with him only two knights and two cross-bow-men, met three Turks, nobly caparisoned, in one of the principal streets. Rushing bravely upon them, he slew the riders in his own royal fashion, and made booty of two horses. The rest of the Turks who were found in the town, were put to the rout in spite of their resistance, and dispersing in different directions, sought to make their escape even where there was no regular road. The king also commanded the parts of the walls which were broken down to be made good, and placed sentinels to keep watch lest the town should be again attacked.

CHAPTER XXIII - *Of the wonderful acts of the king in battle, by which, with the Divine aid, he overthrew numbers of the enemy, and returned safe out of the midst of them to his own army*

These matters settled, the king went down to the shore, where many of our men had taken refuge on board the galleys. These the king exhorted by the most cogent arguments to return to the battle, and share with the rest whatever might befall them. Leaving five men as guards on board each galley, the king led back the rest to assist his hard pressed army; and he no sooner arrived, than with all his fury he fell upon the thickest ranks of the enemy, driving them back and routing them, so that even those who were at a distance and untouched by him, were overwhelmed by the throng of the troops as they retreated. Never was there such an attack made by an individual. He pierced into the middle of the hostile army, and performed the deeds of a brave and distinguished warrior. The Turks at once closed upon him and tried to overwhelm him. In the meantime our men, losing sight of the king, were fearful lest he should have been slain, and when one of them proposed that they should advance to find him, our lines could hardly contain themselves. But if by any chance the disposition of our troops had been broken, without doubt they would all have been destroyed. What however was to be thought of the king who was hemmed in by the enemy, a single man opposed to so many thousands? The hand of the writer faints to tell it, and the mind of the reader to hear it. Who ever heard of such a man? His bravery was ever of the highest order, no adverse storm could sink it; his valor was ever blooming, and if we may, from a few instances, judge of many, it was ever indefatigable in war. Why then do we speak of the valor of Antseus, who regained his strength every time he touched his mother earth, for Antseus perished when he was lifted up from earth in the long wrestling match. The body of Achilles also, who slew Hector, was invulnerable, because he was dipped in the Stygian waves; yet Achilles was mortally wounded in the very part by which be was held when they dipped him. Likewise Alexander, the Macedonian, who was stimulated by ambition to subjugate the whole world, undertook a most difficult enterprise, and with a handful of choice soldiers fought many celebrated battles, but the chief part of his valor consisted in the excellence of his soldiers. In the same manner, the brave Judas Maccabeus, of whose wars all the world discoursed, performed many wonderful deeds, worthy for ever to be remembered, but when he was abandoned by his soldiers in the midst of a battle, with thousands of enemies to oppose him, he was slain, together with his brothers. But King Richard, inured to battle from his tenderest years, and to whom even famous Roland could not be considered equal, remained invincible, even in the midst of the enemy, and his body, as if it were made of brass, was impenetrable to any kind of weapon. In his right hand he brandished his sword, which in its rapid descent broke the ranks on either side of him. Such was his energy amid that host of Turks, that, fearing nothing, he destroyed all around him, mowing men down with his scythe as reapers mow down the corn with their sickles. Who could describe his deeds? Whoever felt one of his blows had no need of a second. Such was the energy of his courage that it seemed to rejoice at having found an occasion to display itself. The sword wielded by his powerful hand, cut down men and horses alike, cleaving them to the middle. The more he saw himself separated from his men, and the more the enemy sought to overwhelm him, the more did his valor shine conspicuous. Among other brave deeds which he performed on that occasion, he slew by one marvelous stroke an admiral, who was conspicuous above the rest of the enemy by his rich caparisons. This man, by his gestures seemed to say that he was going to do something wonderful, arid whilst he reproached the rest with cowardice, he put spurs to his horse and charged full against the king, who waving his sword as he saw him coming, smote off at a single blow not only his head, but his shoulder and right arm. The Turks were terror-struck at the sight, and giving way on all sides, scarcely dared to shoot at him from a distance with their arrows. The king now returned safe and unhurt to his friends, and encouraged them more than ever with the hope of victory. How were their minds raised from despair when they saw him coming safe out of the enemy's ranks! They knew not what had happened to him, but they knew that without him all the hopes of the Christian army would be in vain. The king's person was stuck all over with javelins, like a deer pierced by the hunters, and the trappings of his horse were thickly covered with arrows. Thus, like a brave soldier, he returned from the contest, and a bitter contest it was, for it had lasted from the morning sun to the setting sun. It may seem indeed wonderful and even incredible, that so small a body of men endured so long a conflict; but by God's mercy we cannot doubt the truth of it, for in that battle only one or two of our men were slain. But the number of the Turkish horses which lay dead on the fields is said to have exceeded fifteen hundred and of the Turks themselves more than seven hundred were killed, and yet they did not carry back King Richard, as they had boasted, as a present to Saladin but, on the contrary, he and his brave followers performed so many deeds of valor in the sight of the Turks, that the enemy themselves shuddered to behold them.

CHAPTER XXIV - *How Saladin ridiculed his men for having boasted that they would seize King Richard, and how they, in self-defense, replied that they had never seen so brave a soldier*

In the meantime, our men having by God's grace escaped destruction, the Turkish army returned to Saladin, who is said to have ridiculed them by asking where Melech Richard was, for they had promised to bring him a prisoner? "Which of you," continued he, "first seized him, and where is he? Why is he not produced?" To whom one of the Turks that came from the furthest countries of the earth, replied: "In truth, my lord, Melech Richard, about whom you ask, is not here we have never heard since the beginning of the world that there ever was such a knight, so brave and so experienced in arms. In every deed at arms, he is ever the foremost in deeds, he is without a rival, the first to advance, and the last to retreat we did our best to seize him, but in vain, for no one can escape from his sword; his attack is dreadful to engage with him is fatal, and his deeds are beyond human nature."

CHAPTER XXV - *How the king was ill from his fatigue and exertions in the battle*

From the toil and exertion of the battle. King Richard and several others who had exerted themselves the most, fell ill, not only from the fatigue of the battle, but the smell of the corpses, which so corrupted the neighborhood, that they all nearly died.

CHAPTER XXVI - *Saladin sends word to the king, whilst he was sick, that he was coming to seize him. Richard sends to Casarea for assistance from the French, who refuse to come*

In the meantime Saladin sent word to the king that he would come with his Turks and seize him, if he could only be sure that Richard would await his approach. The king replied instantly, that he would wait for him there, without stirring one foot from where he was, provided only that he had strength, to stand upright and to defend himself. Such was the king's courage, that it could not be overcome by any disasters. When the king, however, came to reflect on his actual situation, and the illness by which he was disabled, he thought it not expedient to be too secure when the serpent was in his neighborhood; he therefore sent Count Henry to Caesarea, with a message to the French, who had previously come thither, that they should join him and assist in defending the Holy Land, signifying also to them his present complaint, and the aforesaid message of Saladin. But the French refused to render him the least assistance; indeed, as far as they were concerned, he might have been destroyed by the multitude of the enemy, if he had not agreed to a truce which in some particulars was open to reprehension. So great was the multitude of the Turks, that what chance could so small a body of men have had against them, even if they had not been sick? It was therefore agreed that Ascalon should be destroyed, rather than that so dangerous a hazard should be run for if the enemy, meeting with no opposition, had seized the king lying ill upon his bed, Ascalon would of course have been taken possession of without resistance but would Tyre or Acre have been safe?

CHAPTER XXVII - *How the king wished to return to Acre to be cured, but, on the people opposing it, he asked of Saladin a truce for three years, which was granted*

In the meantime the king began to be anxious about his health, and after long reflection he sent for his relation Count Henry, with the Templars and Hospitallers, to whom he explained the enfeebled state of his body, and protested that in consequence of the vitiated atmosphere, and the bad state of the fortifications, he must immediately leave the place. He then appointed some of them to go and take charge of Ascalon, and to others to guard Joppa, whilst he went himself to Acre to be cured, as was now absolutely necessary for him. To this proposition they all with one heart and one voice made objection, saying, that they could not possibly guard Joppa or any other fortress after he was gone and persisting in this refusal, they kept aloof, and no longer acted in concert with the king. Richard was vexed and embarrassed by this conduct, and it gave him the most bitter pain that none of them sympathized with his intentions or wishes. He then began to waver as to what he should do, but in all his deliberations he came only to the same conclusion, that there was none of them to sympathize with his misfortunes. Seeing, then, that all left him, and that none took the slightest interest in the common cause, he ordered proclamation to be made, that whoever wished to receive the king's pay should come together to give him their help. At once two thousand footmen and fifty knights came forward. But the king's health now began to get so bad, that he despaired of its being re-established wherefore, in his anxiety both for the others and for himself, he thought it best, of all the plans which suggested themselves, to ask a truce, rather than to leave the land a prey to devastation, as many others had done, by sailing home in numbers to their own country. Thus the king, perplexed and hesitating what he had best do, requested Saphadin, the brother of Saladin, to mediate between them, and obtain the most honorable terms of truce in his power. Now Saphadin was a man of extraordinary liberality, who on many occasions paid great honor to the king for his singular virtues; and he now with great zeal procured for Richard a truce on the following conditions; namely, that Ascalon, which had always been a cause of annoyance to Saladin's government, should be destroyed, and not rebuilt for the space of at least three years, beginning at the following festival of Easter; but at the end of that time, whoever could get possession of it might fortify it that the Christians should be allowed to in habit Joppa without let or molestation, together with all the adjoining country, both on the sea-coast and in the mountains that peace should strictly be observed between the Christians and Saracens, each having free leave to come and go wherever they pleased; that pilgrims should have free access to the Holy Sepulchre, without any payment or pecuniary exaction whatever, and with leave to carry merchandise for sale through the whole land, and to practice commercial pursuits without opposition. This treaty was presented in writing to King Richard, who gave it his approbation, for in his weak condition, and having so few troops about him, and that too within two miles of the enemy he did not think it in his power to more favorable terms. Whoever entertains a different opinion concerning this treaty, I would have him know that he will expose himself to the charge of perversely deviating from the truth.

CHAPTER XXVIII - *How the king and Saladin corresponded amicably with one another by means of messengers*

When therefore the king, in his present emergency, had settled matters in the way described, he, in his magnanimity, which always aimed at something lowly and difficult, sent ambassadors to Saladin, announcing to him, in the presence of numerous of his chiefs, that he had only asked for a truce of three years for the purpose of revisiting his country, and collecting more men and money, wherewith to return and rescue all the land of Jerusalem from his domination, if indeed Saladin should have the courage to face him in the field. To this Saladin replied, calling his own Holy Law and God Almighty to witness, that he entertained such an exalted opinion of King Richard's honor, magnanimity, and general excellence, that he would rather lose his dominions to him than to any other king he had ever seen, always supposing that he was obliged to lose his dominions at all. Alas! how blind are men, whilst they lay plans for many years to come, they know not what to-morrow may bring forth the king's mind was looking forward into the future, and he hoped to recover the sepulchre of our Lord.

CHAPTER XXIX - *How the king went to Cayphas for his health*

The truce having been reduced to writing, and confirmed by oaths on both sides, the king went to Cayphas in the best manner he could, to take medicine and get himself cured.

CHAPTER XXX - *How the French, by the king's agency, for their malice, were forbidden to visit the Holy Sepulchre, whilst the others had permission*

In the meantime the French, who had been long enjoying a holiday at Acre, were getting ready to return home but though they had venomously opposed the truce, they now, before leaving the country, wished to complete their pilgrimage by visiting our Lord's sepulchre. The king, remembering their backwardness to assist him at Joppa, as we have related, and also on many other occasions, sent messengers to request that neither Saladin nor Saphadin, his brother, would allow any one to visit the Holy Sepulchre who did not bring a passport from either himself or Count Henry. The French were much vexed at this, and foiled of their object, soon afterwards returned to their own country, carrying back nothing with them but the reproach of ingratitude. The king, hearing that the greater part of the French who did their utmost to defame him were gone home, and that the mouths of his slanderers were stopped, caused it to be announced by proclamation, that whoever wished might visit our Lord's tomb, and bring back their offerings to help in repairing the walls of Joppa.

CHAPTER XXXI - *Of the first company who made the pilgrimage to Jerusalem, led by Andrew de Chavegui, and of the alarm occasioned by their indiscretion on the way*

The people were now arrayed to visit Jerusalem in three companies, each of which was placed under a separate leader. The first was led by Andrew de Chavegui; the second by Ralph Teissun and the third by Hubert bishop of Salisbury. The first company then advanced under Andrew bearing letters from the king. But, for their sins, they fell into a snare on the journey for when they reached the Plain of Ramula, they by common consent dispatched messengers to inform Saladin that they were coming with letters from King Richard, and that they wished to have a safe-conduct, coming and going. The messengers were noble men, and energetic in character, but on this occasion they well nigh incurred the charge of neglecting their duty their names were William des Roches, Girard de Tourneval, and Peter de Pratelles. When they came to "the Tower of the Soldiers," they halted there to procure the authority of Saphadin for proceeding further; but there they fell asleep, and slept till sunset, and found on awaking that all the pilgrims, on whose behalf they came, had passed by and were gone on before them. The whole number crossed the plains and were approaching the hills, when Andrew de Chavegui and the rest, looking behind them, saw their own messengers coming after them as fast as they were able. Seeing this, they halted in much alarm, considering that they were in great danger of being put to death, for the army of the Turks had not yet departed, and their messengers, who ought to have brought back for them a safe-conduct from the Saracens, were now behind them. When therefore these came up, the others blamed them for their neglect, and told them once more to make haste on before, and do as they had been instructed. The messengers went on with all speed to Jerusalem, and found about 2,000 Turks, or more, encamped without the city. They inquired for Saphadin, and when they had found him, they explained what had happened, and he, rebuking them smartly, said it was evident that they did not value their lives a rush, as they had come into the middle of a hostile army without passport or safeguard of any kind. It was now sunset, and the other pilgrims came up, not knowing what they ought to do, and having no arms to defend themselves. The Turks grinned and frowned on them as they passed, and it was manifest by their looks what enmity they harbored in their hearts, for the face is after the index of the mind and our men at that moment were so confounded that they wished themselves back again at Tyre, or even Acre, which they had just left. Thus they passed the night, near a certain mountain, in a state of great alarm.

CHAPTER XXXII - *How the Turks wished to take vengeance on our pilgrims, but Saladin and his chiefs would not allow it*

The next day certain of the Turks appeared before Saladin, and earnestly entreated of him that they might be allowed to take vengeance on the Christians who were now in their power, for the death of their friends, fathers, brothers, sons, and relations who had been slain, first at Acre, and afterwards at other places, now, as they said, that they had so

good an opportunity. Saladin sent for the Turkish chiefs to consult about this request, and Mestoc, Saphadin, Bedridin, and Dorderin were speedily in attendance. When the subject was placed before them, it was their unanimous opinion that the Christians should have leave to come and go, without injury or hindrance. "For," said they to Saladin, "it would be a deep stain upon our honor, if the treaty which has been made between you and the king of England should, by our interference, be broken, and the faith of the Turks for ever afterwards be called in question." In consequence of these observations, Saladin gave orders immediately that the Christians should be taken care of, and escorted to the city and back again without molestation. To discharge this commission, Spahadin was at his own request deputed; and under his protection the pilgrims had free access to the Holy Sepulchre, and were treated with the greatest liberality, after which they returned joyfully to Acre.

CHAPTER XXXIII - *Of the second company of pilgrims who went to Jerusalem, escorted by Ralph Teissun*

On their return, the second company of pilgrims stationed between the castle of Arnald and Ramula, set forth, led by Ralph Teissun. Now Saladin, as we have before stated, had posted his men to keep diligent guard over the roads whenever any of the pilgrims were on their way to Jerusalem, in consequence of this precaution, we traveled freely and unmolested, and crossing the hill country, arrived at the Mountain of Delight, where, seeing in the distance the city of Jerusalem, we knelt down and gave humble thanks to God, as is the custom of pilgrims. From the same spot we saw also Mount Olivet after which all advanced with joy, and those who had horses rode forward with speed, that they might the sooner gratify their desire of saluting the Holy Sepulchre. Moreover, as those horsemen who had gone before told us, Saladin allowed them to see and kiss the true Cross of our Lord, which formerly had been carried to battle. But we who were on foot, and came in the last, saw what we could, viz. in the first place we saw our

Lord's monument, where oblations were made but, as the Saracens took these away, we did not offer much, but gave part to the French and Syrian slaves, whom we there saw in servitude, laboring in the duties assigned to them. From thence we proceeded to Mount Calvary, where our Lord was crucified, and where there was a stone in which our Lord's cross had been fixed in Golgotha. When we had kissed this with reverence, we proceeded to the church built on Mount Zion, on the left side of which was the place from which Mary, the Holy mother of God, passed from this world to the Father. This spot we saluted with tears running down our cheeks, and then hastened to see the holy table at which Christ condescended to eat bread. This also we kissed fervently, and then we all departed together, in haste for it was no longer safe for us to go anywhere, except in a body, on account of the treachery of the unbelievers, for the Turks had secretly strangled three or four of our men who had strayed into the passages of the crypts. From thence we hastened to the sepulchre of the Blessed Virgin Mary, mother of God, in the middle of the

valley of Jehoshaphat, near Siloe, and kissed it with devout and contrite hearts. After which, with minds not altogether free from apprehension, we entered the vaulted chamber in which our Lord and Redeemer was kept prisoner during the night, to be crucified the next morning. This we saluted devoutly, whilst the tears ran down our cheeks, and then took our leave in haste, and the Turks also spurned us from them not a little, and we grieved for the pollutions with which the holy places were defiled by the horses of the unbelievers who used them for stables. We now took leave of Jerusalem and returned to Acre.

CHAPTER XXXIV – *Of the third company of pilgrims, led by Hubert Walter, bishop of Salisbury, to whom, Saladin showed much honor, and granted every thing he asked for*

The third company, led by the bishop of Salisbury, was now not far from Jerusalem, and Saladin sent out his people to receive the bishop honorably, and to conduct him wherever he pleased, to visit the holy places. Moreover, in acknowledgment of his prudent and honorable character, and his other merits, which had long before been known to Saladin, he was requested to take up his residence in the sultan's palace, and to be entertained at his expense. The bishop refused, saying, "By no means, for we are but pilgrims." Saladin enjoined his servants to show every attention to the bishop and his men, and sent him many presents; afterwards, also, he invited them to an interview, that he might behold his manner and deportment, and he allowed him to have a sight of the Holy Cross and they sat and conversed together a long time. Saladin, therefore, asked him about the king of England, and what the Christians said of his Saracens. To which the bishop replied, "In truth, as concerns my lord the king, I will only say what justice demands, that he has no equal among all the knights in the world, either for valor or for liberality in giving; for he is in every thing distinguished for every excellent quality. In short, my lord, in my humble opinion, if any one, bating your majesty's sins, were to bring your virtues into comparison with those of King Richard, and were to take both of you together, there would not be two other men in the world that could compete with you." Saladin listened patiently to the bishop, and at last replied, "I have long since been aware that your king is a man of the greatest honor and bravery, but he is imprudent, not to say foolishly so, in thrusting himself so frequently into danger, and shows too great recklessness of his own life. For my own part, of however large territories I might be the king, I would rather have abundance of wealth, with wisdom and moderation, than display immoderate valor and rashness." The conversation then took a familiar turn between the two, and Saladin told the bishop to ask for any thing he liked, and it should be given him. The bishop reply, asked if he might have until the next day to consider what he should ask. Which being granted, he then requested, that, whereas divine service was but half performed before at our Lord's tomb, which he had just visited, in the barbarous way of the Syrians, it might be allowed for the future, that two Latin priests with two deacons, to be maintained by the offerings of the faithful, should perform divine service in conjunction with the Syrians and an equal number at Bethlehem, and also at Nazareth. This petition was one of great importance, and as we believe, agreeable to God. The sultan assented to the request and the bishop instituted two priests in the aforesaid places, together with two deacons, rendering to God a service where there had been none before. After this, the pilgrims obtained the sultan's license, and returned from Jerusalem to Acre.

CHAPTER XXXV - *How the pilgrims, having fulfilled their pilgrimage, set sail for their own country, but suffered many shipwrecks and hardships on the way*

The people had now completed the pilgrimage to which they had devoted themselves, and preparing their fleet to return home, they spread their sails to the winds, and committed themselves to their ships. The fleet speedily set sail, and the ships were wafted in different directions, according to the variety of the winds. For a long time they were tossed about on the waves, and some of them reached different ports in safety; others were driven about, and in danger of being shipwrecked; others, again, died on their voyage, and found their grave in the depths of the ocean; others also were seized with incurable diseases, and never recovered or returned to their own country. Others, moreover, who endured in safety to the end, through the loss of their fathers, brothers, relations, and friends, who had perished of disease or by the sword, are believed to have endured a severe species of martyrdom, and diverse passions pierced their breasts as with a sword. Each, in his own way, we must admit it, endured a kind of martyrdom; every one, in short, of those, who with simple and devout hearts had exposed themselves for the love of God to this distant pilgrimage. Some, however, with loquacious garrulity, were accustomed afterwards to complain that the pilgrims had done little good in the land of Jerusalem, because they had not freed the city but they did not know what they were saying, for they were inquiring about things of which they have no personal knowledge or experience. We, however, who have seen, and who know all of it by our own eye-sight, claim to be believed in our accounts of the tribulations and miseries which those men endured. Wherefore, we state confidently, in the hearing of those also who were present that 100,000 Christians perished in that pilgrimage, for the sole reason that, in the hope of divine reward, they had separated themselves from women, deeming it wicked by sacrificing their purity to obtain bodily health and thus they opposed patience even to the corruption of the flesh, that the purity of their minds might remain unimpaired. We know also, for certain, that by sickness and famine combined, there died more than 300,000, in the siege of Acre, and afterwards, in the same city. Who, however, can doubt of the salvation of the souls of such noble and excellent men, who daily heard divine service from the lips of their own chaplains? These surely may be supposed to have gone to heaven.

CHAPTER XXXVI - *How the king, before setting sail for some, exchanged ten noble Turkish captives for William de Pratelles, who had suffered himself to be captured to save the king, saying that himself was Melech*

Meanwhile King Richard's ship was made ready, and every thing necessary, both in arms and provisions, prepared for the voyage. The king then, out of mere liberality, and impelled by his nobleness of mind alone, redeemed William de Pratelles, who, as we have before related, suffered himself to be captured to save the king, by exchanging for him ten of the most noble Turks, though they would gladly have given a large sum of money to retain him but the king's generosity would not condescend in any way to be tarnished.

CHAPTER XXXVII - *How King Richard set sail to return home, and of the misfortunes which he met with*

Every thing was now settled, and the king was already on the point of embarking, when determining before he went, to leave nothing behind him that might detract from his honor, he ordered proclamation to be made that all who had claims on him should come forward, and that all his debts should be paid fully, and more than fully, to avoid all occasion afterwards of detraction or complaint. What sighs and tears were there when the royal fleet weighed anchor! A blessing was invoked on the king's many acts of benevolence, his virtues and his largesses were set forth, and the numerous excellences combined in one man. How then did the lamentations of all resound as they exclaimed, "O Jerusalem, bereft now of every succour! How hast thou lost thy defender! Who will protect thee, should the truce be broken, now that King Richard is departed?" Such were the words of each, when the king, whose health was not yet fully re-established, and who was the subject of all their anxious wishes, went on board and set sail. All night the ship ran on her way by the light of the stars, and when morning dawned, the king looked back with yearning eyes upon the land which he had left, and after long meditation, he prayed aloud, in the hearing of several, in these words, "O holy land, I commend thee to God, and if his heavenly grace shall grant me so long to live, that I may, in his good pleasure, afford thee assistance, I hope, as I propose, to be able to be some day a succour to thee." With these words he urged the sailors to spread their canvass to the winds that they might the sooner cross over the expanse of sea that lay before them; ignorant indeed of the tribulations and sorrows that awaited him, and the calamities that he was to suffer from the treachery that had long before been transmitted to France, by which it was contrived that he should be wickedly thrown into prison, though he justly suspected no such evil in the service of God, and in so laborious a pilgrimage how unequally was he recompensed for his exertions in the common cause ! His inheritance was seized by another, his castles in Normandy were unjustly taken, his rivals made cruel assaults upon his rights without provocation, and he only escaped from captivity by paying a ransom to the emperor of Germany. To gather the money for his ransom, the taxes were raised to the uttermost a large collection was levied upon all his land, and every thing was distracted for the chalices and hallowed vessels of gold and silver were gathered from the churches, and the monasteries were obliged to do without their utensils neither was this unlawful according to the decrees of the holy fathers, nay, it was even a matter of necessity, inasmuch as no saint, many though there be, ever during life suffered so much for the Lord as King Richard in his captivity in Austria and in Germany, he who had gained so many triumphs over the Turks was nefariously circumvented by the brethren of his own faith, and seized by those who agreed with him in name only as members of the creed of Christ. Alas, how much more are secret snares to be feared than open discord, according to the proverb, "It is easier to avoid a hostile than a deceitful man." Oh, shame be it said, that one whom no adversary could resist, nor the whole force of Saladin could conquer, was now seized by an ignoble people, and kept a prisoner in Germany. Oh, how painful is it for those who have been nurtured in liberty, to be placed at the beck of another! But out of that captivity, by God's usual mercy, his own activity, and the care of his faithful servants, he was at length set at liberty for a large sum of money, because he was known to be a man of great power. At last restored to his native soil and the kingdom of his ancestors, in a short time he restored all to tranquility. He then crossed over into Normandy, to avenge himself on the wanton aggressions of the king of France, his rival and when he had more than once defeated him, he powerfully recovered with sword and spear his alienated rights, even with augmentation.

BIOGRAPHICAL NOTICE OF JOINVILLE

The family of Joinville was, in the thirteenth century, one of the most distinguished in Champagne. About the middle of the preceding century, Etienne, surnamed Devaux, an ancestor of the author of these memoirs, became very powerful. He espoused the countess de Joigny, who brought him the fief so named, together with several other manors, as a marriage portion and he was the first who built the castle of Joinville.

The uncle and father of Joinville covered themselves with glory; the first, during the reign of Philip Augustus, when in attendance upon the count of Flanders, at the conquest of Constantinople: the second, during the minority of St. Louis, in defending the town of Toyes against the joint efforts of almost all the lords of France.

John lord of Joinville, author of the following memoirs, was eldest son to Simon lord of Joinville, by Beatrice of Burgundy, his second wife. Biographers differ as to the date of his birth. Du Cange places it in 1220; De la Ravaliere in 1224 and De la Bastie as late as 1228. The authors of the "Biographie Universelle" decide in favor of the middle period. He was betrothed during the life of his parents to Alicia, daughter of Henry count de Grand Pre, by Marie de Garlande. The articles of marriage were agreed to in the month of June, 1231, in the presence of Thibaud count of Champagne, the principal conditions of which were, that the countess and her son Henry should give, in consideration of this alliance, three hundred lives yearly, in land, and that in return Alicia should renounce all claim to the succession of her father and mother.

It was likewise stipulated that Simon lord of Joinville, father to John, should so manage that Geoffrey de Joinville, his son, should approve of and ratify the sentence of separation which the archbishop of Rheims had pronounced between him and the countess of Grand Pre from which we may conjecture, that this marriage was concluded to appease the quarrel which this divorce bad caused between the two families.

The articles were only signed by the countess of Grand Pre, in the absence of her son but the count of Champagne pledged himself for his duly executing them. This was not, however, so soon accomplished, nor was the marriage completed until after the year 1239 at which period John lord of Joinville having succeeded his father in his estates, and in the sense chalship of Champagne, was unmarried for in this year he promised Count Thibaud, king of Navarre, not to ally himself with the count de Bar, nor take his daughter to wife. Beatrice, mother to John, made the count a similar promise for her son.

His marriage with Alicia must have taken place instantly afterward for, in a deed of the year 1240, the lady of Joinville is styled sister to Henry count de Grand Pre. It had probably been deferred until then on account of the youth of the lord de Joinville, who thus speaks of himself: "That when the treaty between the king, Saint Louis, and the count de la Marche, was concluded, he had not then put on his helmet." That is to say, he had not then borne arms, nor received the order of knighthood and that when he put on the cross to march to the Holy Land with his king, he was very young.

That was the first occasion he made use of to display his valor, and show to all the world that he was no way degenerated in courage and virtue from his ancestors. The crusade had been proclaimed throughout France, and St. Louis, his queen and children, with the brothers to the king, and the principal barons of the realm, had already put on their armor, and covered their shoulders with the mark of our redemption, to recover the Holy Land from the hands of the infidels, and to carry the war into their country.

John lord of Joinville followed the examples of his ancestors, who had signalized themselves in these illustrious conquests, took the cross, and determined to accompany the king. But as this enterprise was attended with danger, and would probably be of long duration, he wished, before he set out, to make a settlement of his affairs, and leave every one satisfied with his conduct, so that he might be in the proper condition to deserve the fruits and pardons which these crusaders merited through the concessions of the sovereign pontiff. Having assembled his friends and neighbors, he gave them to understand, that if any one had the smallest subject of complaint against him, or if he had wronged him in the slightest manner, he was ready to make him all the satisfaction that could be wished for. On the other hand, as his mother, Beatrice, was still living, and enjoyed the greater part of his fortune as her dower, he found himself obliged to mortgage the principal part of the remainder of his lands, to supply the expenses of his equipment for so long a voyage, and of so considerable an enterprise, so that there scarcely remained to him twelve hundred lives of yearly rent in land.

He set out from his castle of Acinville after the Easter of 1248, accompanied by ten knights, whom he kept in his pay among whom were three bannerets,—namely, Hugh de Landricourt, Hugh de Til-chatel, lord of Conflans, and Peter de Pontmolain. He journeyed in company with John lord of Aspremont, Gosbert d'Aspremont and his brothers, who were his cousins, and the count de Sarrebruche, all of whom had in like manner put on the cross. They embarked at Marseilles and sailed to Cyprus, where they found the king of France, who had arrived there a short time before. It was there the lord de Joinville first entered into the service and pay of this great king, whose good graces and affection he so much gained that this prince would have him always near his person, employing him in the most important negotiations, and considering him as one of his confidential and faithful counselors. From the day he entered into the service of the king, in the island of Cyprus, he scarcely ever quitted him until his death, and was always attendant on him for the space of twenty, two years.

This would be the place to relate his adventures, his combats, and his travels; how he landed in Egypt, and was attacked by the Saracens, how he repulsed them how he was wounded, and then caught the epidemical disorder of the. army; how he was made prisoner by the enemy, saved and delivered from their hands; how he accompanied the king to Acre, who again retained him and his knights in his pay in short, after having been absent on these expeditions the space of seven years, he returned to France with the king. But as this narration would be of considerable length, and as he himself has written the history, I pass it over, and shall only mention some others of his principal actions. On his return to France, he took leave of the king at Beaucaire, whence, having visited the dauphiness of Vienne his relation, the count de Chalons his uncle, and the count de Bourgognehis cousin-german, he arrived at his castle of Joinville. After residing there some time, he went to Soissons to meet the king, who received him with so much kindness and friendship that the whole court was surprised and became jealous of him. It was about this time that Thibaud II king of Navarre and count of Champagne employed him to request of the king his daughter Isabella and this negotiation he managed with so much address and prudence that, in spite of great difficulties, the marriage was concluded, and celebrated at Melun with royal magnificence, in the year 1255.

This service, in addition to others, gained him the affections of the king of Navarre, who presented him with many gifts, among which was the donation to him and his heirs, dated January 1258, of all the rights and royalties of the village of Germany, as an augmentation of fief, on condition of paying homage liege. In the following year he subscribed the testament of Ebles de Geneva, son to Humbert count of Geneva, in which, however, he adds no title to his name, which may cause a doubt whether this John de Joinville, or de Genville, as he is called, be our seneschal. He was, afterward, almost constantly at the court of the king of Navarre, his lord, and accompanied him, in the year 1267, when this prince did homage to the bishop of Langres for the towns of Bar sur Aube, Bar sur Seine, and some others, which he held under the church, in presence of William lord de Grancey, Renier Vitardore, and Eustache de Conflans, marshals of Champagne, and other lords of that country.

The king, St. Louis, having convoked at Paris all his barons, on the subject of a new crusade, summoned thither the lord de Joinville, at that time suffering under a quartan ague. On his arrival, the king, and Thibaud king of/Navarre, pressed him to put on the cross, and undertake, with them /an expedition to Africa; but he excused himself on the plea of the poverty and distress of his subjects and vassals, who had been harshly treated by the exactions made on them by the king of France's officers during his former expedition. He acted sometime afterward as president in the extraordinary assemblies and assizes held at Troyes, as the person best qualified, in the year 1271. During the journey which was made to Arragon in 128.3, by King Philip the Hardy, who had the wardship of Jane queen of Navarre and countess of Champagne, sole daughter to King Henry, he was appointed by him governor and guardian of that country. He was present likewise at the assizes of Champagne in the years 1291 and 1296 and in the year 1303 he is named, with John de Joinville lord of Ancerville, Anseau de Joinville, and other great barons of France and Champagne, in the summons of Philip the Fair to meet him at Arras the 5th of August, and attend him in his war against Flanders.

He was also one of the lords and barons of Champagne, who formed a league, in the month of November, 1314, against this same king, on account of a subsidy which he had undertaken to raise from the nobles of his realm. This dispute was settled the ensuing year by the king, Louis Hutin, who, by his letters, dated from the Bois de Vincennes, the 17th day of May, 1315, appointed commissioners to inquire into their privileges. The king immediately after issued a summons for the nobles of his realm to assemble at Arras in the month of August, to assist him in his war against the Flemings but the lord de Joinville was ordered, by a private letter from the king, to be at Authie by the middle of June. This was, however, too short notice for him to make his preparations, and he wrote to the king his excuses, alleging the impossibility of being at the appointed place by the time fixed, and promising at the same time to join the army as speedily as he could. And in the list of those men-at-arms who were in the company of my lord the count of Potiers, and received at Arras and elsewhere by his two marshals, M. Regnaut de Lor and the Borgne de Ceris, his name appears, with one knight and six esquires.

The letter which he wrote to the king on the subject of this summons was as follows:

"To his good lord, Louis, by the grace of God, King of France and Navarre, John lord of Joinville, seneschal of Champagne, sends health and his willing service. Dear sire, it is indeed true, as you inform me, that it has been reported you had made up matters with the Flemings; and, as we believed it, sire, we have not made any preparations to obey your summons, which you sent me, sire, acquainting me that you should be at Arras to redress the wrongs the Flemings have done you and in this I think you act well and may God give you his assistance! And as you have ordered me and my people to be at Authie by the middle of June, sire, I inform you that that cannot well be done for your letters only arrived the second Sunday in June, eight days before we ought to have been at the rendezvous. My people shall be got ready as soon as possible, to go whithersoever you please. Sire, do not be displeased that at the beginning of this letter I have only called you my good lord, for I have never done otherwise to my lords your ancestors and predecessors in the government, whose souls may God pardon! Written the second Sunday of June, the same day that your letter was brought me, in the year 1315."

This letter was folded, and sealed with a seal of yellow wax, of the size of a large golden crown, having an impression of a knight armed with his sword and shield, and the coat of arms and housing of his horse blazoned with the arms of Joinville around it, instead of an inscription, was a border of flowers de luce, similar to that which is on the coins of St. Louis. The lord de Joinville must have been ninety or ninety-two years old in this year of 1315; for since his marriage was arranged in 1231, and consummated in 1240, he could not then have been younger than twenty years. A late author assures us, that he lived upwards of one hundred years and in a title-deed of the abbey of St. Urbain, near Joinville, dated on the morrow of Easter, in the year 13 by which he grants to Robert, the abbot, and to the monks of that monastery, certain fields and woods, he says, that he had been engaged so long in the country of the infidels, other parts for which God, out of his mercy, had preserved his body and mind in greater health and vigor to a longer period of time than had been allotted to any of his predecessors.

Although no deed has been found that marks precisely the time of his death, it must have been about the year 1318 for in that year his son Anceau was in possession of the estate of Joinville, and of the office of seneschal of Champagne, as we shall see hereafter. There is a tradition at Joinville that this lord was of an extraordinary stature and strength of body, and that his head was of an enormous size, as large again as that of any of his contemporaries, and that it may now be seen at Joinville with one of his thigh-bones. This agrees with what he writes himself of his constitution and habit of body, saying that he had "la tete grosse, et une froide fource," meaning a cold stomach; for which cause, his physicians had ordered him to drink his wine pure, and to warm it. With regard to the qualities of his mind, it will be sufficient to say, that the great king, Saint Louis, appointed him one of his principal counselors and ministers of state besides, he says of himself that he had a subtle wit.

These memoirs, which Joinville finished in 1309, and published after the death of Philip the Fair, have always been highly esteemed by the public. Although they include a space of but six years, they give us sufficient information respecting the military system of those days, and the principles of administration adopted by St. Louis. They present to us a faithful picture of the customs and manners of our ancestors they charm us but the affecting simplicity of style, which is one of its greatest merits and if we wish to become acquainted with the noble mind of St. Louis, it is in them displayed with the most exact truth.

Among the different editions of these memoirs (in French), the two most approved of are that of Du Cange, printed in 1668, and the one published by the late Mr. Capperonnier in 1761. Whatever may be the merit of the edition of 1761, we prefer that of Du Cange. The public opinion, as well as that of several learned friends, has determined us to make this choice. It is not surprising that the edition of Du Cange has preserved its great reputation; for that of. 1761, notwithstanding the glossary which has been added to it, would not be intelligible for three-fourths of its readers, who, unless perfectly well versed in the old French language, would be fatigued and disgusted with it.

The remarks with which Du Cange has enriched this edition, clear up a number of important facts contained in the memoirs of Joinville, and throw the greatest light on many points connected with the customs and institutions of that period. They seemed too precious to be withheld from our readers, and are, therefore, subjoined to the present edition.

A DISSERTATION ON JOINVILLE'S LIFE OF ST. LOUIS

The life of St. Louis, written by the lord de Joinville, has always been considered as one of the most precious monuments of our history and as a work that contains many of those qualifications which we are accustomed to wish for in the lives of private persons. The author was of very considerable rank by his birth, his connections, his employments, and still more from his personal merit. He had not only lived under the reign of the prince whose life he has written, but was moreover personally attached to him for twenty-two years, and, by consequently following him in his expeditions, had participated in the most, important events of his reign. The air of candor and good faith that accompanies his recitals prejudices the reader in his favor; the scrupulous attention he shows not to mention facts of which he was not a witness, and only to touch on such as he relates from the report of others, as his history requires this attention, I repeat, ought to convince us, that the lord Joinville had no other intention than to transmit to posterity nothing but what he was perfectly well informed of.

His history is not, like the greater part of the chronicles of those times, a simple recital of what passed in France and elsewhere during the reign of St. Louis; it makes us intimately acquainted with that monarch it gives us a just idea of his heart and head, and paints equally well the great man, the great saint, and the great king. The friendship and confidence with which St. Louis honored the lord de Joinville; the intimate familiarity, if I may be allowed the expression, to which he had admitted him, have furnished many curious details, which, although improper for a general history, are not the less agreeable or instructive, since they more distinctly display the characters of the principal persons whom the historian successively offers to our view.

So many interesting motives to the French will not suffer them to see with indifference the attempt that has been made to tear from their hands one of their principal historians, by endeavoring to make the history of the lord de Joinville pass for a romance, not composed till the fifteenth century. For upwards of two hundred years, when it was first printed, no one had ever thought of suspecting its authenticity, when an unjust criticism appeared in the posthumous works of a learned man (Jo Hardouin), more celebrated, however, for the singularity of his ideas, than for the extent of his erudition. He maintains, that the Life of St. Louis, generally attributed to the lord de Joinville, is the work of an author very much posterior to him, who has forged the name of the supposed author of it.

I pass over these objections in silence; they will have no weight, until it shall be granted that the greater part of ecclesiastical and profane authors have been supposititious writers.

JOINVILLE'S HISTORY OF SAINT LOUIS
DEDICATION

May it please you to know, most noble and potent lord, that my late most excellent lady, your mother, whose soul may God pardon, from the great affection she bore me, and from her knowing with how much loyalty and love I had served and attended the deceased king, St. Louis, her spouse, in several countries, had most earnestly entreated me, that in honor to God, I would collect and write a small book or treatise of the holy actions and sayings of the above-mentioned King St. Louis. This I very humbly promised her to execute to the best of my power and because you, my most excellent and potent lord, are his eldest son and heir, and have succeeded to the crown and kingdom of our late lord and king, St. Louis, I send this book to you, not knowing any one living to whom it can more properly belong, in order that you and all others who may read it, or hear it read, may profit by imitating the examples and deeds which it contains, and may God our Father and Creator be worshipped and honored by it.

JOINVILLE'S PREFACE

In the name of the most holy and most sovereign Trinity, the Father, Son, and Holy Ghost, I, John lord of Joinville, high steward of Champagne, do invite and cause to be formed into a book, the life and most pious acts and sayings of my late lord, St. Louis, king of France, from what I personally saw or heard during the space of six whole years that I was in his company, as well in the holy expedition and pilgrimage beyond sea as since our return thence. This book will be divided into two parts. The first will show how the above-mentioned king, St Louis, governed himself according to the precepts of God and of our holy mother the church, to the profit and advancement of this kingdom.

The second part will speak of his gallant chivalry and deeds of arms, that the one may follow the other, to enlighten and exalt the understandings of such as shall read or hear it. The contents of both parts will show plainly that no man of his time, from the beginning of his reign unto the end of it, ever lived a more godly or conscientious life than he did.

It seems however to me, that sufficient respect has not been shown him, inasmuch as he has not been ranked among the martyrs, for the great vexations he suffered on his pilgrimage for the honor of the cross during the six years that I attended him for, as our Lord God died for the human race on the cross, so in like manner died the good king St. Louis, at Tunis, with the cross on his breast. Because nothing is to be preferred to the salvation of the soul, I shall begin this first part which speaks of his righteous doctrine and holy conversation, which is food for the soul

MEMOIRS OF LOUIS IX, KING OF FRANCE
BY JOHN LORD DE JOINVILLE

FIRST PART

This holy man, King St. Louis, loved and feared God during his life above all things, and, as is very apparent, was in consequence favored in all his works. As I have before said that our God died for his people, so in like manner did St. Louis several times risk his life and incur the greatest dangers for the people of his realm, as shall be touched on hereafter.

The good king, being once dangerously ill at Fontainebleau, said to my Lord Louis, his eldest son, "Fair son, I beseech thee to make thyself beloved by the people of thy kingdom; for, in truth, I should like better that a Scotsman, fresh from Scotland, or from any other distant and unknown country, should govern the subjects of my realm well and loyally, than that thou shouldst rule them wickedly and reproachfully."

The holy king loved truth so much, that even to the Saracens and infidels, although they were his enemies, he would never lie, nor break his word in any thing he had promised them, as shall be noticed hereafter. With regard to his food, he was extremely temperate; for I never in my whole life heard him express a wish for any delicacies in eating or drinking, like too many rich men but he sat and took patiently whatever was set before him.

In his conversation he was remarkably chaste for I never heard him, at any time, utter an indecent word, nor make use of the devil's name, which, however, is now very commonly uttered by every one, by which I firmly believe is so far from being agreeable to God, that it is highly displeasing to him.

He mixed his wine with water by measure, according to the strength of it and what it would bear. He once asked me, when at Cyprus, why I did not mix water with my wine. I answered what the physicians and surgeons had told me, that I had a large head and a cold stomach, which would not bear it. But the good king replied, that they had deceived me, and advised me to add water for that if I did not learn to do so when young, and was to attempt it in the decline of life, the gout and other disorders, which I might have in my stomach, would greatly increase or, perhaps, by drinking pure wine in my old age, I should frequently intoxicate myself; and that it was a beastly thing for an honorable man to make himself drunk.

My good lord the king asked me at another time, if I should wish to be honored in this world, and afterward to gain paradise to which I answered, that I should wish it were so. "Then," replied he, "be careful never knowingly to do or say any thing disgraceful, that should it become public, you may not have to blush, and be ashamed to say I have done this, or I have said that." In like manner he told me never to give the lie, or contradict rudely whatever might be said in my presence, unless it should be sinful or disgraceful to suffer it, for oftentimes contradiction causes coarse replies and harsh words, that bring on quarrels, which create bloodshed, and are the means of the deaths of thousands.

He also said, that every one should dress and equip himself according to his rank in life, and his fortune, in order that the prudent and elders of this world may not reproach him, by saying such a one has done too much, and that the youth may not remark, that such a one has done too little, and dishonors his station in society. On this subject, I remember once the good lord king, father to the king now on the throne, speaking of the pomp of dress, and the embroidered coats of arms that are now daily common in the armies. I said to the present king, that when I was in the Holy Land with his father, and in his army, I never saw one single embroidered coat or ornamented saddle in the possession of the king his father, or of any other lord. He answered, that he had done wrong in embroidering his arms and that he had some coats that had cost him eight hundred Parisian lives. I replied, that he would have acted better if he had given them in charity, and had his dress made of good sendal, lined and strengthened with his arms, like as the king, his father, had done.

The good king, once calling me to him, said he wanted to talk with me, on account of the quickness of understanding he knew I possessed. In the presence of several, he added, "I have called these two monks, and before them ask you this question respecting God" "Seneschal, what is God V "Sire," replied I, "he is so supremely good, nothing can exceed him." "In truth," answered the king, "that is well said for your answer is written in the little book I have in my hand. I will put another question to you, whether you had rather be 'mezeau et ladre' or have committed, or be about to commit, a mortal sin?" But I, who would not tell a lie, replied "that I would rather have committed thirty deadly sins than be a leper."

When the two friars were gone away, he called me to him alone, making me sit at his feet, and said, "How could you dare to make the answer you did to my last question?" When I replied, "Were I to answer it again, I should repeat the same thing," he instantly said,—"Ah, foul musart! Musart, you are deceived for you must know there can be no leprosy so filthy as deadly sin, and the soul that is guilty of such is like the devil in hell. It is very true," he added, "that when the leprous man is dead, he is cured of that disorder; but when the man who has committed a deadly sin dies, he is not assured for certain that he had sufficiently repented of it before his death, to induce the goodness of God to pardon him for which cause he must have great fears lest this leprosy of sin may endure for a length of time, even so long as God may remain in paradise.

"I therefore entreat of you, first for the love of God, and next for the affection you bear me, that you retain in your heart what I have said, and that you would much rather prefer having your body covered with the most filthy leprosy than suffer your soul to commit a single deadly sin, which is of all things the most infamous."

He then inquired if I washed the feet of the poor on Holy Thursday. On which I said, "Oh, for shame, no and never will I wash the feet of such fellows." "This is in truth," replied he, "very ill said, for you should never hold in disdain what God did for our instruction for He who is lord and master of the universe, on that same day, Holy Thursday, washed the feet of all his apostles, telling them, that he who was their master had thus done, that they, in like manner, might do the same to each other. I therefore beg of you, out of love to him first, and then from your regard to me, that you would accustom yourself to do so."

He loved every one who, with uprightness of heart, feared and loved God; insomuch that from the great reputation he had heard of my brother Sir Gilles de Bruyri, who was not a Frenchman, for his fear and love of God, as was the truth, he appointed him constable of France.

In like manner, from the favorable report which he had heard of Master Robert de Sorbon being a courageous and discreet man, he made him one of his personal attendants, and permitted him to partake of his table. One time, as we were sitting near each other, and eating and drinking at the king's table, we conversed together in a low voice, which the good king observing, reprimanded us by saying, "You act wrong thus to whisper together speak out, that your companions may not suspect you are talking of them to their disadvantage, and railing at them. When eating in company, if you have any things to say that are pleasant and agreeable, say them aloud, that every one may hear them if not, be silent."

When the good king was in a cheerful mood, he frequently put questions to me in the presence of Master Robert and once he said, "Seneschal, now tell me the reason why a discreet man is of more worth than a valiant man." Upon this a noisy dispute arose between Master

Robert and me and when we had long argued the question, the good king thus gave his judgment. "Master Robert, I should not only like to have the reputation of a discreet man, but to be so in reality, and your other distinctions you may keep for discretion is of such value, that the very word fills the mouth. On the contrary," added the good king, "it is most wicked to take the goods of others for the surrendering of them to their rightful owners is so grievous that the pronouncing of it tears the palate, from the number of rrr's that are in the word which rrr's signify the rents of the devil, who daily draws to him all those who wish to give away the chattels of others they have seized upon. The devil does this with much subtlety, for he seduces the usurers and despoilers, and urges them to give their usuries and rapines to the church, in honor of God, which they ought to restore to the proper owners, who are well known to them." When thus conversing, he told me to say in his name to King Thibaut, his son-in-law that he must look well to his actions, and not overcharge his soul, thinking to acquit himself by the large sums which he gave, or should leave to the monastery of father-preachers in Provins for the discreet man, as long as he lives, ought to act like to the faithful executor of a will. First, he ought to restore and make amends for any wrongs or misdeeds done to others by the deceased and from the residue of the fortune of the dead he should give alms to the poor, in the name of God, as the Scripture plainly show.

The holy king was, one Whitsun holidays, at Corbeil, accompanied by full 300 knights, and also by Master Robert de Sorbon and myself. After dinner, the king went into the meadow above the chapel, to speak with the earl of Brittany, father to the present duke, whose soul may God receive, when Master Robert, taking hold of my mantle, in the presence of the king and the noble company, asked my opinion, whether, if the king should seat himself in this meadow, and I were to place myself on a bench above him, I should, or should not, be blamable to which I answered, "Yes, most certainly." "Why, then," added he, "do not you think yourself blame-worthy for being more richly dressed than the king?" "Master Robert," replied I, "saving the king's honor and yours, I am in this respect blameless for the dress I wear, such as you see it, was left me by my ancestors, and I have not had it made from my own authority. It is you, on the contrary, that deserve being reprimanded for you are descended from bondmen, on both sides, have quitted the dress of your ancestors, and have clothed yourself in finer camlet than what the king now wears."

I then took hold of his sur coat and compared it with what the king had on, saying, "Now see, if I did not tell the truth." The king, upon this, undertook the defense of Master Robert, and to save his honor as much as he could, declared the very great humility he possessed, and how kind he was to every one.

After this conversation, the good king called to him my Lord Philip, father to the king now on the throne, and King Thibaut, his son-in-law, and seating himself at the door of his oratory, he put his hand on the ground, and said to his sons, "Seat yourselves here near me, that you may be out of sight." "Ah, sir," replied they "excuse us, if you please for it would not become us to sit so close to you." The king, then addressing me, said, "Seneschal, sit down here," which I did, and so near him that my robe touched his. Having made them sit down by my side, he said, "You have behaved very ill, being my children, in not instantly obeying what I ordered of you and take care that this never happen again." They answered, that they would be cautious it should not.

Then turning towards me, he said, that he had called us to him to confess to me that he had been in the wrong in taking the part of Master Robert; "but," continued he, "I did so from seeing him so much confounded, that he had need of my assistance you must not, however, think or believe that I did it from the conviction of his being in the right; for, as the seneschal said, every one ought to dress himself decently, in order to be more beloved by his wife, and more esteemed by his dependants." The wise man says, we ought to dress ourselves in such manner that the more observing part of mankind may not think we clothe ourselves too grandly, nor the younger part say we dress too meanly.

You shall now hear a matter of information which the good king made me to understand. When returning from Asia, we were driven near to the isle of Cyprus by a wind called Garbun, which is not one of the principal winds that rule the sea and our vessel struck with such force on a rock as frightened our sailors, who, in despair, tore their clothes and beards. The good king leaped out of his bed barefooted, with only a gown on, and ran to throw himself on his knees before the holy sacrament, like one instantly expecting death. Shortly after, the weather became calm. On the morrow, the king called me and said, "Seneschal, know that God has shown to us a part of his great power for one of these trifling winds, which scarcely deserves a name, had almost drowned the king of France, his queen, children, and family; and St. Anceaune declares, they are the menaces of our Lord, as if God had said, "Now see and feel that if I had willed it, you would all have been drowned." The good king added, "Lord God, why dost thou menace us for the threat thou utter is neither for thy honor nor profit and if thou hadst drowned us all, thou wouldst not have been richer nor poorer thy menaces, therefore, must be intended for our advantage, and not for thine, if we be capable of understanding and knowing them. By these threatenings," said the holy king, we ought to know, that if we have in us the smallest thing displeasing to God, we should instantly drive it from us and, in like manner, we should diligently perform every thing that we suppose would give him pleasure and satisfaction. If we thus act, our Lord will give us more in this world and in the next than we ourselves can imagine. But should we act otherwise, he will do to us as the master does to his wicked servant for if the wicked servant will not correct himself, in consequence of the menaces he receives, his master punishes him in his body, and in his goods until death, or farther were it possible. In such wise will our Lord punish the perverse sinner who shall not be reclaimed by the threats which he hears and he will be the more heavily stricken in body and goods."

This holy king, and good man, took infinite pains, as you shall hear, to make me firmly believe the Christian laws which God has given us. He said, we should so punctually believe every article of the faith that for any thing that may be done against us personally we ought not to act or say any thing contrary to them. He added, that the enemy of mankind, the devil, is so subtle, that when any persons are near dying, he labors with all his power to make them depart with doubts of the articles of our faith for he knows well that he cannot deprive a man of the good works which he may have done; and that he loses the soul if the man die in the true belief of the Catholic faith. For this reason every one should be on his guard, and have such a steady belief, that he may say to the enemy when he comes to tempt him, "Go thy way, thou enemy of mankind; thou shalt never take from me what I so firmly believe, namely, the articles of my religion; I had rather that thou shouldst cut off all the members of my body for I am determined to live and die in the faith." Whoever acts thus conquers the enemy with the staff with which he meant to slay him.

The good king, however, said that faith in God was of such a nature that we ought to believe in it implicitly, and so perfectly as not to depend on hearsay. He then asked me if I knew the name of my father; I answered, that his name was Simon. "And how do you know that?" said he. I replied that I was certain of it, and believed it firmly, because my mother had told it me several times. "Then," added he, "you ought perfectly to believe the articles of the faith which the apostles of our Lord have testified to you, as you have heard the Credo chanted every

Sunday." He told me that a bishop of Paris whose Christian name was William, informed him that a very learned man in sacred theology once came to converse with, and consult him, and teat when he first opened his case he wept most bitterly. The bishop said to him, "Master, do not thus lament and bewail, for there cannot be any sinner, however enormous, but that God has the power to pardon." "Ah," replied the learned man, "know, my lord bishop, that I cannot do any thing but weep for I am much afraid that, in one point, I am an unbeliever, in not being well assured with respect to the holy sacrament that is placed on the altar, according to what the holy church teaches and commands to be believed. This is what my mind cannot receive and I believe," added he, "that it is caused by the temptation of the enemy."

"Master," answered the bishop, "now tell me, when the enemy thus tempts you, or leads you into this error, is it pleasing to you?" "Not at all," said he "on the contrary, it is very disgusting, and displeases me more than I can tell you."

"Well, I ask you again," said the bishop, "if ever you accepted of money or worldly goods, to deny, with your mouth, the holy sacrament on the altar, or the other sacraments of the church?" "You may be truly assured," answered the learned man, "that I have never accepted money, or worldly goods, for such purposes and that I would rather have my limbs cut off, one by one, while I was alive, than in any way to deny these sacraments."

The bishop then remonstrated with him on the great merit which he gained in the suffering of such temptations, and added, "You know, master, that the king of France is now carrying on a war against the king of England. You know, likewise, that the castle situated nearest to the frontiers of each monarch is La Rochelle, in Poitou; now tell me, if the good king of France was to nominate you governor of the castle of La Rochelle, on the frontiers, and to make me governor of the castle of Montlehery, which is in the heart of France, to whom would the king, at the end of the war, feel himself most obliged, you or me, for having prevented the loss of his castles?"

"Certainly, sir," replied the learned man, "I should suppose it would be me, and for this good reason, that I had well guarded La Rochelle, as being in a more dangerous situation." "Master," answered the bishop, "I assure you that my heart is like the castle of Montlehery; for I am perfectly convinced of the truth respecting the holy sacrament displayed on the altar, as well as the other sacraments, without having the most trifling doubt on their subject. I must however tell you, that whatever good-will God the Creator bears me, because I believe his commandments without doubting, he will have double satisfaction in you, for having preserved to him your heart in the midst of perplexity and tribulation and that for no earthly good, nor for any distress that adversity might bring on your body, you would ever deny or abandon your faith in his religion. It is for this reason, I say, that your state is more pleasing to him than mine and I am much rejoiced thereat, and entreat that you will keep it in your remembrance, for he will succour you in your distress."

The learned man, on hearing these words, threw himself on his knees before the bishop, and felt his mind much at ease, and was well contented with the bishop's comfortable advice.

The holy king related to me that the Albigeois once came to the count de Montfort, who was guarding that country for the king, and desired he would come and see the body of our Savior, which had become flesh and blood in the hands of the officiating priest, to their very great astonishment. But the count replied, "Ye who have doubts respecting the faith may go thither but, with regard to me, I implicitly believe every thing respecting the holy sacrament, according to the doctrines of our holy mother church. In return for this faith, I hope to receive a crown greater than the angels, who see the Divinity face to face, which must make them firm in their belief."

At another time, the holy king told me, that during a great disputation at the monastery of Clugny, between the monks and Jews, an ancient knight happened to be present, who requested the abbot of the monastery to allow him to say a few words, which with difficulty was granted him. The old knight, raising himself on his crutches, desired the most learned clerk and the first rabbi of the Jews to come near him, which being done, the knight put the following question to the rabbi: "Do you believe in the Virgin Mary, who bore our Savior Jesus Christ in her womb, and then in her arms, and that she was a virgin when delivered, and is now the mother of God?" The Jew replied, that he did not believe one word of all this. The knight said, "Very stupidly hast thou answered, and foolhardy art thou, when disbelieving all I have asked, thou hast entered the monastery and house of God, for which truly thou shalt now pay;" and lifting up his crutch, he smote the Jew such a blow on the ear as felled him to the ground. The other Jews, seeing their rabbi wounded, fled away, and thus ended the disputation between the monks and the Jews.

The abbot advanced to the knight, and said, "Sir knight, you have done a foolish thing, in thus striking the Jew;" but the knight answered, "You have committed a much greater folly in permitting such an assembly, and suffering such a disputation of errors; for here are numbers of very good Christians, who might have gone away unbelievers in consequence of the arguments of the Jews."

"I therefore tell you," continued the king, "that no one, however learned or perfect a theologian he may be, ought to dispute with the Jews; but the layman, whenever he hears the Christian faith contemned, should defend it, not only by words, but with a sharp-edged sword, with which he should strike the scandalizes and disbelievers, until it enter their bodies as far as the hilt."

The king's mode of living was such that every day he heard prayers chanted, and a mass of requiem, and then the service of the day, according to what saint it was dedicated to, was sung. It was his custom to repose himself daily on his bed after dinner, when he repeated privately, with one of his chaplains, prayers for the dead, and every evening he heard complains.

One day a good Cordelier friar came to the king, at the castle of Hieres, where we had disembarked, and addressed him, saying, that he had read in the Bible, and other good books which spoke of unbelieving princes but that he never found a kingdom of believers or unbelievers was ruined but from want of justice being duly administered. "Now," continued the Cordelier, "let the king, who I perceive is going to France, take care that he administer strict and legal justice to his people, in order that our Lord may suffer him to enjoy his kingdom, and that it may remain in peace and tranquility all the days of his life."

It is said that this discreet Cordelier, who thus lessoned the king, is buried at Marseilles, where our Lord, through him, does many fair miracles.

This Cordelier would not remain longer with the king than one day, in spite of all the entreaties that were made him. The good king was not forgetful of what the friar had told him, to govern his realm loyally according to the laws of God, but was anxious that justice should be done to all, according to the manner you shall hear.

It was customary after the lord de Neeles, the good lord de Soissons, myself, and others that were about the king's person, had heard mass, for us to go and hear the pleadings at the gateway, which is now called the Court of Requests, in the palace at Paris. When the good king was in the morning returned from the church, he sent for us, and inquired how things had passed, and if there were any matters that required his decision. And when we told him that there were some, he sent for the parties, and asked them why they would not be contented with the sentence of his officers, and then instantly made their differences up to their satisfaction, according to the custom of this godly king.

Many times have I seen this holy saint, after having heard mass in the summer, go and amuse himself in the wood of Vincennes when, seating himself at the foot of an oak, he would make us seat ourselves round about him, and every one who wished to speak with him came thither without ceremony, and without hindrance from any usher or others. He then demanded aloud if there were any who had complaints to make and when there were some, he said, "My friends, be silent, and your causes shall be dispatched one after another." Then, oftentimes, he called to him the lord Peter de Fontaines, and the lord Geoffroy de Villette, and said to them, "Dispatch these causes;" and whenever he heard any thing that could be amended in the speeches of those who pleaded for others, he most graciously corrected them himself. I have likewise seen this good king off times come to the garden of Paris, dressed in a coat of camlet, a sur coat of tire main, without sleeves, and a mantle of black scandal, and have carpets spread for us to sit round him, and hear and discuss the complaints of his people with the same diligence as in the wood of Vincennes.

I remember all the prelates of France once assembled at Paris, to speak with the good St. Louis, and to make him a request which, when he was told, he went to the palace to hear what they had to say. The meeting being full, it was the bishop Guy d'Auseure, son to the lord William de Melot, who addressed the king, by the unanimous assent of the other prelates, as follows:—"Sire, know that all these prelates, who are here assembled in your presence, instruct me to tell you that you are ruining Christendom, and that it is sinking in your hands."

The king, upon this, crossed himself, and said, " Bishop, inform me how this happens, and by what cause." "She," answered the bishop, "it is because no notice is taken of excommunicated persons for at this moment a man would rather die in a state of excommunication than be absolved, and will no way make satisfaction to the church. It is for this reason, sire that they unanimously call on you, in the name of God, and in conformity to your duty, that you would be pleased to command your bailiffs, provosts, and other administrators of justice, that wherever in your realm they shall find any one who has been excommunicated a whole year and a day, they constrain him to be absolved by the seizure of his goods."

The holy man replied, that he would most cheerfully order this to be done to every one who should be found unjust towards the church, or towards his parents. The bishop said, it only belonged to them to be acquainted with their own cause of complaint. To this, the good king said, he would not act otherwise, and that it would be blamable before God, and against reason, to force those who had been injured by churchmen to absolve themselves without being heard in their own defense. And he quoted, as an example, the count of Brittany, excommunicated as he was, having pleaded for seven years against the prelates of Brittany, and at last brought the business before our holy father the pope, who gave judgment against them in favor of the count. "Now, should I have constrained the count to seek absolution instantly after the expiration of the first year, he would have been forced to allow to these prelates their demands whether he would or not, and I should, by so doing, have behaved wickedly towards God and towards the count of Brittany."

After the prelates had heard this, they were satisfied with the favorable answer the king had made them and from that time I have never heard that there was further question about it.

The peace which St. Louis made with the king of England was contrary to the opinion of his whole council, who said to him, "Sire, it seems to us that you are doing wrong to your realm by giving up so much of its territory to the king of England, to which he appears to us not to have any right, since his father lost it by a legal sentence." The king replied, that he knew well the king of England had no right to it; but that, for a good reason, he thought he was bound to give it to him, adding, "We have married two sisters our children, therefore, are cousins-german, and it is fitting that there should be union among us. It has likewise given me great pleasure to make peace with the king of England, for he is at present my vassal, which was not the case before."

The uprightness of this good king was very apparent in the case of the lord Reginald de Trie, who brought to the holy man letters which declared he had given to the heirs of the countess of Boulogne, lately deceased, the county of Dammartin, which letters were disfigured and the seals broken. All that remained of the seals were one-half of the legs of the king's effigies and the chantel on which the royal feet were placed.

The king showed these letters to us who were of his council, to have our advice on the occasion. We were unanimously of opinion that the king was not bounden to put these letters into execution, and that the persons mentioned in them ought not to enjoy that county. The king instantly called to him John Sarrazin, his chamberlain, and asked for the letter which he had commanded him to draw up. When he had examined it, he looked at the seal, and at the remains of that on the letters of Sir Reginald, and then said to us, "My lords, this is the seal I made use of before I went to the Holy Land, and the remnant on these letters so much resembles the whole seal that I dare not, without sinning against God and reason, retain the county of Dammartin." He then called for the lord Reginald de Trie, and said, "My fair sir, I restore to you the county which you demand."

SECOND PART

Here begins the second part of this present book, in which, as I have before said, you shall hear of grand facts of chivalry.

In the name of the all powerful God, this good king, St. Louis, as I have frequently heard say, was born on the feast day of St. Mark the apostle and evangelist. On this day, crosses were carried in processions in several parts of France, and were called "the black crosses," a sort of superstition among the people, in commemoration of the great multitudes who died as it were crucified in the expeditions of their holy Ugrimages; that is to say, in Egypt and before Carthage. This caused much grief and moaning in this world and at present there is great joy in paradise among those who died for the faith of God in these devout pilgrimages.

He was crowned t the first Sunday in Advent, on which Sunday the mass begins with these words, "Ad te levavi animam meam," which is as much as to say, "Good Lord God, I have raised my heart and soul toward thee, I put my trust in thee." In these words the good king had great confidence, as respecting himself personally, for the great charge he had just undertaken. He had the fullest trust in God from his infancy to his death for at the end of his latter days, he called upon God and his saints, and especially on St. James and St. Genevieve as his intercessors. In return he was protected by God, in regard to his soul, from his earliest years to his death, and also in respect to the good doctrine he received from his mother, who taught him to believe in God, and to love and fear him in his youth and he has, ever since that time, lived a virtuous and holy life. His mother caused him to be attended by religious persons, who preached to him the word of God on Sundays and feast-days. Many times has he related that his mother should frequently say that she would rather he was in his grave, than that he should commit a mortal sin.

It was needful that God should help him in his youth for his mother was from Spain, a foreign country, and remained in France without any of her own family, relations, or friends. The barons of France thus seeing him an infant, and his mother a foreigner, without any support but from God, made the count of Boulogne, uncle to the king just dead, their leader, and considered him as their lord and master. It happened therefore, after the coronation of this good king, that by way of beginning the rebellion, some of these great barons of France required of the queen-dowager, that she would give them lands appertaining to the crown of France and because she would not consent, urging, as an excuse, that it was not for her to dismember the kingdom of France contrary to the will of her son, who was now crowned king, these barons assembled at Corbeil. The holy king told me that when he and his mother were at Montlehery, they dared not go to Paris until the inhabitants came with a large force of men-at-arms to escort them thither and he added, that the whole road from Montlehery to Paris was filled on all sides with men-at-arms, who besought the Lord that he would grant the king long life and prosperity, and that he would defend him against all his enemies. And this God did in different places, and at different times, as you shall hear in the course of this history.

While the barons were assembled at Corbeil they practiced among themselves, and resolved, with one accord, to raise up the count of Brittany against the king. They promised him, in order to act more treacherously to the good king, that they would obey the royal summons and if the king should send them to make war against the earl of Brittany, they would not bring with them more than two knights each, that the count might the more easily conquer the good king Louis, and his mother, who was a foreigner, as you have before heard.

This plot the barons put into execution, according to the engagement which they had entered into with the count of Brittany and I have heard many say, that the count would have destroyed and subdued the king and his mother, if it had not been for God's assistance, which never failed him. The count Thibaut de Champagne, as it were by divine permission, put himself and his forces in motion, to wait on the good king when he was in such distress and danger. In good truth, he set off with full three hundred knights, perfectly well equipped, and, through God's grace, arrived in good time for, by this timely reinforcement of the count of Champagne, the count of Brittany was forced to surrender himself to the king, and beg his mercy. The good king had no desire of revenge, and considering the victory he had obtained was gained through the power and will of God, in sending to him so opportunely the count of Champagne, received the count of Brittany into favor, and thenceforward the king traveled throughout his kingdom in security. Because incidents frequently happen that deserve mention, I shall at times leave the principal matter of my history to relate them; but, notwithstanding this, you shall hear of some things necessary to be related, for the better understanding the matters I treat of. I will therefore advance with truth.

The good count Henry le Large had, by the countess Mary his wife, who was sister to the king of France, and to Richard king of England, two sons; the elder was called Henry, and the second Thibaut. Henry had put on the cross, and had accompanied King Philip and King Richard to the Holy Land, where these three besieged the city of Acre, and took it.

Immediately after the capture, King Philip returned to France, for which he was greatly blamed. King Richard remained in Palestine, and performed very great feats of arms against the unbelievers and Saracens. They were so much in dread of him, that, as it is written in the history of this expedition to the Holy Land, whenever Saracen children cried, their mothers said to them, "Be quiet, be quiet; here is King Richard coming to fetch you" and, instantly, through the fear which these Saracen children had of the name of King Richard, they became quiet. In like manner, when the Saracens or Turks were riding in the fields, and their horses started at a bush or shadow, and took fright, they said to their horses, sticking spurs into their sides, "What, dost think King Richard is there?" All this clearly proves that he performed grand deeds of arms against them, to make him so much dreaded

This King Richard gained so great renown by his valor that he gave to Count Henry of Champagne, who, as I have before said, had remained with him, the queen of Jerusalem for his wife. Henry of Champagne had by her two daughters, the elder of whom was queen of Cyprus, and the other was married to Sir Ayrart de Brienne, from whom a noble progeny descended, as is apparent in France, and in Champagne.

Of the wife of my before said lord, Sir Ayrart de Brienne, I will not say more at present, but speak of the queen of Cyprus, because it is right to continue my subject properly, and thus proceed.

After the good king had conquered the count of Brittany, through the aid of Count Thibaut de Champagne, the barons of France, indignant against Count Thibaut, agreed among themselves to disinherit him, as being a son of the second son of Champagne, and to send for the queen of Cyprus. This, however, did not seem to them to be for their advantage and for this reason, and because some of the barons foreseeing they could not accomplish their ends, undertook to be mediators of a peace between Count Peter of Brittany and Count Thibaut of Champagne, the matter was so warmly pushed forward, that for greater solidity of peace, Count Thibaut promised to espouse the daughter of Count Peter of Brittany. A day was fixed on for this ceremony, when the young lady was to be conducted to an abbey belonging to the Preaching Friars near Chateau Thierry, called Yalserre, when the count of Champagne was to marry her. And thus, as I have heard, the count of Brittany set out attended by the barons of France, who were almost all his relations, to conduct the damsel to the monastery of Yalrerry, and sent to summon the count of Champagne, then at Chateau Thierry, to come and marry the lady, according to his engagement, which he was well inclined to do. But suddenly there came to him Sir Geoffrey de la Chappelle bringing letters from the king, the contents of which were as follows.

"Sir Thibaut de Champagne,—I have learnt that you have entered into engagements to marry the daughter of the count Peter of Brittany. I therefore send to require of you, that for the sake of all you love in France, you do not perform them. The reason of my desiring it is well known to you: I have never found any one more willing to do me evil than the count of Brittany."

When Count Thibaut had read these letters, although he had left Chateau Thierry, he instantly returned thither.

The count Peter of Brittany, and the French barons, in opposition to the king of France, were waiting for the count of Champagne at Yalserre and perceiving that he had deceived them, in the first burst of their rage against him, they sent for the queen of Cyprus, who shortly afterward joined them.

Immediately on her arrival, they, with one accord, having discussed the matter, sent each of them to collect as many men-at-arms as they possibly could, and resolved to make an inroad by way of France into the territories of Count Thibaut, even into Champagne and Brie.

They had a good understanding with the duke of Burgundy, who had for his wife the daughter of Robert, count de Dreux and who likewise engaged, on his part, to enter the county of Champagne from Burgundy. A day was appointed for their assembling all together before the city of Troyes, in order to take it but all this was known to good King Louis, who, in like manner, summoned his men at arms to accompany him to the aid of Count Thibaut de Champagne.

The barons, in fact, burnt and pillaged the whole country they marched through, as did their ally the duke of Burgundy. When the count of Champagne thus saw himself and his country attacked on all sides, he burnt and destroyed several of his towns, such as Epernay, Vertus, and Sezanne, that his enemies might not find them well furnished with provisions and stores, and turn them against him.

The citizens of Troyes, finding their good master and lord, the count of Champagne, had left their town, instantly sent to Simon, lord of Joinville, father to the lord de Joinville of the present day, and whose name is inscribed in the prologue of this book, to desire that he would come to their assistance. That good gentleman did so. His people were immediately informed of the intelligence that had been brought him, and before day they were in the city of Troyes, where, for his part, he performed such wonders in aiding the citizens that the barons failed to take it.

The barons were forced to march beyond the town, and fix their quarters in the meads with the duke of Burgundy. When the king of France knew where they were lodged, he marched his army straight to combat them which the barons learning, they sent to entreat that he would withdraw his army, for that they were going to fight the count of Champagne, and the duke of Lorraine and their forces, with 300 knights less than were with the count and the duke of Lorraine. But the king replied that they should no way fight with his vassals without his being personally engaged in their defense. This answer threw the barons into confusion, and speedily after, they sent again to say, they would cheerfully persuade the queen of Cyprus to offer terms of peace to Count Thibaut of Champagne. The king's answer was that he would not listen to any proposals for peace, nor suffer the count of Champagne to do so, until they should have quitted the county of Champagne.

On hearing this, they instantly inarched away, and at one march quartered themselves under Juilli. The king lodged at Ylles, whence he had driven them and the barons perceiving the king was so closely pursuing them, they decamped from Juilli, and quartered at Langres, which is in the county of Nevers, and attached to their party. Thus did the good king, St. Louis, make up the differences between the queen of Cyprus and the count of Champagne, in spite of the enterprise of the barons; and peace was concluded between them in such wise, that the count of

Champagne gave to the queen of Cyprus, for her rights of succession, 2,000 lives of landed annual revenue and the king paid her, in behalf of the count of Champagne, the sum of 40,000 livres for the reimbursement of her expenses. To repay these 40,000 livres the count of Champagne sold to the king the following fiefs and lordships; namely, the fief of the county of Blois; the fief of the county of Chartres; the fief of the county of Sancerre; the fief of the viscount of Chateaudun. Some said that the king held them only as a security for the repayment, but that is not the truth, for I put the question to the good king in Palestine, and he told me he held them by purchase.

The lands which the count de Champagne gave to the queen of Cyprus were part of the present county of Brienne and the county of Joigny, because the grandmother of the count de Brienne was daughter to the queen of Cyprus, and wife to the great count, Walter de Brienne. And that you may know whence came the fiefs which the count of Champagne sold to the king, I shall inform you, that the great count Thibaut, who is interred at Laigny, had three sons, the eldest of whom was named Henry, the second Thibaut, and the third Stephen. Henry was afterwards count of Champagne and of Brie, and surnamed Henry the Liberal for generous and liberal was he towards God and man. Towards God he was apparently liberal, by his founding the church of St. Stephen at Troyes, as well as many other to each of which he daily made great gifts, as is well known throughout Champagne.

Towards man he was equally generous, as is notorious from his conduct to Arthault of Nogent, and in many other instances too tedious to relate but I must mention that of Arthault of Nogent. This Arthault was a citizen in whom, for a time, Count Henry had the greatest confidence and Arthault increased so much in riches that he built the castle of Nogent. Now it chanced that Count Henry was desirous of descending from his castles of Troyes to hear mass at St. Stephens church on Whitsunday on the lower steps of the entrance to the church, he found a poor knight on his knees, who with a loud voice cried out, "Sir count, I request of you, in the name of God, that you would give me herewith to portion my two daughters that are by my side, for I am unable to do it." Arthur de Nogent, who was behind the count, replied to the knight, "Sir knight, you do wrong to make such a request to my lord; for he has given away so much, he is no longer able to be generous."

The count, on hearing this, turned round to Arthault and said, "Sir Yilain, you do not speak truth when you say I have no longer wherewithal to give, for I have you in my disposal, and I give you to him. Here, sir knight, I give this man to you, and warrant him your bondsman." The poor knight was greatly surprised, and instantly seizing the citizen by his hood, said he would not let him go until he should have ransomed himself handsomely. Arthault was forced to pay a fine of 500 livres.

The second brother to Henry the Liberal was Thibaut count de Blois, and the third, Stephen count de Sancerre but these two brothers held their counties and lordships under their elder brother Henry the Liberal, and after him under his heirs, who possessed the county of Champagne until this Count Thibaut sold them to the king, St. Louis, as has been mentioned.

Let us now return to our more immediate subject, and say, that shortly after this King Louis held a great and open court at Saumur in Anjou, which I shall speak of, having been present. I can assure you that it was the grandest sight I ever witnessed, the best ornamented and prepared. At the king's table were seated the count de Poitiers, whom he had knighted on the last St. John's day; the count John de Dreux, whom he had lately knighted; the count de la Marche, and the count Peter of Brittany.

At another table, before that of the king on the side where count de Dreux was seated, the king of Navarre dined. He was most richly dressed in cloth of gold, in coat, mantle, girdle, clasp and cap of fine gold, to whom I was the carver. The count served the king, St. Louis, and his brother, and the count de Soissons cut up the meat. Sir Ymbert de Beljeu, who was afterwards constable of France, Sir Honor rat de Coucy, and Sir Archibald de Bourbon were the guards of the king's table and there were behind these barons, full thirty of their knights in cloth of silk, to serve under them. There were likewise behind these knights a great many ushers of arms, and of the apartments, who bore the arms of the count de Poitiers, worked on fendal.

The king was dressed as magnificently as it was possible, but it would be tedious to enter into the particulars of his habiliments. I have heard several persons declare, that they never before saw at any feast so many surcoats and other dresses of cloth of gold as at this.

After this feast, the king conducted the count of Poitiers to that city, to recover the fiefs and lordships. It happened immediately after the king's arrival there, that the count de la Marche, who had even dined at the king's table at Saumur, secretly assembled a large body of men-at-arms to wage war against the king until he should gain his object, and kept himself at Lusignan near to Poitiers. The good king wished to have been in Paris, but he was forced to remain at Poitiers fifteen days without daring to venture beyond its walls. It was said that the king and the count of Poitiers had made a disadvantageous peace with the count de la Marche. It was necessary, therefore, for the king, in order to make up matters with the count de la Marche, to hold a parley with him and the dowager queen of England his wife, mother to the monarch on the throne.

It was not long after the king was returned from Poitiers to Paris, that the king of England and the count de la Marche united together to make war on good St. Louis, and to collect as large a body of men-at-arms as they could. They assembled in Gascony, before the castle of Taillebourg, which is situated on a dangerous river called the Charente, near which there was only one narrow stone bridge that could be passed over.

King Louis, on hearing this, marched an army against them towards Taillebourg; and his men no sooner saw the host of the enemy, who had the castle of Taillebourg on their side, than with great peril they hastened to cross the bridge, and others passed over the river in boats, and began to charge the English. Heavy blows were given on each side, which the good king beholding, he with much danger joined them indeed the risk was very considerable, for the English were more numerous than the French who passed the river, by one hundred to one.

Notwithstanding this superiority, when the English found that the king of France had crossed the river, they took fright, as it seemed God willed, and made for the city of Saintes, which they entered. It happened in the confusion, that several of our men entered that city with them, and were made prisoners.

I have heard from some among them, that during that night there was much discord between the king of England and the count de la Marche in Saintes, as they were informed and that the king of England should tell the count that he had sent for him, under promise that he would find great aid in France and that, perceiving the fallacy of his information, he should return to Gascony, whence he had come. The count de la Marche thus deserted, and knowing that he could not amend himself for the evil he had done, surrendered himself, his wife and children, prisoners to the king, who gained, on consenting to a peace, many considerable territories from the count. I know not what quantity, for I was not present at the treaty, not having then put on the coat of mail but I have heard, that with the lands the king acquired, the Count de la Marche gave him an a quittance for ten thousand livres parisis, which he was wont to receive from him annually.

Shortly after this, the good king was taken grievously ill at Paris; and so bad was his state, that I have heard that one of the ladies who nursed him, thinking it was all over, wanted to cover his face with a cloth, but that another lady, on the opposite side of the bed (so God willed it), would not suffer his face to be covered, or buried as it were, declaring continually that he was alive.

During the conversation of these ladies, our Lord worked upon him, and restored to him his speech. The good king desired them to bring him a crucifix, which was done; and when the good lady, his mother, heard that he had recovered his speech, she was in the utmost possible joy but when she came and saw that he had put on the cross she was panic-struck, and seemed as if she would rather have seen him dead.

In the like manner as the king had put on the cross, so did Robert, count d'Artois; Alphonso, count of Poitiers; Charles, count d'Anjou, who was afterwards king of Sicily; all three brothers to the king; Hugh, duke of Burgundy; William, earl of Flanders; his brother Guion de Flandres, who died shortly after at Compiegne; the valiant count Hugh de St. Pol; his nephew, Sir Walter, who behaved most gallantly beyond sea, and would have gained great renown had longer life been granted him. The count de la Marche, whom we have lately mentioned, was also of the number; Sir Hugh le Brun and his son; the count de Salebruche; Sir Gauberfe d'Apremont and his brothers, in whose company, being my cousins, I, John de Joinville, crossed the sea in a small ship which we hired. We were twenty knights ten of whom accompanied me, and ten came with my cousins. This event took place after Easter, in the year of grace 1248.

Before my departure, I summoned all my men and vassals of Joinville, who came to me the vigil of Easter day, which was the birthday of my son John, lord of Ancarville, by my first wife, sister to the count of Grand Pre. During that whole week I was occupied in feasts and banquets with my brother de Vaucouleur, and all the richment of that part of the country, where, after eating and drinking, we amused ourselves with songs, and led a joyous life. When Friday came, I addressed them thus:—" Gentlemen, know that I am about to go to the Holy Land, and it is uncertain whether I may ever return should there be any of you" therefore, to whom I have done wrong, and who thinks he has cause for complaint, let him come forward; for I am willing to make him amends, as I am accustomed to do to those who have complained of me or my people."

I did this according to the usual manner of my country and my lands and in order that they might not be awed by my presence while they consulted together, I withdrew, and would only listen to what they might say to me without the restraint of fear. I likewise adopted this measure, because I was unwilling to carry with me one single penny wrongfully and to fulfill any demands that might be made, I had mortgaged to friends a great part of my inheritance, so that there did not remain at the utmost more than twelve hundred livres of yearly revenue from my lands for my lady-mother was still living, who held the best of my estate in dower.

I set out, I before said, with my nine knights, having three banners and I have mentioned the things above, because if it had not been for the aid and assistance of God, who never forgot me, I should never have been able to support such a burden as I bore for six years, the time I was on my pilgrimage in the Holy Land.

When I was on the point of departure, John, lord d'Apremont, and the count de Salebruche, sent to me to inquire if I were willing to join parties, and embark together, for that they were ready to march, and their company consisted of ten knights. I cheerfully assented, and we ordered a vessel to he hired for us at Marseilles, which carried us, our arms and horses.

You must know, that before the king left the realm, he summoned all the barons to Paris, and there made them renew their fealty and homage, and swear loyalty to his children, should any unfortunate event happen to himself during this expedition to the Holy Land. He summoned me also but I, who was not his subject, would not take the oath besides, it was not my intention to remain behind.

When I was nearly ready to set out, I sent for the abbot of Cheminon, who was at that time considered as the most discreet man of all the White Monks, to reconcile myself with him. He gave me my scarf and bound it on me, and likewise put the pilgrim's staff in my hand. Instantly after, I quitted the castle of Joinville without ever re-entering it, until my return from beyond sea. I made pilgrimages to all the holy places in the neighborhood such as Bliecourt, St. Urban, and others near to Joinville, on foot without shoes, and in my shirt. But as I was journeying from Bliecourt to St. Urban, I was obliged to pass near to the castle of Joinville I dared never turn my eyes that way for fear of feeling too great regret, and lest my courage should fail on leaving my two fine children and my fair castle of Joinville, which I loved in my heart. Being suddenly called upon by the count de Salbruche, my brother in arms, with our knights and attendants, we went to dine at La Fontaine Archeveque before Dongeux and there the abbot of St. Urban, to whom may God show mercy gave to me and my knights very handsome jewels. We then took our leave of him, and went straight to Auxonne, where we embarked with our armor on the Soane for Lyons: our cavalry and war-horses were led along its banks. When we came to Lyons, we embarked on the river Rhone to go to Aries le Blanc. I remember well that on its banks we saw the remains of a castle called La Roche-gluy, which castle the king had caused to be demolished on account of the lord of it, named Roger, having a very ill-famed reputation of stopping and plundering all merchants and pilgrims that passed that way.

It was the month of August in this same year that we embarked at the rock of Marseilles, and the ports of the vessel were opened to allow the horses we intended carrying with us to enter. When we were all on board, the port was caulked and stopped up as close as a large ton of wine, because when the vessel was at sea, the port was under water. Shortly after the captain of the ship cried out to his people on its prow, "Is your work done? Are we ready?" They replied, "Yes: in truth, we are."

When the priests and clerks embarked, the captain made them mount to the castle of the ship, and chant psalms in praise of God, that he might be pleased to grant us a prosperous voyage. They all, with a loud voice, sang the beautiful hymn of "Yeni Creator," from the beginning to the end and while they were singing, the mariners set their sails in the name of God. Instantly after, a breeze of wind filled our sails, and soon made us lose sight of land, so that we only saw sea and sky, and each day we were at a farther distance from the places from which we had set out.

I must say here, that he is a great fool who shall put himself in such dangers, having wronged any one, or having any mortal sins on his conscience for when he goes to sleep in the evening, he knows not if in the morning he may not find himself under the sea.

I will tell you the first marvel that befel us at sea. It was a great round mountain which we met with about vespers, off Barbary when we had passed it, we made all the sail we could the whole night, and in the morning we supposed we must have run fifty leagues, or more, but we found ourselves again off this large mountain. We were, of course, much alarmed, and continued to make all the sail we could that day and the following night, but it was all the same, we still had the mountain near at hand. We were more astonished than ever, and thought we ran great risk of our lives for the sailors told us that the Saracens of Barbary would come and attack us. A very discreet churchman, called the dean of Mauru, came forward and said, "Gentlemen, I never remember any distress in our parish, either from too much abundance, or for want of rain or any other plague, but that God and his mother delivered us from it, and caused every thing to happen as it could be wished, when a procession had been made three times with devotion on a Saturday." Now this day was a Saturday, and we instantly began a procession round the masts of the ship. I remember well that I was forced to be supported under my arms, because I was at the time very sick. Immediately afterwards we lost sight of this mountain, and arrived at Cyprus the third Saturday after we had made our procession.

We found, on our landing at Cyprus, that the good king, St. Louis, was already there, and had laid in provisions in great abundance. You would have taken his cellars, at a distance, for great houses formed of casks of wine, placed one on the other, which his purveyors had bought two years before, and had left in the open fields. In like manner was the wheat, barley, and other grain in large heaps, which, from their immense size, appeared like mountains and in truth many would have supposed them such for the rains which had battered their sides had made the corn grow, so that there was nothing to be seen but green corn. When the army of the king came to remove the grain, in order to its being sent to Egypt, and to take off the crust of green corn, they found the corn underneath as fine and fresh as if it had been just threshed.

The good king was impatient to set sail, so that if it had not been for his barons, and near relations, who prevailed on him to wait the arrival of forces that were daily expected, he would have embarked alone, or with a very small company.

While the king remained in Cyprus, the great cham of Tartary sent him an ambassador, who paid him many fine compliments among others, the chain of Tartary sent him word that he was ready and at his command to assist him in the conquest of the Holy Land, and to deliver Jerusalem from the hands of the Saracens and Pagans. The king received this embassy with kindness, and, in return, sent ambassadors to the cham of Tartary, who were two years before they returned. The king of France sent likewise to the cham a tent in the form of a chapel it was of fine scarlet cloth, very rich, and handsomely made, with the intent to see if he could induce the cham and his subjects to embrace our faith and religion and, as a further inducement, he had embroidered on the inside of the tent the Annunciation of the Virgin mother of God, with other mysteries of our faith. Two Black Monks, who understood the Saracen language, had charge of this tent, and to exhort the Tartars, and show how they ought to put their belief in God.

The two monks shortly returned, thinking to meet the king at Acre but he was already in Caesarea, upon which they went back to France. To say how the other ambassadors, whom the king had sent to the king of Barbary, were received, would be to tell of wonders, as I heard them related to the king from their own mouths. I have likewise frequently inquired of them concerning their adventures but I will not say any thing of them at present, for fear of breaking in upon the principal matter, which I had already begun.

You must know that when I quitted France, to join this expedition to the Holy Land, I did not possess more than 1,200 livres of yearly revenue, and yet I took charge of nine other knights and three banners. On my arrival at Cyprus I had but twelve score livres in gold and silver, after paying the freight of the ship, so that many of my knights told me they would leave me if I did not better provide myself with money. I was somewhat cast down in courage on hearing this, but had ever my confidence in God and when the good king St. Louis heard of my distress, he sent for me, and retained me in his service, allowing me, like a kind lord, 800 livres Tournois. I instantly returned thanks to God, for I had now more money than I had need of.

It is now necessary that I speak of the state and power of the princes beyond sea, and I shall first begin with the sultan of Connie. This sultan is the most powerful king of all pagan land, and had a most marvelous work achieved for he had melted part of his gold, and made it into large vessels after the manner of the earthen pots in which wine is preserved in those countries, each of which held about a ton of wine. He afterwards had these pots broken, and the pieces lay in one of his castles, which was open for every one to see and touch these broken masses of gold. It was said that he had six or seven of these large golden pots. His great riches were apparent in a pavilion which the king of Armenia sent to the king of France when he was at Cyprus, for it was estimated at 500 livres. The king of Armenia sent word that it had been given to him by one of the serrais of the sultan of Connie. Now you must know that these serrais have the care and management of the pavilions of the sultan, and their employment is to clean every day the apartments of his different palaces.

This king of Armenia was vassal to the sultan of Connie and went to the grand cham of Tartary to complain that the sultan had made war upon him, and kept him in vassalage, and at the same time to entreat he would support and succour him. He consented to become vassal to the cham of Tartary, if he would supply him with a large body of men-at-arms against the sultan of Connie.

The cham of Tartary was willing to do this, and sent him a considerable force, with which the king of Armenia marched against the sultan, whose army was nearly equal to his but the Armenians and Tartars defeated the troops of their enemy; and in consequence of this the king of

Armenia was no longer vassal nor subject to the sultan. This victory, which he had gained by the assistance of the Tartars, increased his renown so much in Cyprus, that many of our people went to Armenia to seek for profit in these engagements but of them we had never after any intelligence.

Of the sultan of Babylon, "I shall say, that he imagined the king was about to make war on the sultan of Hamault, his ancient enemy he was therefore waiting for the king to join his forces against the sultan of Hamault but when he perceived that the king did not advance, he departed, and went to lay siege to the city of Hamault, in which the sultan resided."

The sultan, thus finding himself besieged, knew not how to act for he was aware, that if the sultan of Babylon should remain long, he must conquer and overthrow him. He, however, practiced so successfully by gifts and promises with one of the varlets of the chamber of the sultan of Babylon that he poisoned his master. The manner of his doing it was as follows:—The varlet, who in their language is officially called Serais, knowing that the sultan after playing at chess was frequently used to lie down on mats that were at the foot of his bed, poisoned one of these mats and it chanced that the sultan, having thrown aside part of his dress, lay on the mat with his naked legs, and turning about rubbed a sore he had on one of them against the poisoned part. The venom instantaneously took effect through this sore, and his whole body became so much affected that he lost the use of that side. When the venom was come towards the head, he continued for two days without eating or drinking, and this was the cause that the sultan of Hamault remained in peace, for the sultan of Babylon was obliged to be carried back to his own country by his people.

As soon as the month of March was come, it was proclaimed, by orders of the king that all vessels should be laden and ready to sail whenever the king should command. All things being ready, the king, the queen, and their households embarked on board their different ships. On the Friday preceding Whitsunday, the king ordered every one to follow him on the morrow, and proceed to Egypt and on the morrow, being Saturday, every vessel made sail, which was a pleasant sight to see, for it seemed as if the whole sea, as far as the sight could reach, was covered with cloth, from the great quantity of sails that were spread to the wind, there being 1,800 vessels great and small.

The king, followed by the other vessels, came on Whitsunday to the point of Lymesson, where he landed, and heard mass but of full 2,800 knights, who had embarked to follow the king, there were now only 700 with him on shore. A horrible wind that blew from Egypt had made the remainder alter their course, and had separated them from the company of the king, and driven them on the coast of Acre and other strange countries at a great distance, so that the king did not see them again for a long time. He and his companions were much grieved at their loss, for they believed them drowned, or in great danger at least.

On the morrow of Whitsunday, the wind was favorable, and the king and we who were with him made sail, in God's name, to pursue our route. It happened that in our course we met the prince of Morea and the duke of Burgundy, who has sojourned in the Morea. The king arrived with his fleet on the Thursday after Whitsuntide at Damietta, where a great company was waiting for us.

On the shore we saw the whole force of the sultan, who was handsome men to look at. The sultan wore arms of burnished gold of so fine a polish, that when the sun shone on them, he seemed like a sun himself. The tumult and noise they made with their horns and nacaires was frightful to hear, and seemed very strange to the French.

The king, perceiving this, called together his barons and counselors to consult on what should be done. They advised him to wait until the whole of his force should arrive; for he had not now with him a third part, owing, as I before said, to the contrariety of the wind. But the king would not consent, saying, that by such conduct he should encourage the enemy and likewise because there was not any port near in those seas whither he might retire, and wait in safety the return of those who had been dispersed by the storm. He added that a strong gust of wind might arise and separate them from each other in these foreign countries, as had happened to his other knights on Whitsunday last. They acceded, therefore, to his proposal, that on the Friday preceding Trinity Sunday the king should disembark, and combat the Saracens, if it were not their fault. The king ordered the lord John de Belmont to cause a galley to be given to the lord Airart de Brienne, with whom I was, to land us and our men-at-arms, because the large ships could not approach near enough to the shore. Thus was it the will of God that I should quit my ship, and enter a small galley, which I thought I had lost, and wherein eight of my horses were. This galley had been given me by Madame de Baruth, cousin-german to the count de Montbelial.

The lord Airart de Brienne and I, fully armed, went to the king on the Friday, to ask for the galley which he had ordered for us but Sir John de Belmont replied, in the presence of the king, that we should not then have it from which may be known, that the good king had as much trouble in keeping his own people in peace together, as in his ill-fortunes and losses.

When our people saw that we were not bringing back the galley, they dropped into the boat with all their weight, and when the sailors perceived the boat was gradually sinking, they retired into the ship, abandoning my knights in the boat. On seeing this, I called out to the captain, and asked how many there were overweight for the boat. He said, too many by eighteen so armed. I then instantly discharged so many from the boat, and put them in the ship with my horses. As I was thus arranging these men-at-arms, a knight, belonging to the lord Airart de Brienne, named Plouquet, wanting to descend from the ship to the boat as it was pushing off, fell into the sea and was drowned.

We then began to sail after the boat of the king's large ship and made for land but when those attached to the king, who were hastening to land like ourselves, saw that we made more speed than they, they cried out for us to wait for the arrival of the standard of St. Denis, I would not attend to them, and continued advancing towards a large battalion of Saracens and Turks, consisting of 6,000 men, at least, on horseback. The moment they saw us on shore they spurred their horses full gallop toward us but we struck our spears and shields into the sand with their points against them, which as soon as they perceived, and that we were advancing inland, they suddenly wheeled about and fled.

That discreet man Sir Baldwin de Eheims, as soon as I was landed, sent one of his squires to desire I would wait for him. I made answer, by his messenger, that I would cheerfully do so, for that so valiant a man as he was well deserved waiting for and he was thankful for this attention as long as he lived. He shortly after joined our company, with a thousand knights at least. You must know that when I first landed I had not any one person with me, neither friend nor servant, of all those I had brought from France. Notwithstanding this, God always assisted me with his grace, for which I ever praise him.

On our left the count de Japhe, cousin German to the count de Montbelial, and of the lineage of the house of Joinville, drew up his men. This count Japhe had disembarked in a most grand manner for his galley was all painted with inside and without with escutcheons of his arms, which were a cross patee gules on a field or. There were full three hundred sailors on board the galley, each bearing a target of his arms, and on each target was a small flag with his arms likewise, of beaten gold. It was a sight worthy to be viewed when he went to sea, on account of the noise which these flags made, as well as the sounds of the drums, horns, and Saracen nacaires, which he had in his galley.

The moment his vessel grounded on the sand, and as near as she could be brought to the land, he himself, his knights and men-at-arms disembarked, well armed at all points, and posted themselves by our side. The count de Japhe instantly ordered his pavilions to be pitched, which when the Saracens saw was about to be done, they again returned, spurring their horses against us ; but finding we were not any way intimidated, and that we were firmly waiting for them, they turned their backs and galloped away.

On our right, the galley bearing the standard of St. Denis arrived within a crossbow-shot of us and it happened that as she was touching the ground, a Saracen rode against the crew full speed. I know not why he did so, whether he could not stop his horse, or expected support from his countrymen, but the poor creature was very soon destroyed and cut to pieces.

When the good king St. Louis learnt that the standard of St. Denis was landed he quitted his vessel, which was already close to the shore, without waiting until he could disembark from it, and against the will of the legate, who was with him, leaped into the sea, which was up to his shoulders, and advanced to the land, his shield on his neck, his helmet on his head, and lance in hand. On joining his men, he observed the Saracen army, and asked who they were. On being told they were Turks and Saracens, he wanted to make a course alone against them, but his attendants would not permit it, and made him remain quiet until his whole army should be assembled and armed.

A messenger, called Coullon, was sent thrice to the sultan of the Saracens, to inform him of the arrival of the king of France but no answer was returned, because the sultan was ill. The Saracens, hearing of this, abandoned the city of Damietta, believing their sultan was dead. When the king heard this news, he sent one of his knights to Damietta to know the truth of it, who, on his return, related that the sultan was really dead, and that the Saracens had fled from Damietta, for he had entered their houses that were empty.

Upon this, the king had the legate called, with all the prelates of the army, and ordered the "Te Deum laudamus" to be sung throughout. The king and his army, shortly after, mounted their horses, and went to take up their quarters in Damietta. The Turks were ill advised to retreat so suddenly without destroying the bridges which they had made of boats, which would have distressed us mixed. But in another way they did us great mischief, by setting fire to all parts of the Soulde, where their merchandise and plunder had been deposited, which they burnt, for fear we might make any advantage of them. It would be the same thing if fire were set to the Petit Pont of Paris, which God preserve from such an accident!

Now let us ask ourselves, what grace did not God the Creator show us in preserving us from death and danger on our landing, and when we joyfully advanced to our enemies who were on horseback? What other greater grace did not our good Lord show us in delivering up Damietta without any risk of our lives, and which we never could have gained but by starving the garrison? These graces, we may say, were wondrous great, and apparent to every one.

King John had indeed taken it by famine in the times of our ancestors but I doubt if the good Lord God may not say as much of us as he did of the children of Israel, when he had conducted and led them into the land of promise for which he reproached them, saying, "Et pro nikilo kabuerunt terram desiderabilem, et quae sequuntur." He said this, because they had forgotten him, who had showered down on them so much good. He had saved them, and brought them out of the captivity of Pharaoh, and given them the land of promise. Thus may he say of us, who forgot him, as shall hereafter be told.

I shall begin with the person of the king himself, who assembled all the barons and prelates that had accompanied him, and asked their advice what he should do with the riches he had found in Damietta, and how he should divide them? A patriarch who was present spoke first, and said, —"Sire, it seems right to me, that you should reserve the wheat, barley, rice, and all other provisions, in order that the city may not suffer famine and that you should order proclamation to be made throughout the army, that all other goods and furniture should be carried and deposited in the house of the legate, under pain of excommunication." This advice was acceded to by the barons and all present, and put in execution.

The furniture that was carried to the legate's house was found, on valuation, not worth more than six thousand livres. When all had been brought thither, the king and the barons sent to seek for the good and discreet man, Sir John de Yaleri. On his arrival, the king told him what had been done, and that his council had advised that the legate should give him the six thousand livres at which the goods had been valued, which he would carry to his house, in order that he might dispose of them in the manner he should see right, and where he should think them best employed.

"Sire," replied Sir John, "I most humbly thank you for the honor you do me but, under your good pleasure, I will not accept your proposal never, please God, will I alter good and ancient customs, and such as our predecessors have followed in the Holy Land; for, whenever any city, or other considerable booty, was gained from the enemy, the king never received but one-third of all the riches or goods that were found in the city, and the pilgrims had two parts. This was the custom followed by King John, when formerly he took Damietta and thus, as I have heard my elders say, did the king of Jerusalem act before King John's time, without failing in any one point. Now, consider if you be willing to give me two parts of the grain and other provisions which you have retained, and most cheerfully will I divide and distribute them among the pilgrims, in honor of God."

The king did not agree to this advice, and matters remained as before, which made many discontented with the king, because he had broken through good ancient customs.

The king's officers, when they were at their ease, and comfortably lodged in the city of Damietta, instead of well treating and entertaining the merchants, and those who followed the army with provisions, hired out to them stalls and workmen at as dear a rate as they possibly could. This conduct was spread abroad to distant countries and those who would have supplied the army with provisions delayed doing so, which was a great evil and loss.

The barons, knights, and others, who ought to have attended to their money concerns, and to have practiced economy, as a resource in times of need, began to give sumptuous banquets in rivalship to each other, with the utmost abundance of the most delicious meats. The commonalty likewise gave themselves up to debauchery, and violated both women and girls. Great were the evils in consequence for it became necessary for the king to wink at the greatest liberties of his officers and men. The good king even told me, that at a stone's throw round his own pavilion were several brothels kept by his personal attendants. Other disorders were going forward, and to a greater extent than any person had hitherto seen.

But let us return to our principal object. After we had remained some time in this city of Damietta, the sultan laid siege to it on the land side with a numerous army. The king and his men-at-arms were soon properly drawn out. In order to prevent the Turks from taking possession of the camp we had on the plain, I went to the king fully armed, whom I found in the same state of preparation, as well as all his knights seated around him on benches and most humbly requested that he would permit me and my people to make a course against the Saracens. But the moment Sir John de Belmont heard me, he cried out with a loud voice, commanding me, in the king's name, not to dire to quit my quarters until I should be so ordered by the king.

You must know that there were with the king eight good and valiant knights, who had several times won the prize of arms, as well on this side of the sea as on the other, and they were usually called the good knights. Among them were Sir Geoffrey de Sargines, Sir Mahom de Marly, Sir Philip de Nantuel, and Sir Ymhert de Beaujeu, constable of France but these were not present when I made my request, being on the plain without the city, as well as the master of the cross-bows, with a large body of men-at-arms to prevent the Turks from approaching our main army. It happened that Sir Walter d'Entrache having caused himself to be well armed, and his lance and shield to be given to him, mounted his horse and one of the sides of his pavilion being raised, stuck spurs into his horse, and rode full gallop against the Turks. He thus quitted his pavilion, attended only by one of his people, named Castillon but his horse flung him to the ground, and ran off, covered with his arms, full speed to the enemy; for the greater part of the Saracens were mounted on mares, which caused the horse to play these tricks and run away. I heard from those who said they had witnessed it, that while the lord d'Entrache lay on the ground, four Turks came to him and, as they crossed him backward and forward, gave him heavy blows with their clubs, and would have killed him, if the constable of France had not gone to his succour with a body of king's troops which were under him. He was led back to his pavilion, but so much bruised by the blows he had received, that he was speechless. He was soon attended by the physicians and surgeons; and because they did not think him in any danger of death, they bled him in the arm, from which fatal consequences ensued.

Towards evening, Sir Aubert de Nancy desired I would accompany him on a visit to him, for that he was a man of great renown and valor this I very willingly did, and we went together. On our entering his tent, one of his squires came to us, and desired we would tread softly, lest we might awaken him. We followed this advice, and found him lying on his mantle of mine ever, which covered him but, on approaching his face, we saw he was dead.

We, and several more, were much grieved at the loss of such a man but when it was told the king, he replied, that he did not wish for any one's service who would not attend to him, and obey his orders better than the lord d'Entrache had done; and that through his own fault he had caused his death.

I must inform you that the sultan gave for every head of a Christian that was brought to him a besant of gold and these Saracen traitors entered our camp during the night, and wherever they found any asleep they cut off their heads. They once surprised the watch of the lord de Courtenay, and cut off his head, leaving the body lying on a table. They were likewise well informed of the manner of our encampment for the engagements between us brought each party near to the other in the evenings and the Saracens, in consequence of this knowledge, entered the camp as soon as the guard had made its round, and committed many disorders and murders.

The king, when he heard of this, gave orders for those who were wont to go the rounds on horseback henceforward to do so on foot; by this means the army was in security; for we were so closely encamped that we touched each other, and there were no void spaces.

We remained a long time in and before Damietta for the king had none in his council who advised him to march further, until his brother, the count de Poitiers, whom the storms had driven, as before mentioned, to Acre, was returned for he had with him the arriere ban of France. From fear that the Turks might force the camp with their cavalry, the king ordered it to be surrounded with deep ditches and on their banks there were numerous parties of cross-bows and others, who watched during the nights.

The feast of St. Remy had passed without the army receiving any news from the count de Poitiers or his men. This alarmed the king greatly, and the army was in much distress for they began to fear, from his not coming, that he was either dead, or in very great danger. I then recollected the worthy dean of Mauru, and told the legate how, by means of the three processions which lie made us perform when at sea; we were delivered from the great peril we were in, as I have already related. The legate believed what I said and ordered three processions to be proclaimed throughout the army, to be put into practice the three following Saturdays.

The first procession began at the house of the legate, and proceeded to the church of our Lady in the town of Damietta. This church had been a mosque of the Turks and Saracens but the legate had consecrated it to the honor of the Mother of God, the glorious Virgin Mary. Thus was it continued for two Saturdays and each time the legate preached a sermon. The king and the great lords attended, to whom, after they had heard the sermon, the legate gave absolution. Before the third Saturday, the count de Poitiers arrived with his men, and fortunately for him he did not come earlier; for during the space of the two preceding Saturdays there were such continued storms at sea before Damietta, that twelve score vessels, great and small, were wrecked and sunk, and their crews drowned. Had the count de Poitiers arrived at that time, he would have run great risk of suffering a similar fate and I believe it would have been so, if God had not assisted him.

There was much joy in the whole army on the arrival of the count de Poitiers, the king's brother and shortly after the king assembled his barons and council, and asked them what route he should pursue, whether to Alexandria or to Babylon? The count Peter of Brittany, with several other barons were of opinion that the king should march to Alexandria, because there was a good harbor for boats and vessels, to bring provision to the army. But this plan was not approved of by the count d'Artois, who said he would never march to Alexandria until he should have been at Babylon, which was the seat of empire in Egypt. He added, among other reasons, that whoever wished to kill a snake should begin with the head. To this opinion the king assented, and gave up the former plan.

At the beginning of Advent, the king and his whole army began their march toward Babylon, according to the advice given by the count d'Artois. On the road near to Damietta, we met a branch of the great river and the king was advised to halt a day, until a dam should be thrown across, that the army might pass. This was easily done and the river was stopped so level that it did not overflow, and might be crossed with facility.

What did the sultan do? He sent craftily to the king five hundred of his best-mounted troops, saying they were come to assist him, but in reality to delay him as much as possible. On St. Nicholas's day, the king commanded his army to mount their horses, and forbade any of his people to dare to hurt, in any way, one of the Turks or Saracens whom the sultan had sent to him. Now it happened, that when the Saracens perceived the king's army was in motion, and heard that the king had forbidden any one to touch them, they advanced with great courage in a body toward the Templars, who had the van of the army. One of these Turks gave a knight in the first rank so heavy a blow with his battle-axe as felled him under the feet of Sir Reginald de Bicher's horse, who was marshal of the Templars.

The marshal, seeing this, cried out to his men-at-arms,—"Now, companions, attack them, in the name of God for I cannot longer suffer thus." He instantly stuck spurs into his horse, and charged the Saracens, followed by the whole army. The horses of the Turks were worn down and tired, while ours were fresh and hearty, which caused their misfortune for I have since heard that not one escaped being slain or drowned in the sea.

It is proper that I say something here of the river which runs through Egypt, and which comes from the terrestrial paradise for such things should be known to those who are desirous of understanding the subject I am writing on. This river differs from all others, for the more brooks fall into a large river, the more it is divided into small streamlets, and spread over a country but this river has not such aids, and seems always the same. When arrived in Egypt, it spreads its waters over the country. About the period of St. Remy's day, it expands itself into seven branches, and thence flows over the plains. When the waters are retired, the laborers appear, and till the ground with ploughs without wheels, and then sow wheat, barley, rice, and cumin, which succeed so well that it is not possible to have finer crops.

No one can say whence this annual increase of water comes, except from God's mercy. Were it not to happen, Egypt would produce nothing, from the very great heat of that country for it is near to the rising sun, and it scarcely ever rains but at very long intervals.

This river is quite muddy, from the crowds of people of that and other countries who, towards evening, come thither to seek water to drink. They put into their vessels which hold it four almonds or four beans, which they shake well, and on the morrow it is wondrous clear and fit to drink. When this river enters Egypt, there are expert persons, accustomed to the business, who may be called the fishermen of this stream, and who in the evenings cast their nets into the water, and in the mornings frequently find many spices in them, which they sell into these countries dearly, and by weight such as cinnamon, ginger, rhubarb, cloves, lignum-aloes, and other good things. It is the report of the country, that they come from the terrestrial paradise, and that the wind blows them down from these fine trees, as it does in our forests the old dry wood. What falls into the river is brought down with it, and collected by merchants, who sell it to us by weight.

I heard in the country of Babylon, that the sultan had frequently attempted to learn whence this river came, by sending experienced persons to follow the course of it. They carried with them a bread called biscuit, for they would not have found any on their route, and on their return reported, that they had followed the course of the river until they came to a large mountain of perpendicular rocks, which it was impossible to climb, and over these rocks fell the river. It seemed to them, that on the top of this mountain were many trees and they said they had seen there many strange wild beasts, such as lions, serpents, elephants, and other sorts, which came to gaze at them as they ascended the river. These travelers, not daring to advance further, returned to the sultan.

Now, to pursue my subject, this river, on entering Egypt, spreads its branches over the plain one of them flows to Damietta, another to Alexandria, another to Tunis, and another to Rexi. To this branch which runs by Rexi, the king of France marched with his whole army, and encamped between the Damietta branch and that of Rexi. We found the sultan encamped with his entire force on the opposite bank of the Rexi branch, to prevent and oppose our passage. It was easy for him to do this, for none of us could have crossed unless we had stripped ourselves naked, as there were no other means to pass.

The king determined to have a causeway made, to enable him to pass over to the Saracens and to guard those employed on it, he had built two beffrois, called chas-chatells. There were two towers in front of these beffrois, and two houses in their rear, to receive the things the Saracens threw upon their machines, of which they had sixteen that did wonders. The king ordered eighteen machines to be constructed, under the direction of a man named Jousselin de Courvant, who was the inventor and undertaker and with these engines did each army play on the other. The king's brother was on guard over the cats in the daytime, and we other knights guarded them at night.

These chas-chatells were finished the week before Christmas, and then the causeway was set about in earnest but as fast as we advanced, the Saracens destroyed it. They dug, on their side of the river, wide and deep holes in the earth, and as the water recoiled from our causeway it filled these holes with water, and tore away the banks; so that what we had been employed on for three weeks or a month, they ruined in one or two days; they also very much annoyed, by their arrows, our people who were carrying materials for the dam.

The Turks, after the death of their sultan, who died of the disorder he was seized with when before Hamault, chose for their chief a Saracen named Sacedun, son of the sheik, whom the emperor Ferrait had made a knight.

Shortly after this, Sacedun sent part of his army to cross near Damietta, and to a small town called Sourmesac, which is on the Rexi branch, that from that quarter they might fall on us. On Christmas day, whilst I and all my people were at dinner with my companion Pierre Avalon, the Saracens entered our camp, and slew many of our poor soldiers who had strayed into the fields.

We instantly mounted our horses to attack them and well timed was it for my lord Perron, our host, who had quitted the camp on the first alarm for before we could overtake him, the

Saracens had made him prisoner, and were carrying him off with his brother, the lord Du Val. We pushed our horses forward, attacked the Saracens, and rescued these two good knights, whom they had already, by their blows, struck to the ground, and brought them back to the camp. The Templars who were within hearing, formed a bold and determined rear-guard.

The Turks continued to make repeated attacks on us in that quarter with much courage, until our army had closed up the canal toward Damietta, from that branch to the one of Rexi.

This Sacedun, chief of the Turks, was held to be the most able and courageous of all the infidels. He bore on his banners the arms of the emperor who had made him a knight; his banner had several bends, on one of which he bore the same arms with the sultan of Aleppo, and on another bend on the side were the arms of the sultan of Babylon. His name was, as I said before, Sacedun, son of the sheik, which signifies the same in their language as to say the son of the old man. His name had great weight with them for they are a people it is said who pay much honor to such old men as have in their youth been especially careful to preserve their characters from reproach. This chief, as it was told the king by his spies, boasted that on St. Sebastian's day next coming, he would dine in the king's tent.

When the king heard this, he replied, that he would take good care to prevent it. He then drew his army in closer array, orders for which were given to the men-at-arms; and to the count d'Artois, brother to the king, was given the command of the beffrois and machines. The king, and the count d'Anjou, who was afterwards king of Sicily, took on them the guard of the army, on the side of Babylon and the count de Poitiers, with me, seneschal of Champagne, had the guard on the side towards Damietta.

Not long after this, the chief of the Turks, before named, crossed with his army into the island that lies between the Rexi and Damietta branches, where our army was encamped, and formed a line of battle, extending from one bank of the river to the other. The count d'Anjou, who was on the spot, attacked the Turks, and defeated them so completely that they took to flight, and numbers were drowned in each of the branches of the Nile.

A large body, however, kept their ground, whom we dared not attack, on account of their numerous machines, by which they did us great injury with the divers things cast from them. During the attack on the Turks by the count d'Anjou, the count Guy de Ferrois, who was in his company, galloped through the Turkish force, attended by his knights, until they came to another battalion of Saracens, where they performed wonders. But at last he was thrown to the ground with a broken leg, and was led back by two of his knights, supporting him by the arms.

You must know there was difficulty in withdrawing the count d'Anjou from this attack, wherein he was frequently in the utmost danger and was ever after greatly honored for it.

Another large body of Turks made an attack on the count de Poitiers and me but be assured they were very well received, and served in like manner. It was well for them that they found their way back by which they had come but they left behind great numbers of slain. We returned safely to our camp without having scarcely lost any of our men.

One night the Turks brought forward an engine, called by them la perriere a terrible engine to do mischief, and placed it opposite to the chas-chatells, which Sir Walter de Curel and I were guarding by night. From this engine they flung such quantities of Greek fire that it was the most horrible sight ever witnessed. When my companion, the good Sir Walter, saw this shower of fire, he cried out, "Gentlemen, we are all lost without remedy for should they set fire to our chas-chatells we must be burnt; and if we quit our post we are for ever dishonored from which I conclude, that no one can possibly save us from this peril but God, our benignant Creator; I therefore advise all of you, whenever they throw any of this Greek fire, to cast yourselves on your hands and knees, and cry for mercy to our Lord, in whom alone resides all power."

As soon, therefore, as the Turks threw their fires, we flung ourselves on our hands and knees, as the wise man had advised and this time they fell between our two cats into a hole in front, which our people had made to extinguish them and they were instantly put out by a man appointed for that purpose. This Greek fire, in appearance, was like a large ton, and its tail was of the length of a long spear; the noise which it made was like to thunder; and it seemed a great dragon of fire flying through the air, giving so great a light with its flame, that we saw in our camp as clearly as in broad day. Thrice this night did they throw the fire from la perriere, and four times from cross-bows.

Each time that our good king St. Louis heard them make these discharges of fire, he cast himself on the ground, and with extended arms and eyes turned to the heavens, cried with a loud voice to our Lord, and shedding heavy tears, said, "Good Lord God Jesus Christ, preserve thou me, and all my people" and believe me, his sincere prayers were of great service to us. At every time the fire fell near us, he sent one of his knights to know how we were, and if the fire had hurt us. One of the discharges from the Turks fell beside a chas-chatells, guarded by the men of the

Lord Courtenay, struck the bank of the river in front, and ran on the ground toward them burning with flame. One of the knights of this guard instantly came to me, crying out—"Help us, my lord, or we are burnt for there is a long train of Greek fire, which the Saracens have discharged, that is running straight for our castle."

We immediately hastened thither, and good need was there for as the knight had said, so it was. We extinguished the fire with much labor and difficulty for the Saracens, in the mean time, kept up so brisk a shooting from the opposite bank, that we were covered with arrows and bolts.

The count of Anjou, brother to the king, guarded these castles during the day, and annoyed the Saracen army with his cross-bows. It was ordered by the king, that after the count of Anjou should have finished his daily guard, we, and others of my company, should continue it during the night. We suffered much pain and uneasiness for the Turks had already broken and damaged our tandies and defenses. Once these Turkish traitors advanced their perriere in the daytime, when the count d'Anjou had the guard, and had brought together all their machines, from which they threw Greek fires on our dams, over the river, opposite to our tandies and defenses, which completely prevented any of the workmen from showing themselves and our two chas-chatells were in a moment destroyed and burnt. The count d'Anjou was almost mad at seeing this for they were under his guard, and like one out of his senses, wanted to throw himself into the fire to extinguish it, whilst I and my knights returned thanks to God for if they had delayed this attack to the night, we must have all been burnt.

The king, on hearing what had happened, made a request to each of his barons, that they would give him as much of the largest timbers from their ships that were on the coast as they could spare, and have them transported to where the army lay; for there was not any timber near fit to make use of. After the king had made this request, they all aided him to the utmost and before the new chas-chatells were finished the timber employed was estimated to be worth upwards of 10,000 livres. You may guess from this that many boats were destroyed, and that we were then in the utmost distress.

When the chas-chatells were completed, the king would not have them fixed, or pointed, until the count of Anjou resumed the guard: he then ordered that they should be placed on the exact spot where the others had been burnt. This he did to recover the honor of his said brother, under whose guard the two others had been destroyed. As the king had ordered, so it was done which the Saracens observing, they brought thither all their machines, and, coupling them together, shot at our new chas-chatells vigorously. When they perceived that our men were afraid of going from one castle to the other, for fear of the showers of stones which they were casting, they advanced the perriere directly opposite to them, and again burnt them with their Greek fires. I and my knights returned thanks to God for this second escape. Had they waited until night to make the attack, when the guard would have devolved to us, we must all have been burnt with them.

The king, seeing this, was, as well as his army, much troubled, and he called his barons to council, to consider what should be done for they now perceived themselves that it would be impossible to throw a causeway over the river to cross to the Turks and Saracens, as our people could not make such advance on their side, but they were more speedily ruined by the Turks on the other.

Sir Humbert de Beaujeu, constable of France, then addressed the king, and said, that a Bedouin had lately come to him to say, that if we would give him 500 golden besants, he would show a safe ford, which might easily be crossed on horseback. The king replied, that he most cheerfully granted this, provided he spoke the truth but the man would on no account show the ford before the money demanded was paid.

It was determined by the king, that the duke of Burgundy, and the nobles beyond sea his allies, should guard the army from the alarms of the Saracens whilst he, with his three brothers, the counts of Poitiers, Artois, and Anjou, who was afterward king of Sicily, as I have said before, should with their attendants on horseback make trial of the ford the Bedouin was to show them. The day appointed for this purpose was Shrove-Tuesday, which, when arrived, we all mounted our horses, and, armed at all points, followed the Bedouin to the ford.

On our way thither, some advanced too near the banks of the river, which being soft and slippery, they and their horses fell in and were drowned. The king seeing it, pointed it out to the rest, that they might be more careful and avoid similar danger. Among those that were drowned was that valiant knight Sir John D'Orleans, who bore the banner of the army. When we came to the ford, we saw, on the opposite bank, full 300 Saracen cavalry ready to defend this passage. We entered the river, and our horses found a tolerable ford with firm footing, so that by ascending the stream we found an easy shore, and, through God's mercy, we all crossed over with safety. The Saracens, observing us thus cross, fled away with the utmost dispatch.

Before we set out, the king had ordered that the Templars should form the van, and the count d'Artois, his brother, should command the second division of the army but the moment the count d'Artois had passed the ford with all his people, and saw the Saracens flying, they stuck spurs into their horses and galloped after them for which those who formed the van were much angered at the count d'Artois, who could not make any answer, on account of Sir Fouequault du Melle, who held the bridle of his horse and Sir Fouequault, being deaf, heard nothing the Templars were saying to the count d'Artois, but kept bawling out "Forward, forward!"

When the Templars perceived this, they thought they should be dishonored if they allowed the count d'Artois thus to take the lead, and with one accord they spurred their horses to their fastest speed, pursuing the Saracens through the town of Massoura, as far the plains before Babylon but on their return the Turks shot at them plenty of arrows, and other artillery, as they repassed through the narrow streets of the town. The count d'Artois and the lord de Coucy, of the name of Raoul, were there slain, and as many as 300 other knights. The Templars lost, as their chief informed me, full fourteen score men-at-arms and horses. My knights, as well as myself, noticing on our left a large body of Turks who were arming, instantly charged them and when we were advanced into the midst of them, I perceived a sturdy Saracen mounting his horse, which was held by one of his esquires by the bridle, and while he was putting his hand on the saddle to mount, I gave him such a thrust with my spear, which I pushed as far as I was able, that he fell down dead. The esquire, seeing his lord dead, abandoned master and horse; but, watching my motions, on my return struck me with his lance such a blow between the shoulders as drove me on my horse's neck, and held me there so tightly that I could not draw my sword, which was girthed round me. I was forced to draw another sword which was at the pommel of my saddle, and it was high time but, when he saw I had my sword in my hand, he withdrew his lance, which I had seized, and ran from me.

It chanced that I and my knights had traversed the army of the Saracens, and saw here and there different parties of them, to the amount of about 6,000, who, abandoning their quarters, had advanced into the plain. On perceiving that we were separated from the main body, they boldly attacked us, and slew Sir Hugues de Trichatel, lord d'Escoflans, who bore the banner of our company. They also made prisoner Sir Raoul de Wanon, of our company, whom they had struck to the ground. As they were carrying him off, my knights and myself knew him, and instantly hastened, with great courage, to assist him, and deliver him from their hands. In returning from this engagement the Turks gave me such heavy blows, that my horse, not being able to withstand them, fell on his knees and threw me to the ground over his head. I very shortly replaced my shield on my breast, and grasped my spear, during which time the Lord Errat d'Esmeray, whose soul may God pardon advanced towards me, for he had also been struck down by the enemy and we retreated together towards an old ruined house to wait for the king, who was coming, and I found means to recover my horse.

As we were going to this house, a large body of Turks came galloping towards us, but passed on to a party of ours whom they saw hard by as they passed, they struck me to the ground, with my shield over my neck, and galloped over me, thinking I was dead; and indeed I was nearly so. When they were gone, my companion, Sir Errart, came and raised me up, and we went to the walls of the ruined house. Thither also had retired Sir Hugues d'Escosse, Sir Ferreys de Loppei, Sir Regnault de Menoncourt, and several others and there also the Turks came to attack us, more bravely than ever, on all sides. Some of them entered within the walls, and were a long time fighting with us at spear's length, during which my knights gave me my horse, which they held, lest he should run away, and at the same time so vigorously defended us against the Turks, that they were greatly praised by several able persons who witnessed their prowess.

Sir Hugues d'Escosse was desperately hurt by three great wounds in the face and elsewhere. Sir Raoul and Sir Ferreys were also badly wounded in their shoulders, so that the blood spouted out just like to a ton of wine when tapped. Sir Errart d'Esineray was so severely wounded in the face by a sword, the stroke of which cut off his nose that it hung down over his mouth. In this severe distress, I called to my mind St. James, and said, "Good Lord St. James, succour me, I beseech thee and come to my aid in this time of need." I had scarcely ended my prayer, when Sir Errart said to me, 'Sir, if I did not think you might suppose it was done to abandon you, and save myself, I would go to my lord of Anjou, whom I see on the plain, and beg he would hasten to your help, "Sir Errart," I replied, "you will do me great honor and pleasure, if you will go and seek succour to safe our lives ; for your own also is in great peril" and I said truly, for he died of the wound he had received. All were of my opinion that he should seek for assistance and I then quitting hold of the rein of his bridle, he galloped towards the count d'Anjou, to request he would support us in the danger we were in.

There was a great lord with him who wished to detain him, but the good prince would not attend to what he urged, but, spurring his horse, galloped towards us followed by his men. The

Saracens, observing them coming, left us but when on their arrival they saw the Saracens carrying away their prisoner, Sir Raould de Wanon, badly wounded, they hastened to recover him, and brought him back in a most pitiful state.

Shortly after, I saw the king arrive with all his attendants, and with a terrible noise of trumpets, clarions, and horns. He halted on an eminence, with his men-at-arms, for something he had to say and I assure you I never saw so handsome a man under arms. He was taller than any of his troop by the shoulders and his helmet, which was gilded, was handsomely placed on his head and he bore a German sword in his hand.

Soon after he had halted, many of his knights were observed intermixed with the Turks their companions instantly rushed into the battle among them and you must know, that in this engagement were performed, on both sides, the most gallant deeds that were ever done in this expedition to the Holy Land for none made use of the bow, cross-bow, or other artillery. But the conflict consisted of blows given to each other by battle-axes, swords, butts of spears, all mixed together. From all I saw, my knights and myself, all wounded as we were, were very impatient to join the battle with the others.

Shortly after one of my esquires, who had once fled from my banner, came to me, and brought me one of my Flemish war-horses I was soon mounted, and rode by the side of the king, whom I found attended by that discreet man, Sir John de Valeri. Sir John seeing the king desirous to enter into the midst of the battle, advised him to make for the riverside, on the right, in order that in case there should be any danger, he might have support from the duke of Burgundy and his army, which had been left behind to guard the camp and likewise that his men might be refreshed, and have wherewith to quench their thirst for the weather was at this moment exceedingly hot.

The king sent orders for his barons, knights, and others of his council, to quit the Turkish army, and on their arrival, demanded their counsel, what was best to be done. Several answered, that the good knight, Sir John de Valeri, now by his side, would give him the best advice. Then, according to the former opinion of Sir John de Valeri, which many agreed was good the king turned to the right hand, and advanced toward the river.

As this was doing, Sir Humbert de Beaujeu, constable of France, came up, and told the king that his brother, the count d'Artois, was much pressed in a house at Massoura, where, however, he defended himself gallantly, but that he would need speedy assistance and entreated the king to go to his aid. The king replied, "Constable, spur forward, and I will follow you close." I also, the lord do Joinville, said to the constable, that I would be one of his knights, and follow him in such a case as this.

All of us now galloped straight to Massoura, and were in the midst of the Turkish army, when we were instantly separated from each other by the greater power of the Saracens and Turks. Shortly after, a sergeant at mace of the constable, with whom I was, came to him, and said the king was surrounded by the Turks, and his person in imminent danger. You may suppose our astonishment and fears, for there were between us and where the king was full one thousand or twelve hundred Turks, and we were only six persons in all. I said to the constable, that since it was impossible for us to make our way through such a crowd of Turks, it would be much better to wheel round and get on the other side of them. This we instantly did. There was a deep ditch on the road we took between the Saracens and us and, had they noticed us, they must have slain us all but they were solely occupied with the king, and the larger bodies perhaps also they might have taken us for some of their friends. As we thus gained the river, following its course downward between it and the road, we observed that the king had ascended it, and that the Turks were sending fresh troops after him. Both armies now met on the banks, and the event was miserably unfortunate for the weaker part of our army thought to cross over to the division of the duke of Burgundy, but that was impossible from their horses being worn down, and the extreme heat of the weather. As we descended the river, we saw it covered with lances, pikes, shields, men and horses, unable to save themselves from death.

When we perceived the miserable state of our army, I advised the constable to remain on this side of the river, to guard a small bridge that was hard by "for if we leave it," added I, "the enemy may come and attack the king on this side and if our men be assaulted in two places, they must be discomfited."

There then we halted and you may believe me when I say, that the good king performed that day the most gallant deeds that ever I saw in any battle. It was said, that had it not been for his personal exertions, the whole army would have been destroyed but I believe that the great courage he naturally possessed was that day doubled by the power of God, for he forced himself wherever he saw his men in any distress, and gave such blows with battle-axe and sword, it was wonderful to behold.

The lord de Courtenay and Sir John de Salenay one day told me, that at this engagement six Turks caught hold of the bridle of the king's horse, and were leading him away but this virtuous prince exerted himself with such bravery in fighting the six Turks, that he alone freed himself from them and that many, seeing how valiantly he defended himself, and the great courage he displayed, took greater courage themselves, and abandoning the passage they were guarding, hastened to support the king.

After some little time, the count Peter of Brittany came to us who were guarding the small bridge from Massoura, having had a most furious skirmish. He was so badly wounded in the face that the blood came out of his mouth, as if it had been full of water, and he vomited it forth. The count was mounted on a short, thick, but strong horse, and his reins and the pommel of his saddle were cut and destroyed, so that he was forced to hold himself by his two hands round the horse's neck for fear the Turks, who were close behind him, should make him fall off. He did not, however, seem much afraid of them, for he frequently turned round, and gave them many abusive words, by way of mockery.

Towards the end of this battle, Sir John de Soissons and Sir Peter de Nouille, surnamed Cayer, came to us they had suffered much from the blows they had received by remaining behind in the last battle. The Turks, seeing them, began to move to meet them, but observing us who were guarding the bridge, with our faces towards them, suffered them to pass, suspecting that we should have gone to their succour, as we certainly should have clone. I addressed the count de Soissons, who was my cousin-german: "Sir, I beg that you will remain here to guard this bridge. You will act right in so doing for, if you leave it, the Turks whom you see before you will advance to attack us, and the king may thus have his enemies in front and rear at the same moment." He asked, if he should stay, would I remain with him to which I most cheerfully assented.

The constable, hearing our conversation and agreement, told me to defend this bridge, and not on any account to quit it, and that he would go and seek for succour. I was sitting quietly there on my horse, having my cousin Sir John de Soissons on my right and Sir Peter de Nouille on my left hand, when a Turk, galloping from where the king was, struck Sir Peter de Nouille so heavy a blow with his battle-axe on the back as felled him on the neck of his horse, and then crossed the bridge full speed to his own people, imagining that we would abandon our post and follow him, and thus they might gain the bridge. When they perceived that we would on no account quit our post, they crossed the rivulet, and placed themselves between it and the river on which we marched towards them in such-wise that we were ready to charge them, if they had further advanced.

In our front were two of the king's heralds the name of one was Guillaume de Bron, and that of the other John de Gaymaches; against whom the Turks, who, as I have said, had posted themselves between the rivulet and river, led a rabble of peasants of the country, who pelted them with clods of earth and large stones. At last, they brought a villainous Turk, who thrice flung Greek fires at them and by one of them was the tabard of Guillaume de Bron set on fire; but he soon threw it off, and good need had he, for if it had set fire to his clothes, he must have been burnt. We were also covered, with these showers of stones and arrows which the Turks discharged at the two heralds.

I luckily found near me a gaubison of coarse cloth which had belonged to a Saracen, and turning the slit part inward, I made a sort of shield, which was of much service to me for I was only wounded by their shots in five places, whereas my horse was hurt in fifteen. Soon after, as God willed it, one of my vassals of Joinville brought me a banner with my arms, and a long knife for war, which I was in want of and then, when these Turkish villains, who were on foot, pressed on the heralds, we made a charge on them, and put them instantly to flight.

Thus when the good count de Soissons and myself were returned to our post on the bridge, after chasing away these peasants, he rallied me, saying, "Seneschal, let us allow this rabble to bawl and bray; and, by the 'Cresse Dieu,'" his usual oath, "you and I will talk over this day's adventures in the chambers of our ladies."

It happened that towards evening, about sunset, the constable, Sir Hymbert de Beaujeu, brought us the king's crossbows that were on foot and they drew up in one front, while we, horsemen, dismounted under shelter of the cross-bows. The Saracens, observing this, immediately took to flight, and left us in peace. The constable told me that we had behaved well in thus guarding the bridge and bade me go boldly to the king, and not quit him until he should be dismounted in his pavilion. I went to the king, and at the same moment Sir John de Yaleri joined, and requested of him, in the name of the lord de Chastillon, that the said lord might command the rear guard, which the king very willingly granted. The king then took the road to return to his pavilion, and raised the helmet from his head, on which I gave him my iron skull-cap, which was much lighter, that he might have more air.

Thus as we were riding together, Father Henry, prior of the hospital of Ronnay, who had crossed the river, came to him and kissed his hand, fully armed, and asked if he had heard any news of his brother, the count d'Artois. "Yes," replied the king, "I have heard all;" that is to say, that he knew well he was now in paradise. The prior, thinking to comfort him for the death of his brother, continued, "Sire, no king of France has ever reaped such honor as you have done for with great intrepidity have you and your army crossed a dangerous river to combat your enemies and have been so very successful, that you have put them to flight and gained the field, together with their warlike engines, with which they had wonderfully annoyed you, and concluded the affair by taking possession this day of their camp and quarters."

The good king replied, that God should be adored for all the good he had granted him and then heavy tears began to fall down his cheeks, which many great persons noticing, were oppressed with anguish and compassion, on seeing him thus weep, praising the name of God, who had enabled him to gain the victory.

When we arrived at our quarters, we found great numbers of Saracens on foot holding the cords of a tent which some of our servants were erecting, and pulling against them with all their might. The master of the Temple, who had the command of the vanguard and myself charged this rabble and made them run away. The tent remained, therefore, with us not, however, that there was any great fight, for which reason many boasters were put to shame. I could readily mention their names, but I abstain from doing so because they are deceased and we ought not to speak ill of the dead. Of Sir Guyon de Malvoisin I am willing to speak, for the constable and I met him on the road, returning from Massoura, bearing himself gallantly, although hard pressed by the Turks, who closely pursued him for after they had dispersed the count of Brittany and his battalion, as I have before said, they followed the lord Guyon and his company. He had not suffered much in this engagement, for he and his people had most courageously behaved which is not to be wondered at, when, as I have heard from those who knew him and his family, almost all his knights were of his kindred and lineage, and his men-at-arms his liege vassals. This gave them the greater confidence in their chief.

After we had discomfited the Turks, and driven them out of their quarters, the Bedouins, who are a powerful people, entered the camp of the Saracens and Turks, and seized and carried off whatever they could find, and all that the Saracens and Turks had left behind them. I was much surprised at this for the Bedouins are subjects and tributary to the Saracens but I never heard that they were treated the worse by the Saracens for what they had thus pillaged. They said it was their usual custom to fall on the weakest, which is the nature of dogs for when there is one dog pursued by another, and a shouting made after him, all the other dogs fall on him.

As my subject requires it, I shall say something concerning these Bedouins, and what sort of people they be. The Bedouins reside in deserts and mountains, and have no great faith in Mahomet, like the Turks, but believe in the religion of Aly, who, they say, was uncle to Mahomet. They are persuaded that when any one of them dies for the service of his lord, or when attempting any good design, his soul enters a superior body, and is much more comfortable than it was before this makes them ready to die at the command of their superiors or elders. These Bedouins do not reside in town or city, but always lie in the fields and deserted places, where, whenever the weather is bad, they, their wives and children, make themselves habitation, by sticking into the ground poles connected by hoops, like to what women use in drying their washed clothes and over these hoops they throw skins of their large sheep, which they call skins of Somas, tanned with alum. The Bedouins have large pelisses of coarse hair, which cover their whole bodies, and when evening comes, or when it is cold or wet, they wrap themselves up in them, and retire to rest. Those who follow war have their horses feeding near them during the night, and have only to take off their bridles, and let them eat. In the morning they spread their pelisses to the sun, and, when dry, rub them, so that they do not appear as if they had been wetted. They never are armed for combat, for they say, and believe, that no one can die but at his appointed hour they have likewise a mode of cursing, alluding to their faith, when they swear at their children, saying, "Be thou accursed, like him who arms himself for fear of death." In battle they use only a sword, made after the Turkish manner, and are clothed in linen robes like to surplices. They are an ugly race, and hideous to look at for their hair and beards are long and black. They live on the superabundance of the milk from their herds and their numbers are not to be counted for they dwell in the kingdoms of Jerusalem, Egypt, and throughout all the lands of the Saracens and infidels, to whom they are tributary.

Now I am on the subject of the Bedouins, I must say that I have seen, since my return from the Holy Land, some calling themselves Christians, who hold similar faith with the Bedouins for they maintain that no man can die before his determined time, happen what may, which is a falsehood. I consider such a belief the same as if they should say that God had not the power to assist or hurt us, nor to lengthen or abridge our lives, which is heresy. On the contrary, I declare that we ought to put our whole faith in him who is all-powerful, and may, according to his good pleasure, send us death sooner or later. This is the opposite to the faith of the Bedouins, who firmly believe the day of death to each person is determined infallibly, without any possibility of prolonging or shortening the time.

To return to the original matter, and continue my history. In the evening of this severe engagement that I spoke of, and when we had taken up our quarters in those from whence we had driven the Saracens, my people brought me, from the main army, a tent, which the master of the Templars, who had the command of the van, had given me. I had it pitched on the right of those machines we had won from the enemy, as each of us was eager for repose indeed we had need of it, from the wounds and fatigues we had suffered in the late battle.

Before daybreak, however, we were alarmed by the cries of "To arms, to arms!" and I made my chamberlain rise, who lay by my side, to go and see what was the matter. He was not long in returning, much frightened, and crying out, "My lord, up instantly; for the Saracens have entered the camp, both horse and foot, and have already defeated the guard which the king had appointed for our security, and to defend the engines we had won from them."

These engines were in front of the king's pavilions, and of us who were near to him. I immediately rose, threw a cuirass on my back, and put my iron skull-cap on my head una having roused our people, wounded as we were, we drove the Saracens from the engines which they were so anxious to recover.

The king, seeing that scarcely any of us had armor on, sent Sir Walter de Chastillon, who posted himself between us and the Turks, for the better guard of the engines. After for Walter had several times repulsed the enemy, who made frequent attempts during the night to carry off these engines, the Saracens, finding they could not succeed, retreated to a large body of their horse, that were drawn up opposite to our lines, to prevent us from surprising their camp, which was in their rear.

Six of the principal Turks dismounted, armed from head to foot, and made themselves a rampart of large stones, as a shelter from our cross-bows, and from thence shot volleys of arrows, which often wounded many of our men. When I and my men-at-arms who had the guard of that quarter saw their stone rampart, we took counsel together, and resolved that, during the ensuing night, we would destroy this rampart and bring away the stones.

Now I had a priest called John de Waysy, who, having overheard our counsel and resolution, did not wait so long, but set out alone towards the Saracens, with his cuirass on, his cap of iron, and his sword under his arm. When he was near the enemy, who neither thought of nor suspected any one coming against them thus alone, he rushed furiously on, sword in hand, and gave such blows to these six captains, that they could not defend themselves, and took to flight, to the great astonishment of the other Turks and Saracens.

When the Turks saw their leaders fly, they stuck spurs into their horses, and charged the priest, who was returning to our army, whence had sallied fifty of our men to oppose them, as they were pursuing him on horseback the Turks would not meet them, but wheeled off two or three times. It happened, however, that during these wheelings, one of our men threw his dagger at a Turk, and hit him between the ribs he carried off the dagger, but. it caused his death. The other Turks, seeing this, were shier than before, and never dared to approach while our men were carrying away the stones of the rampart. My priest was well known ever after by the whole army, who said when they saw him, "That is the priest who, single-handed, defeated the Saracens."

These things happened during the first day of Lent and this same day the Saracens elected another chief, in the place of their late chief, Secedun, of whom mention has been made, and who died in the battle of Shrove-Tuesday at the same time, probably, that the good count d'Artois, brother to the king St. Louis, was slain. This new chief found among the other dead the body of the count d'Artois, who had shown great intrepidity in this battle, magnificently dressed, becoming a prince and this chief took the count's coat of armor, and, to give courage to the Turks and Saracens, had it hoisted before them, telling them it was the coal-armor of the king their enemy, who had been slain in battle adding, "My lords, this should make you exert yourselves the more, for body without head is nothing, nor is an army without prince or chief to be feared. I advise, and you ought to have confidence in me, that we increase the force of our attacks on them and on Friday next we must conquer and gain the battle, since they have now lost their commander." All who heard him cheerfully agreed to follow his advice.

You must know that the king had many spies in the Saracen army, who, having overheard their plans, knew their intentions, and how they meant to act. Some of them informed the king of the intended attack of the enemy, and that they believed him dead and the army without a leader.

Upon this, the king summoned all his captains, and commanded them to have their men-at-arms completely armed, and ready drawn up before their tents at midnight, and then to advance as far as the lines which had been made to prevent the Saracens entering the camp on horseback, although they were so constructed that they might pass them on foot. This was punctually executed according to the king's orders.

You may suppose that the plan the Saracen chief had proposed and adopted he lost no time in putting into execution.

On the Friday morning, by sunrise, 4,000 knights, well armed say mounted, were drawn up in battalions, alongside our army, which lay on the banks of the river toward Babylon, and extending as far as a town called Ressil. When the Pagan chief had thus drawn up his 4,000 knights in front of our army, he then brought another large body of Saracens on foot and in such numbers that they surrounded all the other side of it. After doing this, he drew up at a short distance other bodies in conjunction with the power of the sultan of Babylon, to succour and aid each of the two former, as occasion might occur.

The chief of the Saracens, having now completed the arrangement of his army, advanced on horseback alone, to view and make his observations on the manner in which the king's army was formed and where he saw ours was the strongest or weakest, he strengthened or diminished his own. After this he ordered 3,000 Bedouins, whose nature and character I have described, to march in front of the troops under the command of the duke of Burgundy, which were posted between the two branches of the Nile, thinking that part of the king's army might be under the duke, and his own so much the weaker, and that these Bedouins would effectually prevent the duke from affording any support to the king.

All these operations of the infidel chief took him up until about mid-day. This done, he ordered the nacaires and drums to be loudly sounded, according to the mode of the Turks, which is certainly very surprising to those who have not been accustomed to hear them ; and then both horse and foot began to be in motion on all sides. I will speak first of the battalion under the count d'Anjou, which received the first attack, being posted the nearest to Babylon. The enemy advanced in a chequered manner, like to a game of chess for their infantry ran towards our men, and burnt them with Greek fires, which they cast from instruments made for that purpose. On the other hand, the Turkish cavalry charged them with such rapidity and success, that the battalion of the count d'Anjou was defeated. He himself was on foot among his knights, very uncomfortably situated.

"When news was brought to the king of the danger his brother was in, nothing could check his ardour nor would he wait for any one, but, sticking spurs to his horse, galloped into the midst of the battle, lance in hand, to where his brother was, and gave most deadly blows to the

Turks, hastening always to where he saw the greatest crowd. He suffered many hard blows; and the Saracens covered all his horse's tail and rump with Greek fires. You may be assured that at such a time he had God in his heart and mind and in good truth our Lord in this distress befriended him, and so far assisted him, that the king rescued his brother, the count d'Anjou, and drove the Turks before him without the lines.

Next to the battalion of the count d'Anjou was that commanded by Sir Guy de Guivelins, and his brother Baldwin, which joined the battalion of that bold and gallant man Sir Walter de Chastillon. He had with him numbers of chivalrous knights and these two battalions behaved so vigorously against the Turks, that they were neither any way broken nor conquered.

The next battalion, however, fared but badly, under the command of Friar William de Sonnac, master of the Temple, who had with him the remnant of the men-at-arms that had survived the battle of Shrove-Tuesday, which had been so severely murderous. The master of the Temple, having but few men, made of the engines that had been taken from the enemy, a sort of rampart in his front; this, nevertheless, availed him nothing, for the Templars having added to them many planks of fir-wood, the Saracens burnt them with their Greek fires and seeing there were but few to oppose them, they waited not until they were destroyed, but vigorously attacking the Templars, defeated them in a very short time. It is certain, that in the rear of the Templars there was about an acre of ground so covered with bolts, darts, arrows, and other weapons, that you could not see the earth beneath them, such showers of these had been discharged against the Templars by the Saracens. The commander of this battalion had lost an eye in the preceding battle of Shrove-Tuesday and in this he lost the other, and was slain God have mercy on his soul!

Sir Guy de Malvoisin, a bold and valiant captain of another battalion, was severely wounded in the body and the Saracens perceiving his gallant conduct and address, shot Greek fire at him incessantly, so that at one time when he was hit by it, his people had much difficulty to extinguish it. But notwithstanding this, he stood bold and firm, unconquered by the Pagans.

From the battalion of Sir Guy de Malvoisin, the lines which enclosed our army descended to where I was, within a stone's cast of the river, and passed by the division of the lord William earl of Flanders, which extended to that branch of the river which entered the sea. Our battalion was posted opposite, and on that bank of the river where Sir Guy de Malvoisin was. The Saracens, observing the appearance of the division of the earl of Flanders fronting them, dared not make any attack on us, for which I thanked God, as neither my knights nor myself could put on any armor, on account of the wounds we had received in the engagement of the Tuesday, which rendered it impossible to wear any defensive clothing.

The Lord William of Flanders and his battalion did wonders they gallantly and fiercely attacked the Turks on horseback and on foot, and performed great deeds of arms. Seeing their prowess, I ordered my cross-bows to shoot strongly at the Turks, who were on horseback at this engagement; and the moment they felt themselves or horses wounded by the arrows, they instantly took flight, and abandoned their infantry. The earl of Flanders and his division, observing the Turks fly, passed the lines, and charged the Pagans, who were on foot, killing great numbers, and bringing off many targets. Among others, Sir Gaultier de la Horgne, who bore the banner of the count d'Aspremont, displayed much courage.

Adjoining this battalion was that of my lord the count de Poitiers, brother to the king; it was composed solely of infantry, and the only person on horseback was the count, which was unfortunate for him for the Turks defeated this battalion, and made the count prisoner. They would surely have carried him away, had not the butchers, and all the other traffickers, men and women, who supplied the army with provision, hearing that the Turks were carrying off the count de Poitiers, set up a great shout, and rushed on the Saracens with such fury that they rescued the count de Poitiers, and drove the Turks beyond the lines.

The next battalion to that of the count de Poitiers was the weakest of the whole army, and commanded by Sir Josserant de Brancon, whom my lord de Poitiers had brought with him to Egypt. This division was also formed of dismounted knights, Sir Josserant and his son Sir Henry being the only persons on horseback. The Turks broke this battalion on all sides, on which Sir Josserant and his son fell on the rear of the Turks, and cut them down with their swords. They pressed the enemy so much that they frequently turned on them again, leaving the main body of his men. In the end this would have been fatal for the Turks must have slain the whole, if Sir Henry de Cone, a wise and valiant knight of the division under the duke of Burgundy, well knowing the weakness of the lord de Brancon's battalion, had not, every time he saw the Turks make their charge on it, ordered the king's cross-bows to shoot at them. He exerted himself so effectually that the lord de Brancon escaped from this danger, but lost twelve of the twenty knights whom it was said he had, without counting other men-at-arms. He himself, however, was the victim of the wounds he received in the service of God, who, we are bound to believe, has well rewarded him for it.

This lord was my uncle, and I heard him on his death-bed say, that he had in his time been in thirty-six battles or warlike skirmishes, and had borne off the prize of arms in most. Of some of them I have a remembrance for once being in the army of the count de Maseon, who was his cousin, he came to me and a brother of mine on a Good Friday, and said to us, "Come my nephews with all your men, and join us in charging these Germans, who are destroying the monastery of Maseon."

We were instantly on horseback, and hastened to attack the Germans, whom, with hard blows of sword and lance, we drove from the monastery, where many were killed and wounded. When this was done, the good man fell on his knees before the altar, and cried with a loud voice to our Lord, praying that he would be pleased to have mercy on his soul, that he might die for his service, to the end that he might be entitled to the reward of paradise. I have related this that you may know, as I firmly believe, that God has granted to him the request he then made.

After this battle was ended, the king summoned all his barons, knights, and other great lords, to whom, when assembled, he thus kindly addressed himself: "My lords and friends, you have all now witnessed the great grace which God our Creator has of late shown us, and continues to do so daily, for which we are bounden to return him our thanksgiving. Last Tuesday, which was Shrovetide, we, aided by him, dislodged our enemies from their quarters, of which we have gained the possession. This Friday, which is now passed we have defended ourselves against them, very many of us being without arms, while they were completely armed on horseback, and on their own ground." Many more fair speeches did he make and the good king dwelt much upon what had passed, to comfort and give them courage and faith in God.

In pursuing the subject-matter of my book it is necessary now and then to make digressions, and to inform you of the manner in which the sultan supported his men-at-arms, and how his armies were supplied. It is true that the greater part of his chivalry was composed of foreigners, whom the merchants trading by sea had bought when young, and whom the Egyptians purchased by order of their sultan. They came mostly from the east; for when an eastern king* had defeated in battle another neighboring monarch, the victor, and his people, seized the subjects of the vanquished, whom they sold to merchants, who bought them, as I have said, to sell again in Egypt. The children born from these captives the sultan supported and educated, and when their beards appeared, they were taught to draw the bow, by way of amusement and when he was in a jocund mood they displayed their skill before him.

As they increased in strength, their small bows were exchanged for others of greater weight, and proportioned to their powers. These youths bore the arms of the sultan, and were called his Bahairiz. When their beards were grown, the sultan made them knights and their emblazonments were like his, of pure gold, save that to distinguish them, they added bars of vermilion, with roses, birds, griffins, or any other difference as they please. They were called the band of La Hauleca, which signifies the archers of the king's guard and were always about the person of the sultan to defend him. When the sultan went to war they were quartered near him as his body-guard.

He had, beside these, other guards still nearer to his person, such as porters and minstrels, who played upon their instruments from the break of day until the sultan rose and in the evenings sounded the retreat. Their instruments made so loud a noise, that those who were near them could not hear each other speak and their notes were distinctly heard throughout the army. During the daytime, they dared on no account play on them, without express orders from the commander of the Hauleca.

When the sultan wanted any thing, or wished to give orders to his men-at-arms, he mentioned it to the above commander, who ordered the minstrels to sound their Saracen horns, drums, and nacaires and to this sound the whole of the chiefs drew up before their sultans tent, to whom the commander of the Hauleca told the good pleasure of the sultan, which they instantly obeyed to the utmost of their power. Whenever the sultan went personally to war, he nominated from such of the knights of the Hauleca as showed the most courage and abilities an admiral or captain over the men-at-arms, and according as they rose in merit, the more the sultan gave them; by which means every one of them tried who should surpass the other to the utmost.

The manner of the sultan's acting towards them was, that whenever any one of the knights of the Hauleca had, by his prowess and chivalry, gained a sufficiency, so that he was no longer in want, and could live independent, the sultan, for fear lie should dethrone or kill him, had him arrested and thrown into prison, where he was secretly put to death, and then he took possession of all the fortune his wife and children might have had left to them. An example of this happened while I was in that country; for the sultan had imprisoned those who, by their valor and address, had made prisoners of the counts of Montfort and Bar and from envy and jealousy, and from his dread of them, had them put to death. He acted in like manner to the Boudendars, who are his subjects for when they had defeated the king of Armenia, and came to inform him of the event, they found him hunting wild beasts. Having dismounted to make their obeisance, and thinking, as they had behaved so well, they should be recompensed, he eyed them maliciously, and said he should not return their salute, for they had made him lose his chase and ordered their heads to be struck off.

To return to our subject. The sultan, lately deceased, had left a son, who was twenty-five years old, well informed, prudent, and already full of malice. The last sultan, fearing he might dethrone him, kept him at a distance from his person and had given him a kingdom in the East but the moment his father was dead, the admirals of Babylon sent for him, and made him their sultan. On taking possession of his dignity, he deprived the constable, marshals, and seneschals of his father of their golden wands, and the offices which they held, and gave them to those whom he had brought with him from the East.

This caused great discontent in those who had been removed, as also in those of the council of his late father, who suspected strongly that he would act by them, after seizing their wealth, in -the same manner as the sultan had done by those who had taken the counts of Montfort and of Bar, as already related. They therefore unanimously agreed to put him to death, and found means of obtaining from those called La Hauleca, who were the sultan's guard, a promise to murder him.

After the two battles I have mentioned, which were marvelously sharp and severe, the one on Shrove-Tuesday, and the other the first Friday in Lent, another great misfortune befel our army. At the end of eight or ten days, the bodies of those who had beep slain in these two engagements, and thrown into the Nile, rose to the top of the water. It was said, this always happens when the gall is burst and rotten. These bodies floated down the river until they came to the small bridge that communicated with each part of our army and the arch was so low it almost touched the water, and prevented the bodies passing underneath. The river was covered with them from bank to bank, so that the water could not be seen a good stone's throw from the bridge upward.

The king hired one hundred laborers, who were full eight days in separating the bodies of the Christians from the Saracens, which were easily distinguishable the Saracen bodies they thrust under the bridge by main force, and floated them down to the sea but the Christians were buried in deep graves, one over the other. God knows how great was the stench, and what misery it was to see the bodies of such noble and worthy persons lying so exposed. I witnessed the chamberlain of the late count d'Artois seeking the body of his master, and many more hunting after the bodies of their friends but I never heard that any who were thus seeking their friends amidst such an infectious smell ever recovered their health. You must know, that we ate no fish the whole Lent but eelpouts, which is a gluttonous fish, and feeds on dead bodies. From this cause, and from the bad air of the country, where it scarcely ever rains a drop, the whole army was infected by a shocking disorder, which dried up the flesh on our legs to the bone, and our skins became tanned as black as the ground, or like an old boot that has long lain behind a coffer. In addition to this miserable disorder, those affected by it had another sore complaint in the mouth, from eating such fish that rotted the gums, and caused a most stinking breath. Very few escaped death that were thus attacked and the surest symptom of its being fatal was a bleeding at the nose, for when that took place none ever recovered.

The better to cure us, the Turks, who knew our situation, fifteen days afterward attempted to starve us, by means I shall now tell you. These villainous Turks had drawn their galleys overland, and launched them again below our army, so that those who had gone to Damietta for provision never returned, to the great astonishment of us all. We could not imagine the reason of this, until one of the galleys of the earl of Flanders, having forced a passage, informed us how the sultan had launched his vessels, by drawing them overland, below us, so that the Turks watched all galleys going toward Damietta, and had already captured fourscore of ours, and killed their crews.

By this means all provision was exceedingly dear in the army and when Easter arrived, a beef was sold for eighty livres, a sheep for thirty livres, a hog for thirty livres, a mud of wine for ten livres, an egg for sixpence, and every thing else in proportion.

When the king and his barons saw this, and that there was not any remedy for it, they advised the king to march the army from near Babylon, and join that of the duke of Burgundy, which was on the other bank of the river that flowed to Damietta. For the security of his retreat, the king had erected a barbican in front of the small bridge I have so often mentioned and it was constructed in such wise that it might be entered on each side on horseback. As soon as this barbican was finished, the whole host armed; for the Turks made a vigorous attack, observing our intentions to join the duke of Burgundy's army on the opposite side of the river.

During the time we were entering the barbican, the enemy fell on the rear of our army, and took prisoner Sir Errart de Valeri but he was soon rescued by his brother, Sir John de Yaleri. The king, however, and his division never moved until the baggage and arms had crossed the river and then we all passed after the king, except Sir Gaultier de Chastillon, who commanded the rear-guard in the barbican.

When the whole army had passed, the rear-guard was much distressed by the Turkish cavalry; for from their horses they could shoot point blank, as the barbican was low. The Turks on foot threw large stones and clods of earth in their faces, without the guard being able to defend themselves. They would infallibly have been destroyed, if the count d'Anjou, brother to the king, and afterwards king of Sicily, had not boldly gone to their rescue, and brought them off in safety.

The day preceding Shrovetide I saw a thing which I must relate. On the vigil of that day died a very valiant and prudent knight, Sir Hugh de Landricourt, one under my banner and during his burial, six of my knights talked so loud they disturbed the priest as he was saying mass on this I arose, and bade them be silent for it was unbecoming gentlemen thus to talk whilst the mass was celebrating. But they burst into laughter, and told me they were talking of marrying the widow of Sir Hugh, now in his bier. I rebuked them sharply, and said such conversation was indecent and improper, for that they had too soon forgotten their companion.

Now it happened on the morrow, when the first grand battle took place, although we may laugh at their follies, God took such vengeance on them, that of all the six not one escaped death, and remained unburied. The wives of the whole six re-married. This makes it credible, that God leaves no such conduct unpunished. "With regard to myself, I fared little better, for I was grievously wounded in the battle of Shrove-Tuesday. I had, besides, the disorder in my legs and mouth before spoken of, and such a rheum in my head it ran through my mouth and nostrils. In addition, I had a double fever, called a quartan, from which God defend us and with these illnesses was I confined to my bed the half of Lent.

My poor priest was likewise as ill as myself and one day when he was singing mass before me as I lay in my bed, at the moment of the elevation of the host, I saw him so exceedingly weak that he was near fainting but when I perceived he was on the point of falling to the ground, I flung myself out of bed, sick as I was, and taking my coat, embraced him, and bade him be at his ease, and take courage from him whom he held in his hands. He recovered some little but I never quitted him until he had finished the mass which he completed, and this was the last, for he never after celebrated another, but died. God receive his soul!

To return to our history. It is true there were some parleys between the councils of the king and of the sultan, respecting a peace and a day was appointed for the further discussion of it. The basis of the treaty was agreed on,—namely, that the king should restore to the sultan Damietta and the sultan should surrender to the king the realm of Jerusalem. He was also to take proper care of the sick in Damietta, and to give up the salted provision that was there, for neither Turk nor Saracen eat of it, and likewise the engines of war but the king was to send for all these things from Damietta.

The end of this was, that the sultan demanded what security the king would give him for the surrender of Damietta and it was proposed that he should detain as prisoner one of the king's brothers, either the count de Poitiers, or the count d'Anjou, until it were effected. But the Turks refused to accept of any other hostage than the person of the king.

To this the gallant knight, Sir Geoffry de Sergines, replied, that the Turks should never have the king's person and that he would rather they should all be slain than it should be said they had given their king in pawn and thus matters remained.

The disorder I spoke of very soon increased so much in the army that the barbers were forced to cut away very large pieces of flesh from the gums, to enable their patients to eat. It was pitiful to hear the cries and groans of those on whom this operation was performing; they seemed like to the cries of women in labor, and I cannot express the great concern all felt who heard them.

The good king, St. Louis, witnessing the miserable condition of great part of his army, raised his hands and eyes to heaven, blessing our Lord for all he had given him, and seeing that he could not longer remain where he was, without perishing himself as well as his army, gave orders to march on the Tuesday evening after the octave of Easter, and return to Damietta. He issued his commands to the masters of the galleys to have them ready to receive on board the sick, and convey them to Damietta. He likewise gave his orders to Josselin de Corvant, and to other engineers, to cut the cords which held the bridges between us and the Saracens but they neglected them, which was the cause of much evil befalling us.

Perceiving that every one was preparing to go to Damietta, I withdrew to my vessel, with two of my knights, all that I had remaining of those that had accompanied me, and the rest of my household. Towards evening, when it began to grow dark, I ordered my captain to raise the anchor, that we might float down the stream but he replied, that he dared not obey me, for that between us and Damietta were the large galleys of the sultan, which would infallibly capture us.

The king's seamen had made great fires on board their galleys, to cherish the unfortunate sick and many others in the same state were waiting on the banks of the river for vessels to take them on board. As I was advising my sailors to make some little way, I saw, by the light of the fires, the Saracens enter our camp, and murder these sick that were waiting on the banks of the Nile and as my men were raising the anchor, and we began to move downward, the sailors who were to take the sick on board advanced with their boats but seeing the Saracens in the act of killing them, they retreated to their large galleys, cut their cables, and fell down on my small bark.

I expected every moment they would have sunk me but we escaped this imminent danger, and made some way down the river. The king had the same illness as the rest of his army, with a dysentery which, had he pleased, he might have prevented, by living on board his larger vessels but he said, he had rather die than leave his people. The king, observing us make off, began to shout and cry to us to remain, and likewise ordered some heavy bolts to be shot at us, to stop our course until we should have his orders to sail.

I will now break the course of my narration, and say in what manner the king was made prisoner, as he told me himself. I heard him say, that he had quitted his own battalion and men-at-arms, and, with Sir Geoffry de Sergines, had joined the battalion of Sir Gaultier de Chastillon, who commanded the rear division. The king was mounted on a small courser, with only housing of silk and of all his men-at-arms, there was only with him the good knight Sir Geoffry de Sergines, who attended him as far as the town of Casel, where the king was made prisoner. But before the Turks could take him, I heard say, that Sir Geoffry de Sergines defended him in like manner as a faithful servant does the cup of his master from flies for every time the Saracens approached him, Sir Geoffry guarded him with vigorous strokes of the blade and point of his sword, and it seemed as if his courage and strength were doubled.

By dint of gallantry he drove them away from the king, and thus conducted him to Casel, where, having dismounted at a house, he laid the king in the lap of a woman who had come from Paris, thinking that every moment must be his last, for he had no hopes that he could ever pass that day without dying.

Shortly after arrived Sir Philip de Montfort, who told the king that he had just seen the admiral of the sultan, with whom he had formerly treated for a truce and that if it were his good pleasure, he would return to him again, and renew it. The king entreated him so to do, and declared he would abide by whatever terms they should agree on.

Sir Philip de Montfort returned to the Saracens, who had taken their turbans from their heads, and gave a ring, which lie took off his finger, to the admiral, as a pledge of keeping the truce, and that they would accept the terms as offered and of which I have spoken.

Just at this moment a villainous traitor of an apostate sergeant, named Marcel, set up a loud shout to our people, and said, "Sir knights, surrender yourselves the king orders you by me so to do, and not to cause yourselves to be slain." At these words, all were thunderstruck and thinking the king had indeed sent such orders, they each gave up their arms and staves to the Saracens.

The admiral, seeing the Saracens leading the king's, knights as their prisoners, said to Sir Philip de Montfort, that he would not agree to any truce, for that the army had been made prisoners. Sir Philip was greatly astonished at what he saw, for he was aware that, although he was sent as ambassador to settle a truce, he should likewise be made prisoner, and knew not to whom to have recourse. In Pagan countries, they have a very bad custom, that when any ambassadors are dispatched from one king or sultan to another, to demand or conclude a peace, and one of these princes dies, and the treaty is not concluded before that event takes place, the ambassador is made prisoner, wherever he may be, and whether sent by sultan or king.

You must know, that we who had embarked on board our vessels, thinking to escape to Damietta, were not more fortunate than those who had remained on land for we were also taken, as you shall hear. It is true, that during the time we were on the river, a dreadful tempest of wind arose, blowing towards Damietta, and with such force that, unable to ascend the stream, we were driven towards the Saracens. The king, indeed, had left a body of knights, with orders to guard the invalids on the banks of the river but it would not have been of any use to have made for that part, as they had all fled. Towards the break of day, we arrived at the pass where the sultan's galleys lay, to prevent any provisions being sent from Damietta to the army, who, when they perceived us, set up a great noise, and shot at us and such of our horsemen as were on the banks, with large bolts armed with Greek fire, so that it seemed as if the stars were falling from the heavens.

When our mariners had gained the current, and we attempted to push forward, we saw the horsemen whom the king had left to guard the sick flying towards Damietta. The wind became more violent than ever, and drove us against the bank of the river. On the opposite shore were immense numbers of our vessels that the Saracens had taken, which we feared to approach for we plainly saw them murdering their crews, and throwing the dead bodies into the water, and carrying away the trunks and arms they had thus gained.

Because we would not go near the Saracens, who menaced us, they shot plenty of bolts upon which, I put on my armor, to prevent such as were well aimed from hurting me. At the stern of my vessel were some of my people, who cried out to me, "My lord, my lord our steersman, because the Saracens threaten us, is determined to run us on shore, where we shall be all murdered." I instantly rose up, for I was then very ill, and, advancing with my drawn sword, declared I would kill the first person who should attempt to run us on the Saracen shore. The sailors replied, that it was impossible to proceed, and that I must determine which I would prefer, to be landed on the shore, or to be stranded on the mud of the banks in the river. I preferred, very fortunately, as you shall hear, being run on a mud bank in the river to being carried on shore, where I saw our men murdered, and they followed my orders.

It was not long ere we saw four of the sultan's large galleys making toward us, having full a thousand men on board. I called upon my knights to advise me how to act, whether to surrender to the galleys of the sultan or to those who were on the shore. We were unanimous, that it would be more advisable to surrender to the galleys that were coming, for then we might have a chance of being kept together whereas, if we gave ourselves up to those on the shore, we should certainly be separated, and perhaps sold to the Bedouins, of whom I have before spoken. To this opinion, however, one of my clerks would not agree, but said it would be much better for us to be slain, as then we should go to paradise but we would not listen to him, for the fear of death had greater influence over us.

Seeing that we must surrender, I took a small case that contained my jewels and relics, and cast it into the river. One of my sailors told me, that if I would not let him tell the Saracens I was cousin to the king, we should all be put to death. In reply, I bade him say what he pleased. The first of these galleys now came athwart us, and cast anchor close to our bow. Then, as I firmly believe, God sent to my aid a Saracen, who was a subject of the emperor. Having on a pair of trousers of coarse cloth, and swimming straight to my vessel, he embraced my knees, and said,

"My lord, if you do not believe what I shall say, you are a lost man. To save yourself, you must leap into the river, which will be unobserved by the crew, who are solely occupied with the capture of your bark." He had a cord thrown to me from their galley on the escort of my vessel, and I leaped into the water followed by the Saracen, who indeed saved me, and conducted me to the galley; for I was so weak I staggered, and should have otherwise sunk to the bottom of the river.

I was drawn into the galley, wherein were fourteen score men, besides those who had boarded my vessel and this poor Saracen held me fast in his arms. Shortly after, I was landed, and they rushed upon me to cut my throat indeed, I expected nothing else, for he that should do it "would imagine he had acquired honor.

This Saracen who had saved me from drowning would not quit hold of me, but cried out to them, "The king's cousin! The king's cousin!"

I felt the knife at my throat, and had already cast myself on my knees on the ground but God delivered me from this peril by the aid of the poor Saracen, who led me to the castle where the Saracen chiefs were assembled.

When I was in their presence, they took off my coat of mail and from pity, seeing me so very ill, they flung over me one of my own scarlet coverlids, lined with mine ever, which my lady-mother had given me. Another brought me a white leathern girdle, with which I girthed my coverlid around me. One of the Saracen knights gave me a small cap, which I put on my head; but I soon began to tremble, so that my teeth chattered, as well from the fright I had had as from my disorder.

On my complaining of thirst, they brought me some water in a pot but I had no sooner put it to my mouth, and began drinking, than it ran back through my nostrils. God knows what a pitiful state I was in for I looked for death rather than life, having an impost fume in my throat. When my attendants saw the water run thus through my nostrils, they began to weep and to be very sorrowful.

The Saracen who had saved me asked my people why they wept they gave him to understand, that I was nearly dead, from an impost fume in the throat which was choking me. The good Saracen, having always great compassion for me, went to tell this to one of the Saracen knights, who bade him to be comforted, for that he would give me something to drink that should cure me in two days. This he did and I was soon well, through God's grace, and the beverage which the Saracen knight gave me.

Soon after my recovery, the admiral of the sultan's galleys sent for me, and demanded if I were cousin to the king, as it was said. I told him I was not, and related why it had been reported, and that one of my mariners had advised it through fear of the Saracens in the galleys, for that otherwise they would put us to death. The admiral replied that I had been very well advised, or we should have been all murdered without fail, and thrown into the river. The admiral again asked me, if I had any acquaintance with the emperor Ferry of Germany, then living, and if I were of his lineage; I answered truly, that I had heard my mother say I was his second cousin. The admiral replied that he would love me the better for it.

Thus, as we were eating and drinking, he sent for an inhabitant of Paris to come to me, who, on his entrance, seeing what we were doing, exclaimed, "Ah, sir, what are you about?" "What am I about!" replied, "When he informed me, on the part of God, that I was eating meat on a Friday. On which, I suddenly threw my trencher behind me and the admiral, noticing it, asked of my friendly Saracen, who was always with me, why I had left off eating. He told him, because it was a Friday, which I had forgotten. The admiral said that God could never be displeased, because I had done it unknowingly. You must know, that the legate who had accompanied the king frequently reproached me for fasting when thus ill, and when there was not any statesman but myself left with the king, and that I should hurt myself by fasting. But notwithstanding this, and that I was a prisoner, I never failed to fast every Friday on bread and water.

A CONTINUATION OF THE SECOND PART OF THE MEMOIRS OF JOHN LORD DE JOINVILLE

On the Sunday after we had been made prisoners, the admiral ordered all that had been taken on the Nile to be brought from the castle, on the banks of the river. In my presence, my chaplain was dragged from the hold of the galley but, on coining to the open air, he fainted, and the Saracens killed him instantly before my eyes, and flung him into the stream. His clerk, from the disorder he had caught when with the army, being unable to stand, they cast a mortar on his head, killed him, and flung him after his master.

In the like manner did they deal with the other prisoners for as they were drawn out of the hold of the galleys wherein they had been confined, there were Saracens purposely posted, who, on seeing any one weak or ill, killed him and threw him into the water. Such was the treatment of the unfortunate sick. Seeing this tyranny, I told them, through the interpretation of my Saracen, that they were doing very wrong and contrary to the commands of Saladin the pagan, who had declared it unlawful to put to death any one to whom they had given salt and bread. They made answer, that they were destroying men of no use, for that they were too ill with their disorders to do any service.

After this they brought before me my mariners and said they had all denied their faith. I replied I did not believe it, but that their fears of death might have caused them to say so, and that the moment they found themselves in another country they would return to their own religion.

The admiral added to this, that he believed firmly what I said, for that Saladin had declared that a Christian was never known to make a good pagan, nor a good Saracen a Christian. The admiral, soon after, made me mount a palfrey, and we rode side by side over a bridge to the place where St. Louis and his men were prisoners.

At the entrance of a large pavilion we found a secretary writing down the names of the prisoners by orders of the sultan. I was there forced to declare my name, which I no way wished to conceal, and it was written down with the others. As we entered this pavilion the Saracen, who had preserved my life, and had always followed me, said, "Sir, you must excuse me, but I cannot follow you further. I advise and entreat that you will never quit the hand of this young boy whom you have with you, otherwise the Saracens will murder him." The boy's name was Bartholomew de Montfaucon, son to the lord Montfaucon de Bar.

When my name was written down, the admiral led me and the little boy to the tent where were the barons of France, and more than ten thousand other persons with them. On my entrance, every one seemed to testify great pleasure at seeing me again and for some time nothing could be heard for their noisy joy, as they concluded I had been murdered.

Thus as we were together, hoping, through the grace of God, we should not long remain in this state, a rich Saracen led us into another tent, where we had miserable cheer. Numbers of knights and other men were confined in a large court, surrounded with walls of mud. The guards of this prison led them out one at a time, and asked each if he would become a renegado: those that answered in the affirmative were put aside, but those who refused, instantly had their heads cut off.

Shortly after, the council of the sultan sent for us, and demanded to whom it was most agreeable they should deliver the sultan's message. We unanimously answered, by means of an interpreter, who spoke both French and Saracen, to the count Peter of Brittany. This was the message: "My lords, the sultan asks by us if you wish to be free and what you are willing to give for your liberty?"

To this the earl of Brittany replied, that we all heartily wished to be delivered from the hands of the sultan, who had made us suffer most unreasonably. But when the council of the sultan asked if we would not be willing to give for our ransom some of the castles of the barons of the Holy Land, the earl of Brittany answered, that we could not possibly comply for these castles and strong places belonged to the emperor of Germany, now on the throne, and who would never consent to the sultan holding any fiefs under him.

The council then asked if we would not surrender some of the castles belonging to the Knights Templars, or to the hospital of Rhodes, for our deliverance. The earl replied that that was equally impossible for it would be contrary to the accustomed oath which the governors or lords of such castles take on their investiture, when they solemnly swear to God that they will never surrender these castles for the deliverance of any man whatever.

The Saracens then spoke together, saying, that it did not appear we had any desire to regain our liberty and that they would send us those who well knew how to use their swords, to treat us as the others had been dealt with, and on that they left us.

Not long after the sultan's council had departed, a tall old Saracen, of goodly appearance, came to us, accompanied by a great multitude of young Saracens, each of whom had a large sword by his side, which alarmed us much. The old Saracen asked us, by means of an interpreter, who spoke and understood our language well, if it were true that we believed in one only God, who had been born for our salvation, was crucified to death, and after three days rose again to save us. We answered, that what we had heard was perfectly true. On this he replied, that since it was so, we ought not to be cast down for any persecutions we might suffer for his sake and that we had not as yet endured death for him, as he had done for us and since he had the power to raise himself from the dead, it would not be long before he would deliver us.

The old Saracen then went away with all the young men, without doing any thing more, which rejoiced me exceedingly; for I really thought the intent of his visit was to cut our heads off. It was not long after this before we heard news of our deliverance.

The sultan's council soon returned to us again, and said the king had exerted himself so effectually, that he had succeeded in obtaining our liberty. They ordered us to send four of our company to hear and know the terms on which we were to have our freedom. To this end we deputed the lords John de Valeri, Philip de Montfort, Baldwin de Ebelin, seneschal of Cyprus, and his brother, the constable of Cyprus, who was one of the handsomest and best-informed knights I ever knew and who loved greatly the people of that country.

These four knights were not long in bringing us the terms of our liberty. In order to try the king, the sultan's council had made the same demands from him as from us but it pleased God that the good king, St. Louis, made similar answers to what we had done through the mouth of Count Peter of Brittany. The council, seeing the king would not comply with their demands, threatened to put him in the bernicles, which is the greatest torture they can inflict on any one. The bernicles are formed of two thick blocks of wood fastened together at the top and when they use this mode of torture, they lay the person on his side, between these two blocks, passing his legs through broad pins; they then fix the upper block on the sufferer, and make a man sit on him, by which means all the small bones of his legs are broken or dislocated. To increase the torture, at the end of three days they replace his legs, which are now greatly swollen, in the bernicles, and break them again, which is the most cruel thing ever heard and they tie his head down with bullock's sinews, for fear he should move himself while in them.

The good king held all their menaces cheap, and said that since he was their prisoner they might do to him whatever they pleased. The Saracens finding they could not conquer the king by threats, came to him, and asked how much money he would give the sultan for his ransom, in addition to Damietta, which was to be surrendered. The king replied, that if the sultan would be contented with a reasonable ransom, he would write to the queen to pay it for himself and his army. The Saracens asked why he wanted to write to the queen. He answered, that it was but reasonable he should do so, for that she was his wife and companion. The council then went to the sultan to know what sum he required from the king and on their return told the king, that if the queen would pay a million of golden besants equal at that time to 500,000 livres, she would, by so doing, obtain the king's liberty. The king then asked them, on their oath, should the queen pay these 500,000 livres, would the sultan consent to his deliverance. On this they again returned to the sultan to know if he would bind himself by such a promise, and brought back his answer, that he was very willing so to do.

The council then took their oaths to the punctual fulfillment of this agreement, which, when done, the king engaged to pay cheerfully, for the ransom of his army, 500,000 livres and that for his own ransom he would surrender the town of Damietta to the sultan for he was of a rank whose bodily ransom could not be estimated by the value of money.

When the sultan heard the good disposition of the king, he said, "By my faith, the Frenchman is generous and liberal, when he does not condescend to bargain about so large a sum of money, but has instantly complied with the first demand. Go, and tell him from me," added the sultan, "that I make him a present of 100,000 livres, so that he will have only to pay 400,000."

The sultan then commanded that all of the principal nobles, and great officers of the king, should be embarked in four of the largest galleys, and conducted to Damietta. In the galley on board of which I was shipped, were the good count Peter of Brittany, William count of Flanders, John, the good count de Soissons, Sir Hymbert de Beaujeu, constable of France, and those two excellent knights and brothers, Sir Baldwin and Sir Guy Ebelin.

The captain of the galley made us land before a large house which the sultan had erected on the banks of the river where there was a handsome tower made of poles of firewood, and covered with painted cloth. At the entrance a great pavilion had been pitched, where the admirals of the sultan left their swords and staves whenever they wanted to speak with him. Passing this pavilion, there was another very handsome gateway that led to the great hall of the sultan, and adjoining was a tower like unto the first, by which they mounted to the chamber of the sultan. In the midst of this lodgment was a handsome lawn, on which was another tower larger than the others, whence the sultan made his observations on the surrounding country, and on each army. There was in this lawn an alley that led to the river, at the end of which the sultan had made a summer-house on the strand to bathe himself. This summer-house was formed of trelliswork, covered with Indian linen, to prevent any one seeing what passed with inside. All the towers were likewise covered with cloth.

We arrived before this lodging on the Thursday preceding the feast of the Ascension of our Lord. Near to it the king had landed, to hold a parley with the sultan in a pavilion, and it was then agreed that the ensuing Saturday the king should go to Damietta.

Just as we were on our departure for Damietta, to surrender to the sultan, the admiral of the present sultan's father showed great dissatisfaction with the reigning monarch. Although he had been the principal author of his having been sent for on his father's death at Damietta, to succeed to the throne, he had much disappointed the admiral by dismissing him from his office of constable and others from their marshalships and seneschalships, to provide for those who had accompanied him to Egypt.

They therefore held a council, when he said,—"My lords, you see how much the sultan has dishonored us, by depriving us of those governments and honors with which his father had entrusted us. Such conduct, you may be assured, will induce him, when once master of the castle and fortresses of Damietta, to have us arrested and put to death in his prisons, through fear that in process of time we may take our revenge on him as his grandfather did to the admiral and the others who had made the counts de Bar and de Montfort prisoners. It will be therefore more to our advantage that we destroy him before he escape out of our hands."

This was unanimously assented to and they instantly went to practice with the band of the Hauleca, who, as I have said before, are those who have the guard of the sultan's person. They made to them remonstrances on the subject similar to those which they had made among themselves, and required of them to slay the sultan, which they promised to do.

One day the sultan invited the knights of the Hauleca to dine with him. After the dinner, when he had taken leave of his admirals, and was about to retire to his chamber, one of these knights, who bore the sultan's sword, struck him a blow on the hand, which cut up his arm between the four fingers. The sultan, turning to his admirals, who had been the instigators of it, said, "My lords, I make my complaint to you against the knights of the Hauleca, who have endeavored to kill me, as you may see by my hand." They all replied, that it was much better he should be slain than that he murder them, as he would assuredly do if once in possession of the fortresses of Damietta.

The conspirators acted with great caution, for they ordered the sultan's trumpets and nacaires to sound for the assembling of the army to know the sultan's will. The admirals and their accomplices told them, Damietta was taken, that the sultan was marching thither, and ordered them to arm and follow him. Instantly all armed, and set off, full gallop, towards Damietta. We were much frightened, on noticing what was going forward, for we really believed Damietta had been stormed.

The sultan, though wounded, being aware of the malice of his enemies, who had conspired against his person, fled to the high tower near his chamber which I mentioned for those of the Hauleca had already destroyed his other pavilions, and were surrounding that in which he had hidden himself. Within this tower were three of how ecclesiastics, who had dined with him, who bade him descend. He replied, he would willingly descend, if they would answer for his safety but they replied that they would make him come down by force, for that he was not yet arrived at Damietta. They then discharged some Greek fire into the tower, which being made only of fir and linen cloth, as I have before said, the whole was in a blaze and I promise you, I never beheld so fine nor so sudden a bonfire.

When the sultan saw the fire gaining ground on all sides, he descended into the lawn, of which I have spoken, and ran for the river but in his flight one of the Hauleca struck him a severe blow on the ribs with a sword, and then he flung himself, with the sword in him, into the Nile. Nine other knights pursued and killed him while in the water, near the side of the galley.

One of the foresaid knights, whose name was Faracataic, seeing the sultan dead, cut him in twain, and tore the heart from his body. On coming to the king with his hands all bloody, he said, "What wilt thou give me who have slain thine enemy, who, had he lived, would have put thee to death. But the good king St. Louis made no answer whatever to this demand."

The deed being done, about thirty of them entered our galley with their swords drawn and their battle-axes on their necks. I asked Sir Baldwin Ebelin, who understood Saracenic, what they were saying. And he replied, that they said they were come to cut off our heads and shortly after I saw a large body of our men on board confessing themselves to a monk of La Trinite, who had accompanied the count of Flanders. With regard to myself, I no longer thought of any sin or evil I had done, but that I was about to receive my death in consequence, I fell on my knees at the feet of one of them, and making the sign of the cross, said, "Thus died St. Agnes." Sir Guy d'Ebelin, constable of Cyprus, knelt beside me, and confessed himself to me and I gave him such absolution as God was pleased to grant me the power of bestowing but of all the things he had said to me, when I arose up I could not remember one of them.

We were confined in the hold of the galley, and laid heads and heels together. We thought it had been so ordered because they were afraid of attacking us when we were in a body, and that they would destroy us one at a time. This danger lasted the whole night. I had my feet right on the face of the count Peter of Brittany, whose feet, in return, were beside my face. On the morrow we were taken out of the hold, and the admirals sent to inform us that we might renew the treaties we had made with the sultan. Those who were able went thither but the earl of Brittany, the constable of Cyprus, and myself, who were grievously ill, remained on board.

The earl of Flanders, the count de Soissons, and the others who had gone to parley with the admirals, related to us the convention for our delivery and the admirals promised, that as soon as Damietta should be surrendered to them, they would give liberty to the king and the other great personages now prisoners.

They told them, that had the sultan lived, he would have had the king beheaded, with the others and that, contrary to the treaties entered into, and the promises made to the king, he had already transported to Babylon several of their most considerable men that they had slain the sultan, because they knew well that the moment he should have been master of Damietta he would have had them instantly murdered, or would have put them to death when in confinement.

By this new agreement, the king was to swear to leave at their disposal 200,000 livres before he quitted the river, and the other 200,000 he should pay in Acre. They declared they would detain, for their security, all the sick in Damietta, the cross-bows, armors, machines, and salted meats, until the king should send for them, and should have paid the balance of his ransom.

The oath, which was on this occasion to be taken by the king and the admirals, was drawn up and on the part of the admirals it ran thus that in case they failed in their conventions with the king, they would own themselves dishonored like those who for their sins went on a pilgrimage to Mecca, bareheaded, or like to those who divorced their wives, and took them again. By their law, no one can divorce his wife and cohabit with her again, before he has witnessed some other person lying in bed with her. The third oath was that they would own themselves blasted and dishonored like a Saracen who should eat pork.

The king accepted the above oaths, because Master Nicolle, of Acre, who knew their manners well, assured him they could not swear more strongly. After the admirals had taken the oath above mentioned, they had one such as they wished him to take written down, and gave it to the king. This oath had been drawn up according to the advice of some renegado Christians, whom they had with them. It ran thus, that in case the king did not fulfill the conventions he had entered into with them, he might be deprived for ever of the presence of God, of his worthy mother, of the twelve apostles, and of all the saints of both sexes in Paradise. This oath the king took. The other was, that if the king broke his word he should be reputed perjured, as a Christian who had denied God, his baptism, and his faith and in despite of God would spit on his cross, and trample it under foot. But when the king heard this oath read, he declared he would never take it.

The admirals, hearing the king had refused to take the oath which they had required of him, sent in haste for Master Nicolle, of Acre, to tell him they were greatly dissatisfied with him, and discontented with the king for that they had sworn every oath he had desired, and now, in his turn, he had refused to comply with the oaths offered to him on their part. Master Nicolle told the king that he was certain, that unless he took the oaths as prescribed, the Saracens would behead him and all his people.

The king replied, that they might act according to their pleasure, but that for his part he would rather die a good Christian than live under the anger of God, his blessed mother, and his saints. At that time, the patriarch of Jerusalem was with the king; he was eighty years old, or thereabout, and had once before gained the good-will of the Saracens for the king, and was then come to him to assist in his delivery from them. It was the custom among the Pagans and Christians that in case any two princes were at war with each other, and one of them should die during the time ambassadors were sent to either, the ambassadors were, in such case, to remain prisoners, whether in pagan land or in Christendom and because the sultan, lately murdered, had granted a safe-conduct to this patriarch, he was become a prisoner to the Saracens as well as ourselves.

The admirals perceiving the king was not to be frightened by their menaces, one of them said to the others, that it was the patriarch who had thus advised him and if they would allow him to act, he would force the king to take the oath, for he would cut off the head of the patriarch, and make it fly into the king's lap. The rest would not agree to this but they seized the good patriarch, and tied him to a post in the presence of the king, and bound his hands behind his back so tightly, that they soon swelled as big as his head and the blood spouted out from several parts of his hands. From the sufferings he endured, he cried out, "Ah! sire, sire, swear boldly for I take the whole sin of it on my own soul, since it is by this means alone you may have the power to fulfill your promises." I know not whether the oath was taken at last but however that may be, the admirals at length held themselves satisfied with the oaths of the king and his lords then present.

When the knights of the Hauleca had slain the sultan, the admirals ordered their trumpets and nacaires to sound merrily before the king's tent and it was told the king, that the admirals had hoi den a council and were very desirous to elect him sultan of Babylon. The king one day asked me, if I were of opinion, that if the kingdom of Babylon had been offered him, he ought to have taken it? I answered, that if he had, he would have done a foolish thing, seeing they had murdered their lord. Notwithstanding this, the king told me he should have scarcely refused it.

This project only failed from the admirals saying among themselves, that the king was the proudest Christian they ever knew and that, if they elected him sultan, he would force them to turn Christians, or have them put to death. This they said from observing, that whenever he quitted his lodgings, he made the sign of the cross on the ground, and crossed his body all over. The Saracens added, that if their Mahomet had allowed them to suffer the manifold evils that God had caused the king to undergo, they would never have had any confidence in him, nor paid him their adorations.

Not long after the conventions had been completed between the king and the admirals, it was determined that on the morrow of the feast of the Ascension of our Lord, Damietta should be surrendered to the Turks, and the king and all the other prisoners set at liberty. Our four galleys were anchored before the bridge of Damietta, where a pavilion had been pitched for the king's landing.

About sunrise of the appointed day, Sir Geoffry de Sergines went to the town of Damietta to deliver it to the admirals, and instantly the flags of the sultan were displayed from the walls. The Saracen knights entered the town, and drank of the wines they found there, insomuch that the greater part was drunk. One of them came on board our galley with his naked sword reeking with blood, telling us that he had killed six of our countrymen, which was a brutal thing for any knight or other to boast of.

Before the surrender of Damietta, the queen had embarked with all our people on board the ships, except the poor sick, whom the Saracens were bound by their oath to take care of, and give up on the payment of 200,000 livres, as has been mentioned. They were also to restore the war machines, salted meats, which they never eat, and our armor; but these infidel dogs, on the contrary, killed all the sick, and cut to pieces the machines and other things which they had promised to take care of and restore at the proper time and place. They made a great heap of the whole, and set it on fire and it was so immense, the fire blazed from the Friday to the Sunday following.

After they had thus killed, destroyed, and set fire to all they could lay hands on, we that ought to have had our liberties at sunrise remained until sunset without eating or drinking, and the king suffered equally with us. The admirals were disputing together, and seemed inclined to put us to death. One of them, addressing the others, said, "My lords, if you will believe me and these beside me, we will kill the king and all the great persons with him, and then for forty years to come we need not fear them for their children are young, and we have possession of Damietta, which will likewise be our security."

Another Saracen, named Secrecy, a native of Morentaigne, opposed this, and remonstrated with the others, that if they should slay the king, just after they had killed their sultan, it would be said that the Egyptians were the most disloyal and iniquitous race of men in the world. The admiral who was desirous of our deaths, replied by palliating arguments. He said, that indeed they had been to blame in slaying their sultan, because it was contrary to the law of Mahomet, who had commanded them to guard their sovereign as the apple of their eye, and he showed them this commandment written down in a book which he held in his hand. "But," added he, "listen, my lords, to another commandment," and, turning over the leaves of his book, read to them the commandment of Mahomet, that for the security of the faith, the law permitted the death of an enemy. Then, turning his speech to his former purpose, he continued, "Now consider the sin we have committed in killing the sultan, against the positive command of our prophet, and the great evil we shall again do if we suffer the king to depart, and if we do not put him to death, in spite of the assurances of safety he may have had from us, for he is the greatest enemy to our law and religion."

One of the admirals that were against us, thinking we should be slain, came to the bank of the river, and shouted out in Saracen to those who were on board our galleys, and taking off his turban made signs, and told them, they were to carry us back to Babylon. The anchors were instantly raised, and we were carried a good league up the river. This caused great grief to all of us, and many tears fell from our eyes, for we now expected nothing but death.

However, as God willed it, who never is forgetful of his servants, it was agreed among the admirals, about sunset, that we should have our liberty, and we were in consequence brought back to Damietta. Our galleys were moored close to the shore, and we requested permission to land but they would not allow it until we had refreshed ourselves, for the Saracens said it would be a shame for the admirals to discharge us fasting from their prison.

Shortly after they sent us provision from the army that is to say, loaves of cheese that had been baked in the sun to prevent the worms from collecting in them, with hard eggs, which had been boiled four or five days, and the shells of which, in honor to us, they had painted with various colors. When we had eaten some little, they put us on shore, and we went towards the king, whom the Saracens were conducting from the pavilion where they had detained him, toward the water-side. There were full 20,000 Saracens on foot surrounding the king, girded with swords.

It chanced that a Genoese galley was on the river opposite to the king, on board of which there appeared but one man, who, the moment he saw the king, whistled, and instantly fourscore cross-bows, well equipped, with their bows bent and arrows placed, leaped on the deck from below. The Saracens no sooner saw them, than, panic struck they ran away like sheep, and not more than two or three stayed with the king.

The Genoese cast a plank on shore, and took on board the king, his brother the count d'Anjou, who was afterward king of Sicily, Sir Geoffry de Sergines, Sir Philip de Nemours, the marshal of France, the master of the Trinity, and myself. The count de Poitiers remained prisoner with the Saracens until the king should send the 200,000 livres which he was bound to pay before he quitted the river.

The Saturday after the Ascension, which was the morrow of our deliverance, the earl of Flanders, the count de Soissons, and many other great lords, came to take leave of the king. He entreated them to delay going until his brother, the count de Poitiers, should have his liberty but they replied it was not possible, for their galleys were on the point of sailing.

They embarked on board their galleys on their return to France, and with them was the earl of Brittany, who was grievously sick. He did not live three weeks, but died at sea.

The king, uneasy at the situation of his brother, was very anxious to pay the 200,000 livres and the whole of Saturday and Sunday were employed in it. They paid the money according to weight and each weighing was to the amount of 10,000 livres. Towards evening of the Sunday, the king's servant, occupied in this payment, sent him word they still wanted 30,000 livres. There were then with the king only the count d'Anjou, the marshal of France, the master of the Trinity and myself, all the rest being engaged in paying the ransom. I said to the king it would be much better to ask the commander and marshal of the Knights Templars to lend him the 30,000 livres to make up the sum, than to risk his brother longer with such people.

Father Stephen d'Outricourt, master of the Temple, hearing the advice I gave the king, said to me, "Lord de Joinville, the counsel you give the king is wrong and unreasonable for you know we receive every farthing on our oath and that we cannot make any payments but to those who give us their oaths in return."

The marshal of the Temple, thinking to satisfy the king, said, "Sire, don't attend to the dispute and contention of the lord de Joinville and our commander. For it is as he has said; we cannot dispose of any of the money entrusted to us, but for the means intended, without acting contrary to our oaths, and being perjured. Know, that the seneschal has ill-advised you to take by force, should we refuse you a loan but in this you will act according to your will. Should you, however, do so, we will make ourselves amends from the wealth you have in Acre." When I heard this menace from them to the king, I said to him, that if he pleased I would go and seek the sum, which he commanded me to do.

I instantly went on board one of the galleys of the Templars, and, seeing a coffer, of which they refused to give me the keys, I was about to break it open with a wedge in the king's name but the marshal, observing I was in earnest, ordered the keys to be given me. I opened the coffer, took out the sum wanting, and carried it to the king, who was much rejoiced at my return. Thus was the whole payment of the two hundred thousand livres completed for the ransom of the count de Poitiers. Before it was all paid, there were some who advised the king to withhold it until the Saracens had delivered up his brother but he replied, that since he had promised it, he would pay the whole before he quitted the river.

As he said this, Sir Philip de Montfort told the king, that the Saracens had miscounted one scale weight, which was worth ten thousand livres. The king was greatly enraged at this, and commanded Sir Philip, on the faith he owed him as his liege man, to pay the Saracens these ten thousand livres, should they in fact not have been paid. He added, that he would never depart until the uttermost penny of the two hundred thousand livres was paid.

Several persons, perceiving the king was not as yet out of danger from the Saracens, often entreated him to retire to a galley that was waiting for him at sea, to be out of their hands, and at length prevailed on him so to do, for he said that he believed he had now fulfilled his oath.

We now began to make some way at sea, and had advanced a full league without saying a word to each other on the concern we felt to have left the count de Poitiers in prison. In a very short time, Sir Philip de Montfort, who had remained to make good the payment of the ten thousand livres, approached us, calling out to the king, "Sire, sire, wait for your brother the count de Poitiers, who is following you in this other galley." The king then said to those near him, "Light up, light up!" and there was great joy among us all on the arrival of the king's brother. A poor fisherman having hastened to the countess of Poitiers, and told her he had seen the count at liberty from the Saracens, she ordered twenty livres parisis to be given him, and each then went to his galley.

Before I quit the subject of Egypt, I wish not to forget any occurrences that happened while we were there. I shall first speak of Sir Gaultier de Chastillon, and say, that I heard from a knight, that he had seen him post himself with his drawn sword in a street at Casel, where the king was made prisoner, and, whenever any Turks passed that street, he attacked and drove them before him with hard blows as they fled, they discharged arrows at him, with which he was covered ; and, when Sir Walter had put them to flight, he picked the arrows out of his body, and re-armed himself. He was a long time thus engaged and the knight saw him rise in his stirrups, and call out, "Ha! Chastillon, chevalier, where are my good companions?" but not one was with him.

One day afterward, as I was conversing with the admiral of the galleys, I inquired of all his men-at-arms if there were any one who could give me an account of what was become of him, but I could hear nothing. At length, I met with a knight called Sir John Frumons, who told me, that as they were carrying him prisoner, he saw a Turk on the horse of Sir Gaultier de Chastillon, whose tail and rump were covered with blood and when he asked him what was become of the knight to whom that horse belonged, he replied, that he had cut his throat while on horseback, and that he was thus covered with his blood.

There was a most valiant man in our army whose name was Sir James du Chastel, bishop of Soissons, who when he saw we were going towards Damietta, and that every one was impatient to return to France, preferred living with God to returning to where he was born. In consequence, he made a charge on the Turks, as if he alone meant to combat their army but they soon sent him to God, and placed him in the company of martyrs, for they killed him in a very short time.

Another thing I witnessed. As the king was waiting on the river the completion of the payment of the ransom for his brother, the count de Poitiers, a handsome and well dressed Saracen came up, and presented him with some lard in pots, and a variety of sweet-smelling flowers, telling the king it was the children of the nazac of the sultan of Egypt, who had been murdered, that sent him this gift.

The king, hearing the Saracen address him in French, asked him where he had learnt it.

He replied that he was a Christian renegado on which the king bade him withdraw, for he would not say any more to him. I took him aside, and inquired who he was, and why he had become a renegado. The Saracen told me, "that he was born in Provence, and had followed King John to Egypt, where he was married, and had a very considerable property." I said to him, "And do you not know, that if you were to die in such a state, you would descend straight to hell, and be damned forever?" He replied, "that he knew it well, and that there was not a better religion than that of the Christians but I fear, were I to return with you, I should suffer great poverty, and be continually reproached all my days by being called 'Renegado, renegado' I had rather, therefore, live at my ease, like a rich man, than become such an object of contempt."

I remonstrated with him, that it was much better to suffer the scorn of the world, since at the day of judgment every evil deed would be made manifest to all, and then damnation would follow. But all this was to no purpose, and when he quitted me I never saw him more.

You have had related the great persecutions and miseries the good king St. Louis and we all suffered in Egypt. You must know also, that the good queen was not without her share, and very bitter to her heart, as you shall soon hear. Three days before she was brought to bed, she was informed that the good king, her husband, had been made prisoner, which so troubled her mind, that she seemed continually to see her chamber filled with Saracens ready to slay her and she incessantly kept crying out, "Help, help" when there was not a soul near her. For fear the fruit of her womb should perish, she made a knight watch at the foot of her bed all night without sleeping. This knight was very old, not less than eighty years, or perhaps more and every time she screamed he held her hands, and said, "Madam, do not be thus alarmed; I am with you quit these fears."

Before the good lady was brought to bed, she ordered every person to leave her chamber except this ancient knight, when she cast herself out of bed on her knees before him, and requested that he would grant her a boon. The knight, with an oath, promised compliance. The queen then said, "Sir knight, I request, on the oath you have sworn, that should the Saracens storm this town and take it, you will cut off my head before they seize my person." The knight replied, that he would cheerfully so do, and that he had before thought of it, in case such an event should happen.

The queen was, shortly after, delivered of a son in the town of Damietta, whose name was John, and his surname Tristan, because he had been born in misery and poverty. The day she was brought to bed it was told her, that the Pisans, the Genoese, and all the poorer commonalty that were in the town, were about to fly and leave the king.

The queen sent for them, and addressed them,—"Gentlemen, I beg of you, for the love of God, that you will not think of quitting this town for you well know if you do, that my lord the king, and his whole army, will be ruined. At least, if such be your fixed determination, have pity on this wretched person who now lies in pain, and wait until she be recovered, before you put it into execution."

They answered they could not remain longer in a town where they were dying of hunger. She said, they should never die of hunger; for that she would buy up all the provision that was in the place, and retain it henceforward in the name of the king. This she was obliged to do and all the provision that could be found was bought up, which, on her recovery a little time after, cost her upwards of three hundred and sixty thousand livres to feed these people. Notwithstanding this, the good lady was forced to rise before she was perfectly recovered, and set out for the city of Acre, for Damietta was to be surrendered to the Turks and Saracens.

It should be known, that although the king had suffered such a variety of woes, his attendants, when he embarked, had not made any preparations for him on board, such as robes, bed, bedding, and other necessary things. He was thus forced, for six days, to sleep on mattresses, until we arrived at Acre. The king had not any other habiliments but two robes which the sultan had caused to be made for him they were of a black silken staff, lined with squirrel skins, with a number of golden buttons.

While we were on our voyage to Acre, on account of illness, I was always seated near the king and it was then he related to me how he had been taken, and how, through the aid of God, he had accomplished his own ransom and ours. I was likewise obliged to tell him how I had been captured on the river, and how a Saracen had saved my life. The king said, I ought to feel myself under the greatest obligations to our Lord, who had delivered me from such imminent dangers. At times, the good and holy king bewailed bitterly the death of his brother the count d'Artois.

He one day inquired what his brother the count d'Anjou was doing, and complained, that notwithstanding they were in the same galley, he never once thought of being in his company a single day. When the king was told that he was playing at tables with Sir Walter de Nemours, he arose hastily, though from his severe illness he could scarcely stand, and went staggering to where they were at play, when, seizing the dice and tables, he flung them into the sea, and was in a violent passion with his brother for so soon thinking of thus amusing himself by gaming, forgetful of the death of his brother the count d'Artois, and of the great perils from which the Lord had delivered them. But Sir Walter de Nemours suffered most, for the king flung all the money that lay on the tables after them into the sea.

After these words, the Poitiers edition contains a whole chapter, which is wanting in the edition of Menard, in the following terms:—

"When we arrived before Acre, the citizens came out to meet the king as far as the shore with grand processions and received him joyfully."

"I attempted to mount the palfrey that had been brought for me from the town; but I was no sooner mounted than I fainted, and should have fallen to the ground had it not been for him who brought the horse, who held me tight, and with much difficulty I was led to the king's house. I remained some time at a window without any one taking the least notice of me, and of all those whom I had brought to Egypt I had occupy with me, a young boy, called Bartholomew, the bastard-son of the lord Ame de Montbelliar, lord of Montfaucon, of whom I have before spoken."

"As I was there waiting, a youth came to me dressed in scarlet striped with yellow, and, having saluted me, asked if I did not know him. On my saying I did not, he told me he was a native of Chasteau-Descler that belonged to my uncle. He asked if I would take him into my service, for he was without a master. This I readily agreed to, and retained him as my varlet. He soon after brought me clean coffees, and combed my hair exceedingly well. At this time, the king sent for me to come to dinner; I went, attended by my new varlet, who carved before me, and found means to get a sufficiency for himself and the young boy."

"After the dinner this varlet, whose name was Guillemin, obtained for me a lodging near the baths, that I might wash and clean myself from the filth I had gained in prison. Towards evening, he put me into a bath but I had no sooner entered it than I again fainted and fell backwards in the water, so that with much trouble they drew me out alive, and carried me to my chamber. You must know, that I had only a poor jacket for my dress, nor any money in my pocket to buy better clothing, or to support me in my illness. This affected me very much, and I suffered more from the extreme indigence I was in, than from the pains of my disorder."

"As I was in this distress, most fortunately a knight came to visit me, whose name was Sir Peter de Bourbrainne, and seeing my miserable state, he comforted me to the best of his power, and caused cloth to be given me to new-dress myself, by a merchant o Acre, to whom he gave his own security for the due payment."

"At the end of three days, when I was somewhat better and stronger. I went to the king, who blamed me much for having been so long absent, and charged me, as I valued his love, not to fail partaking of his meals morning and evening, until he should determine to remain there, or return to France. While with the king, I complained to him of the lord Peter de Courcenay, who owed me 400 livres of my pay, and refused to give it me and the king ordered the 400 livres to be instantly paid me, to my great joy, for I did not possess a single farthing.

"When I had received my money, Sir Peter de Bourbrainne advised me to keep only forty livres for my expenses, and to give the remainder to the governor of the palace of the Templars to keep for me, which I willingly did. Having spent the forty livres, I sent for as much more; but this governor bade them tell me, that he had not any money of mine, and, what was worse, that he did not know me."

On the receipt of this answer, I went to the master of the Templars, whose name was Father Regnaut de Yichiers, to whom I carried intelligence of the king, and then told him the treatment I had met with, and complained to him of the governor of the palace, for not restoring to me the money I had entrusted to his care. But I had no sooner ended, than he flew into a violent passion, and said, "Lord de Joinville, I love you very much, but I shall cease doing so, if you hold such language, for it seems to be insinuated, by what you complain of, that our brotherhood are all thieves." I replied, that so far from being silent, I would make the matter public, for that I was in such want of my money I had not a penny to support me, and, without a word more, left him.

"I can assure you I was during four days in the utmost uneasiness about my money, and knew not to what saint to make my vows, to recover it. These four days I did nothing but run about, seeking means to regain it. On the fifth the master of the Templars accosted me with a smile, and told me he had found my money, and instantly gave me the amount, to my great joy, as I was in very great need of it and I took good care, in future, not to trouble these monks with the keeping of my cash."

At this place I must relate some great persecutions and evils that befel me when at Acre, but from which those two, in whom I had my whole confidence, our Lord God and the blessed Virgin Mary, relieved me. This I say as an encouragement to such as may read my book, to have a perfect confidence in God, and patience in their adversities and tribulations, when he will aid them, as he has done me, many and many times.

On the king's arrival before Acre, the inhabitants of that city came out in grand procession to meet him on the sea-shore, and received him with much joy. Soon after, the king sent for me, and expressly commanded me, as I valued his love, to come and eat with him morning and evening, until he should determine whether to return to France or to remain there.

I was lodged with the rector of Acre, for there the bishop had fixed my residence, and was most grievously ill. Of all my servants, there was but one that was not confined to his bed with sickness like myself; nor had I any to comfort me, by once offering me something to drink. The more to enliven me, I saw daily pass my window twenty corpses for burial and when I heard the chant, "Libera me Domine." I shed floods of tears, and cried out to God that he would mercifully save me and my household from the pestilence that then raged. And this he did.

Not long after the king's arrival at Acre he summoned his brothers, and all the other nobles, on a certain Sunday, and, when assembled, he addressed them: "My lords, I have called you together, to give you some news from France. In truth, my lady-mother, the queen, has sent for me, and it is necessary that I return with the utmost haste, for my kingdom is in great danger, inasmuch as there exists neither peace nor truce with the king of England. The people here wish to detain me, assuring me that if I depart their country will be destroyed, and insist on following me. I beg you will maturely consider what I have said, and give me your opinions within eight days."

On the Sunday following, we all presented ourselves before the king to give him our opinions, as he had charged us, whether he should depart or stay. Sir Guion de Malvoisin was our spokesman, and said, "Sire, my lords your brothers, and the other nobles now present, have fully considered your situation, and they are of opinion, that you cannot remain longer in this country with honor to yourself or profit to your kingdom. For, in the first place, of all the knights whom you led to Cyprus, amounting to 2,800, not one hundred remain. Secondly, you have not any habitation in this country, nor have your army any money for these reasons, which we have maturely weighed, we unanimously advise that you return to France to reinforce yourself with men-at-arms, and supply yourself with money, so that you may hastily repair again hither, and take vengeance on the enemies of God and of his holy religion."

The king was not pleased with this advice of Sir Guy, but demanded from each person his private opinion on the business, beginning with the counts d'Anjou, de Poitiers, and the other nobles near him. All of them replied, they agreed in the advice of Sir Guy de Malvoisin. The count de Japhe was hard pressed to give his opinion, for he had castles and possessions in those countries ; but when the king insisted on having it, he said, that if the king could keep the field, it would redound more to his honor to remain, than thus discomfited to return. I, who was the fourteenth in rank, answered in my turn that I was of the same opinion with the count de Japhe; moreover, giving these additional reasons, that it was reported the king had not as yet expended any of the money from the royal treasury, but had employed that which was in the hands of the clerks of finance and that the king should send to the Morea, and the adjoining countries, to seek powerful reinforcements of men-at-arms, who, when they should learn the high pay the king was willing to give, would hasten to join him from all parts, and by this means the king might deliver the multitude of poor prisoners who had been captured in the service of God, which would never be the case unless it were done as now proposed.

You must know that at this moment none reproved me for my opinion, but many began to weep, for there was scarcely one among us who had not some of his relations in the prisons of the Saracens.

Sir William de Belmont spoke next, and said that my advice was very good, and that he agreed in it. When all had delivered their opinions, the king was much confounded at their diversity, and took eight days more to declare which he should follow. When we had left the presence of the king, the great nobles made a violent attack on me, and, through jealousy and envy, said, "Ha! Certainly the king must be mad, if he do not follow your opinion, lord de Joinville, in preference to that of the whole French council." But to this I made not any reply.

The tables were soon after laid for dinner, and the king, who had usually made me sit down near him when his brothers were absent and during the repasts had conversed with me, did not now open his lips, nor even turn his face toward me. I then thought he was displeased with me for having said that he had not employed his own money, when he had expended such very large sums. After he had said grace, and returned thanks to God for his dinner, I retired to a window near the head of the kings bed, and, passing my hand through the grating, remained there musing. I said to myself, that if the king should now return to France, I would go to the prince of Antioch, who was a relation of mine.

While I was thus meditating, the king leant on my shoulders, and held my head between his hands. I thought it was Sir Philip de Nemours, who had been fretting me all the day for the advice which I had given the king, and said to him, M Sir Philip, do leave me quiet in my misfortune." As I turned round, the king covered my face with his hands, and I then knew it was the king from an emerald on his finger. I wished to make some reparation, as one that had improperly spoken but the king made me be silent, and continued, "Now, lord de Joinville, tell me how you, who are so young a man, could have the courage to advise me to remain in these countries contrary to the opinion of all my greatest nobles?" I replied, that if I had advised him well, he should follow it; if the contrary, he ought not to think more on what I had said. u And will you remain with me, if I should stay?" "Yes, certainly," answered I, "were it at my own or at another's expense." The king said that he was pleased with the advice I had given, but ordered me to tell this to no one.

I was so rejoiced that whole week with what he had told me that I was insensible to my illness, and defended myself boldly against the other lords when they attacked me.

You must know, in these countries the peasant is called Poulain, and I was told by my cousin Sir Peter d'Avallon, that I was called Poulain, because I had advised the king to remain with the Poulains. This information he gave me, that I might defend myself against those who should call me so, and tell them that I would rather be a Poulain than such recreant knights as themselves.

On the Sunday we all again assembled in the presence of the king, who began by signing himself with the cross, saying that it was from the instructions of his mother he did so, who had thus ordered him, and likewise to invoke the name of God and the aid of his Holy Spirit, whenever he was about to make a speech. He then continued: "My lords, I feel equally thankful to those who have advised our return to France as to those who have recommended our stay here. But, since I last saw you, I have fully considered this matter, and believe, that should we remain here, my kingdom will not the sooner be in great danger from it; for my lady-mother the queen has a sufficiency of men-at-arms to defend it. I have thought much on what the knights of this country say, that if I depart, the kingdom of Jerusalem will be lost, since no one will remain here after me. Now, my lords, having told my resolution, let such speak out boldly who wish to remain with me and I promise to give them emoluments, that the fault shall not be mine but their own, if they do not remain. Those that may not choose to stay, God be with them."

When the king had done speaking, several were as if thunderstruck, and began to weep bitterly. After the king had declared his resolution, he gave permission to his brothers to return to France but I know not if he did this at their requests, or whether it was the will of the king. This passed about St. John Baptist's day.

Shortly after the departure of his brothers for France, the king was impatient to learn what success those who had stayed with him had met with in recruiting his men-at-arms. On the feast-day of St. James, whose pilgrim I was, for the manifold kindness he had shown me, the king, after mass, retired to his chamber, and called to him the chiefs of his council, namely, Sir Peter the chamberlain, who was the most loyal and upright man I ever saw of the king's household, that good knight Sir Geoffry de Sergines, the discreet Sir Giles le Brun, and others, among whom was that prudent man, to whom the king, after the death of Sir Hymbert de Beaujeu, had given the constable's sword. He asked them what numbers and sort of men they had collected for the reinforcement of his army, and with warmth continued,—"You know that it is about a month since I have declared my intention to stay here, and I have not as yet had intelligence that you have raised any reinforcements of knights or others."

To this Sir Peter the chamberlain replied, in the name of the council—"Sire, we have not hitherto done any thing, nor do we think we shall ever accomplish it for every one demands such a price, and so great pay, that we are afraid of promising to give them what they ask." The king would know to whom they had spoken, and those who had demanded such great pay. They unanimously replied, that it was I, and that I would not be satisfied with a trifle. All this I overheard, as I was in the king's apartment and the council had told the king these things of me, because I had advised him, contrary to their opinion, to remain, and had thus prevented their return to France.

The king sent for me on my entrance, I cast myself on my knees before him; when, making me rise and seat myself, he said,—"Seneschal, you know full well the confidence I have in you, and how much you are beloved by me. My council, notwithstanding this, assure me, that you are so hard to deal with, that they cannot satisfy you in regard to the pay they are willing to give you. How is this?"

"Sire," replied I, "I know not what they may have reported to you; but in regard to myself, if I demand a good salary, I cannot avoid it for you know, that when I was made prisoner on the Nile, I lost every thing I had, except what was on my body, and I cannot maintain my people on a little."

The king then asked how much I would have for the support of my company until next Easter, which was nearly half a year. I answered two thousand livres. "Now tell me," continued the king, "have you no knights here with you?" "Yes, sire, I made Sir Peter de Pontmolain remain, who is the third under my banner and he costs me four hundred livres." The king, then reckoning on his fingers, said, "Your knights and men-at-arms then cost you twelve hundred livres." I then said, "Consider, sire, if I must not require full eight hundred livres to equip myself with horses and armor, and to provide a table for my knights until Easter." The king then told his council that he could not think my demands extravagant; and said to me, that he retained me in his service.

Not long after this, the emperor of Germany sent an embassy to the king, with credential letters, to say that he had written to the sultan of Babylon, of whose death he was ignorant, to give credit to those he sent to him, and, cost what it would, to deliver the king of France and his army from their captivity. But I well remember, that several said they believed the emperor wished to find them still prisoners for they suspected, that his motive in sending this embassy was to cause us to be more straightly confined, and more heavily oppressed. When the ambassadors found us at liberty, they returned to the emperor.

After this embassy was departed, there arrived at Acre another from the sultan of Damascus to the king. The sultan complained, in his letter, of the admirals of Egypt, for having put to death their sultan, who was his cousin. He offered, if the king would assist him against them to deliver up the kingdom of Jerusalem, which they held. The king replied to these ambassadors, that if they would retire to their lodgings, which had been prepared for them, they should shortly have an answer on the subject on which the sultan of Damascus had written to him. To this they consented and the king resolved, in council, to send his answer by the ambassadors: but that they should be accompanied by a monk, called Father Yves le Breton, who was of the order of Preaching Friars.

Father Yves was sent for, and dispatched to the ambassadors, of the sultan, to say, the king had ordered him to accompany them to Damascus, to inform the sultan what were the king's intentions respecting the Saracens. This Father Yves did but I must relate an incident which I heard from him. On going from the king's residence to the lodgings of the ambassadors, he met a very old woman in the street, having in her right hand a porringer full of fire, and in her left a phial of water. Father Yves asked, "Woman, what art thou going to do with this fire and water which thou art carrying." She replied, that with the fire she wished to burn paradise, and with the after to drown hell, so that there should be never more a paradise or hell. The friar asked why she uttered such words. "Because," she said, "I wish not that any one should do good for the reward of paradise, nor avoid evil from fear of hell but every good ought to be done from the perfect and sincere love we owe to our Creator, God, who is the supreme good, and who loved us so much that he suffered death for our redemption which death he submitted to for the sin of our first father, Adam, and for our salvation."

During the king's residence at Acre, there came likewise to him ambassadors from the prince of the Bedouins, called the Old Man of the Mountain. After the king had attended mass in the morning, he would hear what these ambassadors had to say. On their entrance, the king caused them to be seated, to deliver their message when one of the chiefs began by asking the king if he were acquainted with their lord, the prince of the mountain. The king said he was not he had never seen him, although he had heard much spoken of him. The chief continued: "Sire, since you have heard my lord spoken of, I wonder much that you have not sent him such of your people as should have made him your friend, in like manner as the emperor of Germany, the king of Hungary, the sultan of Babylon, and many other princes have yearly done for they know well that they would not be allowed to exist or reign, but during his good pleasure. For this cause he has dispatched us hither to advertise you, that he wills you should act in the like manner, or at least that you acquit him of the tribute he pays annually to the grand master of the Temple, or of the Hospital, and if you do this, he will consider it as paid to himself. My lord says truly, that should he destroy the master of the Temple, or of the Hospital, there would soon be others as good, and for this reason he is unwilling to risk his people's lives where little is to be gained."

The king replied, that he would consider what they had said, and if they would return in the evening they should have his answer. When they came again before the king, it was about vespers, and they found the master of the Temple on one side of him, and the master of the Hospital on the other. The king, on their entrance, ordered them to repeat what they had before said to him, as well as the demand which they had made in the morning. They replied, that they should not think it right to repeat what they had said, except in the presence of such as had heard them in the morning. The masters of the Temple, and of the Hospital, on this ordered them to repeat it. The chief then repeated what he had said before to the king, as has been mentioned.

The masters, on hearing it, bade them come and confer with them in the morning, and they should then know the king's pleasure. On the morrow, when they were before the masters of the Temple and Hospital, they told them, that their lord had very foolishly and impudently sent such a message to the king of France, and had used such harsh expressions, that were it not unbecoming the honor of the king, on the account of their being invested with the character of ambassadors, he would have had them thrown into the filthy sea of Acre, and drowned, in despite of their master. "And we command you," continued the masters, "to return to your lord, and to come back within fifteen days with such letters from your prince, that the king shall be contented with him and with you."

Before the fifteen days were expired, the same ambassadors returned from the prince of the mountain, and addressing the king, said, "Sire, we are come back from our lord, who informs you, that as the shirt is the part of dress nearest to the body, he sends you this, his shirt, as a gift, or a symbol that you are the king for whom he has the greatest affection, and which he is most desirous to cultivate and, for a further assurance of it, here is his ring that he sends you, which is of pure gold, and hath his name engraven on it and with this ring our lord espouses you, and understands that henceforward you be as one of the fingers of his hand."

Among other presents sent to the king were an elephant of crystal, figures of men of different crystals, the whole set in fine pieces of amber with borders of pure gold. You must know that when the ambassadors opened the case that contained all these fine things, the whole apartment was instantly embalmed with the sweet odor of their perfumes.

The king, desirous not to be behindhand in making a return for these presents from the old prince of the mountain, sent to him, by his ambassadors, and by Father Yves Le Breton, who understood the Saracenic, great quantities of scarlet robes, cups of gold, and other vessels of silver. When Father Yves was in the presence of the prince of the Bedouins, he conversed with him on the articles of his faith but, as he afterward reported to the king, he found he did not believe in Mahomet, but followed the religion of Aly, who was, he said, the uncle of Mahomet. He told him, that it was Aly to whom Mahomet was indebted for all the honors he enjoyed; and that, when Mahomet had made his great conquests over mankind, he quarreled with and separated from Aly, who perceiving the pride of Mahomet, and that he wished to trample upon him, began to draw as many as he could to his doctrines, and retired to a part of the deserts and mountains of Egypt, where he gave them a different creed from that of Mahomet. Those who support the religion of Aly call those who follow Mahomet unbelievers, as the Mahometans in like manner style the Bedouins infidels. Each party, in this respect, says the truth, for in fact they are both unbelievers.

One of the points of doctrine of Aly consists in the belief, that when any one is killed by the command or in the service of his superior, the soul of the person so killed goes into another body of higher rank, and enjoys more comforts than before. It is for this reason that the Bedouins of the mountain are ambitious to be killed in the service of their prince, in the expectation of enjoying the above recompense.

Another point is that no man can die before his predetermined day. This the Bedouins so firmly believe, that they never go in armor to battle for, if they did, they would think they were acting contrary to the dogmas of their faith. When they swear at their children, they usually say, "Mayest thou be cursed like him who arms himself for fear of death," which, they think, every one should be ashamed of. This is an absurd error; for it supposes that God, who is all-powerful, cannot abridge or lengthen life at his pleasure. It is also false, for in Him alone resides omnipotency.

While Father Yves Le Breton was on his embassy to the Old Man of the Mountain, he one day found at the head of the prince's bed a small book, in which were written many of the excellent words that our Savior had said to Peter during his residence on earth, and prior to his passion. Father Yves, having read them, said, "Ah! my lord! the frequent reading of this book will do you much good for, small as it may be, it contains many excellent things."

The Old Man of the Mountain replied, that he frequently read it, as he had great faith in St. Peter. He continued, "In the beginning of the world, the soul of Abel, after his brother Cain had murdered him, entered the body of Noah and the soul of Noah, on his decease, went into the body of Abraham and after Abraham it entered the body of St. Peter, who is now under the earth."

Yves, hearing him thus talk, argued with him on the absurdity of his belief, and showed him many fair promises and commandments of God, but he would never have any faith in them. Father Yves reported to the king, that when the prince of the Bedouins took the field, he was preceded by a man carrying his battle-axe, the handle of which was covered with silver and this handle served as a case for a number of sheep knives. The bearer cried out with a loud voice in his language, "Turn back ! fly from before him who carries the deaths of kings in his hands."

I have delayed informing you of the answer which the king made to the ambassadors from Damascus. It was to this effect that the king would send to the admirals of Egypt to know if they were willing to re-establish the truce they had promised, but which they had already broken, as has been said, and, should they refuse, the king would very willingly join his forces, and assist him in revenging the murder of his cousin the sultan of Babylon.

After this, the king, during the time he was at Acre, sent Sir John de Vallance to the admirals in Egypt, to require them to make such satisfaction to the king for the outrages they had committed, contrary to treaty, that he should be contented with them. This admirals promised to do, but on condition that he would unite himself with them against the sultan of Damascus before mentioned. To gain the king's heart, after that wise man Sir John de Vallance had strongly remonstrated with and severely blamed them for the wrongs they had done contrary to their law, and for breaking the truce they had solemnly sworn to keep, they sent to the king all the knights whom they had detained in their prisons. They likewise sent him the bones of the count Walter de Brienne, that they might be buried in consecrated ground.

Sir John de Vallance brought back with him 200 knights, without including great numbers of common people who had been confined in the Saracen prisons. On his arrival at Acre, Madame de Secte, cousin-german to the count de Brienne, received his bones, and had them interred well and honorably in the church of the Knights Hospitallers at Acre. The funeral service was grand, and attended by every knight, who made his offering of a waxen taper and a silver penny. The king offered a taper, and a golden bezant of the coinage of Madame de Secte, which caused every one to wonder, for he was never before known to make an offering of any coin but his own. He did this, however, out of compliment to Madame de Secte.

Among the knights whom Sir John de Vallance had brought with him from Egypt, I was acquainted with forty at least, attached to the count of Champagne, who were in a most ragged and dirty condition. These forty I had new dressed at my own expense, and, clothed in coats and surcoats of green, I conducted them to the presence of the king and entreated that he would detain them in his service.

The king, having heard my request, made not a word of reply but one of his council then present reproved me, saying, that I did very ill to make such requests to the king, who had already exceeded the state of his income by 7,000 livres. I replied, that misfortunes make people speak for that among us of Champagne we had lost in the service of the king at least five-and-thirty knights bannerets of the count of Champagne, adding, that the king would not act properly if he did not retain them, seeing the want he was in of knights. As I said this, I began to weep, when the king appeased me, by granting what I had asked; he retained all the knights, and added them to my battalion.

When the king had given audience to the ambassadors from the admirals of Egypt who had accompanied Sir John de Vallance, and learnt that they were impatient to return, he told them, that he would not enter into any negotiation with them for a truce until they should have restored all the heads of the Christians which were hanging on the walls of Quassere, from the time the counts of Montfort and of Bar were made prisoners. They were likewise to send him all children whom they had taken when young, and had forced to deny the Christian religion and believe in their faith and, beside these two articles, they were to send an acquittance for the 200,000 livres which were still owing to them.

The king ordered Sir John de Vallance to return with the ambassadors, on account of his consummate wisdom and valor, to announce this answer to the admirals.

About this time the king left Acre, and went to Caesarea with all his people, and had the walls and fortifications of that place repaired, which the Saracens had broken down and destroyed. Caesarea is full twelve leagues from Acre, on the road to Jerusalem. I know not how it happened, except by the will of God who can do as he lists, but during the year that the king stayed at Caesarea to repair it, no attack was made upon him, nor harm done to him, nor to the few men-at-arms that were left at Acre.

I have before said that ambassadors had come to the king from the great cham of Tartary during our residence at Cyprus. They assured the king they were come to assist him in the conquest of Jerusalem from the Saracens. The king sent them back, and with them two notable Friars Preachers, who carried as a present to the cham of Tartary a tent in the form of a chapel, the lining of which was of scarlet cloth, embroidered over with the history of our religion; the Annunciation of the angel Gabriel, the Nativity, the Baptism of our Lord, the Passion, the Ascension, and the Descent of the Holy Ghost. The king sent also chalices, books, ornaments, and every thing necessary for saying mass; and, as I have since heard these ambassadors tell the king, they embarked for the port of Antioch, and in going from thence to the place where the cham of Tartary resided, they were occupied for a whole year, traveling ten leagues a day. They found the country through which they passed subject to the Tartars, and saw in different towns on their road large mounds of bones.

The ambassadors inquired how they could have conquered so large a tract of country, and destroyed such numbers of people, whose bones they had seen piled up. The Tartars described to them their manners, beginning from their first origin, saying they were sprung from a great berrie in a plain where nothing grew. This berrie was placed under a rock, so very high that no one could pass it, and pointed toward the east. The Tartars told them, that between this, and other rocks towards the extremity of the earth, were enclosed the people of Gog and Magog, who were to attend Antichrist when he should come, at the end of the world, to make a general destruction.

From this same berrie came the Tartars that are subject to Prester John II on the one side, and to the emperor of Persia on the other, which empire was joined to them also by a narrow tract of land.

There were many infidel nations intermixed with them, to whom they were forced to pay a yearly tribute, for themselves and for the pasturage of their herds, which were their sole nourishment.

The Tartars added, that this Prester John, the emperor of Persia, and the other kings to whom they were tributary, held them in great abhorrence and hatred for when they carried them their tribute, they would not receive it in their presence, but turned their backs on them. This conduct was the cause that one of their wise men went from berrie to berrie, stating to the inhabitants the wretched condition they were in, and remonstrating on the base slavery they were suffering from various princes, and recommended that they should take counsel together on the best means of extricating themselves from the debasing condition in which they were now kept. This wise man worked so effectually on their minds, that there was a general assembly appointed at the berrie nearest to the lands of Prester John. After many remonstrances, this wise man prevailed on them to act as he should advise they only requested him to be prudent in adopting the best means to accomplish his purposes.

He told them, they would never be successful until they should have a king to be master and lord over them, and whom they must obey in whatsoever he commanded. The manner in which he proposed they should elect a king was as follows of the fifty-two tribes of which the Tartars were composed, each tribe should bring him an arrow marked with the name and seal of the tribe. This was agreed to by all the people and when done, the whole fifty-two arrows were placed before a child of five years old, and from the tribe whose arrow the child should pick, the king was to be chosen.

The child having taken an arrow, all the tribes were ordered to retire and fifty-two men, the most learned and valiant, were selected from the tribe to whom the arrow belonged, among whom was their adviser; and each of them holding an arrow apart signed with his name, they made a child of five years old take one of these arrows, the owner of which was to be their king or ruler. By accident the choice of the child fell on the arrow of him who had proposed the measure, to the great joy of the whole nation. Having caused silence to be proclaimed, he said— "Gentlemen, if you wish that I should be your lord, you will swear by Him who made the heavens and earth, that you will obey my commands." And they all took the oath.

After this, he gave them many useful instructions, very excellent for keeping a nation in peace at home. One of his regulations was, that no one should seize the goods of another without his will, nor to his loss and that no one should strike another, under pain of his hand being cut off". Another, that no one should force the wife or daughter of any one, under penalty of death. Many other good laws did he promulgate for the preservation of peace among them.

Having given them these instructions, he remonstrated with them on their ancient enemy Prester John, and how great his hatred was against them and, in conclusion, said, "Now, as I am determined to attack him, I order you all to be ready tomorrow to follow me. Should it so happen that we be defeated, which God forbid, each of you must do the best he can to save himself. Should the victory be ours, I strictly command that it be followed up with courage, should the combat last three days and three nights, without any one daring to think of pillage, but all must be solely occupied with destroying and putting to death the enemy for when the victory shall be completely gained, I will so honorably divide the plunder among you, that every one shall be satisfied." He was heard with pleasure, and his orders unanimously obeyed.

On the morrow, according to what had been proposed, so did they act. They made a very severe inroad on their enemies, and according to the will of God, who is all powerful, they defeated them, and put to death every one that had defensive arms in his hand. But those that wore a religious dress, and the priests, were spared. The rest of the nation, under Prester John, who were not engaged in battle, submitted, and placed themselves under their dominion.

A wonderful thing happened after this conquest. A great chief of one of the tribes before spoken of was missing from the Tartars three days, without any thing being known of him. On his return, he told his people that ho thought he had been absent but one night, and that he had not suffered hunger or thirst. He related, that he had ascended a marvelous high hill, where he had seen the handsomest race of men, and the finest dressed, that he had ever beheld in his life. In the centre of this hill a king was seated on a throne of gold, who was superior in beauty and dress to all the others on his right and left were six kings richly adorned with jewels, and with crowns on their heads. Near to him, on his right, was a queen on her knees, who begged and entreated him to consider his people. On his left a most beautiful youth knelt, having two wings as brilliant as the sun and around the king were great numbers of handsome winged attendants.

The king called him to him, and said, "Thou art come from the host of the Tartars." "Sire," replied I, "I am." "Thou wilt return thither and tell the chain of Tartary that thou hast seen me, who am the Lord of heaven and earth and that I order him to render me thanks and praise for the victory I have granted him over Prester John and his nation and thou wilt tell him from me, that I give him power to subdue the whole earth." "Sire," answered the chief, "how will the cham of Tartary believe me." "Thou wilt tell him he shall believe in thee from the following circumstance that thou shalt go and combat the emperor of Persia with three hundred of thy men, and that, through me, thou shalt vanquish the emperor of Persia, although he will advance to combat thee with three hundred thousand men-at-arms and upwards. But before thou think of fighting with the emperor of Persia, thou wilt demand of the cham of Tartary, that he give up to thee all priests, the monks, and the commonalty who have remained of those taken in the battle with Prester John and thou wilt believe all they shall say and show to thee, for they are my people and my servants." "Sire," replied the Tartar chief, "I shall never find my way, unless you cause me to be conducted." The king, on this, turned round, and said, "Come hither, George; go and conduct this man to his quarters, and let him be restored safe" and instantly this chief was transported among the Tartars.

On his return, all the host of the Tartars came to see him, and made him good cheer. He very soon demanded the priests and monks from the cham of Tartary, according to the instructions he had received from the king on the mount, who were granted to him. This prince of the Tartars received very kindly the doctrines they taught, and all his people were baptized. When this ceremony was over, he selected 300, made them confess themselves and get ready, and thence marched to attack the emperor of Persia, whom he defeated, and drove out of his kingdom and possessions. He fled as far as Jerusalem and it was he who vanquished our people, and made the count Gautier de Brienne prisoner, as you shall hear related. The subjects of this Christian prince increased so much, according to the information I had from those whom the king had sent as ambassadors to Tartary that they counted in his army 800 chapels on wheels.

But let us now return to my principal subject. During the time the king was fortifying Caesarea, as I have before noticed, there came to him a knight called Sir Elenars de Seningaan, who said he had set out from the kingdom of Norone, where he had embarked, and coasting Spain, had passed the Straits of Morocco and that he had run great hazards and suffered much evil before he could come to us. The king retained this knight, with ten others of his companions. I heard him say, that the nights in the land of Norone, during the summer, were so short, that you could see in the latest part of them. When this knight became acquainted with the country, he and his people began to hunt the lions, many of which they took, but not without much bodily danger.

Their manner of hunting was on horseback and when they found a lion, they shot at him at a proper distance from their bow or cross-bow. On the lion being wounded, he ran at the first he saw, who instantly spurred his horse to a full gallop, dropping as he fled some piece of old cloth or coverlid, which the lion seized and tore to pieces, imagining it was the man he was in pursuit of. As the lion was employed in tearing the cloth, others advanced and shot at him, which made him again pursue them they kept dropping old cloths, and shooting at him alternately, until they killed him. Thus did they destroy many lions.

Another most noble knight came to the king when he was at Caesarea, who said he was of the house of Coucy. The king said, he was his cousin by his descent from one of the sisters of King Philip, who had been married to the emperor of Constantinople. The king retained this knight, and nine others, for one year on the expiration of which, he returned to Constantinople, whence he had come. While he was with us, I heard him tell the king, that the emperor of Constantinople had once formed an alliance with the king of the Commains, to have their assistance to conquer the emperor of Greece, whose name was Yataiche and he added, that the king of the Commains, to have greater faith in the professions of the emperor of Constantinople, caused him and their people on both sides to be blooded, and made each drink alternately of the others blood, in sign of brotherhood, saying they were now brothers of the same blood. It was thus we were forced to do with this knight and his companions; and our blood, being mixed with wine, was drunk by each party, as constituting us all brothers of the same blood.

They performed another ceremony, by driving a dog between them and us, as we were divided into two bodies, and then cutting him to pieces with their swords, saying, "Let those be thus mangled who shall fail in their engagements to each other."

Another wonderful story this knight of Coucy told the king. He said, that in the country of the Commains, when a great and powerful prince died, on his decease an immense grave was made, and the dead person, most richly adorned, was seated in a magnificent chair within the grave, and the finest horse he had possessed, together with one of his officers, were let down alive in the grave. The officer, before he descended, took leave of the king and the other great personages present, when the king gave to him a large quantity of gold and silver coin, which he placed in a scarf round his neck, the king making him promise that on his arrival in the other world he would restore to him his money, which he faithfully engaged to do. After this, the king gave him a letter addressed to the first of their monarchs, in which he told him that the bearer of it had well and faithfully served him, and on that account entreated he would properly reward him. When this was done, the grave was filled up over the corpse, the living officer, and the horse, and covered with planks well nailed together. Before night there was a considerable mound of stones piled over the grave, in memory of those whom they had interred.

When it was near Easter I left Acre, and went to visit the king at Caesarea, where he was employed in fortifying and enclosing it. On my arrival, I found him in conversation with the legate, who had never left him during this expedition to the Holy Land. On seeing me, he quitted the legate, and coming to me, said, "Lord de Joinville, is it really true that I have only retained you until this ensuing Easter? Should it be so, I beg you will tell me how much I shall give you from this Easter to that of this time twelve months."

I replied, that I was not come to him to make such a bargain and that I would not take more of his money but I would offer other terms, which were, that he should promise never to fly into a passion for any thing I should say to him, which was often the case, and I engaged that I would keep my temper whenever he refused what I should ask.

When he heard my terms, he burst into laughter, and said that he retained me accordingly then, taking me by the hand, he led me before the legate to his council, and repeated the convention that had been agreed to between us. Every one was joyous on hearing it, and consequently I remained.

I will now speak of the acts of justice, and the sentences of the king, which I witnessed during his stay at Caesarea. The first was on a knight who had been caught in a house of ill fame he gave him the alternative, that the prostitute with whom he had been found should lead him in his shirt through the army, with a cord tied to his private parts, one end of which cord the prostitute was to hold or, should he not like this, he should forfeit his horse, armor, and accoutrements, and be driven from and banished the king's army. The knight preferred the loss of his horse and arms, and banishment from the army. When I saw the horse was forfeited, I requested to have him for one of my knights who was a poor gentleman but the king said my request was unreasonable, for that the horse was well worth from fourscore to a hundred livres, which was no small sum. I answered, "Sire, you have broken our convention in thus replying to my request." The king laughed, and said, "Lord de Joinville, you may say what you please, but you shall not put me in a passion the sooner." However, I did not get the horse for my poor gentleman.

The second act of justice I witnessed was on some of my knights who, one day, had gone to hunt the animal called an antelope, which is something like a roe-buck. The Knights Hospitallers had sallied out to meet my knights, fought with them, and did them much mischief, for which outrage I went to lay my complaints before their commander, taking with me those of my knights who had been wounded. The commander, having heard my accusation, promised to do me justice, according to the rules and customs of the Holy Land, which were, to make the brethren who had been guilty of this outrage, eat upon their cloaks, in the presence of those who had been ill-used, who should afterwards carry away their cloaks.

The commander did indeed make the guilty eat on their cloaks before me and some of my knights, but when we demanded of the commander that they should rise up, he wanted to refuse; however, he was forced to it at last for we seated ourselves to eat with the brethren, which they would not suffer, and they were obliged to rise with us to eat with the other brethren at table, leaving us their cloaks.

Another act of justice was on a king's sergeant called Goullu, who laid his hands on one of my knights, and rudely pushed him. I went to complain of this to the king, who told me I might as well be quiet, since the sergeant had only pushed the knight. But I replied, that I would not be quiet, and would quit his service unless justice were done me for that it was highly indecent for any sergeant to lay his hands on a knight. The king, hearing this, did me the usual justice, which was, that, according to the custom of the country, the sergeant should come to my lodgings, barefooted, and in his shirt, with a sword hanging on his wrist, when, having knelt before the knight whom he had injured, he was to offer the sword by the hilt, and say to him—

"Sir knight, I crave your mercy for having laid hands on you, and have brought this sword, which I now offer to you for you to cut off my hand, if it shall so please you." I then entreated the knight to pardon him, which he did. Several other judgments I witnessed that were executed according to the rites and customs of the Holy Land.

You have before heard how the king had sent to inform the admirals of Egypt, that unless they made him satisfaction for the outrages they had committed, he would not abide by any truce that had been made with them. Ambassadors, in consequence, had arrived from the admirals, with letters, to assure the king that they would do all he had desired.

A day was appointed for the king and these ambassadors to meet at Jaffa, when they were to promise the king, on their oaths, that they would surrender Jerusalem up to him. In return, the king and his nobles were to swear, on their part, to aid and assist the admirals against the sultan of Damascus. It happened, that on the sultan of Damascus hearing that we were become the allies of his enemies in Egypt, and that a day was appointed for the ratification of the treaties at Jaffa, he sent upwards of 20,000 Turks to guard the passes but this did not prevent the king from putting himself in motion to march to Jaffa.

When the count of Jaffa learnt that the king was coming, he put his castle into such a good state, that it resembled a well-defended town at each bulwark of his castle were posted 500 men, each with a target and penoncel with his arms. It was a beautiful sight to see for his arms were of fine gold, with a cross-patee gules, richly worked.

We encamped on the plain, near to this castle of Jaffa, which was situated on an island near the sea-shore and the king began to fortify and enclose a village adjacent to the castle, wherever the shore would permit it. The king, by way of encouraging his workmen, said to them, "I have more than once carried the hod myself to gain a pardon." The admirals of Egypt were afraid to advance, on account of the passes being so well guarded by the sultan of Damascus however, they sent to the king all the heads of the Christians that had been exposed on the walls of Cairo, in compliance with the demand which he had made for them. Those heads he caused to be buried in consecrated ground. They likewise sent him all the children they had detained, and whom they had forced to abjure their faith to God, together with an elephant, which last the king had transported to France.

As the king and his whole army were lying before Jaffa, fortifying themselves against those in the castle, news was brought the king that the army of the sultan of Damascus had taken the field, and was in ambush waiting to attack him and that one of their admirals had advanced to reap and despoil the corn of a Karet, within three leagues of the army. The king instantly sent thither to reconnoiter, and followed in person but the admiral no sooner saw us appear than he took to flight, pursued by some of our men full gallop. A young gentleman of our army came up with them, and gallantly unhorsed two Turks with the point of his lance, without breaking it. The admiral perceiving that this gentleman was alone, turned about, but he received such a stroke from him with his spear as wounded him desperately in the body, when the young man returned to the army. The admirals of Egypt, learning that the king and his army were at Jaffa, sent other ambassadors to him, to appoint a day when they would meet him without fail. The king having fixed on a day, they promised faithfully to be punctual in concluding all the different businesses that were in agitation. While we were waiting for this day of meeting with the admirals from Egypt, the count d'Eu came to the king bringing with him the good knight Arnold de Guynes, and his two brothers, whom, with eight other knights, the king retained in his service, and created the count d'Eu a knight, who was at that time but a very youth.

At the same time, the prince of Antioch and his mother waited on the king, to whom he paid much respect, and received them with every honor. The king made the prince of Antioch a knight, though but sixteen years old but I never saw, at that age, so discreet a youth. When he was knighted, he requested the king to allow him and his mother a private audience, which being granted, he spoke as follows: "Sire, it is very true that my mother here present keeps me in ward, and has the power of so doing for four years to come, by which she has the enjoyment of all things, and I have nothing. I think, however, that she ought not to suffer my lands to be wasted and this I say because my city of Antioch is falling to ruin in her hands. I therefore supplicate you, sire, to remonstrate with her on this matter, and to prevail on her to allow me money and men that I may succour my people who are in that city, as she is bounden in justice to do."

When the king had heard the prince's demand, here demonstrated so effectually with his mother that she complied with his wishes, and the prince returned to Antioch, where he did wonders. From that time, in honor to the king, he quartered his arms, which are gules with the arms of France.

As it is very praiseworthy and pleasant to relate, in order that they may be known, the deeds and virtues of any excellent prince, we will here speak of the good count of Jaffa, Sir Gautier de Brienne. He performed in his lifetime most gallant deeds of chivalry, and kept possession of his county of Jaffa for many years, although continually attacked by the Egyptians, and without enjoying any revenues but what he gained in his excursions against the Saracens and other enemies of the Christian faith.

He once defeated a large body of infidels, who were transporting many bales of different sorts of silken cloths, which having taken and brought home, he divided the whole among his knights, without keeping any part for himself. His way of life was, after parting with his knights in the evening, to enter his chapel, where he was long employed in prayer and thanksgiving to his God. He afterwards went to bed to his wife, who was a wondrous good lady, and sister to the king of Cyprus.

You have before heard of the Tartar prince having, through the aid of God, defeated the emperor of Persia and his army of 300,000 men, with only 300, and afterwards driving him out of his kingdom. We now know the road that this emperor of Persia, whose name was Barbaquan, took. He fled to the kingdom of Jerusalem and on his arrival did great damage to it for he took the castle of Tabarie that belonged to Sir Eudes de Montbeliar and put to death as many of our people as he could find in the hospitia without Acre, and without Jaffa. After doing as much mischief as he could, he marched toward Babylon, to receive succors from the sultan of Babylon, who was to join his forces and attack us. Upon this, the barons of the country assembled with the patriarchs, and determined to offer combat to the emperor before he should form his junction with the sultan of Babylon. They sent to the sultan of La Chamelle for his assistance, who was one of the best and most loyal knights in all pagan land. He came to them, and was most honorably received at Acre, which they left together, and sat down before Jaffa.

When this army arrived at Jaffa, the chiefs entreated the count Gautier to join them, and march against the emperor of Persia. He replied, that he would cheerfully do so if the patriarch would absolve him from an excommunication which he had lately denounced against him, because he would not surrender a tower of his castle of Jaffa called the Tower of the Patriarch, and which the patriarch claimed as belonging to him. The patriarch would not absolve him: nevertheless, the count did not fail to accompany us. The army was divided into three battalions the first was given to Count Gautier, the second to the sultan of La Chamelle, and the third to the patriarch and barons of the country. In the battalion of Sir Gautier were the Knights Hospitallers.

When these three battalions had been properly arrayed, they moved forward, and advanced within sight of the enemy; who, on noticing their approach, formed their army likewise into three divisions. Count Gautier de Brienne, observing this maneuver, cried out, "My lords, what are we about? We allow our enemies time to draw up their men in array, and increase their courage by seeing us thus remain inactive. I beg of you, in the name of God, instantly to charge them." But not one would pay him the least attention, or advance. He then went up to the patriarch, and again demanded absolution, but it was refused him.

With the count was a most learned man, the bishop of Ranid, who had done many gallant deeds of chivalry in company with the count. The bishop said to him, "Do not let your conscience be uneasy at this excommunication of the patriarch, for he is very much in the wrong and, from the powers I possess, I absolve you from it, in the name of the Father, Son, and Holy Ghost. Amen." He then added, "Come now, let us charge the enemy." Sticking spurs into their horses, they fell on the battalion of the emperor of Persia that formed the rear, but it was too numerous for those who had followed the count. Very many were slain on each side notwithstanding this, the count was made prisoner, for his battalion most shamefully fled, and several, from despair, threw themselves into the sea. One cause of this despair was owing to a battalion of the emperor of Persia falling on that of the sultan of La Chamelle, who fought and defended himself with such great valor, although he was much weaker in numbers than the enemy that out of 2,000 men there did not remain more than fourscore, so that he was forced to make his retreat to the castle of La Chamelle.

The emperor of Persia, concluding that his victory was complete, resolved to besiege the sultan in his castle of La Chamelle. But the sultan, observing his approach, like a wary soldier, assembled his garrison, and said, "Gentlemen, if we allow ourselves to be besieged we are undone: it will be better therefore that we attack them." In consequence, he ordered out a party, badly armed, to march in the hollow of a valley, and to fall on the rear of the enemy. This was executed, and a great slaughter made of women and children. The emperor hearing a sudden noise in his rear, as he was advancing near the castle, turned about, with the intent to put a stop to it, but this was no sooner done, than the sultan made a sally with his whole garrison, and fought them so desperately, that the emperors army, which at first consisted of 25,000 men, being attacked in front and rear, was defeated, and not one man or woman escaped being put to death.

You must know, that the emperor of Persia, before he marched to lay siege to the castle of La Chamelle, had carried the good count of Jaffa, Sir Gautier de Brienne, before the city of

Jaffa, and had him hung by the arms to a gallows that was in front of the castle, declaring publicly that he would never take down their count until they should have surrendered to him the castle. As the poor count was thus suspended, he cried with a loud voice to his people never to surrender the castle for any thing they might see done to him for should they so do the emperor would put them all to the sword.

The emperor, perceiving he could not gain any thing more, sent Count Gautier to the sultan of Babylon as a present, with the commander of the Knights Hospitallers, and many other noble personages whom he had made prisoners. He ordered 300 of his knights to escort Count Gautier and the other prisoners as far as Babylon, which turned out fortunately for them since by this they avoided being included in the butchery of the emperor of Persia and his army before the castle of La Chamelle, as has been before told.

When the merchants of Babylon heard that their sultan detained Count Gautier in his prisons, they assembled, and made a clamorous petition to the sultan, that he would execute the count of Jaffa, for that he had destroyed several of their companions, and had frequently done them much mischief. In compliance with their request, the sultan ordered the body of Count Gautier to be delivered to them, in order that they might take their own revenge on him. These traitorous dogs entered the prison of the count and cut him into pieces, making him thus suffer martyrdom, for which we may imagine he is now glorious in paradise.

But to return to the sultan of Damascus. He withdrew the men he had at Gadres, and, entering Egypt made an attack on the admirals. By the fortune of war, one of his battalions defeated one of the admirals, and in another instance the chance was just the reverse. On this account, the sultan of Damascus returned to Gadres, very badly wounded in the head and other places. While he stayed there, the admiral sent him ambassadors, who made a peace between them, so that we seemed a subject of mockery to both sides; for, from that time forward, we enjoyed neither peace nor truce from the sultan, nor from the admirals. You must know that we could never muster in our army more than about 1,400 men-at-arms fit for service.

As soon as the sultan of Damascus had concluded a peace with the admirals of Egypt, he collected all his men from Gadres, and marched his whole army, amounting to 20,000 Saracens and 10,000 Bedouins, within sight of us. They passed within two leagues, but never made any attack. The king, the master of his artillery, and the whole army were on the watch for three days, lest they should attempt to fall on us when we were unprepared.

On St. John's day, next after Easter, while the king was at sermon, one of the men attached to the master of the artillery entered the king's chapel armed and told him that the Saracens had surrounded the master of the cross-bows in the plain. I instantly requested of the king permission to go thither, to which he consented, and gave me 500 men-at-arms, whom he named. As soon as we were without the camp, and were perceived by the Saracens who were pressing round the master of the cross-bows, they retreated to an admiral that was posted on a small hillock with at least 1,000 men. The battle now began between the Saracens and the company of the master of the cross-bows and as the admiral saw his men fail, he sent thither fresh reinforcements, in like manner did the master of the cross-bows to his men. While they were thus fighting, the legate and the barons of the country told the king, it was great madness to allow me to take the field and he thereon sent to order me back, together with the master of the cross-bows.

The Turks now retired and we returned to the army but many were much surprised that the Turks let us return quietly without an attack and accounted for it by saying, that their horses were almost starved by having remained a whole year at Gadres.

Some other Turks, who had left Jaffa, came to Acre, and sent to inform the lord d'Asur, who was constable of Jerusalem, that if he did not send them 50,000 besants they would destroy the gardens round the town. The lord d'Asur made answer, that he would give them nothing. Upon this, they drew up their battalions, and advanced along the sands so near to the town of Acre as to be within cross-bow shot. The lord d'Asur then quitted the town and marched to the mount, where was the church-yard of St. Nicholas, to defend the gardens and when the Turks approached, a body of foot sallied out of Acre, and kept up a brisk discharge of arrows against them but for fear of the dangers they might incur, the lord d'Asur sent them orders by a young knight from Genoa to retire within the walls.

As the Genoese knight was retiring with his body of infantry, a Saracen, suddenly moved by his courage, came boldly up to him, and said in his Saracenic tongue, that if he pleased, he would tilt with him. The knight answered with pride that he would receive him but, when he was on the point of beginning his course, he perceived on his left hand eight or nine Saracens, who had halted there to see the event of the tournament. The knight, therefore, instead of directing his course toward the Saracen who had offered to tilt with him, made for this troop, and striking one of them with his lance, pierced his body through, and killed him dead on the spot. He retreated to our men, pursued by the other Saracens, one of whom gave him a heavy blow on his helmet with a battle-axe. In return, the knight struck the Saracen so severely on the head that he made his turban fly off. You must know, that these turbans save them from many hard blows; and for this reason, they always wear them when they go to battle. Another Saracen thought to have given the knight a mortal blow with his Turkish blade, but he twisted his body in such wise that it missed him and the knight, by a back-hand blow on the Saracen's arm, made his sword fall to the ground, and he then made a good retreat with the infantry. These three famous actions did the Genoese knight perform in the presence of the lord d'Asur, and before all the principal persons of the town, who were assembled on the battlements.

The Saracens withdrew from before Acre and as they had heard the king was strengthening and enclosing Sajecte, and had but few men-at-arms with him, they marched thither. As soon as the king learnt their intentions, not having a sufficient force to oppose them, he retired with the master of his artillery, and as many as the place would hold, into the castle of Sajecte, which was very strong, and well enclosed few, however, could be lodged within it from the smallness of its extent. The Saracens arrived soon after, and entered Sajecte without any opposition, for the walls were not then finished, and slaughtered full 2,000 of the poorer sort of our army having done this, and pillaged the town, they marched off toward Damascus.

The king was much grieved on hearing that the Saracens had destroyed all his works at Sajecte, but he could not help it on the contrary, the barons of the country were rejoiced at it and the reason was, that the king intended, after he had finished at Sajecte, to enclose a mound, on which formerly had stood a castle in the time of the Maccabees, and which was on the road from Jaffa to Jerusalem. The barons opposed its being enclosed, because it was five leagues from the sea, and they said, and said truly, that it could never be victualled without certain risk of the provision being seized on the road thither by the Saracens, as they were more numerous. The barons remonstrated with the king, that it would be preferable in point of honor and in all other respects, to repair Sajecte, than to undertake a large and new building so far from the sea. To this the king assented.

During the king's stay at Jaffa, he was told that the sultan of Damascus would allow him to visit Jerusalem in perfect security. The king would most willingly have gone thither, but his great council dissuaded him from it, as it would leave the city in the hands of the enemy. The lords of the country likewise were unwilling to consent to this and cited to him the example of

King Philip, who, when he departed from Acre on his return to France, left the command of his whole army to Hugh, duke of Burgundy, grandfather to the duke lately deceased.

In those times, and when Duke Hugh of Burgundy and King Richard of England were residing in Acre, they received intelligence that they might take Jerusalem on the morrow, if they pleased for that a large army of knights from Egypt was gone to the assistance of the sultan of Damascus, in his war at Nessa against the sultan of that place. The duke of Burgundy and the king were soon prepared to march thither; and when they had divided their army, the king of England led the first battalion, followed by the duke of Burgundy, and by such of the king of France's army as had remained after his departure. But when they were near to Jerusalem, and on the point taking it, intelligence came from the duke of Burgundy's division, that he had turned back merely out of envy, and to prevent its being said, that the English had taken Jerusalem. As this intelligence was discussing, one of the king of England's officers cried out, "Sire, sire, only come hither, and I will show you Jerusalem." But the king, throwing down his arms, said with tears, and with hands uplifted to heaven, "Ah! Lord God, I pray thee that I may never see thy holy city of Jerusalem, since things thus happen, and since I cannot deliver it from the hands of thine enemies."

This example was laid before the king St. Louis, because he was the greatest monarch in Christendom and if he should perform a pilgrimage to Jerusalem, without delivering it from the enemies of God, every other king, who might wish to make a similar pilgrimage, would think he had amply performed it without seeking to do more than the king of France had done.

This Richard, king of England, performed such deeds of prowess when he was in the Holy Land, that the Saracens, on seeing their horses frightened at a shadow or bush, cried out to them, "What, dost think King Richard is there?" This they were accustomed to say, from the many and many times he had conquered and vanquished them. In like manner, when the children of the Turks or Saracens cried, their mothers said to them, "Hush, hush or I will bring King Richard of England to you" and from the fright these words caused they were instantly quiet.

I must say something more of this Hugh, duke of Burgundy. He was personally brave and chivalrous, but never reputed very wise toward God or man, as appears from what has just been told of him and, in allusion to him, the great king Philip said, when he was told that the count John de Chalons had a son whom he had christened Hugh, "May God, out of his goodness, make him a preuhomme as well as a preudhomme." There is much difference between these two characters, for many a knight among the Christians and Saracens is bold enough, but of little discretion, who neither fears nor loves God and it was said that God had been very gracious to that knight, who, by his actions, showed he united both these qualities. But the person of whom I am speaking might well be called a preudhomme, for he was sufficiently bold and personally enterprising, but not mentally so, for he feared not to sin, nor to behave ill toward his God.

Of the immense sums it cost the king to enclose Jaffa it does not become me to speak, for they were countless. He enclosed the town from one side of the sea to the other and there were twenty-four towers, including small and great. The ditches were well scoured, and kept clean both within and without. There were three gates, one of which the legate was ordered to build, as well as the wall that connected it with the next gate. To form some estimate of what the king's expenses might have been, I was once asked by the legate how much I thought the gate and wall he had erected cost him. When I replied that I estimated the gate at five hundred livres, and the wall three hundred, he told me I was very far from the amount, and added, that as God might help him, the gate and wall had cost him full thirty thousand livres. We may guess from this sum how great was the expense for the remainder.

When the king had finished the fortifications of Jaffa, he was desirous of doing the same to Sajecte, and repairing its walls, to put it in a similar state to what it had been in before the Saracens destroyed it. In consequence, he gave orders for the march of the army thither on the festival of St. Peter and St. Paul. While the king and his army were before the castle of Asur, he summoned his council in the evening, and told them he was very anxious to take from the Saracens the city of Naples, which is called in the Holy Scriptures Samaria.

The Knights Templars, barons and admirals of the country, advised him to it, as what he was in duty bound to do but added, that he ought not personally to expose himself there, for fear of any unfortunate accident, saying that if he were made prisoner or killed, the whole country would be lost.

The king replied that he would not allow his army to march thither without his accompanying it, and from this disagreement the enterprise was no more thought of. We continued our march along the sands to Acre, where the king and his whole army were lodged that night.

On the morrow, a great troop of Armenians, who were on their pilgrimage to Jerusalem, came to me, and entreated, through a Latin interpreter, that as I was about the king's person, I would show them the good king Louis. I went to the king, and told him that large body of people, from Upper Armenia, going to Jerusalem, were very desirous to see him. He burst into laughter, and bade me bring them to him. I instantly obeyed, and they followed me eagerly. When they had seen him, they recommended him to God, as he did the same to them in return.

The next day the king and his army marched to a place called Passe-poulain, about a league distant from Acre, where are many beautiful springs of water, with which the sugarcanes are irrigated.

When I was lodged, one of my knights said to me, "Sir, you are now much better quartered than you were before Saint Sur." Upon which another of my knights, who had fixed on my lodgings the preceding day, replied, "You are too foolhardy in thus blaming me to my lord" and having said this, he sprang on the other knight, and seized him by the hair. Astonished at the presumption of the knight, who had thus in my presence seized his companion, I ran to them, and gave the aggressor a hard blow between the shoulders, which made him quit his hold of the knight's hair. I then ordered him to quit my lodgings instantly, for that never more, as God might help me, should he be of my household.

The knight went away making great moan to Sir Gilles le Brun, then constable of France, who shortly after came to me to entreat I would take my knight again, for that he was sorely repentant of his folly. I told him I could not do any thing until the legate had absolved me from my oath. The constable then went to the legate, told him the case, and requested him to give me absolution from the oath I had sworn but the legate said he had not the power to absolve me, seeing that I was justified in making such an oath, and that the knight had richly deserved it by his conduct. This story I wished to introduce into my book, as an example to all not to make any oaths without very sufficient grounds for so doing for the wise man says, that those who swear on every occasion will probably as often forswear.

On the day following, the king marched his army before the city of Sur, which is called Thiry in the Bible. When there, the king was pressed to march and take a city hard by called Belinas his council advised him to it, but not to go thither in person, to which, with some difficulty, he was persuaded. It was determined that the count d'Anjou should march thither, with Sir Philip de Montfort, the lord of Sur, Sir Gilles le Brun, constable of France, Sir Peter the chamberlain, the masters of the Temple and of the Hospital, and their men-at-arms. During the night we armed ourselves and a little before day saw the plain in which was situated the city of

Belinas, called in Scripture Caesarea Philippi. There is within the city a beautiful fountain named Le Jour, and on the plain before the place, another fine spring, called Dain. From these two springs issue rivulets, which unite at some distance and form the river Jordan, in which our Lord Jesus Christ was baptized.

By the advice of the count d'Anjou, and the masters of the Templars and Hospitallers, it was ordered, that the battalion of the king, in which I then was, with my knights, as were also the forty knights from Champagne, whom the king had put under my command, Sir Geoffry de Sergines, and the other brave men that were with us, should march between the castle and town; that the barons and landholders of the country should enter the town on the left, the Hospitallers on the right, and the master of the Templars, with his division, was to enter the place from the road by which we had come. Each body was now in motion and as we approached the back parts of the city we found many of our countrymen dead, whom the Saracens had killed and thrown over the walls. You must know the line we were to take was very dangerous for, in the first place, there were three walls to pass, and a bank so steep and broken, that no one could keep his saddle. On the top of this bank, which we were to ascend, was a large body of Turks on horseback. Perceiving that our people were at one place breaking down the walls, I wished to advance towards them skirmishing. As I was doing this, one of our men attempted to leap the wall, but he fell under his horse, which was also thrown down. When I saw this I dismounted, and, taking my horse by the bridle, ascended boldly towards the Turks but as God willed it, they fled and left us the place. On the top there was a road cut in the rock which led to the city; and the Saracens within the place no sooner saw us masters of the rock than they took to flight, and gave up the city without opposition to our army.

While I was on the top of this mount, the master of the Templars, hearing that I was in great danger, hastened to me. I had with me the Germans, who, when they saw the Turks fly for the castle, which was at some distance from the town, began to pursue them, in spite of me, and although I cried out to them they were doing wrong, for we had accomplished what we had been ordered to perform.

The castle was seated above the town, but without the suburbs, and nearly half a league up Mount Libanus. There are very high rocks to pass before you arrive at the castle and when the Germans found they were very rashly pursuing the Turks, who had gained the castle, well knowing all the turnings of the rocks, they returned to rejoin us but the Saracens, observing them retreating, dismounted, and. falling on them as they descended the rocks, gave them many severe blows with their battle-axes, insomuch that they drove them back in disorder to where I was. My men seeing the mischief the Saracens did to the Germans, whom they closely pursued, began to be frightened, and to take alarm but I told them that if they quitted their position I would break them, and prevent them ever after from receiving the king's pay. They replied, "Lord de Joinville, we are much worse off than you are for you are on horseback, and can escape when and where you please but we who are on foot are in the greatest danger of being killed, should the Saracens come hither." Upon this I dismounted among them, to give them more courage, and sent my war-horse to the battalion of the Templars, which was a long cross-bow-shot distant.

As the Saracens were thus driving the Germans before them, one of my knights received a bolt from a cross-bow in the throat that laid him dead at my feet, upon which another of my knights, called Sir Hugh d'Escosse, uncle to the dead knight, desired I would assist him to carry his nephew down from the mount, that he might be buried but I refused, for the knight had joined the Germans in pursuing the Saracens, contrary to my will and orders. If, therefore, he suffered for it, I was no way to blame. So soon as Sir John de Yalenciennes heard the danger we were in, and that my division was in disorder, he hastened to Sir Olivier de Termes, and the other captains from Languedoc, and addressed them, "My lords, I beg of you, and indeed command, in the king's name, that you join me to assist the seneschal of Champagne."

A knight, whose name was Sir William de Beaumont, came to him, and said that I was killed but, notwithstanding this, the good Sir Olivier de Termes did not the more spare himself, for he was determined to know the truth, whether I was alive or dead, that he might give the king certain information of it, and gallantly ascended the mount, when I went to him. Sir Olivier, when on the mount, saw the great danger we were in, and that we could not descend the way we had got up he therefore gave us good advice, and made us descend a slope of the hill, as if we were going to Damascus, saying that the Saracens would suppose, by this maneuver, that we meant to fall on their rear. When we had got into the plain, Sir Olivier ordered a large heap of corn that was stacked on the ground, to be set on fire, and by this means, and our own exertions, through the good counsel of Sir Olivier de Termes, we escaped, and arrived on the morrow in safety at Sajecte, where the king was. We found the good and holy man had ordered the bodies of those Christians that were slain to be buried, and that he himself had assisted in carrying their corpses to the grave. Some of the bodies were in such a state of corruption, that divers of the carriers were obliged to stop their nostrils, but the good king never did this. When we came to him, he had caused our lodgings and quarters to be ready prepared for us.

"While we were before Sajette, some merchants came to the king, and brought him intelligence that the king of Tartary had taken the city of Baldac, with the apostle of the Saracens, who was lord of the town, and was called the Caliph of Baldac."

"The manner of its capture was as follows:—The king of Tartary had laid his plans with much secrecy and caution, and after he had besieged the place, sent to inform the caliph, that in order to preserve peace and be on good terms with him, he was desirous that a marriage should take place between their two children. The caliph, having consulted his council, replied, that he was satisfied with the proposal. In return, the king of Tartary requested that he would send to him forty of his principal counselors to treat of and agree to this marriage. This the caliph complied with but the king of Tartary detained them, and sent word they were not enough, and that forty more of the richest of the caliph's subjects must also be sent for the greater security of the articles of the marriage. The caliph, believing what he said was the truth, sent him forty more, as he had desired, and even a third time the same number of his principal subjects."

"When the Tartar king had thus got six score of the best captains, and the principal and most wealthy of the caliph's subjects, he thought the remainder must consist of such common people as could not resist him, and would be unable to defend themselves."

"Upon this, he ordered the six score personages to be beheaded, and attacked the town so briskly that he took it, with the caliph its lord."

"Having gained the town, he wished to cover his disloyalty and treason by throwing the blame on the caliph, whom he confined in an iron cage. He made him fast until the last extremity, when the king came to him, and asked if he were hungry. Yes, indeed, am I, replied the caliph, and not without cause.' The king then ordered a large golden platter filled with jewels and precious stones to be offered to him, and asked him, Caliph, dost thou know these rich jewels and treasure which thou seest before thee?" 'Yes,' said the caliph, for they had been his own. The king again asked, if he much loved these jewels and on the caliph answering in the affirmative, he replied, "Well, since then thou lovest these treasures so much, take of them as much as thou wilt, and eat them, to appease thy hunger." The caliph said they were not food to eat. Now, answered the king of Tartary, ' thou mayest at present see thy great fault; for if thou hadst given of thy treasures, which thou lovest so dearly, to subsidize soldiers in thy defense, thou mightiest have held out against me but that which thou prizes the most has failed thee in thy need."

During this time, being one day in the presence of the king, I asked his leave to make a pilgrimage to our Lady of Tortosa, which was then very much in request. Great numbers of pilgrims went thither daily, for it was said to have been the first altar erected in honor of the mother of God. Our Lady performed there many wonderful miracles and one in particular on a poor man that was a demoniac, having lost his senses, for he was possessed by a wicked spirit. It happened, that one day he was brought to this altar of our Lady at Tortosa and as his friends who had brought him were praying to our Lady to cure him, and restore his senses, the devil whom the poor creature had in his body replied, "Our Lady is not here but in Egypt, whither she is gone to aid the king of France and the Christians, who land this day on the Holy Land, to make war on the Pagans, who are on horseback to receive them."

What the devil had uttered was put down in writing and when it was brought to the legate, who was with the king of France, he said to me that it was on that very day we had arrived in Egypt and I am sure the good Lady Mary was of the utmost service to us.

The king very readily gave me leave to make this pilgrimage, and at the same time charged me to buy for him a hundred- weight of different colored camlets, which he was desirous to give to the Cordeliers on his return to France. From this, I guessed that it would not be long before he set out on his return thither.

When I arrived at Triple, the end of my pilgrimage, I made my offerings to God, and to our Lady of Tortosa, and afterward bought the camlets according to the king's orders. My knights, seeing me thus occupied, asked what I intended doing with so many camlets. I induced them to believe that I made these purchases to gain a profit from reselling them.

The prince of that country, hearing of our arrival, and knowing that I was come from the king's army, gave us a most honorable reception, and offered us magnificent presents. We returned him our most humble thanks, but would accept of nothing but a few relics, which I brought to the king with his camlets.

You must know that the queen had heard that I had been on a pilgrimage, and had brought back some relics. I sent her by one of my knights four pieces of the camlets which I had purchased and when the knight entered her apartment, she cast herself on her knees before the camlets, that were wrapped up in a towel, and the knight, seeing the queen do this, flung himself on his knees also. The queen, observing him, said, " Rise, sir knight, it does not become you to kneel, who are the bearer of such holy relics." My knight replied, that it was not relics, but camlets, that he had brought as a present from me. When the queen and her ladies heard this, they burst into laughter, and the queen said, "Sir knight, the deuce take your lord for having made me kneel to a parcel of camlets."

Soon after the king's arrival at Sajecte, he received the news of the death of the queen his mother, which caused him such grief that he was two days in his chamber without suffering any one to see him. On the third, he sent one of his valets to seek me and, on my presenting myself, he extended his arms, and said, "Ah, seneschal, I have lost my mother!"

"Sir," replied I, "I am not surprised at it, for you know there must come a time for her death; but I am indeed greatly so, that you who are considered as so great a prince should so outrageously grieve for you know," continued "a that the wise man says, whatever grief the valiant man suffers in his mind, he ought not to show it on his countenance, nor let it be publicly known, for he that does so gives pleasure to his enemies and sorrow to his friends."

I thus appeased him a little; and he gave orders that most magnificent religious services should be performed in the country in which he then was, for the salvation of the soul of the late queen. He sent likewise to France a load of jewels and precious stones to the national churches, with letters from him to entreat they would pray to God for him and for the soul of the late queen his mother.

The Poitiers edition adds: "After I had quitted the apartment of the king, the lady Mary de Bonnes-Vertus came to entreat that I would wait on the queen to comfort her, for that she was in marvelous great grief. When I was in her chamber, and saw her weeping so very bitterly, I could not refrain from saying to her that the proverb was very true which said, "We ought never to believe in the tears of women,' for that the lamentation she was making was for the woman she hated the most in this world. She replied, that it was not for her she wept, but for the extreme melancholy of the king, as well as for her daughter, afterwards queen of Navarre, who would now be under the guardianship of men. The reason why the queen disliked the queen dowager, was the continued rudeness of her behavior to her for she would not suffer her son to keep company with his queen, and prevented it as much as lay in her power. When the king made any excursions through his kingdom, in company with the two queens, Queen Blanche had him separated from his queen, and they were never lodged in the same house. It happened one day, during a stay which the court made at Pontoise, that the king as lodged in the story above the apartments of his queen, and he had given orders to his ushers of the chamber, whenever he should go to lie with his queen, and his mother was coming to his, or to the queens chamber, to beat the dogs until they cried out when the king heard them, he hid himself from his mother. Now one day Queen Blanche went to the queen's chamber, where her son had gone before to comfort her, for she was in great danger of death, from a bad delivery, and he hid himself behind the queen to avoid being seen but his mother perceived him, and, taking him by the hand, said, 'Come along you will do no good here,' and put him out of the chamber. Queen Margaret observing this and that she was to be separated from her husband, cried aloud, 'Alas! will you not allow me to see my lord, neither when I am alive nor dying?' In uttering these words she fainted, and her attendants thought she was dead the king likewise believed it, and instantly returned to her, and recovered her from her fainting-fit."

Not long after this the king attended to his affairs, but was undetermined whether to remain longer where he was, or to return to France. While he was thus hesitating, and during his stay at Sajecte, which he had almost enclosed, he called the legate, who had accompanied it, and bade him make many processions, requesting God to enlighten him, and let him know his will, whether he should return to France or remain in Palestine. Some little time after these processions were over, the principal persons of the country and myself were going to amuse ourselves in a meadow, when the king called me to him. The legate was with him, who said to me, in the presence of the king,—"Seneschal, the king is very much satisfied with the good and agreeable services you have done him, and earnestly wishes for your honor and advancement. He orders me to tell you, as he knows it will give you much pleasure at heart that his intention is to return to France on this side Easter that is coming."

I replied, "May our Lord induce him to act always according to his will." When I had said this, the legate left the king, and desired I would accompany him to his lodgings, to which I willingly assented. He made me enter his closet, when, bursting into tears, he clasped my hands and said—"Seneschal, I am greatly rejoiced, and thank God for that you have thus escaped from the imminent dangers you have been in during your stay in this country and, on the other hand, I am much concerned and grieved at my heart, that I shall be forced to quit such good and religious companions, to return among such a set of wretches as the court of Rome consists of. But I will tell you that my intention is to remain one year, after your departure, at Acre, to expend all money in enclosing the suburbs of that place, which I shall continue to do as long as my means shall last to avoid having any reproaches made against me."

On my return to the king the next day, he commanded me to arm myself and my knights on the morrow. When I was armed, I asked him what was his pleasure for us to do. He then said, to escort the queen and his children to Sur, which was full seven leagues distant. I would not say any thing against this, in spite of the great dangers we should run, for at that time we had neither peace nor truce with the Egyptians, nor with those of Damascus. We set out, and through the mercy of God, arrived in the evening at Sur without any accident or hindrance.

Soon after the patriarchs and barons of the country who had for a length of time attended on the king, seeing that he had enclosed Sajecte with high walls and large towers, and that the ditches were well cleansed within and without, waited on him to render him their most humble thanks and praise for the great good and the honor he had conferred on Palestine for he had rebuilt, from the ground, Sajecte, Caesarea, Jaffa, and had greatly strengthened the city of Acre with high walls and towers.

They addressed him as follows: "Sire, we perceive very clearly that your stay with us cannot be much prolonged, with any kind of profit to the kingdom of Jerusalem. We would therefore advise you to go to Acre, where you may make your preparations for departure during this ensuing Lent, so that you may secure a safe passage to France."

The king followed their counsel and went to Sur, whither we had escorted the queen and his family, and at the beginning of Lent we all arrived at Acre.

During the whole of Lent, the king was making his fleet ready for his return to France, which consisted of fourteen ships and galleys. On the vigil of St. Mark, after Easter, the king and queen embarked on board their ship, and put to sea, having a favorable wind for their departure. The king told me he was born on St. Mark's day and I replied, that he might well say he had been born again on St. Mark's day, in thus escaping from such a pestilent land, where he had remained so long.

On the Saturday following, we arrived at the island of Cyprus and there was a mountain hard by the island, called the Mountain of the Cross, which marked at a great distance the situation of the island. On this Saturday, about vespers, there came on such a thick fog from the land that our sailors thought themselves at a greater distance from the shore than they were, for they lost sight of this mountain and it happened, that as they were eager to reach the shore, they struck on the extremity of a sandbank which was clear of the island fortunately it was so, for had we not struck on this bank, we should have run against some dangerous half-covered rocks, and should have been in the utmost peril of being all drowned. We were even now in much danger. All thought themselves lost, and that the vessel must be wrecked but a sailor, casting the lead, found we were no longer aground, on which every one rejoiced and returned thanks to God.

Many on board were kneeling before the holy sacrament that was on the ship's altar, adoring and begging pardon of God, for each expected nothing but death. When day appeared, we saw the rocks on which we should have struck, had it not been for the good fortune of the sandbank. In the morning the king sent for the principal of the ships' captains, who brought with them four divers, fellows who dive naked to the bottom of the sea like fish. The captains ordered the divers to plunge into the sea at this place who did so, and passed under the king's ship. On their reappearance on the opposite side to where they had gone down, we heard each ask the other what he had found. They all reported, that on the part where our vessel had struck on the sand three fathoms of its keel had been beaten off, which account surprised very much the king, and all who heard it. The king asked the mariners for their advice on the occasion, who replied,—" Sire, if you will believe us, you must remove from this ship to another. We know well, that since the keel has suffered such damage, all the ribs of the vessel will have been started, and we very much fear that she will be unable to bear the sea, should there be any wind, without danger of sinking. When you sailed from France, we saw an accident just similar happen to a vessel which had struck on a bank and when she was afterward in a gale of wind she could not withstand it, but opened her sides and was lost all on board perished but a young woman, with an infant child in her arms, who had accidentally remained on one of the ship's timbers, and was saved.

The king having listened to what the mariners said, and the example they brought, I testified to the truth of it for I had seen the woman and child, who had arrived at the city of Baphe, in the house of the count de Joingny, who had all care taken of them for the honor of God.

The king summoned his council to deliberate on what was to be done, and they unanimously agreed to what the mariners had proposed but the king called the captains again to him, and asked them, on the faith and loyalty which they owed him, whether, if the ship were their own, and full of merchandise, they would quit it. They all said they would not for that they would prefer risking their lives to the loss of such a vessel, which would cost them from forty to fifty thousand livres. "Why then," said the king, "do you advise me to quit her?" They replied,— "Sire, you and we are two different sorts of things for there is no sum, however great, that can be had in compensation for the loss of yourself, the queen, and your three children; and we will never advise that you should put yourself in such risk."

"Now," said the king, "I will tell you what I think of the matter. Suppose I quit this ship, there are five or six hundred persons on board, who will remain in the island of Cyprus for fear of the danger that may happen to them should they stay on board and there is not," added the king, "one among them who is more attached to his own person, than I am myself, and if we land they will lose all hopes of returning to their own country. I therefore declare, I will rather put myself, the queen, and my children, in this danger, under the good providence of God, than make such numbers of people suffer as are now with me."

The great mischief that would have happened, if the king had landed, was very apparent, from what befel that puissant knight Sir Olivier de Termes, who was on board the king's ship. Sir Olivier was one of the bravest knights, and most enterprising men of all I was acquainted with in the Holy Land; he was, however, afraid of remaining on board, and therefore went on shore but, rich and mighty as he was, he met with so many difficulties, that it was upwards of a year and a half before he could again rejoin the king. Now, if so rich a man found so many difficulties, what would the number of inferior personages have done, who could not have money to defray their expenses and support themselves?

After God had saved us from this peril, near the island of Cyprus, another befel us ; for there arose so violent a storm, that in spite of all our efforts we were driven back again to the same island, after we had long left it. The sailors cast four anchors in vain, for the vessel could not be stopped until they had thrown out the fifth, which held. All the partitions of the king's cabin were obliged to be destroyed and so high was the wind, that no one dared stay therein for fear of being blown overboard.

The queen came into the king's chamber, thinking to meet him there, but found only Sir Gilles le Brun, constable of France, and myself, who were lying down. On seeing her, I asked what she wished. She said, she wanted the king, to beg he would make some vows to God and his saints, that we might be delivered from this storm, for that the sailors had assured her we were in the greatest danger of being drowned. I replied to her,—"Madam, vow to make a pilgrimage to my lord Saint Nicholas, at Varengeville, and I promise you that God will restore us in safety to France." "Ah! seneschal," answered she, "I am afraid the king will not permit me to make this pilgrimage for the accomplishment of my vow." "At least, then, madam, promise him, that if God shall restore you in safety to France, you will give him a silver ship of the value of five marcs, for the king, yourself, and your children and if you shall do this, I assure you that, at the entreaties of St. Nicholas, God will grant you a successful voyage and I vow for myself, that, on my return to Joinville, I will make a pilgrimage to his shrine barefooted."

Upon this, she made a vow of a silver ship to St. Nicholas, and demanded that I would be his pledge for her due performance of it, to which I assented. She shortly after came to us to say that God, at the intercession of St. Nicholas, had delivered us from this peril.

On the queens return to France, she caused the ship to be made that she had vowed, and had introduced in it the king, herself, her three children, with the sailors, mast and steerage, all of silver, and the ropes of silver thread. This ship she sent me with orders to convey it to the shrine of my lord Saint Nicholas, which I did. I saw it there a long time afterward, when we conducted the king's sister to the emperor of Germany.

We will return to our principal subject, and continue the account of our voyage home. When the king perceived we had escaped from these two perils, he rose from a bench of the vessel, and said to me,—" Now see, seneschal, if God has not clearly manifested his great power, when by a blast of one of these four winds, the king, the queen, our children, and so many other persons, might have been drowned? For our deliverance from this danger, we ought to pay him our sincerest thanks."

The good king talked incessantly of the imminent danger we had been in, and of the power which God had displayed. He said to me, "Seneschal, when such tribulations befall mankind, or other misfortunes of sickness, the saints say they are threatenings from our Lord. I therefore maintain that the perils we have been in are the same kind of threatening from our Lord, who might say, "Now consider how very easily I might have suffered you all to be drowned, had I so willed it." "For this reason," continued the holy king, "we should examine ourselves well that there be nothing in our conduct displeasing to God our Creator and whenever we may find there is any thing wrong, we ought instantly to make ourselves clear of it. When we thus act, God will love us and preserve us from all perils; but, should we follow a contrary behavior after having noticed these menaces, he will afflict us with some grievous malady, perhaps death, and permit us to descend to hell, without hope of redemption."

The good and holy king continued,—"Seneschal, that good man Job said to God, ' Lord God, wherefore dost thou afflict us for if thou destroy us, thou wilt not be the poorer and if thou wert to call us all to thee, thou wouldst not be more powerful nor more rich.' Whence we may see," added he, "that the menaces of God are uttered against us from his great love to us, and for our welfare, not for his own that we may the more clearly discover our faults and demerits, and purify our consciences from all that may be displeasing to him. Let us therefore act in this manner, and we shall be the wiser and better for it."

After having taken water on board at the island of Cyprus, and some other necessary articles, we again set sail when the tempest had ceased, and saw another island called Lampedosa. We landed on it, and catch a great many rabbits. We found there a hermitage among the rocks, with a handsome garden planted with olives, figs, vines, and other fruit trees, with a fine spring of water, that ran through it. The king and his company went to the upper part of the garden, where was an oratory, the roof of which was painted white, with a red cross in the centre. In another chamber, more retired, we found two dead bodies with their hands on their breasts, and only the ribs which held them together. These bodies were laid towards the east, as is the usual custom at interments.

When we had seen and examined every thing, the king and his company returned on shipboard but one of our sailors was missing, and the captain, after considering awhile, said he guessed who it was, and that it was one who was desirous of living there henceforward as a hermit. The king, hearing this, ordered three sacks of biscuit to be left on the shore of this island, in order that the sailor might find them, and they might serve for his sustenance.

The Poitiers edition to this adds: "Afterward, in the course of our voyage, we passed another island, called Pantaleone, which was peopled with Saracens, a part of whom were subject to the king of Sicily, and part to the king of Tunis. When we first saw this island at a distance, the queen entreated the king to have the goodness to order three galleys to bring fruit for her children, which he did, commanding them to make haste, that they might meet him when he should pass the island."

"It fell out, that when the king was opposite to the port of this island, he could not see his galleys. The sailors, to his questions about them, answered, that very probably the Saracens had captured them and their crews but, sire, we would not advise you to wait for them, for you are near the kingdoms of Sicily and Tunis, neither of whose kings bears you any great love and if you will allow us to make sail, we will, before night, place yon out of danger from them, for we shall, in a short time, have passed the straits. In truth, replied the king, c I shall not follow your advice, but order you to turn the helm, that we may seek our people. And, happen what would, we were obliged so to do, and thus lost full eight days in waiting for them, on account of their gluttony, which they were impatient to satisfy.

"This island, which is here called 'Pantaleone' is that named by geographers 'Pantalarea' situated between Sicily and Africa, pretty near to Sousa, a town in the kingdom of Tunis. It belongs to the king of Spain, and is subject to the viceroy of Sicily. The inhabitants, although Catholic Christians, wear the dress and speak the language of the Moors."

Shortly after, an accident happened on board the ship of the lord d'Argones, one of the most powerful lords of Provence. He was annoyed one morning in bed by the rays of the sun darting on his eyes through a hole in the vessel, and calling one of his esquires, ordered him to stop the hole. The esquire, finding he could not stop it with inside, attempted to do it without, but his foot slipping, he fell into the sea. The ship kept on her way, and there was not the smallest boat alongside to succour him. We, who were in the king's ship, saw him, but as we were half a league off, we thought it was some piece of furniture that had fallen into the sea, for the esquire did not attempt to save himself, nor to move. When we came nearer, one of the king's boats took him up, and brought him on board our vessel, when he related his accident. We asked him why he did not attempt to save himself by swimming, nor call out to the other ships for help. He said he had no occasion so to do, for, as he fell into the sea, he exclaimed, "Our Lady of Valbert!" and that she had supported him by his shoulders until the king's galley came to him. In honor of the blessed Virgin Mary, and to perpetuate this miracle, I had it painted in my chapel of Joinville, and also on the windows of the church of Blecourt.

At the end of ten weeks that we had been at sea, we arrived in the port of Hieres, in front of the castle that belonged to the count de Provence, afterward king of Sicily.

The queen, and the whole of the council, advised the king to disembark there, as it was on his brothers land but he declared he would not land before he came to Aigues Mortes, which was his own territory. On this difference, the king detained us there Wednesday and Thursday, without any one being able to prevail on him to land. On the Friday, as he was seated on one of the benches of the ship, he called me to him, and demanded my opinion, whether he ought to and or not. I replied, "Sire, it seems to me that you ought to land for Madame cle Bourbon, being once in this very port, and unwilling to land, put again to sea, to disembark at Aigues Mortes, but she was tossed about for upwards of seven weeks before she could make that harbor." Upon this, the king consented to follow my advice, and landed at Hieres, to the great joy of the queen and all on board.

The king, the queen, and their children took up their residence in the castle of Hieres until horses should be provided for the further continuance of their journey. The abbot of Cluny, who was afterward bishop of Olive, sent the king two palfreys; one for himself, and the other for the queen. It was said at the time, that they were each well worth 500 livres. When the king had accepted of these two fine horses, the abbot requested an audience of him on the morrow, on the subject of his affairs. This was granted, and the next day the abbot conversed a long time with the king, who listened to him very attentively.

When the abbot was gone, I asked the king if he would answer a question I wished to put to him. On his replying in the affirmative, I said, "Sire, is it not true that you have thus long listened to the abbot for the sake of the horses he gave you?" The king said, "It was certainly so." I then continued, that I had asked the question, that he might forbid, on his return to France, those of his council, on their oaths, to receive the smallest gifts from any one who had business to transact in his presence "for be assured," added I, "that if they take presents, they will listen and attend to the givers, even longer than you have done to the abbot of Cluny." The king, calling his council, told them the request I had made, and the reason for my making it. His council, however, said that I had given very excellent advice.

While we were at Hieres we heard of a very good man, a Cordelier friar, who went about the country preaching his name was Father Hugh. The king being desirous of hearing and seeing him, the day he came to Hieres, we went out to meet him, and saw a great company of men and women following him on foot. On his arrival in the town, the king directed him to preach, and his first sermon was against the clergy, whom he blamed for being in such numbers with the king, saying they were not in a situation to save their souls, or that the Scriptures lied. This was true for the Scriptures do say that a monk cannot live out of his cloister, without falling into deadly sins, any more than fish can live out of water without dying. The reason is plain for the religious, who follow the king's court, eat and drink many meats and wines which they would not do were they resident in their cloisters, and this luxurious living induces them more to sin than if they led the austere life of a event.

He afterwards addressed the king, and pointed out to him, that if he wished to live beloved and in peace with his people, he must be just and upright. He said, he had carefully perused the Bible and other holy books, and had always found, that among princes, whether Christians or infidels, no kingdoms had ever been excited to war against their lords, but through want of proper justice being done to the subject. "The king, therefore" added the Cordelier, "must carefully have justice administered equally to every one of his subjects, that he may live among them in peace and tranquility to his last day, and that God may not deprive him of his kingdom with dishonor and shame.

The king had him several times entreated to live with him during his stay in Provence but he replied that he would not on any account remain in the company of the king. This Cordelier only stayed with us one day, and on the morrow departed. I have since heard that his body is buried at Marseilles, where it performs many fine miracles.

After this, the king set out from Hieres, and came to the city of Aix in Provence, in honor of the blessed Magdalen, who is interred a short day's journey off. We visited the place of Le Baume, which is a deep cave in a rock, wherein, it is said, the holy Magdalen resided for a long time, at a hermitage. We passed the Rhone at Beaucaire and when the king was in his own realm I took my leave of him, and went to my niece the dauphiness of Yiennois, thence to my uncle's the count de Chalons, and to the count of Burgundy His son, whence I went to Joinville.

Having made a short stay there, I set out to meet the king, whom I found at Soissons. On my arrival, he received me with such joy as surprised every one. I met there Count John of Brittany, and his wife, the daughter of King Thibault. On account of the dispute that was between the king of Navarre and the heiress of Champagne, for some claims the king of Navarre pretended to have on the country of Champagne, the king ordered them all to Paris, that each side might be heard, and justice properly done between them.

At this parliament King Thibault of Navarre demanded in marriage Isabella, the king's daughter and they had brought me with them that I might in suitable terms make this proposal of marriage, for they had observed the high favor I was in with the king when at Soissons. I went purposely to speak on this subject to the king, who replied, "Seneschal, go first and make peace with the count of Brittany, and when that is done, we will settle the marriage." I answered, "Sire, you should not neglect this matter on any account." But he said, he would not marry his daughter without the consent of his barons, nor until peace were concluded with the count of Brittany.

I immediately returned to Queen Margaret of Navarre, the king her son, and their council, to tell them the king's answer which having heard, they set about concluding a peace with all diligence with the count of Brittany and when that was done, the king gave his daughter Isabella in marriage to the king of Navarre. The wedding was celebrated with pomp and magnificence at Melun, whence King Thibault conducted her to Provins, where they were most splendidly received by the barons.

I will now speak of the state and mode of living of the king, after his return from Palestine. In regard to his dress, he would never more wear mine ever or squirrel furs, nor scarlet robes, nor gilt spurs, nor use stirrups. His dress was of camlet or Persian, and the fur trimmings of his robes were the skins of garnutes or the legs of hares. He was very sober at his meals, and never ordered any thing particular or delicate to be cooked for him, but took patiently whatever was set before him. He mixed his wine with water according to its strength, and drank but one glass. He had commonly at his meals many poor persons behind his chair, whom he fed, and then ordered money to be given to them. After dinner, he had his chaplains who said grace for him and when any noble person was at table with him, he was an excellent companion, and very friendly. He was considered as by far the wisest of any in his council and as a proof of his wisdom, whenever any thing occurred that demanded immediate attention, he never waited for his council, but gave a speedy and decided answer.

Soon after, the good king St. Louis negotiated so successfully that he prevailed on the king and queen of England to come to France with their children to conclude a peace. His council, however, were much against this peace, and said to him, "Sire, we marvel greatly how you can consent to the king of England keeping so large a tract of your territories, which your predecessors have conquered from him for ill conduct, and which it seems you have not duly considered, nor will he be any way grateful for it."

To this the king answered, that he was well aware the king of England and his predecessor had mostly forfeited the lands he held, and that he never meant to restore any thing but what he was in justice bounden to do. But he should make this restoration in order to confirm and strengthen that union which ought to exist between them and their children, who were cousins-german. The king added, "And by thus acting, I think I shall do a very good work for, in the first place, I shall establish a peace, and shall then make him my vassal, which he is not yet, as he has never done me homage."

The king, St. Louis, was the man in the world who labored most to maintain peace and concord among his subjects, more especially between the princes and barons of his realm, in particular between my uncle, the count de Chalons, and his son, the count of Burgundy, who carried on a violent war after our return from Palestine. To make a peace between the father and son, he sent several of his council, at his own costs and charges, into Burgundy, and took such pains, that at length he concluded a peace between them. Through his interference, in like manner, was peace made between the second king Thibault of Navarre, and the counts of Chalons and Burgundy, who carried on a very disastrous war but he sent part of his council thither, who appeased their differences, and concluded a peace.

After this peace another serious war broke out between Count Thibault de Bar and the count of Luxembourg, who had married his sister. They fought a duel with each other below Pigny, when the count de Bar made prisoner the count de Luxembourg, and won the castle of Ligney, that belonged to the latter in right of his wife. To put an end to this war, the king, at his own expense, sent thither his chamberlain, the lord Perron, in whom, of all his courtiers, he put the greatest confidence, who, in conjunction with the king, labored so effectually that peace was restored.

His council sometimes reproved him for the great pains he took to make up the quarrels of foreigners, for that he acted wrong in preventing them from making war on each other, as peace would in consequence be more securely maintained. The king, in answer, told them, they did not advise what was right "for," added he, "if the princes and great barons, whose territories join mine, perceive that I suffer them to make war on each other with indifference, they may say among themselves, that the king of France allows them thus to act, through malice and ingratitude, and on that account they may unite and make an attack on my kingdom, which may suffer from it and I shall, besides, incur the anger of God, who expressly says, ' Blessed are peacemakers, for theirs is the kingdom of heaven."

The Burgundians and Lorrainers perceiving so much goodness in the king, and the great pains he took to keep them at peace, had such an affection for him that they were willing to obey his commands, and with much pleasure pleaded their private disputes in his presence. I saw them frequently come on this business to Paris, to Rheims, to Melun and elsewhere, as the king might happen to be.

The good king loved God and the blessed Virgin with such sincerity that he severely punished every one that was guilty of villainous swearing, or of having used any indecent or beastly expression. I saw him once at Caesarea order a silversmith to be pilloried in his shirt and breeches, to the disgrace of the criminal and I heard that, after his return from Palestine, while I was at Joinville, he caused a citizen of Paris to be burnt, and marked with a hot iron on the nose and under-lip, for having blasphemed. I heard also, from the king's own mouth, that he would willingly be seared with a red-hot iron, and he was little able to bear such an operation, if he could banish from his kingdom all blasphemies and swearing.

I have been constantly with him for twenty-two years, but never in my life, for all the passions I have seen him in, did I hear him swear or blaspheme God, his holy mother, or any of the saints. When he wished to affirm any thing, he said, "Truly it is so" or, "In truth, it is not so." It was very clear that on no earthly consideration would he deny his God for when the sultan and admirals of Egypt wanted to make that the condition, should he break the treaty, he would never consent and when he was told this was the last proposal of the Turks, he replied, that he would rather die than commit such a crime.

I never heard him name or mention the word devil, if it was not in some book that made it necessary and it is very disgraceful to the princes and kingdom of France to suffer it, and hear the name for you will see that in any dispute one will not say three words to another in abuse, but he will add, "Go to the devil," or other bad words. Now it is very shocking thus to send man or woman to the devil, when they are by baptism become the creatures of God. In my castle of Joinville, whoever makes use of this word is instantly buffeted, and the frequency of bad language is abolished there.

The holy king once asked me if I washed the feet of the poor on Thursday before Easter. I said I did not, for that I did not think it very becoming such a person as I was. The good king instantly replied, "Ah, Lord de Joinville, you ought not to disdain nor think unbecoming that which God has done for our example, when he washed the feet of his apostles, he who was their Lord and Master. I believe you would very unwillingly perform what the king of England, now with us, does. On this Holy Thursday, he washes the feet of lepers, and then kisses them."

Before this good king went to bed he was often accustomed to have his children brought to him, and then related to them the brilliant actions and sayings of kings and other ancient princes, telling them to retain them well in their memory, to serve as examples. In like manner, he told them the deeds of wicked men, who, by their luxury, rapine, avarice, and pride, had lost their honors and kingdoms, and that their deaths had been unfortunate. "Such things," added the king, "you will cautiously avoid doing like them that you may not fall under the displeasure of God." He likewise taught them their prayers to the blessed Virgin, and heard them daily repeat the prayers for the day, according to the seasons, in order to accustom them to do the same when they should be more advanced in years, and govern their country.

He was a most liberal almsgiver; for, whenever he traveled through his kingdom, he always visited the churches, the infirmaries, and hospitals. He sought out distressed gentlemen, poor widows, and unmarried girls without fortune and every place where he found distress or want, he gave large sums of money. To poor beggars he ordered meat and drink, and I have often seen him cut the bread and pour out drink to them himself.

During his reign, he built and endowed several churches, monasteries, and abbeys such as Reaumont, the abbey of St. Anthony at Paris, the abbey Du Lis, the abbey De Malboisson, and many more for the Cordeliers and Friars-preachers. He also erected the Maison Dieu at Pontoise, that of Yernon, the house of the Quinze-vingts at Paris, and the abbey of Cordeliers at St. Cloud, which the princess Isabella, his sister, founded at his request. When any benefices became vacant and were in his gift, before he provided for them, he made strict inquiry of proper persons respecting the situation and condition of those who asked for them, and whether they were men of letters and well informed. He would never allow those to whom he gave benefices to hold more than was becoming their state and he never gave them without having duly consulted those well qualified to give him good advice.

You will see below how he punished his bailiffs, judges, and other officers when in fault and the handsome new establishments he formed for the benefit of his kingdom of France. His ordinance runs thus:

"We Louis, by the grace of God, king of France, order that all bailiffs, provosts, mayors, judges, receivers, and others in whatever office they may be, do each henceforth make oath that, during the time he shall hold such office, he will do strict justice to every one, without exception of person, as well to the poor as to the rich, to the stranger as well as to the resident, and will follow such laws and customs as have been found good and approved of. Should any one act contrary to his oath, we will and expressly command that he be punished in body and estate, according to the exigency of the case. We reserve to ourselves, and to our own discretion, the punishments that may be due to our bailiffs, judges, and other officers, and also to those employed under them."

"Our treasurers, receivers, provosts, auditors of accounts, and other officers concerned in our finances, will swear that they will well and loyally guard our rents and domains, with all our rights, liberties, and privileges, without suffering them in any way to be infringed upon or abridged."

"They will not themselves accept of any gift or present, nor permit their clerks or other persons under them to do the same, nor consent to any presents being made to their wives or children, in order to gain their favor. Should any gift have been made, they will instantly and without delay restore it, or have it sent back. In like manner, they will not make any presents to any persons their superiors, to gain their favor and support. They will also swear, that whenever they shall discover any officers, sergeants, or others, who are robbers, and abuse their offices, for which they ought to be dismissed from them, and our service, they will not conceal or disguise their guilt for any gift, favor, promise, or otherwise but that they will punish and correct them, as the case may require, with good faith and equity, and without any malice."

"We will, that the aforesaid oaths be taken before us, and that afterward they be proclaimed publicly before clerks, knights, lords, and the commonalty, in order that they may be better observed, and that those who have taken these oaths may be afraid of committing the sin of perjury, not only for the punishment that may ensue at our hands, but for fear of public disgrace and the judgment of God hereafter."

"We likewise forbid and prohibit all our said bailiffs, provosts, mayors, judges, and others our officers, either to swear by or blaspheme the name of God, his holy mother, or the blessed saints in paradise, or to game with dice, or to frequent taverns, or houses of ill-fame, under penalty of deprivation of office and undergoing such other punishment as their crimes may deserve. We order, likewise, that common prostitutes and women too free of their favors, be put out of private houses, and separated from others of a different behavior and that no person let to hire any house or habitation for them to carry on their libidinous trade and vicious habits of luxury."

"We also forbid and prohibit any of our bailiffs, provosts, mayors, or others our officers, to have the boldness to acquire or purchase, by themselves or others, any lands or possessions in the districts over which they have been appointed to administer justice, without our being previously made acquainted therewith, and our leave and license first had and obtained. Should they act otherwise, we will and declare that such lands and possessions, so acquired, be confiscated to our benefit."

"In like manner, we forbid any of our aforesaid superior officers, so long as they shall be in our service, to marry their sons, daughters, or other relations they may have, to any persons within their bailiwicks or district, without our special permission first obtained. We also include within the above prohibitions of acquisitions of property and marriage, all other inferior judges, or other subalterns of office."

"We likewise forbid any bailiff, provost, or other, to have too great a number of sergeants or beadles, so that the people may be aggrieved thereat."

"We also forbid any of our subjects to be personally arrested or imprisoned for any debts of theirs, but what may be owed to the crown, and that any fine be levied on any of our subjects for debt."

"We likewise ordain that those who may hold our provostships, viscountships, or other offices, do not sell nor transfer them to any other person without our consent. And our Lady in March, that I fell asleep during matin service. In my sleep, I thought I saw the king on his knees before an altar, and that he was surrounded by many prelates who clothed him with a red chasuble, that was of serge of Rheims. When I awakened, I told one of my chaplains, who was a learned man, my dream, who informed me that the king was the next day to put on the cross. I asked him how he knew this he replied, by what I had told him of my vision and that the red chasuble I had seen him clothed with signified the cross of our Lord Jesus Christ, which was dyed with the precious blood he had shed for us and, as the chasuble was of serge of Rheims, the crusade would be of a short duration; and the truth of what he said I should be witness to on the morrow.

Now, on the next day, the king and his three sons did put on the cross and the crusade was a trifling business, as the chaplain had foretold to me the preceding day. This made me consider it as a prophecy. When this was done, the king of France and the king of Navarre pressed me strongly to put on the cross, and undertake a pilgrimage with them but I replied that when I was before beyond sea, on the service of God, the officers of the king of France had so grievously oppressed my people that they were in a state of poverty, insomuch that we should have great difficulty to recover ourselves and that I saw clearly, were I to undertake another crusade, it would be the total ruin of my people. I have heard many say since that those who had advised him to this crusade had been guilty of a great crime, and had sinned deadly. As long as he remained in his kingdom of France, every thing went on well, and all lived peaceably and in security, but the moment he left it things began to decline. They were criminal in another respect, for the good king was so weakened in his body that he could not support the weight of his armor, nor remain long on horseback. I remember that I was once forced to carry him in my arms from the house of the count d'Auxerre as far as the convent of the Cordeliers, when we landed on our return from Palestine.

Of his expedition to Tunis I will say nothing, for I was not of it, and am resolved not to insert any thing in this book but what I am perfectly certain is true. But I will say, that during the time the good king Saint Louis was at Tunis, and before the castle of Carthage, he was seized with a dysentery the lord Philip, his eldest son, was attacked with the same disorder, and a quartan ague. The good king took to his bed, and, well knowing he was about to quit this life for another, called to his children, and, addressing himself to his eldest son, gave them instructions, which he commanded them to consider as his last will, and the objects which they were to attend to when he should be deceased. I have heard that the good king had written out these instructions with his own hand, and that they were as follow:

"Fair son, the first advice that I shall give thee is, that with all thy heart, and above all other things, thou love God, for without this no man can be saved. Be most careful not to do any thing that may displease Him that is to say, avoid sin. Thou oughtest to desire to suffer any torments rather than sin mortally. Should God send thee adversity, receive it patiently, give him thanks for it, and believe that thou hast well deserved it, and that it will turn out to thine honor. Should he grant thee prosperity, be humbly grateful for it but take care thou do not become worse, through pride or presumption, for it behoves us not to make war against God for his gifts. Confess thyself often, and choose such a discreet and wise confessor as may have abilities to point out to thee the things necessary for thy salvation, and what things thou oughtest to shun and mayest thou be such a character, that thy confessor, relations, and acquaintance may boldly reprove thee for any wrong thou mayest have done and instruct thee how thou shouldest act. Attend the service of God, and of our mother church, with heartfelt devotion, more particularly the mass, from the consecration of the holy body of our Lord, without laughing or gossiping with any one. Have always a compassionate heart for the poor, and assist and comfort them as much as thou canst."

"Keep up and maintain good manners in thy kingdom abase and punish the bad. Preserve thyself from too great luxury and never lay any heavy imposts on thy people, unless through necessity forced to it, or for the defense of thy country. If thy heart feel any discontent, tell it instantly to thy confessor, or to any sober-minded person, that is not full of wicked words : thou mayest thus more easily bear it, from the consolation he may give thee. Be careful to choose such companions as are honest and loyal, and not full of vices, whether they be churchmen, monks, seculars, or others."

"Avoid the society of the wicked and force thyself to listen to the word of God, and to retain it in thy heart. Beg continually in thy prayers for pardon, and the remission of thy sins. Love thine honor. Take care not to suffer any one to dare utter words in thy presence that may excite to sin, nor any calumny of another, whether he be present or absent nor any thing disrespectful of God, his holy mother, or of the saints."

"Offer thanks frequently to God for the prosperity and other good things he gives thee. Be upright, and do justice strictly to all, to the poor and to the rich. Be liberal and good to thy servants, but firm in thy orders, that they may fear and love thee as their master. If any controversy or dispute arises inquire into it until thou comest to the truth, whether it be in thy favor or against thee. If thou possess any thing that does not belong to thee, or that may have come to thee from thy predecessors, and thou be informed for a truth that it is not thine, cause it instantly to be restored to its proper owner. Be particularly attentive that thy subjects live in peace and security, as well in the towns as in the country. Maintain such liberties and franchises as thy ancestors have done, and preserve them inviolate for by the riches and power of thy principal towns thy enemies will be afraid of affronting or attacking thee, more especially thy equals, thy barons, and such like."

"Love and honor all churchmen, and be careful not to deprive them of any gifts, revenues, or alms which thy ancestors or predecessors may have granted to them. It is reported of my grandfather Philip, that when one of his counselors told him that the churchmen were making him lose his revenues, royalties, and even his rights of justice, and that he was surprised how he suffered it, the king replied, that he believed it was so, but that God had shown him so much favor, and granted him such prosperity, that he had rather lose all he had, than have any dispute or contention with the servants of his holy church."

"Be to thy father and mother dutiful and respectful, and avoid angering them by thy disobedience to their just commands. Give such benefices as may become vacant to discreet persons of a pure conversation, and give them with the advice of well-advised, prudent persons. Avoid going to war with any Christian power, without mature deliberation and if it can in anywise be prevented. If thou goest to war, respect churchmen and all who have done thee no wrong. Should contentions arise between thy vassals, put an end to them as speedily as possible.

"Attend frequently to the conduct of thy bailiffs, provosts and others thy officers inquire into their behavior, in order that if there may be any amendment to be made in their manner of distributing justice, thou mayest make it. Should any disgraceful sin, such as blasphemy or heresy, be prevalent in thy kingdom, have it instantly destroyed and driven thence. Be careful that thou keep a liberal establishment, but with economy."

"I beseech thee, my child that thou hold me, and my poor soul, in thy remembrance when I am no more, and that thou succour me by masses, prayers, intercessions, alms, and benefactions, throughout thy kingdom, and that thou allot for me a part of all the good acts thou shalt perform."

"I give thee every blessing that father ever bestowed on son, beseeching the whole Trinity of paradise, the Father, the Son, and the Holy Ghost, to preserve and guard thee from all evils, more particularly that thou die not under any deadly sin, and that we may, after this mortal life, appear together before God, to render him praise and thanksgiving, without ceasing, in his kingdom of paradise. Amen."

When the good king St. Louis had finished giving the above instructions to the lord Philip, his son, his disorder so greatly increased, that he asked for the sacraments of the holy church, which were duly administered to him, whilst he enjoyed full life and perfect memory. This was very apparent when they came to the unction for when they chanted the seven penitential psalms, he himself repeated the responses with the assistants, who replied to the priest that was anointing him. I have since heard from my lord the count d'Alencon, his son, that while the good king was in the agonies of death, he made efforts to call on all the saints in paradise to come and aid him in his distress. He in particular called on my lord St. James, in repeating his prayer, which begins "Esto Domine." He prayed to my lord St. Denis of France in words that were nearly as follow—"Lord God, give us grace to have the power of despising and forgetting the things of this world, so that we may not fear any evil." He called, likewise, on St. Genevieve. He then ordered his body to be placed on a bed of ashes, and, crossing his hands on his breast, with eyes uplifted to heaven, rendered his soul back to his Creator, at the very same hour that our Lord Jesus Christ expired on the cross for the salvation of his people.

The death of this holy prince was a melancholy event and worthy of lamentation for he had lived like a saint, had well taken care of his kingdom, and done many religious acts towards God. As an author has his book finely illuminated, that greater honor and respect may be paid to it, so our late holy king had illuminated his country by his great alms, and by the churches and monasteries that he had erected and founded in his lifetime, in which, at this moment, God is praised and adored day and night. The good king departed from this life to another on the morrow after the feast of St. Bartholomew, and his corpse was brought to St. Denis in France, and was buried in the spot he had some time before fixed for his sepulture in which place, God has, through his intercessions, done many and great miracles.

Soon after, by orders from the holy pontiff at Rome, a prelate of France, who was archbishop of Rouen, in company with another bishop, came to St. Denis, where they remained a long time, making inquiries into the life of the good king St. Louis. They summoned me before them, and I stayed there two days in relating all I knew of his life and manners. When they had made every necessary inquiry respecting this good king, they carried with them their report to Rome where, having thoroughly canvassed it, they placed him among the saints in paradise. This was undoubtedly joyful news to France, and ought to be so to the whole kingdom, and a great honor to his descendants, particularly such as may follow his example, but dishonorable to those who shall not and they will be pointed at by the fingers of the public, who will say, the holy man, had he been alive, would never have done such disgraceful acts.

When intelligence of his canonization was brought from Rome, the king appointed a day for the raising of his holy body, which was done by the then archbishop of Rheims, and it was borne by Sir Henry de Villiers, archbishop of Lyon, and by several archbishops and bishops, whose names I do not remember. After its translation, Friar John de Semours preached a public sermon. Among the many traits of the life of this holy king which he dwelt upon, was one which I had told him I mean, his great fidelity to his word for, as I have before said, whenever he had simply given his word to the Saracens on any subject, there was nothing that could prevent him from most strictly keeping it, whatever might be the consequences; nor, for 100,000 livres would he have broken his word. Friar John, in his sermon, detailed the whole life of this good king, as I have edited it. On the sermon being ended, the king and his brothers carried the corpse of their father to the church of St. Denis, assisted by others of their relations, to do honor to the corpse of him who had done them great honor, if they did not deprive themselves of it by their own faults, as I have before said.

I must mention something more in honor to the good king St. Louis. I was on a certain day in my chapel of Joinville, when I thought I saw him resplendent with glory before me. I was very proud to see him thus in my castle, and said to him, M Sire, when you shall depart hence I will conduct you to another of my castles that I have at Chevillon, where you shall also be lodged. Methought he answered me with a smile, "Lord de Joinville, from my affection to you, I will not, since I am here, depart hence so soon." When I awoke, I bethought myself, that it was the pleasure of God, and his own, that I should lodge him in my chapel, and instantly afterward I had an altar erected to the honor of God and of him. I also founded a perpetual mass for every day in honor of God and St. Louis. These things have I told to the king Louis, in order that by my endeavors to please God and my late lord, I might obtain some part of the relics of the real holy body of St. Louis to decorate my chapel of Joinville with, to induce those who shall see his altar to pay greater devotion to the saint.

I now make known to my readers that all they shall find in this little book, which I have declared to have seen and known, is true, and what they ought most firmly to believe. As for such things as I have mentioned as hearsay, they will understand them just as they shall please. And I beseech God, through the prayers of my lord St. Louis, that it may please him to give us such things as he knows to be necessary, as well for the body as the soul. Amen.